HλLF-LIFE® 2

PRIMA OFFICIAL GAME GUIDE

DAVID SJ HODGSON

Prima Games
A Division of Random House, Inc.
3000 Lava Ridge Court
Roseville, CA 95661
1-800-733-3000
www.primagames.com

Product Manager: Jill Hinckley
Editorial Supervisor: Christy Seifert

Valve: Viktor Antonov, Ted Backman, Kelly Bailey, Jeff Ballinger, Matt Bamberger, Aaron Barber, Yahn Bernier, Ken Birdwell, Derrick Birum, Chris Bokitch, Steve Bond, Matt Boone, Charlie Brown, Julie Caldwell, Dario Casali, Yvan Charpentier, Jess Cliffe, John Cook, Greg Coomer, Kellie Cosner, Scott Dalton, Kerry Davis, Jason Deakins, Ariel Diaz, Quintin Doroquez, Martha Draves, Laura Dubuk, Mike Dunkle, Mike Dussault, Rick Ellis, Dhabih Eng, Miles Estes, Minh Le, Adrian Finol, Bill Fletcher, Moby Francke, Pat Goodwin, Chris Grinstead, John Guthrie, Leslie Hall, Damarcus Holbrook, Tim Holt, Brian Jacobson, Erik Johnson, Jakob Jungels, Iikka Keranen, Eric Kirchmer, Marc Laidlaw, Jeff Lane, Tom Leonard, Doug Lombardi, Randy Lundeen, Scott Lynch, Ido Magal, Gary McTaggart, John Morello II, Bryn Moslow, Gabe Newell, Tri Nguyen, Jake Nicholson, Martin Otten, Kristen Perry, Bay Raitt, Alfred Reynolds, Dave Riller, Danika Rogers, David Sawyer, Aaron Seeler, Nick Shaffner, Taylor Sherman, Eric Smith, David Speyrer, Jay Stelly, Mikel Thompson, Kelly Thornton, Carl Uhlman, Bill Van Buren, KayLee Vogt, Robin Walker, Josh Weier, Doug Wood, Matt T Wood, Matt Wright, Chris Ashton, Michael Booth, Matt Campbell, Bryan Cleveland, Phil Robb, Todd Williams

ISBN: 0-7615-4362-7
Library of Congress Catalog Card Number: 2003108428
Printed in the United States of America

04 05 06 07 LL 10 9 8 7 6 5 4 3 2 1

CONTENTS

ACKNOWLEDGMENTS:

Author Special Thanks: To my beautiful wife Melanie; Mum, Dad, Ian, and Rowena; Bryn, Rachel, and Samuel; Jill, Carrie, and Christy at Prima for their help and extraordinary sanity; Bryan "KingHell" Stratton, Holly, and Steve; and N for Neville, who died of ennui.

Valve Special Thanks: The author and Prima would like to extend their heartfelt and sincere thanks to all at Valve Software for their help, patience, and support in making this guide possible. In particular, Jess Cliffe (for managing this project) and Marc Laidlaw (for help and character biographies); and the following Cabals for revealing the easiest, most cunning, and interesting methods of completing the game. Streetwar Cabal: Tom Leonard, John Guthrie, Dario Casali, and Steve Bond. Canals Cabal: David Speyrer, Brian Jacobson, Dave Riller, Josh Weier, and Jeff Lane. Prison Cabal: Robin Walker, Adrian Finol, Charlie Brown, David Sawyer, and Iikka Keranen. Thanks also to Yahn Bernier (map software), plus Kerry Davis and Jason Deakins (QA, help, and tips).

HλLF-LIFE®²
PRIMA OFFICIAL GAME GUIDE

WAKE UP AND SMELL THE ASHES

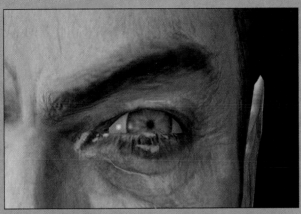

You wake from darkness. An auditory and visual hallucination startles you. A gaunt man clad in an inexpensive gray suit is floating about in your consciousness.

This is a new world, far away from Xen, where an agreement was entered into all those years ago. The G-Man speaks. You listen. "Rise and shine, Mr. Freeman. Rise and shine. Not that I wish to imply that you have been sleeping on the job."

"No one is more deserving of a rest. And all the effort in the world would have gone to waste until... well, let's just say your hour has come again. So nice to have you with us, Mr. Freeman."

"The right man in the wrong place can make all the difference in the world. So, wake up, Mr. Freeman. Wake up and smell the ashes." You emerge from the pit of subconscious slumber. You're a passenger on a train....

GETTING STARTED

HOW TO USE THIS BOOK

Welcome to *Half-Life® 2: Prima Official Game Guide*. The following sections reveal in detail all the necessary elements you need to survive, thrive, and resist the Combine's assorted forces. Before you squeeze into your HEV Suit, thoroughly digest the strategies presented here.

The bulk of this guide is a walkthrough of the single-player adventure. Each chapter has labeled maps and various additional information boxes to further aid your progress:

Tips, Notes, and Cautions: These detail a preferred tactic (Tip), an interesting aside (Note), or a dangerous problem (Caution) nearby.
Entity Encounter: A quick run-down of an enemy the first time you encounter it, along with takedown tactics as applicable.
Additional Investigations: These detail key information and some game script, along with any backstory elements.
G-Man About Town: Your sponsor is keeping a closer eye on you than you may realize. His spying spots are revealed.
Lambda Location: Every time a member of the resistance scrawls a lambda logo on a wall, we show you where the hidden goods are.
Inventory Adaptation: Whenever a new weapon or offensive capability becomes available, these provide a brief description of the item's effectiveness and usage.

GAME INSTALLATION

Insert the *Half-Life 2* CD into your CD-ROM drive. If the CD-ROM drive's Auto-Play feature is enabled, select "Install Half-Life 2" from the menu and follow the instructions. If Auto-Play isn't enabled, double-click on the My Computer icon on your desktop, and then double-click on your CD-ROM drive icon to begin installation. Follow the installation instructions.

If *Half-Life 2* doesn't begin to install immediately, right-click on the CD-ROM drive icon, choose Explore from the pull-down menu, and then double-click on autorun.exe to launch.

SYSTEM REQUIREMENTS
MINIMUM SYSTEM REQUIREMENTS

Supported OS: Windows® XP/ME/2000/98
Processor: 1.2 GHz Intel Pentium or AMD processor
RAM: 256 MB
Video Card: 3D accelerator card (Direct 3D)
Sound Card: Windows-compatible sound device
DirectX Version: DirectX 7 graphics card
Hard Drive Space: 3GB available HD space
Mouse and Keyboard

RECOMMENDED SYSTEM REQUIREMENTS

Supported OS: Windows® XP/2000
Processor: 2.4 GHz or faster Intel Pentium or AMD processor
RAM: 512 MB
Video Card: DirectX 9 graphics card
Mouse and Keyboard

THE MAIN MENU

Use the mouse or the arrow keys to navigate the menu selections. During a game, press [Esc] to access this main menu screen.

MAIN MENU CHOICES

New Game: When selected, you can begin a new game from the start or from the beginning of each game Chapter you have previously completed.
Difficulty: There are three levels: Easy, Medium, and Hard. Difficulty levels are detailed following this list.
Load Game: Select and start a previously saved game.
Save Game: Select New Saved Game in the list to create a new file, or select a previously saved game to overwrite a file.
Resume Game: Return to the current game.
Options: Set the audio and video settings, and customize the keyboard and mouse controls.
Quit: Exit *Half-Life 2*. Remember to save first!

DIFFICULTY DEFINED

Quick descriptions of the settings are listed here, followed by detailed comparisons of how these differences affect gameplay.

Easy: Enemies are weak and easy to defeat.
Normal: Enemies are stronger and have basic combat skills, making them more difficult to defeat.
Hard: Enemies have advanced combat skills, making them deadly opponents.

Easy Comparison to Normal:

- More ammunition is available, your weapons are more powerful, and enemies are weaker.
- You receive 20 percent more ammunition when picking up ammo items.
- You take one-half of the damage values listed in the Bestiary section of this guide, except when damaged by fire, falling, drowning, physics, poison, or sniper.
- You inflict 150 percent of the damage values listed in the Weapons Detail section of this guide.
- You receive automatic aiming assistance (auto-aim).

Hard Comparison to Normal:

- Less ammunition is available, your weapons are slightly less powerful, and enemies are much more dangerous.
- You receive 40 percent less ammunition when picking up ammo items.
- You take 150 percent of the damage listed in the Bestiary section of this guide, except when damaged by fire, falling, drowning, physics, poison, or sniper.
- You inflict 75 percent of the damage values listed in the Weapons Detail section of this guide.
- You receive *no* aiming assistance (auto-aim) from the computer.

CONTROLS

These are the default controls; choose Options at the main menu and access the keyboard and mouse configuration settings.

MOVEMENT COMMANDS

FUNCTION	DEFAULT KEY	NOTES
Move forward	W	Use with Alt for slower movement and quieter walking.
Move backward	S	–
Move left (strafe)	A	Use erratically to avoid gunfire.
Move right (strafe)	D	Use erratically to avoid gunfire.
Jump	Spacebar	Combine with Sprint for longer jump. When underwater, makes you rise.
Duck	Ctrl	Reduces your target profile. Rolls Grenade (if equipped and used).
Sprint	Shift	Cover ground quickly. HEV Sprint meter appears.
Walk	Alt + W, S, A, or D	–
Crawl	Ctrl + W, S, A, or D	Much less noise made. Good for moving past a noise-sensitive enemy.

MOUSE MOVEMENT COMMANDS

FUNCTION	NOTES
Turn left	Continuous use allows you to spin in a circle. The main method of looking around and targeting an enemy.
Turn right	Same as previous, but in opposite direction.
Look up (Swim up)	When swimming, use in conjunction with W.
Look down (Swim down)	When swimming, use in conjunction with W.

MODIFYING STRAFING AND LOOKING

The in-game options allow you to increase or decrease the sensitivity of your strafing and looking; the higher the value, the quicker you will sidestep or swing your head around.

- If you're constantly being hit before you can turn and react to an enemy, try increasing your strafing and looking.

- If you're constantly overshooting enemies when targeting them, try decreasing your strafing and looking.

Once familiar with these maneuvers, experiment with the many subtle moves you can achieve with different key and mouse interactions. For example, sidestep right D and turn left to move away from a target in a circle.

H λ L F - L I F E ²
PRIMA OFFICIAL GAME GUIDE

GETTING
STARTED

VEHICLE MOVEMENT

FUNCTION	DEFAULT KEY	NOTES
Turbo (car)	Shift	Useful for clearing ramps and gaps.
Handbrake (car)	Spacebar	Excellent for sudden stops and quick turns.
Drive forward	W	Accelerates, too.
Reverse	S	–
Turn left	A	Turning controls are reversed in airboat. Combine with handbrake for sharper turn.
Turn right	D	Turning controls are reversed in airboat. Combine with handbrake for sharper turn.

In addition to the controls described in the above table, use the look and mouse button commands to gaze around your vehicle and fire its weapon, if applicable.

WEAPON AND SUIT COMMANDS

FUNCTION	DEFAULT KEY	NOTES
Primary attack	Left Click	Your weapon's main attack.
Secondary attack	Right Click	Your weapon's secondary attack (not available on all weapons).
Reload weapon	R	Use at opportune moments, such as after a battle.
Use	E	Incredibly useful: chats, opens doors, flicks switches, and more.
Squad orders	C	Use while pointing in direction with target reticle and your team moves to that point. Only works with "team following" icon in bottom-right of HUD.
Weapon Category 1	1	–
Weapon Category 2	2	–
Weapon Category 3	3	–
Weapon Category 4	4	–
Weapon Category 5	5	–
Previous weapon	Mouse Up	The easiest way to cycle through weapons.
Next weapon	Mouse Down	The easiest way to cycle through weapons.
Last weapon used	R or Q	Excellent if you're almost out of ammo and want to switch quickly to another preferred weapon.
Gravity Gun	G	Useful; quickly switch between your last weapon and the Zero Point Energy Field Gravity Gun.
Bugbait	n/a	Simply use the Mouse Wheel.
Flashlight	F	Energy meter appears. Use sparingly in dark areas.
HEV Zoom	Z	Excellent zoom capabilities. Use to view unexplored areas ahead.

OTHER COMMANDS

FUNCTION	DEFAULT KEY MAPPING	NOTES
Take screenshot	Prt Sc	Screens are saved within HL2 directory.
Quick save	F5	Extremely useful; utilize as often as appropriate.
Quick load	F6	Allows quick return to action after demise.
Pause game	Pause	Can be used to plan an attack by inspecting area ahead.
Quit Game	n/a	–

SUITING UP: THE HEV AND HUD
THE MARK V HAZARDOUS ENVIRONMENTAL SUIT

This isn't available until it is given to you. It provides limited protection from the elements (including enemy fire). It also displays vital information on the heads-up display (HUD). The suit needs to be recharged periodically; the greater the charge, the more protective power the suit provides. It has the following additional functions.

FLASHLIGHT

The HEV Suit includes a built-in Flashlight. Press the Flashlight key F to turn it on or off. The Flashlight draws energy from the suit battery, so be sure to turn it off when you exit a dark area. The Flashlight recharges automatically. When in use, the energy level is shown in the bottom-left part of the screen.

HEADS-UP DISPLAY

1. Your health (on a scale of 0–100)
2. HEV Suit's protective charge (on a scale of 0–200; normally only available up to 100)
3. Ammo remaining in the current clip
4. Total available ammo
5. Secondary ammo if available
6. Sprint, Flashlight, or Oxygen levels appear here
7. Target reticle
8. Available teammates

The HEV Suit's HUD shows health, available energy, and remaining ammunition. It allows you to select a weapon or item quickly from your inventory. It also alerts you when you are sustaining injury from enemy fire (a red arc in the direction of the attack, allowing you to quickly turn and deal with the situation at hand) and when an environmental hazard such as radioactivity or drowning is threatening your survival.

WEAPON SELECTION

The Weapons Detail section of this guide has exhaustive information on each piece of killing ordnance available. The following information is initial advice on weapon management.

CATEGORIES

Along your journey, you can find and use a variety of weapons ranging from common handguns to multipurpose experimental prototypes. Most weapons offer a primary and secondary fire mode, so become familiar with newly equipped weapons before heading into a firefight. Weapons are stored in one of six slots, easily accessed by pressing the number keys or using the Previous/Next Weapon command.

WEAPON USAGE

1. Weapon categories
2. Remaining health indicator
3. Reticle
4. Remaining in-clip ammunition

Crosshairs: The on-screen crosshairs, also known as the reticle, aim your shots. In addition, the Quick Info reticle provides important status information. The left side of the crosshair circle displays remaining health. The right side displays remaining ammo in the clip.

Primary Fire: The left mouse button (or Enter) fires your weapon. Quickly tap, and then press the fire button down to check whether your weapon can be fired rapidly or not.

Secondary Fire: Some weapons have secondary fire (also known as Alt-Fire) capabilities, such as a Zoom or a grenade launcher. Note that some secondary fire ammunition may not be available immediately.

Reload: Don't forget to Reload (R) when you have a break in combat. You do not waste any ammo remaining in your clip when reloading.

SURVIVING AND THRIVING

You must learn some movement tactics that can save your hide time and time again in combat situations.

MOVEMENT FUNDAMENTALS

The basic movement techniques are the foundation of more advanced moves described later.

CONTINUOUS MOVEMENT

As you begin your adventure, attempt to move continuously; a moving target is more difficult to hit. Perfecting the sidestep, or strafe, is the key to maneuvering while keeping your target within your crosshairs.

CROUCHING

Ducking decreases your target profile and allows you to remain in a smaller amount of cover for a longer period of time. Crouching is also necessary when maneuvering through small ducts or other tiny areas. Combine this with a jump to leap through small windows, or other tight spaces above you.

SPRINTING AND JUMPING

Your suit's new Sprint function is exceptional for moving quickly through an area, but don't dash through a zone you haven't explored fully. You can only sprint for a short amount of time (indicated on screen), so use this power wisely, such as for negotiating a pipe belching hazardous smoke. Try sprinting and jumping to reach a far balcony or ledge, such as leaping an area of sand or gap between balconies. Otherwise, jumping is simply a method of maneuvering across openings. It can also be used to dodge incoming fire.

GRABBING

Most useful when climbing up and down ladders, pressing the E grabs and releases your grip from the ladder, enabling you to quickly move away from a ladder you can sometimes become "stuck" on.

SWIMMING

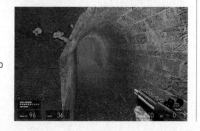

Although not used to the same extent as in the original *Half-Life*, your suit's oxygen tank is set up to give you a small air supply—just enough to venture underwater. Remember you can use

Spacebar to rise to the surface, and your look direction influences whether you swim up or down. When in a panic, point up and move!

STRAFE, DON'T TURN

A distinct technique from turning (which is moving forward and looking), strafing involves moving sideways while keeping your body facing the same direction you are looking. Initially, it is useful for dodging incoming bullets without losing sight of your foe. Strafe left to avoid a bullet, and right to return to your previous position. Practice this. It is especially useful at range, where you can nimbly sidle left and right, avoiding gunfire while continuously targeting an enemy and firing.

STRAFE AROUND CORNERS

The next technique to learn is to strafe around corners. Usually, you would walk slightly past a corner, then turn (by looking). Not so if you want to remain healthy. Instead, just before reaching a corner, turn and face the new passage before proceeding. Then sidestep out and press forward. This allows you to react instantly to any enemies ahead. This example shows avoiding a nasty Barnacle attack with this method.

RUNNING BACKWARD

When facing aggressive and highly intelligent enemies in a limited space, maneuvering backward can be more productive than turning and fleeing. You are able to lay down fire, won't be shot in the back, and can then take cover. Practice maneuvering through the train station or plaza in City 17 at the start of your adventure. Then retrace your steps, this time traveling backward. Once you can maneuver without floundering, you can apply this in the combat zone.

KEY TACTICS

SLIDE AND ATTACK

Putting strafing together with gunfire results in the slide-and-attack technique. You remain the same distance away from your enemy, but shift left and right while keeping your foe targeted, plugging away until your adversary falls. This is a reasonable plan for dealing with semi-intelligent enemies in an enclosed space.

HIDE AND PEEK

Wherever possible, a better way to fight involves diving behind crates or staying at a corner, peeking out to fire, and then returning to cover. You can be fired upon for only a limited amount of time. You do need to re-target your enemy each time you pop out, however, so watch your step when using this technique against fast-moving entities. When entering a room, use this technique if you're in a safe position to quickly determine the threats in the chamber, and then enter.

CIRCLE-STRAFING

The final, and most advanced, technique in combat is the circle-strafe. This must be undertaken in an area large enough to accommodate you as you run around an enemy, circling the foe while keeping your gun targeted directly on him. This way, you can constantly plug bullets into him while remaining difficult to hit. Vary your direction, and maneuver in and out to become even more hard to kill.

GENERAL TECHNIQUES

EXPLORE THOROUGHLY, CLEAR YOUR AREA

During your adventure, inspect every nook and cranny, and remember every junction where you missed a branching pathway, or ladder you didn't have time to climb. Thorough exploration usually solves a seemingly infuriating dead end, such as a gate that you can't open (chances are that a switch or other device lies nearby). Make sure you break open every Supply Crate, check every corner, and stop for a moment to inspect the walls, ceilings, and floors so you don't miss a hidden duct or passage. Don't flee a combat area to another area; try securing each area you're in before continuing, unless the walkthrough instructs you otherwise.

SAVE OFTEN

Saving your game seems like a simple idea, but in the heat of battle you can forget, and then have to replay major portions of a level. Whenever you reach a junction, after every battle or escape, and each time you peek around a corner, view a nasty enemy, and dart back behind cover, you should save.

EXPERIMENT

With weapons as varied as the Zero Point Energy Field Gravity Gun, you'll find that dozens of possible methods exist for completing each area. Using a different weapon to clear the same area produces an entirely different gameplay experience each time you play.

Remember that risky tactics are sometimes the most adrenaline-pumping, so next time you spot a squad of Soldiers and think you can bludgeon them to death with a Crowbar instead of using cover and a submachine gun, save your game and give it a try!

CRATE BLOCKING

In certain situations, you can actually use scenery items to your advantage, such as for destroying enemies, or at the very least blocking their path. Adventuring in *Half-Life 2* isn't a simple matter of completing areas by laying waste to them; preventing enemies from chasing you by blocking their path is another tactic to try.

CARRYING ITEMS

Pressing E enables you to carry an item, although certain heavier items require a little more exertion, and some can't be lifted at all. Play with items to learn their behavior when thrown, shoved, or otherwise manipulated to see which can become valuable weapons, movable cover, or crushing devices to use against the enemy.

FULL-LIFE: STRATEGIES FOR SURVIVAL

Before you begin your mission, make sure you remember at least a couple of the following tips to increase your chances of survival. You should also read up on the characters, enemies, and weapons you'll need to complete this monumental task.

G FOR GRAVITY

Be sure you use the G key to regularly switch between your last weapon and the Gravity Gun. This way you can quickly flick between firepower and scenery item movement. For example, you can shove a wardrobe down some stairs into an enemy, then hit G to switch immediately to the Pistol and finish off the wounded victim. Because the Gravity Gun is used more than any other weapon, flicking between it and your other most effective gun for the situation is quicker than manually cycling through all your firepower.

HEADS UP

Headshots: the only way to defeat your foes. Whenever possible, aim at your enemy's head, if it has one. The damage you inflict is tripled. Furthermore, when dealing with Zombies, you can kill both the Zombie *and* the Headcrab controlling it, whereas if you strike the Zombie's body, the Headcrab usually survives.

GETTING
STARTED

ZOOM, RELEASE, FIRE

With nimble key strokes, you can turn any weapon into a sniper rifle. Press Z to use your suit's Zoom function to inspect an enemy in the distance, get a good view, then fire as you zoom out. You can wing a target from extreme range by using this method.

ANIMOSITY

Zombies and Combine Soldiers just don't get along. Sentry guns programmed to attack will take out Zombies for you. Fast Zombies and Antlions facing off is a sight to behold. An Antlion Guard devastating a Combine Soldier squad is a thrilling and one-sided carnagefest. If there are two types of enemy in a single area, it is sometimes best to let their animosity play out. It saves ammunition too.

HEARING

Listening is just as important as an itchy trigger-finger and a circle-strafe. You can actually hear enemies ahead, behind, or around you if you listen. Sometimes an enemy out of view is still able to be heard, allowing you to react before you see it.

YOUR ENVIRONMENT

LEDGES AND EDGES

Be sure your dexterity is attuned and your game is saved; numerous narrow ledges, cliffsides, and precipices endanger you with a potential death plummet. Keep a steady pace and don't rush these sections.

TELEPORTING

Teleporters are used on more than one occasion to transport you a distance too great to travel on foot. Simply sit back and wait for the teleport operators to do their job. It's probably safe.

OBSTACLES

Whether a group of crates, a duct grating, or a barricade of planks, many obstacles can be removed or maneuvered around by smashing with either the Crowbar or the force of the Gravity Gun.

LADDERS

Climbing ladders can be treacherous until you employ the technique of pressing E to grab and release your grip on a ladder. This lets you negotiate ladders without fear near precipices.

STAIRS

Heading up and down stairs is a simple concept, but always check whether you can see through the stairs and blast incoming enemies from above or below. Also watch for ambushes on stairways.

EXPLOSIVE BARRELS

These barrels are an important offensive tool and the demise of an unwary player. Two bullets will cause a barrel to catch fire after a three-second delay, and three bullets detonate them. Blow them apart to defeat enemies, but watch out for chain reactions.

MOVING VEHICLES

Whether it's the colossal Razor Tren hurtling by you, or a Combine Armored Personnel Carrier (APC) driving in the streets below, large vehicles cannot be entered or driven, and serve only as deadly obstacles. Don't step out in front of them!

DOORS AND GATES

Doors appear in a variety of shapes and types. Although they are easy to operate by pressing E, be aware that a squeaky door opening can alarm enemies. Remember that you can fire through mesh gates.

DUCTS

Air-conditioning ducts are always big enough to crawl through. Arm the Crowbar or a close-assault weapon, and switch on the Flashlight when exploring.

ENERGY WALLS

The Combine has erected large blue walls of energy in various areas around the city to stop citizens (and you) from venturing outside of its control. Some walls can be powered down, but most are dead ends. Watch out for enemy forces, though; they can move through energy walls at will.

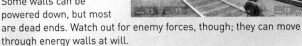

WATER

Once you determine that the liquid you're about to wade into isn't radioactive or swarming with Carnivorous Leeches, you can dive in. Note that your Crossbow and Crowbar work underwater, and you have limited oxygen. Find the surface as fast as you can.

COVER

When engaged in a vicious firefight, make sure you locate cover. Crouching behind it is an excellent plan. Notice what happens to cover when enemy fire hits it; some is destroyed, cars can move, and other cover remains sturdy.

LAMBDA LOGOS

The resistance forces use a lambda logo that they spray-paint or stamp across the walls throughout your adventure, and this is always a sign of a hidden weapon or ammo cache nearby.

VALVES, LEVERS, AND SWITCHES

You'll find devices that must be pressed, turned, or generally fiddled with, and the general rule is to use these devices. Some can't be reset, or require you to hold  instead of tapping it.

RADIOACTIVE SLUDGE

Radioactive waste is extremely dangerous, and a built-in Geiger counter on your HEV Suit warns you of its location (although it is easy to spot). You'll lose significant health if you wade in.

PARASITE ROCKETS

Seen either arcing through the sky leaving a bluish trail, or already embedded in the ground, parasite rockets are named after the Headcrab cargo they unload on impact. If you spot a rocket, prepare for Headcrab combat.

ELECTRICITY

Various disturbances sometimes shake electrical cables free of their moorings, and the shock you can receive is damaging. Stay away from writhing cables, electrified containers, or electrified water.

RAMPS

Scattered throughout the canals and coastal areas are a variety of ramps, which you should approach at maximum velocity; you must jump some ramps just to continue progress. Hit them head-on and fast.

PUZZLES

Don't expect to waltz through this adventure with guns blazing; you must solve a number of brain-teasing puzzles. Fortunately, the walkthrough reveals all of the puzzles and their solutions.

ELEVATORS

Some elevators don't work, and most others are controlled by another character. Look up or down as the elevator moves, and look for the direction of the exit door and turn that way.

GETTING STARTED

FIRE

Moving into fire is never recommended, but it is a useful tool for destroying enemies, mainly the undead Zombie types. Escaping gas, explosive barrels, canisters, gas pumps, and gas cans are all flammable. Stand far back.

SAND

The coastal plains stretching away from City 17 are home to a vicious creature known as the Antlion, and as soon as you stand on sand (whether covered in grass or not), these entities spawn. Stay off the sand!

OCEAN

The ocean is a deadly place that you should not venture into under any circumstances; it teems with schools of Carnivorous Leeches that quickly kill you.

THUMPERS

Large black obelisks are part of the Combine technology that is actually advantageous to be near; they halt Antlions from spawning in a circumference around the device. These can be switched on and off.

CUBBY HOLE COVER

Taking cover behind objects is an excellent option discussed earlier, but you can also use confined spaces to hide without fear of attack from similarly sized enemies, such as this cubby hole too small for a Fast Zombie to enter. Defeat enemies at your leisure.

PLUGS

Powerful devices not yet spliced into the Combine Citadel run off generators, and these are connected by large plugs. It only takes a swift tug (from your hands or Gravity Gun) to unhook such a device.

LASER TRIP-MINES

Watch your step when you spot a faint red or blue laser beam; these are attached to mines on the wall, gun emplacements, or ground turrets. The walkthrough details how to avoid these.

MONITORS

Monitors scattered about the environment range from towering screens attached to large buildings across City 17 to smaller monitors in command rooms inside Nova Prospekt. These have multiple channels; press Ⓔ to flick through them.

COMPUTER TERMINALS

The Combine's giant computer terminals provide command-and-control capabilities and have been installed throughout City 17 and Nova Prospekt. You have no security clearance; only other characters can access these devices.

COMBINE LOCKS

Many doors are sealed by a complex black Combine lock that requires specialist Electro Magnetic Pulse (EMP) devices to unlock. Unfortunately, you do not possess one. Alyx Vance has been known to carry such a lock pick, however.

NON-PLAYER CHARACTERS

These are friendly entities you meet along your way. Talk to them by meeting them and pressing Ⓔ. Continue to press Ⓔ for further conversation, or sometimes combat supplies.

COMBINE GENERATORS

Encased in thick metal frames, City 17's Combine security points and large-scale suppressor weapons are powered by massive generators. To disable them, they must be opened and the inner core orb removed.

DESTINATIONS

CITY 17

The once-bustling metropolis with a rich history and numerous landmarks is now slowly being overrun by the Combine after a surprise attack and Earth's surrender. Combine propaganda is constantly spewed over giant monitors and speakers via the mouthpiece of the surrender and human consul Wallace Breen, while the populace live in squalor, deal with psychotropic foodstuffs, and suffer constant brutal treatment by the Overwatch, the Combine's police forces.

THE KANALS

A crisscrossing maze of conduits, channels, and sewers connects the city to a river system and dam where the city's water supply is pumped (now under Combine control). A rag-tag resistance force uses the dilapidated nature of the canals as an underground railroad of sorts, ferrying those with predisposition for social unrest out to the relative safety of the surrounding countryside—safe, that is, until the Combine began to bomb the area with parasite rockets.

BLACK MESA EAST

The epicenter of the human resistance, this well-hidden compound has been struggling to remain hidden from prying Combine eyes, and is the base for the continuing work by Doctor Eli Vance, a survivor of the original Black Mesa Incident. Ably assisted by his daughter Alyx and colleague Doctor Mossman, this laboratory is buried deep underground and features numerous escape routes should the Combine attack, including a blocked-off passage to the plague town of Ravenholm.

RAVENHOLM

A once-prosperous mining settlement renowned for its minerals, this resistance hotspot was recently discovered by the Combine, who immediately dispatched a number of parasite rockets. The effects on the town were devastating; a plague of Headcrabs descended and ended the lives of townsfolk and many rebels. The only rumored survivor is the pastor of the town's church, Father Grigori, although his whereabouts are currently unknown.

SHOREPOINT

Run by Leon, one of the resistance veterans, this dockyard at the southernmost tip of the coastal region is another rebel stronghold where guerilla-style attacks on the Combine are planned and performed. A constant battle rages to hold this station because of the Combine and monstrous incursions from the coast.

NEW LITTLE ODESSA

The second major settlement along the coast, this was once a fishing hamlet, but has now been turned into a thoroughfare for resistance forces heading toward the main viaduct, a place called Bridge Point which has recently fallen into Combine hands. This stronghold is named after its eccentric leader, Colonel Odessa Cubbage.

LIGHTHOUSE POINT

The northern tip of the coastal road ends at another human settlement under constant Combine attack, and is the key bridge between the ocean wastelands and the gun emplacements of Nova Prospekt. The lighthouse and trio of slowly disintegrating buildings around disguise the importance of this destination.

NOVA PROSPEKT

A gulag where society's least productive members were imprisoned, this rambling prison set high above the ocean cliffs has now been acclimatized to Combine control, and is slowly being integrated into a factory of sorts. Recent intelligence points to this prison becoming a processing plant for citizens deemed troublesome, who are sorted at City 17's train station and transported in confining pods via Razor Tren to Nova Prospekt to face an unknown fate.

THE CITADEL

A towering spire so immense its upper tip cannot be seen through the clouds, this seems to be the focus of the Combine's power. Viewing the Citadel from the outside yields no real knowledge of its internal workings, except for a stream of machines being released periodically from its massive ducts, and a gargantuan wall of dark onyx-like metal that slowly tears through the city, feeding the machine. Perhaps the secrets of the Combine are hidden inside this ominous edifice.

WEAPONS DETAIL

Fighting the Combine requires a variety of specialized equipment. Throughout the adventure, you regularly locate different types of killing weaponry and use them in a variety of offensive operations. This section covers all the weapons you can carry on your person (on-board ordnance), plus essential items to collect (in-game inventory).

ON-BOARD ORDNANCE

Here we reveal and explain each weapon you can carry on your person and access through your HEV Suit's HUD at the top of the screen. They are listed here in the order they appear as you cycle through your inventory.

To determine which weapon to use in terms of damage, compare the "damage inflicted" number listed in this section to the enemy's health detailed in the next section of this guide; this tells you how many shots it takes to defeat a particular foe.

The "chapter located" information refers to the *game's* chapter number, not this book's chapter numbers.

SCENIC DEBRIS

Damage inflicted:
Varies (light)
Description: Various scattered objects, from paint cans to radiators affixed to walls, found throughout your adventure.
Techniques: Look for an object, press E to pick it up, and throw it. The height at which you're looking influences how far the object will travel. Heavier objects cannot be thrown as far as lighter objects. Practice throwing items of different size and weight until you are comfortable with how objects behave. This form of attack is not recommended, as it is incredibly ineffectual.
Targets: Scanners, until the Gravity Gun is acquired, then any human-sized or smaller enemies.

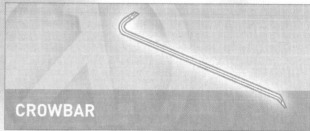

CROWBAR

Chapter located: 2, A Red Letter Day
Damage inflicted: 10
Secondary fire: No

Description: A straight bar of steel, with the working end shaped like a chisel, bent and forked, usually used as a lever.
Techniques: This is the first actual weapon you find, and not too different from a tool picked up during the original Black Mesa Incident. You can swing it at any nearby enemies (especially good for battering Headcrabs if you time the swing to coincide with the beast's jump), and is also useful for breaking apart wooden barricades, and other scenery you don't wish to waste ammunition on. Also use it to bludgeon lone Zombies or Police, and in tight spots (such as ventilation ducts).
Targets: Headcrabs, Metro Police, or Soldiers. (Only attack Combine forces if you have no other choice.)

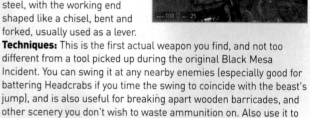

9MM PISTOL

Chapter located: 3, Route Kanal
Damage inflicted: 5
Ammunition (chamber/carried): 18/150
Ammo pick-up amount: 20 (small)/100 (large)
Secondary fire: No

Description: A silver-and-black 9mm Combine-approved handgun with 18 bullets in the clip.
Techniques: This accurate tool, the first weapon you receive that enables you to bring down enemies at range, is more helpful than you may initially realize. Despite the low damage it inflicts, it fires as fast as you can manually pull the trigger—a vital point to learn, allowing upward of three shots per second if your reactions are fast enough. The faster you fire, the less accurate your shots become, so consider target distance versus situational urgency when deciding how quickly to fire.

Targets: Metro Police, Scanners (especially at distance), Barnacles, Headcrabs, and fights with one or two enemies at a time.

.357 MAGNUM

Chapter located: 4, Water Hazard
Damage inflicted: 40
Ammunition (chamber/carried): 6/12
Ammo pick-up amount: 6
Secondary fire: No

Description: A heavy, six-shot silver revolver with incredibly powerful bullets loaded manually into the chamber.
Techniques: Six shots, a lengthy reload time, and no secondary fire may dissuade you from using this. Ignore these shortcomings; the weapon takes down any pedestrian enemy with a single shot, even at range. Ensure an instant kill by aiming at the head. For single assassinations at close or long ranges, there's nothing quite as satisfying as a takedown with a Magnum. If you have incredible dexterity, use the Magnum to shoot incoming grenades back at the attacker. This is the preferred weapon for this tactic because the strength of the shot ricochets the grenade away with extreme force. Employ hit-and-run tactics with this weapon, popping out from cover to kill an enemy, then darting back to relative safety.
Targets: Metro Police and Soldiers, all Zombie types, especially Fast Zombies (headshots only).

SUBMACHINE GUN (SMG)

 PRIMARY FIRE CAPABILITIES   SECONDARY FIRE CAPABILITIES

Chapter located: Chapter 3, Route Kanal
Damage inflicted: 4 per bullet (fires about 13 per sec.)
Ammunition (chamber/carried): 45/225
Ammo pick-up amount: 45 (small)/225 (large)
Secondary fire: Yes
Damage inflicted: 100
Ammunition (chamber/carried): 1/3
Ammo pick-up amount: 1

Description: A compact but powerful Combine-approved submachine gun with integrated secondary grenade-launcher capabilities.
Techniques (Primary): A rapid-fire, all-purpose combat weapon, this is your default ordnance for tackling enemies in the widest variety of combat situations until the Pulse Rifle is obtained. The SMG has a very high rate of fire, but only mid-level damage when it hits, so it is best suited to close-to-mid-range combat. Watch your ammo level; there's a tendency to lay down too many consecutive shots. Use quick and accurate bursts of fire. A good rule of thumb is: the faster the enemy, the shorter and sharper the bursts of SMG fire should be. For Zombies, unload constantly until it falls. For a Headcrab, tap tiny bursts to maximize your ammo supply. This is a fine weapon for circle-strafing.
Targets (Primary): Any enemy confrontation with troops (humanoid size or smaller), Antlions, and three foes or fewer in a group.
Techniques (Secondary): The Alt-Fire for this weapon lobs an explosive Grenade in an arc in the direction you point your weapon. The Grenade instantly explodes on impact. This is a very useful "panic button" for situations that quickly turn ugly (such as when backing up from an ambush), to dispatch two or more enemies very close together, or to remove enemies when it's almost time to reload the SMG's primary fire.
Targets (Secondary): Clumps of enemies just appearing out of doorways or confined in a small chamber. Also able to flush snipers from windows with careful aiming.

12-GAUGE SHOTGUN

 PRIMARY FIRE CAPABILITIES    SECONDARY FIRE CAPABILITIES

Chapter located: 6, "We don't go to Ravenholm"
Damage inflicted: 56* (8 per pellet x 7 pellets per blast)
Ammunition (chamber/carried): 30/6
Ammo pick-up amount: 20
Secondary fire: Yes
Damage inflicted: 84* (12 per pellet x 7 pellets per blast)
(* Varies depending on range)

Description: 12-gauge manual-pump shotgun firing buckshot load.
Techniques: An exceptional close-quarter weapon, Father Grigori's 12-gauge shotgun has tremendous stopping power that can't be beaten (except by the Magnum, which requires more accuracy). However, damage at range tails off considerably; this may be an essential weapon for blasting the Headcrabs off Zombies, but it's unimpressive at mid to long range. It has two additional firing abilities that you should test: The first is the secondary fire, which is a slower-firing burst that uses double the ammunition, but inflicts more damage. Use this on a single, powerful enemy that's in your face. The other firing mode is the out-of-ammo firing; you can manually load and fire a single shot. This takes around half a second per action, and is much slower than backing out of a fight and

completing the chamber reload. Use this technique only when facing an immediate threat and cannot switch to the Magnum. You can also employ hit-and-run tactics with the Shotgun; stepping out of cover, blasting, and returning to hide. Or, let the enemy spot you, hide around a corner, wait for them to appear, and blast them. Reload when no enemies are around; it's better to switch to another weapon than wait for a Shotgun reload in the heat of battle.

Targets: Headcrabs on Zombies, Headcrabs, any entity at close range (less than 20 feet).

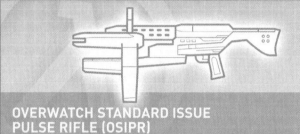

OVERWATCH STANDARD ISSUE PULSE RIFLE (OSIPR)

PRIMARY FIRE CAPABILITIES — SECONDARY FIRE CAPABILITIES

Chapter located: 6, "We don't go to Ravenholm"
Damage inflicted: 8 per bullet (fires about 10 per sec.)
Ammunition (chamber/carried): 30/60
Ammo pick-up amount: 20
Secondary fire: Yes
Damage inflicted: 100*
Ammunition: (chamber/carried): 1/3
Ammo pick-up amount: 1
(* Instant death to each enemy hit by it, up to three hits)

Description: Combine-assembled dual-purpose Overwatch Pulse Rifle with optional energy orb thrust launcher.

Techniques (Primary): An exceptional rapid-fire variant to your SMG, the Overwatch Pulse Rifle (also known as the AR2) is an impressive piece of Combine manufacturing issued to some Soldier classes. Featuring extremely hard-hitting pulses and quick reload, this is a viciously powerful weapon. Use even shorter and more accurate bursts than with the SMG, as constant firing leads to massive ammunition consumption. Highly accurate with almost double the damage of the SMG, this is the choice weapon for intense combat situations at medium to long distance and/or against a large number of opponents. Use this instead of the SMG in long-range encounters specifically.

Targets (Primary): Any enemy of Antlion size or smaller, groups of enemies.

Techniques (Secondary): The secondary fire is a large energy ball with a three-second lifespan. It should be accurately shot at a single incoming enemy in a group. Normally, it travels for two seconds and ricochets, killing enemies for one second. It is usually possible to destroy three enemies with one orb. After three enemies or seconds, the ball dissipates. To best use the limited orb life, you should be relatively close to the enemy before launching it.

Targets (Secondary): Groups of enemies in an enclosed space (never use on single humanoid-sized foes). Single large-scale entities (such as Striders).

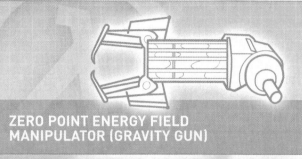

ZERO POINT ENERGY FIELD MANIPULATOR (GRAVITY GUN)

PRIMARY FIRE CAPABILITIES — SECONDARY FIRE CAPABILITIES

Chapter located: 5, Black Mesa East
Damage inflicted: Varies
Ammunition (chamber/carried): N/A
Ammo pick-up amount: N/A
Secondary fire: Yes

Description: Zero Point Energy Field Manipulation device emitting an orange beam with inorganic-management capabilities.

Techniques: Also known as the Physics Cannon and the Gravity Gun, the Zero Point Energy Field Manipulator is the most versatile, helpful, and sometimes devastating weapon you're ever likely to find. How you use this weapon is completely dependent upon your immediate environment, allowing you to be very creative with scenic items, so the walkthrough describes specific scenarios and tactics. The controls are described here, along with some general guidelines for how to apply the Gravity Gun's abilities.

Right-click sucks objects (up to the size of a car) from their location and into the Gravity Gun's field directly in front of you, where you can hold them. Right-click again drops them. Right-click object "pulling" is a long-range technique.

Left-click blasts objects (up to the size of a car) away from you. The blast beam is powerful, but you can substantially increase this power by first sucking (right-click) an object toward you, then blasting it toward your target. Left-click "pushing" is a close-range technique.

Press Ⓖ to swap immediately between the Gravity Gun and the previous weapon used. This is useful for clearing a path while under fire and you need to quickly flick between the Gravity Gun and a regular gun.

Now that you know *how*, you need to know *what* to suck and blast:
- Any object can be pulled or pushed, except for objects bolted to the ground, or organic materials (such as Combine Soldiers or Alyx).
- An object's weight and size determines the force and distance it travels when blasted. Small items (cans, small crates, saw blades) travel fast and long. Medium items (radiators, washing machines) travel fast and short. Large items (cars) can only be pushed.
- Use radiators and similar objects (that don't block your vision) as projectiles against enemies. You can use the same item repeatedly and carry it along. This saves ammo. Saw blades are good, too.
- Stack items to gain access to upper areas.
- Clear areas of debris quickly and effectively.
- Grab items and supplies that you can't otherwise reach.

- Destroy barricades with a left-click blast.
- Manipulate larger items (like cabinets) as shields or to block enemy movement.
- Explosive barrels can be manipulated *carefully*.
- Extra ammo or health can be carried or blasted into areas you know you'll reach later.
- Destroy Manhacks and Rollermines by sucking them in and then blasting them into a wall or the ocean. You can hold the Manhack to use as a chainsaw.
- Grab and blast back incoming grenades and energy orbs (you can't actually grab the orbs, but can manipulate them for multiple kills).
- Catch or deflect large objects falling toward you.

FRAGMENTATION GRENADE

PRIMARY FIRE CAPABILITIES   SECONDARY FIRE CAPABILITIES

Chapter located: 3, Route Kanal
Damage inflicted: 125
Ammunition (chamber/carried): 1/5
Ammo pick-up amount: 1
Secondary fire: Yes

Description: A single-use cylindrical military-issue fragmentation Grenade with four-second fuse.
Techniques: Prime a Grenade with left-click or right-click, and then release it; the trajectory is determined by your target reticle, not how long you hold down the button. In primary fire situations, the Grenade is thrown long through the air in an arcing movement. It lands and explodes after its fuse expires, which starts from the moment you throw the Grenade. The throw is key to flushing out enemies behind cover or around corners. Practice banking Grenades around corners to gauge the proper trajectory for making them detonate at the point you desire.

Secondary fire with Grenades is the advanced tactic of throwing a Grenade a short distance instead of long distance. This is useful when you are around a corner close to your enemy. If you crouch and Alt-Fire, you roll the Grenade across the floor for more precise low-level takedowns of devices such as ground turrets. Also remember that enemy grenades can be picked up (by hand or Gravity Gun) and tossed back at the target (or blown back with a Magnum shot), although your timing must be precise. Finally, grenades are good for flushing enemies out of buildings, or for sneak attacks on a group of enemies unaware of your presence. For example, use another weapon to break a window, then throw in the Grenade, or roll it through a door.
Targets: Enemies behind cover or around corners, stationary enemies, and ground turrets.

ZERO POINT ENERGY GRAVITY GUN (ORGANIC)

PRIMARY FIRE CAPABILITIES   SECONDARY FIRE CAPABILITIES

Chapter located: 13, Benefactory
Damage inflicted: Varies
Ammunition (chamber/carried): N/A
Ammo pick-up amount: N/A
Secondary fire: Yes

Description: Zero Point Energy Field Manipulation device emitting a blue beam with additional organic-management capabilities.
Techniques: Should the Gravity Gun's flux capacitors become modified by Combine technology, both inorganic and organic materials can now be manipulated. In addition to every ability detailed previously, any enemy, whether human or machine, can be sucked, blasted forward, or abused as if it were a barrel or piece of debris. The offensive capabilities of this method of attack are unsurpassed: "bowling" enemies into each other, carrying a suspended enemy as a shield, and hurling scenic objects at your foes.

The Gravity Gun's power to move heavier inorganic objects has also increased, and these make powerful projectiles. For example, you can "yo-yo" energy conduit orbs between enemies, alternately blasting and sucking these projectiles, bank them off walls, and crush them with any large-scale available objects, or even use the flailing bodies of Combine foes as humanoid shields while you advance.
Targets: All Combine forces within the Citadel.

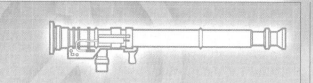

WEAPONS
DETAIL

ROCKET-PROPELLED GRENADE LAUNCHER (RPG)

Chapter located: 7, Highway 17
Damage inflicted: 200
Ammunition (chamber/carried): 1/3
Ammo pick-up amount: 1
Secondary fire: No

Description: A reusable, shoulder-fired, muzzle-loaded, recoilless anti-Combine and antipersonnel RPG firing fin-stabilized Grenade rockets.

Techniques: With only three shots before the ammo is depleted, the RPG's single-shot strikes cannot be wasted, but they are devastating! Attacks are launched with the primary attack only; fire once to launch the rocket. It is heat-seeking, but not very intelligent, and is easily cut down by enemy gunships. For effectiveness, launch, then press and hold left-click to bring out a red laser. Guide the rocket with the laser to your chosen target (ideally placing the dot on the target for the missile to reach).

If attacking a Gunship, which is swift enough to down a rocket if fired directly at it, you must "corkscrew" the rocket by tracing a series of wide circles with your laser for the rocket to follow, and continue this erratic path around and finally into your target. Use this weapon at range! It is the preferred weapon for tackling Gunships and Striders.

Targets: Gunships, flying entities, APCs, Striders, enemies at extreme range.

CROSSBOW

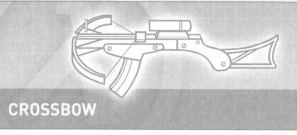

PRIMARY FIRE CAPABILITIES

SECONDARY FIRE CAPABILITIES

Chapter located: 7, Highway 17
Damage inflicted: 100
Ammunition (chamber/carried): 1/10
Ammo pick-up amount: 6
Secondary fire: Yes

Description: Black huntsman-style crossbow with a 250 lb.+ draw weight and bolt speeds over 350 feet per second, with optional scope mounting.

Techniques: The ultimate in stealth sniper weaponry, the long-distance takedowns available from this weapon more than make up for the lengthy reload and low ammunition count. Takedown results are impressive. The primary attack fires, and the secondary fire zooms in on a target to a greater range than your HEV Suit's function (press right-click again to zoom out). If you want to view potential ambush points ahead and can spot an enemy at extreme range, use this hard-hitting, single-strike takedown armament. Be warned that bolts take time to travel, so you must lead any moving targets (meaning you should fire at where the target will move to by the time the bolt arrives, not where the target is when you fire). Bolts also drop in the air as they lose speed and react to gravity, so compensate for this if firing over an extremely long distance. Skewer unwary, stationary foes with this weapon.

Targets: Humanoid targets at extreme range, or on upper platforms or gantries that cannot be reached.

PHERAPODS (BUGBAIT)

PRIMARY FIRE CAPABILITIES

SECONDARY FIRE CAPABILITIES

Chapter located: 8, Sandtraps
Damage inflicted: Immobilization (Combine only), Death (Antlion attack)
Ammunition (chamber/carried): 1/ N/A
Ammo pick-up amount: N/A
Secondary fire: Yes

Description: Pheropod glandular sacs harvested from Antlion Guard (*Myrmidont giganticus*).

Techniques: Once secured from the dissolving remains of an Antlion Guard with the help of Vortigaunt manipulation (harvesting cannot be undertaken by humans), any threat from Antlions (see Bestiary) is immediately nullified. You can now use the Pheropod to herd these creatures into combat, mainly against Combine forces. The primary fire tosses a Pheropod sac (which you have a limitless number of) in an arc like a grenade. The distance it travels depends on where your target reticle is pointing. When the sac lands, it explodes, and any nearby Antlions immediately swarm to that location. If a Combine enemy (not Zombie) is struck by a Pheropod, it is incapacitated for five seconds, wafting the vortex of spray that congeals around him.

This can also be used to incapacitate Combine forces in areas without Antlions; debilitate with the Pheropod, then swap to another weapon to finish off the foe. However, when Antlions are available, they swarm the area and wait for you after killing any enemies. Primary throwing can also be used to send Antlions to specific areas you wish to herd them to. The Secondary fire functionality is a squeeze of the sac, which emits a muffled squelch, and releases Pheropods, attracting all Antlions in the area. This is useful to call back Antlions from an area to congregate near you prior to an assault.

Targets: Combine Soldiers.

IN-GAME INVENTORY

SUPPLY CRATE

Any time you see a small crate marked "supply," immediately destroy it and grab its contents: random ammunition and health items. The actual items inside are determined depending on how well you are playing. If you are desperately in need of health, for example, the crate will usually contain a Health Pack.

AMMUNITION BOX

Dotted around various levels, and also contained in Supply Crates, are ammunition boxes for the various weapons you can pick up and carry. Grab these if you need them, and use their contents wisely—and sparingly in Hard mode!

Following are the different ammunition types available, along with the number of bullets they grant you. Note that "small" ammo refers to clips and limited ammo, while "large" refers to cartons with a bountiful supply.

AMMUNITION

TYPE	NUMBER OF BULLETS
Small Pistol Ammo:	20
Large Pistol Ammo:	100
Small SMG Ammo:	45
Large SMG Ammo:	225
SMG Grenade:	1
Small .357 Magnum Ammo:	6
Large .357 Magnum Ammo:	20
Shotgun Buckshot Ammo:	20
Fragmentation Grenade:	1
RPG Round:	1
Pulse Rifle Ammo:	20
Pulse Rifle Energy Orb Ammo:	1
Crossbow Ammo Bolts:	6

WEAPON DROP

In addition to weapon ammunition, actual weapons can be found lying around, usually near corpses or next to victims you've dropped. If you haven't received the particular weapon yet, it is added to your inventory. If you have the weapon already, ammunition equal to a small ammo box of that particular weapon type is added to your inventory.

INFINITE AMMO CRATE

Always inspect large chests with a particular ammunition emblem on them. These are Infinite Ammo Crates, and are constantly restocked with a particular ordnance, in this case SMG rounds. Bag as many as you need. You can come back to take more if you wish (be sure to do so after every combat).

Dropped items are found near the bodies of fallen Combine troops and Scanners. Soldiers dropping health or Grenades, only do so once every 30 seconds; spacing out kills may help you obtain more health pickups, if you can survive long enough.

If you pick up a weapon that an enemy dropped, you usually recover one magazine's worth of ammo for that weapon. One exception is that Metro Police drop much less ammo if they're armed with an SMG.

THE MARK V HAZARDOUS ENVIRONMENT SUIT (HEV SUIT)

This is a crucial body suit designed to constantly check the health of its wearer and administer painkillers if you are wounded. Your HEV Suit provides a HUD in constant use that shows your health, suit protection, weapon inventory, and enemy attack direction (if you are hit). Its Geiger counter alerts you to areas of radioactivity. Vision enhancement is provided by the suit's Zoom function ([Z]), built-in flashlight ([F]), and a target reticle. A computer informs you of your well-being. Swimming and Sprinting ([Shift]) are also possible. Refer to the Training section for more information on use these features.

HEALTH AND BATTERIES

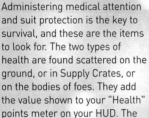

HEALTH VIAL: 10 HEALTH POINTS

HEALTH PACK: 25 HEALTH POINTS

SUIT BATTERY: 15 SUIT POINTS

Administering medical attention and suit protection is the key to survival, and these are the items to look for. The two types of health are found scattered on the ground, or in Supply Crates, or on the bodies of foes. They add the value shown to your "Health" points meter on your HUD. The Battery adds points to your Suit's armor protection ("Suit" on your HUD), and is found in the places health is obtained, as well as from destroyed Scanners.

RECHARGER

HEALTH RECHARGER: UP TO 50 HEALTH POINTS ADDED

HEV SUIT RECHARGER: UP TO 75 SUIT POINTS ADDED

COMBINE RECHARGER: UP TO 150 HEALTH POINTS ADDED, UP TO 150 SUIT POINTS ADDED

Dotted around the walls of your adventure are a number of Rechargers that dispense health, suit battery power, or a combination of both. Use these whenever you see them.

AIRBOAT

Pieced together from the remnants of a dune buggy and a marshland skimmer, this airboat steers similarly to the way you move (use your mouse to look and movement keys to steer). However, when reversing, the fins underneath the boat turn you in the opposite direction to a car, so learn how to accurately reverse before attempting complex maneuvers. The airboat can be abused without falling to pieces; accelerate up the banks of the river, but don't get too crazy, because the boat can land upside down and crush you. The boat's speed is its best asset—until a Combine Gauss Cannon is fitted to the front.

GAUSS CANNON
Chapter located: 4, Water Hazard
Damage inflicted: N/A
Ammunition(chamber/carried): N/A
Ammo pick-up amount: N/A
Secondary fire: Yes

Technique: The front-mounted Gauss Cannon on the airboat is an exceptionally powerful weapon with infinite ammunition, but a finite power supply. The weapon's strength remains constant, but watch the counter because the weapon needs recharging if it hits zero, and only recharges when you aren't firing. Otherwise, fire at everything that moves! It is used in specific combat to down a Hunter-Chopper and strafe Metro Police and APCs, and has a secondary fire Zoom function.

SCOUT CAR

Based off a dune-buggy frame, Eli Vance's transportation across the dangerous coastal zone has been this scout car. Robust and stable, usually landing on all four wheels, it is controlled in a similar manner to the airboat (use your mouse to look, and movement keys to steer).

The scout car is equipped with a turbo that provides a boost for using up sharp inclines and over jumps ([Shift]), and a handbrake ([Spacebar]) that lets you stop suddenly or skid and slide. Once you begin your drive, try both these special maneuvers, and also inspect the rear; there's infinite SMG ammo in this case!

TAU CANNON

Chapter located: 7: Highway 17
Damage inflicted: 15 (shot) 250 (burst)
Ammunition:
(chamber/carried): N/A
Ammo pick-up amount: N/A
Secondary fire: Yes

Technique: Firing this weapon evokes memories of a previous device that Gordon used during the Black Mesa Incident. However, this Tau Cannon is bolted firmly to the right front end of your car. Tap the left-click to fire a stream of beam fire, which is great for knocking back Antlions and firing faster than your regular handgun. Secondary fire (press right-click, hold, then release) is a charged beam that uses a concentrated beam to pull apart anything up to the size of an Antlion. The scout car's Tau Cannon does 15 points of damage per shot. If you charge fully for three seconds, the burst inflicts 250 damage. Combine Gunships are immune to this attack, so use it only for dealing with ground enemies of any size.

TURRET GUN (EMPLACEMENT)

This emplacement turret is used by the Combine Overwatch forces to lay down suppressing fire on groups of rebellious citizens. Turning the tide and using it to shoot rapid-fire pulses directly into the enemy is a simple but effective method of destroying groups of enemies. However, the lack of rotation and peripheral vision exposes you to attacks from the sides or behind. You can't take this weapon from its mount.

SENTRY GUN

The sentry gun, although featuring an unstable tripod base defect that was only noticed after manufacturing, is a definite bonus to have working in your favor; you can employ it in combat situations. The key to placing friendly sentry guns is to make sure there's a long line-of-sight, and aim the 90-degree firing angle through which the sentry gun can swivel toward the widest open area your foes maneuver into.

Always pick up a sentry gun with [E], not the Gravity Gun; otherwise, you'll be unarmed when you drop the sentry gun. You should also open fire on targets the gun spots. Keep a constant check on each sentry gun, because enemy weapons (especially the shotgun) can knock the gun out of its aiming alignment. The more reckless combat veteran can shoot around corners carrying this weapon without being tagged!

Finally, sentry guns placed by Combine forces will attack you and your teammates, but not Combine forces. These can be used only to destroy Zombie enemies. Sentry guns still in storage can be reprogrammed (by Alyx) and used against any enemy forces.

HOPPER

Hoppers take their name from their proximity attack; they "hop" in a single bound from a rooted position toward a target, then explode. These mobile mines are usually concealed by Combine forces in urban warfare situations, but you can use them too. Watch your step, and always clear away Hoppers before securing an area. The color of the device is very important:

- Red Hoppers are active, and will hop and attack you.
- Yellow Hoppers are primed and ready to launch at you, so be extremely careful if you see one of these; suck them from the ground, and with your Gravity Gun handy, use them as improvised Grenades to launch at enemies.
- Blue Hoppers are "friendly" models, which you can set by dropping them on the ground.
- Green Hoppers are friendly mines set by you or your team.

ENERGY ORB

Energy balls (also known as orbs) rising up the conduits in the Citadel can be used as excellent projectile weapons that act like the secondary fire capabilities of the Pulse Rifle. Use the organic variant of the Gravity Gun to manipulate the orbs, bank them around corners, and drive them through opponents. If you are carrying an energy orb and quickly move it around the screen, there are some blurring effects. Pick up these balls from any energy conduit.

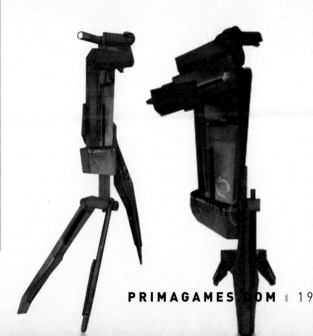

HλLF-LIFE²
PRIMA OFFICIAL GAME GUIDE

HALF-LIFERS: THE CHARACTERS

Your life-or-death struggle against the Combine menace is filled with interesting characters who help or hinder your progress. This chapter provides a biography for each main player, shown in order of appearance.

CAUTION

Biographies of some characters may reveal their allegiances. If you prefer to discover these yourself while you play, be warned.

THE COMBINE

Attracted to Earth by the dimensional rift caused by the Black Mesa Incident, a galactic infection of catastrophic proportions launched an invasive force that overpowered Earth, catching the human population (now called City 17), and the rest of the planet, by surprise.

A peace deal was brokered by former Black Mesa Laboratory Administrator Wallace Breen, leading to a subservient and meager existence for Earth's remaining human population under the oppressive entity known as the Combine. Aside from the Combine's unrelenting absorption and repurposing of Earth's resources to its own nefarious plans, little is known about this omnipresent collective.

GORDON FREEMAN

A native of Seattle, Washington, Gordon Freeman showed great interest and aptitude in the areas of quantum physics and relativity at a young age. His earliest heroes were Einstein, Hawking, and Feynman.

While visiting the University of Innsbruck in the late 1990s, Gordon Freeman observed a series of seminal teleportation experiments conducted by the Institute for Experimental Physics. Practical applications for teleportation became his obsession. In 1999, Freeman received his doctorate from M.I.T. with a thesis paper entitled *Observation of Einstein-Podolsky-Rosen Entanglement on Supraquantum Structures by Induction through Nonlinear Transuranic Crystal of Extremely Long Wavelength (ELW) Pulse from Mode-Locked Source Array.*

Disappointed with the slow pace and poor funding of academic research—and with tenure a distant dream—Gordon looked for a job in the private sector. As fortune would have it, his mentor at M.I.T., Professor Isaac Kleiner, had taken charge of a research project being conducted at a decommissioned missile base in Black Mesa, New Mexico. Kleiner was looking for a few bright associates, and Gordon was his first choice. Considering the source and amount of funds available to the Black Mesa Labs, Gordon suspected that he would be involved in some sort of weapons research, but in the hopes that practical civilian applications would arise in areas of quantum computing and astrophysics, he accepted Kleiner's offer. Apart from a butane-powered tennis ball cannon he constructed at age 6, Gordon had never handled a weapon of any sort—until the Black Mesa Incident.

After battling through a paradimensional rift to a final audience with a figure known only as the G-Man, Freeman agreed to work for him, hoping to become an aide to humanity in the process. It has been years since Gordon's former (and surviving) colleagues have heard from him, and the world has certainly changed since then.

THE G-MAN

First seen: Chapter 1, Point Insertion
Chapter appearances: 1-4, 6, 9, 11, 14
Alignment: Unknown

The so-called "G-Man" is a mysterious agent who may or may not represent a rogue government. He has a gravelly, mocking voice that tends to put emphasis and inflection in odd places—a voice that speeds up and slows down unpredictably, as if he is not quite comfortable with human speech.

ADMINISTRATOR
WALLACE BREEN

First seen: Chapter 1, Point Insertion
Chapter appearances: 1-3, 9-14
Alignment: Hostile

Dr. Breen is the former Administrator of Black Mesa Research Facility, and is now the Interim Administrator of Earth. He is dry, driven by logic, and literal-minded. Not a man who ever sought the spotlight, he finds himself forced to justify the invasion—and his decision to orchestrate Earth's surrender—by lecturing the public on the theory behind his appeasement. In person he is as cold and unfeeling as he appears on the gigantic monitors.

CITIZENS

First seen: Chapter 1, Point Insertion
Chapter appearances: 1-8, 10-12, 14
Alignment: Neutral/Friendly

The downtrodden citizens of City 17 are gloomy and hopeless until Gordon Freeman ignites the revolution. They then become determined fighters, offering assistance and warnings along with covering fire. The "Bestiary" section of this guide has further information on the resistance citizens (and Zombies that many of these city-dwellers turn into).

OFFICER
BARNEY CALHOUN

First seen: Chapter 1, Point Insertion
Chapter appearances: 1, 2, 11, 12
Alignment: Friendly

The stalwart security guard of *Half-Life* is back, working undercover as an officer for the Civil Protection Unit of City 17. Barney as a down-to-earth, fearless, wisecracking buddy: a good guy to have at your back in a fight.

INTRODUCTION

GETTING STARTED

WEAPONS DETAIL

HALF-LIFERS: THE CHARACTERS

THE BESTIARY

CHAPTER 1

CHAPTER 2

CHAPTER 3

CHAPTER 4

CHAPTER 5

CHAPTER 6

CHAPTER 7

CHAPTER 8

CHAPTER 9

CHAPTER 10

CHAPTER 11

CHAPTER 12

CHAPTER 13

CHAPTER 14

ANOMALOUS MATERIALS

HALF-LIFERS:
THE CHARACTERS

ALYX VANCE

First seen: Chapter 1, Point Insertion
Chapter appearances: 1, 2, 5, 6, 9-11, 14
Alignment: Friendly

Alyx Vance is a tough fighter and explorer who grew up in the post-invasion world learning science and mechanics at the knee of her inventor father. The harshness of the environment is tempered by the warmth of her father and the importance of the work she has done to keep the resistance together. She is extremely bright, but strong emotions and a keen intuition also drive her. She knows she doesn't like Dr. Mossman, but she can't quite put her finger on why.

DOCTOR ELI VANCE

First seen: Chapter 2, A Red Letter Day
Chapter appearances: 2, 5, 10, 14
Alignment: Friendly

Like Kleiner, Eli is also a brilliant scientist, but much more of a hands-on, pragmatic inventor of devices. He lost his leg to a Bullsquid while struggling to get Dr. Kleiner over a barrier into the comparative safety of a Combine city. He now works as a figurehead for the resistance, bridging the gap between Kleiner's abstract theories and the practical needs of the revolutionaries. Eli is warm, good-humored, and charismatic, holding everyone around him in the aura of his personal charm. His wife, Azian, was lost in the Black Mesa Incident.

PROFESSOR ISAAC KLEINER

First seen: Chapter 1, Point Insertion
Chapter appearances: 1, 2, 11
Alignment: Friendly

Dr. Kleiner is the quintessential absentminded professor, and an escapee from the Black Mesa Incident. He is wrapped up in theoretical physics while the resistance goes on around him. His speech is mannered and somewhat disconnected; he clearly enjoys talking about the strange concepts behind his work. He bears a soft spot for Alyx Vance, the daughter of his oldest surviving friend. He also has a penchant for exotic (and not to mention ironic) pets: nurturing and studying a de-beaked headcrab named Hedy Lamarr (after the actress and inventor) from birth.

DOCTOR JUDITH MOSSMAN

First seen: Chapter 2, A Red Letter Day
Chapter appearances: 2, 5, 10, 14
Alignment: Unknown

Judith Mossman is a brilliant physicist driven by unquenchable scientific curiosity and professional envy. This combination brought her under the sway of Dr. Breen, who has used her to penetrate Eli's resistance team. Over time she has come to love Eli while being torn by the knowledge that she is expected to betray him. She is intellectually superior but emotionally vulnerable, so she keeps a rigid grip on her emotions and comes off as somewhat chilly.

VORTIGAUNT ALLIES

First seen: Chapter 2, A Red Letter Day
Chapter appearances: 2, 3, 5, 7, 8
Alignment: Friendly

Vortigaunts are a hive-minded, energy-wielding slave race, inadvertently liberated by Gordon Freeman when he destroyed the Xen masters in his initial encounter with them after the Black Mesa Incident. Rather than fall under the dominion of the Combine, those Vortigaunts now stranded on Earth have joined with humans to fight for the freedom of all.

FATHER GRIGORI

First seen: Chapter 6, "We don't go to Ravenholm..."
Chapter Appearance: 6
Alignment: Friendly

Father Grigori sought out the harsh mining town of Ravenholm and did his best to minister to its citizens throughout the Combine invasion and occupation. He is tough, clever with his hands, and somewhat angry after seeing his entire flock struck down or turned to Zombies. There is not a scrap of fear in him. He meets the enemy with a mad laugh and a blaze of shotgun fire.

DOG

First seen: Chapter 5, Black Mesa East
Chapter appearances: 5, 11, 12
Alignment: Friendly

Created by Doctor Eli Vance more than two decades ago to both celebrate and protect his daughter, Alyx, this mechanoid has grown from a four-foot "pup" to a ten-foot-high bipedal armored beast with incredibly powerful fusion-powered appendages, thanks to the Vance family's tinkering. Dog has been programmed to be playful, but also ardently loyal to Alyx (acting as both a pet and bodyguard), and engages in unequalled ferocity when engaging forces of the hated Combine.

COLONEL ODESSA CUBBAGE

First seen: Chapter 7, Highway 17
Chapter appearance: 7
Alignment: Friendly

Odessa Cubbage, a.k.a. The Colonel, is the feisty leader of a small band of rebels located in New Little Odessa. Whether the town was named after him or whether he took the name from the village is uncertain. In fact, much about the Colonel is open to question: from his slightly askew mustache, to his supposedly British accent, which many suspect is as false as the military exploits with which he regales his followers. He seems far too young to have been a Bengal Lancer, or to have served with Rudyard Kipling. There is only one certainty when it comes to Colonel Odessa Cubbage: In times of peril, you will always find him in the basement Headquarters, dispatching firm orders and bravely sending warnings to neighboring outposts, while never exposing himself to the slightest personal harm.

INTRODUCTION

GETTING STARTED

WEAPONS DETAIL

HALF-LIFERS: THE CHARACTERS

THE BESTIARY

CHAPTER 1

CHAPTER 2

CHAPTER 3

CHAPTER 4

CHAPTER 5

CHAPTER 6

CHAPTER 7

CHAPTER 8

CHAPTER 9

CHAPTER 10

CHAPTER 11

CHAPTER 12

CHAPTER 13

CHAPTER 14

ANOMALOUS MATERIALS

THE BESTIARY

THE BESTIARY

Welcome to the bestiary, where the results of field studies regarding the life-forms you encounter are shown. All these creatures (except for the citizens) are hostile to you and the resistance fighters you lead. They are organized into two general groups: monsters and fiends that act independently, and the Combine collective, which attacks only to further its own goals.

CAUTION

The following bestiary lists information, including takedown tactics, of all the enemy entities you will encounter. If you do not wish to learn the full horror that awaits you, avoid reading this chapter.

Each creature's description lists information on where it appears, its health points and damage points, threat level and its type. Following this listing are lengthier descriptions regarding additional notes, attack patterns, and takedown tactics.

The threat level, a ranking from 1 to 5 stars, indicates how wary you should be when clashing with a particular foe.

★	**Negligible apprehension**–inconsequential foe
★★	**Slight trepidation**–possible minor harm
★★★	**Exercise caution**–expect reasonable retaliation
★★★★	**Real threat**–combat is hazardous
★★★★★	**Extreme danger**–powerful entity

Finally, to determine which weapon to use on each entity and how many shots are required for a particular weapon to destroy a foe, check the foe's health and compare it to the damage inflicted by a weapon's ammunition (refer to the "Weapons Detail" section for this information).

PART I: MONSTERS AND FIENDS

Monsters and fiends are subdivided into two classes: "Monstrous" (usually wildlife with animal instincts) and "Parasitic" (either a controlled or controller entity with simple and savage attack patterns).

ANTLION

First seen: Chapter 7, Highway 17
Chapter appearance(s): 7-9
Health: 30
Attack damage: 5 (mandible), 5 (land from jump)
Threat level: ★★★★
Entity type: Monstrous

NOTES AND ATTACK PATTERNS

These vicious predators hunt in herds of two to six (although they do attack on their own). They savage prey with giant mandibles that skewer and rend flesh. Their incisor-coated mouths knock you back

and damage you severely. Twice as fast as a humans and able to fly before pouncing (which is their second attack), these fiends are soon able to overwhelm you. They appear only when you disturb the sand they burrow up from; so avoid combat entirely by staying off beaches and keeping to rocky outcrops.

TAKEDOWN TACTICS

Retreat, run them over with your car, or shoot them with your Gravity Gun to flip them onto their backs while you escape. Antlions attack in waves, so after you kill about five at once, you have a moment to escape before more arrive. Without a car, blast them with fast-firing weapons, and seek higher ground off the sand that alerts them, or look for a black obelisk known as a Thumper that thuds the ground and scares them off.

NOTE

Once you have the Pheropod in your position, Antlions are considered friendly creatures to use as offensive weapons. When they attack an enemy, one single mandible or landing attack kills its target (usually a Combine Soldier).

ANTLION GUARD

First seen: Chapter 8, Sandtraps
Chapter appearance(s): 8, 9
Health: 500
Attack damage: 20 (charging butt), 10 (shove)
Threat level: ★★★★★
Entity type: Monstrous

NOTES AND ATTACK PATTERNS

One of the most feared creatures outside of the Combine Citadel, the Antlion Guard (also known as a Myrmidont), is an enlarged genus of the Antlion family, sporting more earthy tones and a larger elongated head. It scuttles quickly across any surface and relies on a thick, sinewy head to smash into targets, creating horrific blunt-trauma damage. When coupled with a charge, the damage is even more severe.

TAKEDOWN TACTICS

Either use the Gravity Gun to shoot heavy objects, such as high explosive weapons or barrels, at the beast, or use fire from multiple sources. Specifically, an RPG round is excellent at temporarily halting this beast, and an exploding barrel blasted right as the Antlion Guard summons Antlions from the ground defeats all the incoming enemies in a single explosion. If you are attacking an Antlion Guard together with a group of Combine Soldiers, let them wound the beast before finishing it off. Fight blunt attacks with your own heavy projectiles, such as radiators, sinks, or other medium-sized scenic pieces.

NOTE

With appropriate help from a Vortigaunt, you can harvest an Antlion Guard's pheromones and turn them into "bugbait," which attracts Antlions to the carrier, but won't attack him.

BARNACLE

First seen: Chapter 3, Route Kanal
Chapter appearance(s): 3, 4, 6, 9, 10, 12
Health: 35
Attack damage: Special (10 per second)
Threat level: ★
Entity type: Monstrous

NOTES AND ATTACK PATTERNS

A dangerous creature of limited intelligence, the Barnacle uses dark places to surprise its prey. Sticking to the ceiling, usually around a blind corner, the beast unravels a giant elongated tongue to the height of a human's head. Anything caught in this tongue is sucked up and rapidly pulled up into a sickly and slobbering maw.

TAKEDOWN TACTICS

Six pistol shots defeat a Barnacle, after which it drops a disgusting array of partially decomposed body parts. The main threat is when you don't notice them until you are entangled and hoisted up; if this occurs, blast at the mouth.

A better plan, which saves ammunition, is to avoid Barnacle combat altogether by feeding it an object (such as a crate or barrel), then running under the creature to bypass it. Or, push an explosive barrel under the tongue and light it as it gets sucked up—an excellent plan if you encounter a cluster of them.

THE
BESTIARY

CARNIVOROUS
LEECH

First seen: Chapter 7, Highway 17
Chapter appearance(s): 7, 8
Health: N/A
Attack damage: 10 per second of exposure
Threat level: ★★★
Entity type: Monstrous

NOTES AND ATTACK PATTERNS
The most serious reason for staying out of the water along the coastal beaches are the shoals of nasty Carnivorous Leeches. They continuously attack, making short work of you and any Antlions.

TAKEDOWN TACTICS
Simply back up out of the water. Carnivorous Leeches cannot be killed because of their numbers.

HEADCRAB

First seen: Chapter 3, Route Kanal
Chapter appearance(s): 3, 4, 6-13
Health: 10
Attack damage: 5 (bite)
Threat level: ★★
Entity type: Parasitic

NOTES AND ATTACK PATTERNS
This is the parasitic pest responsible for changing citizens across City 17 and beyond into cadavers of filth and depravity. Leaping up to scratch and tear, these whittle you down and then clamp onto your head, possess you, and slowly turn you into a Zombie. Released

during the initial Black Mesa Incident, they have survived and thrived in the intervening years. Their adaptation has caused the Combine to mass-breed them, then fit them into large missiles known as parasite rockets, and launch these into large areas of human resistance, such as the town of Ravenholm.

TAKEDOWN TACTICS
Produce your Crowbar and destroy any lurking Headcrab with a well-timed swing. Three Pistol shots or a quick burst from more powerful weaponry works well, but nothing beats a Crowbar for well-timed ferocity and effectiveness.

POISON HEADCRAB

First seen: Chapter 6, "We don't go to Ravenholm"
Chapter appearance(s): 6, 7, 9, 12
Health: 35
Attack damage: 10 (bite reduces health to 1)
Threat level: ★★★
Entity type: Parasitic

NOTES AND ATTACK PATTERNS
This is a cat-sized, spiderlike entity with a dark gray mottled back. It launches with a meaty maw opening, and if it connects, you're damaged by 10 points, and your health drops to 1! However, Poison Headcrabs alone cannot kill you; other enemies striking you while you're reduced to critical health do this job.

TAKEDOWN TACTICS
This is why it is important to destroy these creatures as a matter of urgency. Your Suit administers antitoxins, slowly rebuilding your health back to its original level (minus the original 10 points of damage the creature caused). Slam furniture into these beasts, pepper them with bullets, or bring out the Crowbar to quickly swat at them. If multiple types of enemies are around, the Crowbar isn't advised.

FAST HEADCRAB

First seen: Chapter 6, "We don't go to Ravenholm"
Chapter appearance(s): 6, 8-12
Health: 10
Attack damage: 5 (bite)
Threat level: ★★★
Entity type: Parasitic

NOTES AND ATTACK PATTERNS

Initially looking similar to the regular Headcrab, a closer inspection reveals spindly elongated legs and a more streamlined, less lumpy appearance. This is a Fast Headcrab; they move more quickly and are more difficult to pin down. Should one clamp on your head and kill you, it not only devours your head, but the skin from your entire body, flaying its victim and eventually transforming its host into a partial skeleton: the Fast Zombie.

TAKEDOWN TACTICS

Shoot or throw objects at a distance as they come toward you. At close range, Crowbar or Pistol shots work well.

ZOMBIE

First seen: Chapter 3, Route Kanal
Chapter appearance(s): 3, 4, 6, 8-12
Health: 50
Attack damage: 10 (single slash), 25 (double slash)
Threat level: ★★
Entity type: Parasitic

NOTES AND ATTACK PATTERNS

Known colloquially in parts of New Mexico as "Mawmen," Zombies are the results of a successful Headcrab attack on a human victim. The Headcrab is attached to the cranium and controls the host body, usually to attack and destroy. They swipe with sharp and filthy claws (sometimes both at the same time for added damage), and are able to throw scenery such as barrels at you with considerable force. However, their slow walk makes them easy to avoid.

TAKEDOWN TACTICS

Firstly, Zombies are vulnerable when they rise from a slumped position and can be easily killed at this point. Secondly, attack a Zombie with regular weaponry (such as the Shotgun or SMG) by aiming directly at the head. If you aim elsewhere and kill the Zombie, the Headcrab will survive and add to your combat time. Once you get the Gravity Gun, use various scenic pieces (ideally sharp, heavy and blunt, or flammable) to sever or crush them.

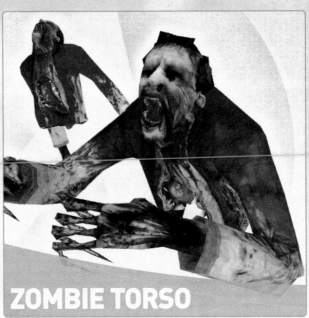

ZOMBIE TORSO

First seen: Chapter 3, Route Kanal
Chapter appearance(s): 3, 4, 6, 8-12
Health: 25
Attack damage: 10 (slash)
Threat level: ★★
Entity type: Parasitic

NOTES AND ATTACK PATTERNS

A Zombie Torso is an undead victim that's suffering further after-death indignities by having a Headcrab control all physical functions. The human has lost the use of its legs, usually resulting from previous combat or severing attacks.

TAKEDOWN TACTICS

Identical to the Zombie's, although the Zombie Torso moves slower, giving you more time to react. If you're attacking regular Zombies with sharp cutting objects and aim at the torso, you may create a Zombie Torso. Blast at the head with a Pistol or other weapon.

POISON ZOMBIE

First seen: Chapter 6, "We don't go to Ravenholm"
Chapter appearance(s): 6, 7, 9, 12
Health: 175
Attack damage: 20 (claw)
Threat level: ★★★
Entity type: Parasitic

NOTES AND ATTACK PATTERNS
A death too hideous for contemplation is to be a host body for up to four Poison Zombies. Bent over, the corpse only moves slowly, but has a nasty close mauling attack. Poison Headcrabs constantly leap back and forth from this wretched victim.

TAKEDOWN TACTICS
Compared to other undead types, the Poison Zombie takes colossal punishment to bring down (at least three Shotgun blasts). Target the Headcrabs first before you defeat the Zombie. However, if you have access to fire, back up and attempt to burn the host first, then deal with the Headcrabs individually. Scenery, Grenades, or Shotgun shells also work well.

FAST ZOMBIE

First seen: Chapter 6, "We don't go to Ravenholm"
Chapter appearance(s): 6, 8, 11, 12
Health: 50
Attack damage: 3 (claw)
10 (jumping slam)
Threat level: ★★★
Entity type: Parasitic

NOTES AND ATTACK PATTERNS
Perhaps the most frightening of the mutant undead, these former humans have been flayed and their dripping corpses commandeered by Fast Headcrabs. They move at extreme speed, leaping from rooftop to rooftop using their powerful legs to gain distance. They close in to land on you, and then swipe you to death.

TAKEDOWN TACTICS
Because they are so quick, don't run; stand your ground and fight. A sharp blade to the head or a single shot by a powerful weapon is the only real way to bring them down. Bring out the Shotgun or Magnum and aim for the head. If you spot any scuttling up drainpipes near your location, you have some extra time to aim and drop them; otherwise, stay cool, find a doorway to help block them off, and stay on the other side and blast the heads off.

PART II: COMBINE COLLECTIVE
The other enemy group serves the Combine, and further divides into three types: Humanoid, Machine, and Synth. Humanoids are human or once-human figures that serve the Combine. Machines are entities created by the Combine and used for their offensive capabilities, and are not sentient. Synths are self-repairing biomechanical organisms constructed deep in the bowels of the Citadel and are usually the Combine's most feared troops.

METRO COPS

First seen: Chapter 1, Point Insertion
Chapter appearance(s): 1-4, 11
Health: 26 (Chapters 1-4), 40 (Chapter 11)
Attack damage: Manhack release
0 (stun baton)
3 (Pistol per shot)
3 (SMG per shot)
Threat level: ★★
Entity type: Humanoid (Overwatch)

NOTES AND ATTACK PATTERNS
Part of the Combine public order force known as Overwatch, these humans clad in riot gear rule City 17 with an iron fist. They can also release a floating, bladed attack robot known as a Manhack.

TAKEDOWN TACTICS

You can use various scenery items, such as explosive barrels or turret guns, to your advantage, but otherwise, a brief half-dozen Pistol shots to the head is perfect for downing a Metro Cop. Switch to your SMG once you obtain it, and always aim for the head. Finally, try to stop the Cops from firing a flare skyward; if they succeed, at least three more Cop reinforcements will deploy.

COMBINE SOLDIER

First seen: Chapter 6, "We don't go to Ravenholm"
Chapter appearance(s): 6-14
Health: 50
Attack damage: 10 (rifle-butt)
3 (SMG per shot)
3 (Shotgun per shot)
3 (Pulse Rifle per shot)
75 (Grenade per detonation)
Threat level: ★★★★
Entity type: Humanoid (Overwatch)

NOTES AND ATTACK PATTERNS

The shock troop of the hated Combine, the Soldier is an intelligent infantryman that works well in a team and has multiple methods of attack, depending on the combat situation. They drop ammunition when they succumb to your fire, and are armed with a Shotgun, SMG, Pulse Rifle, and Grenades. The walkthrough chapters contain multiple methods of defeating them, because combat is never the same twice, but for some basic tactics, try the plans described here, which work for Soldiers and Elites.

TAKEDOWN TACTICS

1. Bring rapid-fire weapons to bear on their heads quickly.
2. Listen to their weapons. If you hear a Shotgun blast, focus on that Soldier first, because they inflict a huge amount of damage.
3. When fighting in dark corridors or tossing explosives around corners, listen for the long beep that indicates a Soldier has been killed.
4. Living Soldiers can be heard via your HEV Suit, and the radio chatter indicates a menace. When combat chatter ceases, Soldiers in the area have been defeated.
5. Listen for the phrase "Outbreak! Outbreak! Outbreak!" during combat. This is the Combine code word to indicate that only one Soldier remains, and combat should be easier from this point.

6. When fighting Soldiers inside structures from the outside, breaking a building's window and throwing in a Grenade causes the most havoc, and sometimes forces them out the building's doors and into your line of sight.
7. Soldiers must reload just like you; if you hear them in the middle of reloading, charge in and cut them down.
8. Combine Elite are particularly dangerous when fighting on structures with a drop nearby; their "orb" attack not only inflicts sizable damage, but it also shoves you a short distance, which can result in a death plummet. Listen for the orb's charging sound, then immediately sidestep so the ball misses you. If you're gifted with quick reactions, use the Gravity Gun to catch the orb and shoot it back at them.
9. Your Pulse Rifle's secondary orb fire is an excellent way of destroying multiple Soldiers. However, you can't collect any ammunition from a Soldier killed this way.
10. Always attempt a ram if you're inside a vehicle and spot Combine Soldiers on the road; it's usually easy to strike them down for an instant kill.
11. Hoppers, plentiful in City 17, are excellent for placing at entrances before a Combine Soldier intrusion; a number will be caught in the explosion.
12. Combine Soldiers standing at extreme range should be destroyed with your Crossbow or RPG.
13. Soldiers carrying shotguns are especially brutal because they can unload into you rapidly, especially when panicked. Pick off these Soldiers first, if possible.
14. Back away from close combat, because the Soldier's rifle-butt attack is vicious and damaging.

COMBINE ELITE

First seen: Chapter 9, Nova Prospekt
Chapter appearance(s): 9-14
Health: 70
Attack damage: 15 (rifle-butt)
3 (Pulse Rifle)
15 (Pulse Rifle Secondary fire orb)
Threat level: ★★★★
Entity type: Humanoid (Overwatch)

THE BESTIARY

NOTES AND ATTACK PATTERNS

Clad in white protective armor and sporting a Pulse Rifle and a single red ocular sensor, the cream of the Combine crop are the sharpshooting Elite. They act in groups of their own kind, or sometimes lead squads of Combine Soldiers. Elite are tougher, fire faster and more accurately than regular humanoid forces, and use a highly damaging orb attack from their pulse rifles (which causes 15 damage per hit). They react to combat in a similar way to Combine Soldiers, and must be treated in the same careful and methodical manner (see the Soldier takedown tactics previously). If you have a choice, deal with Elites before regular forces.

NOTE

Combine Elites drop a special item: a pulse rifle secondary fire orb that is very useful in combat situations. Be sure you pick these up.

STALKER

First seen: Chapter 9, Nova Prospekt
Chapter appearance(s): 9, 13
Health: N/A
Attack damage: N/A
Threat level: ★
Entity type: Humanoid

NOTES AND ATTACK PATTERNS

Humans unfortunate enough to take a train from City 17 to Nova Prospekt are delivered to Combine scientists. These feared experimenters sever higher brain functions, experiment on the lobotomized victim in any number of foul and depraved ways, embed a number of blackened nano-devices in the skin, and slowly watch the victim lose all humanity. Known by the codename "Stalker," these emaciated slaves are sent on any number of menial duties inside the vast edifice known as the Combine Citadel.

TAKEDOWN TACTICS

These are never encountered in the combat zone and therefore pose no threat to you.

ARMORED PERSONNEL CARRIER (APC)

First seen: Chapter 1, Point Insertion
Chapter appearance(s): 1, 3, 4, 7, 8, 11, 12
Health: 750
Attack damage: 5 (minigun per bullet)
25 (missile strike)
Threat level: ★★★★
Entity type: Machine

NOTES AND ATTACK PATTERNS

The Combine APC is a well-armored and sturdy troop carrier armed with a turret-mounted rocket launcher and minigun. APCs cannot be entered, and usually only attack from extreme range.

TAKEDOWN TACTICS

When you are called upon to actually disintegrate an APC, you'll have the weapon for the job mounted to the front of your boat. Strafe the sides of the APC until the vehicle bursts into flames.

HUNTER-CHOPPER

First seen: Chapter 3, Route Kanal
Chapter appearance(s): 3-5
Health: 5,600
Attack damage: 5 (minigun per bullet)
30 (bomb strike at epicenter)
Threat level: ★★★★★
Entity type: Machine

NOTES AND ATTACK PATTERNS

The Hunter-Chopper is the optimal machinery created by human hands (the Combine concentrated on more biomechanical offensive airborne vehicles). The Hunter-Chopper stalks you through most of your adventure through the canal system of City 17, strafing you with highly damaging cannon fire in bursts.

TAKEDOWN TACTICS

While you lack proper armament to defeat it, run to suitable cover between its bursts of cannon fire. Once the gauss cannon has been fitted to your boat, refer to the end of Chapter 4, Water Hazard, for all the combat tips you need to defeat this airborne menace.

MANHACK

First seen: Chapter 3, Route Kanal
Chapter appearance(s): 3, 4, 8-13
Health: 25
Attack damage: 20 (blade)
Threat level: ★★
Entity type: Machine

NOTES AND ATTACK PATTERNS

Usually released by Metro Cops, these nasty robotic hovering devices have gyroscopic sensors to steady themselves in the air. They tend to work in packs, charging you and wounding with rotating blades.

TAKEDOWN TACTICS

Prior to other forms of weaponry, the best way to defeat a Manhack is by timing a Crowbar swing just as it zooms at you, but before it connects. Then follow it with a second, killing blow, knocking the Manhack into a wall if you can. Once you have the Gravity Gun, suck the Manhack into the weapon's field, then shoot it out, ideally into a wall.

NOTE

Manhacks can be used in conjunction with your Gravity Gun like a chainsaw; suck one so it floats in front of you, caught in the Gravity Gun's energy field, then run into enemies with it.

ROLLERMINE

First seen: Chapter 7, Highway 17
Chapter appearance(s): 7, 8
Health: N/A
Attack damage: 10 (shock)
Threat level: ★★
Entity type: Machine

NOTES AND ATTACK PATTERNS

These pulsing orbs are a Combine creation that appear on roads or in buildings, then home in on you, buffeting you and causing nasty electrical damage.

TAKEDOWN TACTICS

If you're in the scout car, the mines buffet it; more than one can cause severe control loss. Bring out the Gravity Gun, suck up each mine, then blast it over a nearby cliff into water, where the devices short-circuit. Note that explosions (from barrels or gas cans) also destroy Rollermines.

SCANNER TYPE I

First seen: Chapter 1, Point Insertion
Chapter appearance(s): 1-5, 13
Health: 30
Attack damage: 25 (dive)
Threat level: ★
Entity type: Machine

INTRODUCTION

GETTING STARTED

HALF-LIFERS

WEAPONS DETAIL

THE BESTIARY

CHAPTER 1

CHAPTER 2

CHAPTER 3

CHAPTER 4

CHAPTER 5

CHAPTER 6

CHAPTER 7

CHAPTER 8

CHAPTER 9

CHAPTER 10

CHAPTER 11

CHAPTER 12

CHAPTER 13

CHAPTER 14

ANOMALOUS MATERIALS

THE BESTIARY

NOTES AND ATTACK PATTERNS

These Scanners harass you from the moment you enter City 17. They constantly watch your movements, relaying a live feed to the Combine Civil Protection units in the field. They do not harm you, but they do blind you with spotlights as they home in on your location.

TAKEDOWN TACTICS

As soon as some become available, you can throw paint cans at the Scanner to destroy it. With the Crowbar, slash at it only when it flies close to you. A better plan is to simply tag it with a Pistol until it begins to smoke. Then it tries to dive-bomb you in a suicide plummet; blast it apart before it reaches you. Once you have the Gravity Gun, simply employ the takedown tactic used to halt Manhacks.

SCANNER TYPE II

First seen: Chapter 11, Anticitizen One
Chapter appearance(s): 11, 12
Health: 30
Attack damage: 3 (per bullet)
25 (dive)
Threat level: ★
Entity type: Machine

NOTES AND ATTACK PATTERNS

This Scanner features a quick-firing machine gun and the usual blinding searchlight. These are slightly more hardy and have multiple purposes: attacking citizens, carrying mobile mines known as Hoppers, and searching for undesirables.

TAKEDOWN TACTICS

Shoot it from the sky before it can drop any cargo, and if you're short on Batteries for your HEV Suit, these drop them; look for Batteries in the debris that falls to earth after a successful kill. In a pinch, remember your Gravity Gun and employ the suck-and-blast plan used against the Manhack.

SENTRY GUN

First seen: Chapter 9, Nova Prospekt
Chapter appearance(s): 9-12
Health: N/A
Attack damage: 3 (per bullet)
Threat level: ★★★
Entity type: Machine

NOTES AND ATTACK PATTERNS

These tripod-mounted sentry guns have a 90-degree firing angle forward and are motion-sensitive, which means as soon as movement from organic beings is sensed, the machine guns atop the sentry mounting activate.

TAKEDOWN TACTICS

Fortunately, the guns are easily toppled. When facing such a device, use Antlions (or a barrel or radiator) as fodder to soak up the gunfire. Move to the side or around the back of the sentry gun, and run into it to knock it over. Or, you can blast it with a Shotgun, or pick it up and drop it. Be careful to pick it up with the gun pointing away from you! Once pushed over, a sentry gun fires a burst and deactivates until placed right-side up. You can also knock over sentry guns with well-placed Grenades or other thrown objects. You can even carry sentry guns to destroy non-Combine forces (place them at 90-degree angles, and refer to the walkthrough for specific strategies).

GROUND TURRET

First seen: Chapter 12, "Follow Freeman!"
Chapter appearance(s): 12
Health: N/A (only destroyed by Grenade)
Attack damage: 3 (per bullet)
Threat level: ★★★
Entity type: Machine

NOTES AND ATTACK PATTERNS

Ground turrets are interior gun emplacements that search for signs of movement on the floor they guard. The turret emits a constant radar range arc visible as blue laser light coming from the front of a floor tile. When it senses something, the turret rises from the ground, and a machine gun unleashes a fixed stream of bullets (about 20 bullets per second—a much higher rate of fire than other enemies with machine guns).

TAKEDOWN TACTICS

The plan of attack is to activate the turret, step to the side out of its range, and roll (using right click) a Grenade into the workings the turret exposes when it rises from the ground. Keep an eye out for the blue laser light that indicates a ground turret nearby.

COMBINE DROPSHIP

First seen: Chapter 4, Water Hazard
Chapter appearance(s): 4, 7, 8, 11, 13
Health: N/A
Attack damage: 3 (per bullet)
Threat level: ★
Entity type: Synth

NOTES AND ATTACK PATTERNS

A giant swooping *thing* featuring eight massive spiderlike legs is a part of the Combine attack force, but doesn't play an offensive role. It transports other Combine forces (APCs, containers full of troops, or Striders) to battle locations, and then returns to the Citadel.

TAKEDOWN TACTICS

Dropships cannot be destroyed by the weapons available to you, but the cargo they carry can (however, the cargo is usually deposited before you can react). Simply ignore the Dropships and concentrate on the forces they release. The wake on the Dropship pushes Grenades away.

COMBINE GUNSHIP

First seen: Chapter 1, Point Insertion
Chapter appearance(s): 1, 7, 8, 12-14
Health: N/A
      3 (direct RPG hits for Easy difficulty)
      5 (direct RPG hits for Normal difficulty)
      7 (direct RPG hits for Hard difficulty)
Attack damage: 3 (per bullet)
Threat level: ★★★★
Entity type: Synth

NOTES AND ATTACK PATTERNS

The Combine Gunship is a blend of biomorphic and mechanical parts created to form the ultimate in airborne assault craft. It has a single jet engine powering a fan that propels it in all directions with extreme grace and maneuverability. It attacks with a fast-firing cannon mounted to the snout of the vehicle.

TAKEDOWN TACTICS

The only weapon powerful enough to take down a Gunship is the RPG. When the gunship finishes a blast of cannon fire, step out of cover and launch a rocket, using the red target laser to maneuver the rocket in a spiraling path known as a "corkscrew." This allows you to avoid the Gunship's cannon, which can easily destroy incoming rockets that aren't flying in an erratic pattern. Continue this corkscrew attack until the machine blows apart after three, five, or seven hits (depending on difficulty level).

COMBINE ADVISOR

First seen: Chapter 2, A Red Letter Day
Chapter appearance(s): 2, 14
Health: N/A
Attack damage: N/A
Threat level: ★
Entity type: Synth

NOTES AND ATTACK PATTERNS
Behold the real face of the Combine. A giant, green, sluglike entity with the gift of telekinesis appears for the briefest of moments on Breen's computer monitors within the Citadel.

TAKEDOWN TACTICS
These are never encountered in the combat zone and therefore pose no threat to you.

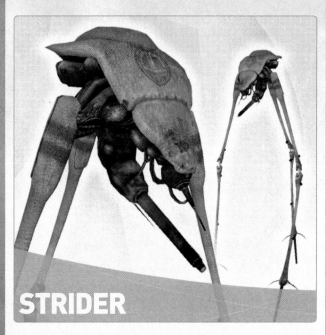

STRIDER

First seen: Chapter 1, Point Insertion
Chapter appearance(s): 1, 11-13
Health: N/A
    3 (direct RPG hits for Easy difficulty)
    5 (direct RPG hits for Normal difficulty)
    7 (direct RPG hits for Hard difficulty)
(Note that Pulse Rifle secondary fire orb attacks, Grenades, and SMG Grenades count as half a direct hit for damage calculation.)

Attack damage: 5 (per bullet)
    Death (warp cannon shot)
    Death (foot skewer)
Threat level: ★★★★★
Entity type: Synth

NOTES AND ATTACK PATTERNS
This giant tripod attacks with two weapons mounted to its snout: a machine-gun-like rapid-fire weapon, and what can only be described as a warp cannon that instantly kills anything it touches. It also attacks with its sharp skewering tripod feet.

TAKEDOWN TACTICS
Instant death and scenic destruction are the result whenever the warp cannon fires its particle beam, so stay out of the shimmering light. Seek cover from the machine-gun fire, and stay clear of the legs, which skewer human-sized foes with their sharp feet. Only use powerful projectiles against Striders. RPGs, Grenades, SMG Grenades, or Pulse Rifle secondary fire orbs are all recommended, and the Strider only attacks you after you hit it if other targets are in the area. Two, four, or six direct strikes are needed to topple one of these colossal fiends. Finally, if fighting a Strider inside the confines of the Citadel, three orb strikes are needed to bring it down.

CRAB-SYNTH AND MORTAR-SYNTH

First seen: Chapter 13, Benefactory
Chapter appearance(s): 13
Health: N/A
Attack damage: N/A
Threat level: ★
Entity type: Synth

NOTES AND ATTACK PATTERNS
You have only the briefest of glimpses of these strange, inhuman contraptions: self-replicating and part-replacing synths, the backbone of the Combine's subsequent armies. Crab Synths with their sharp mandibles are close-quarter ripping fiends, while Mortar Synths utilize biomechanical armaments and shells to wreak havoc on the humans they are about to destroy.

TAKEDOWN TACTICS
These are never encountered in the combat zone and therefore pose no threat to you.

THE BESTIARY

PART III: HUMAN RESISTANCE FORCES

Human resistance forces are a key part of the fight against the Combine. Learning which citizens can actually aid your progress, and how to utilize them in the combat zone, is pivotal to your success.

REPATRIATED CITIZEN

First seen: Chapter 1, Point Insertion
Chapter appearance(s): 1, 3, 11, 12
Health: 40
Attack damage (to enemies): Pulse Rifle 3 (per bullet)
Pistol 3 (per bullet)
SMG 3 (per bullet)
Shotgun 3 (per round)
RPG 50 (per shot)
Grenade 75 (per grenade)

Forced into dilapidated tenement blocks or worse (many citizens are indiscriminately picked from trains or homes and taken for "reevaluation" at a prison known as Nova Prospekt), City 17 citizens live in a constant state of fear and bewilderment, having most of their basic rights removed, such as the right to assemble, grow their own food, and even procreate. Don't expect any help from them until the tide turns in your favor.

RESISTANCE CITIZENS

First seen: Chapter 3, Route Kanal
Chapter appearance(s): 3-8, 11, 12

Resistance Citizens are key to your survival once you uncover the clandestine operation headed by Doctor Eli Vance that pits likeminded freeform fighters against the might of the Combine. During battles against either large entities, such as Gunships or Combine forces on the streets of City 17, you have the extra help of human forces. Their outfits and combat capabilities vary, but all can help you during the most violent and trying times in your adventure.

- **Medic:** When you need health during combat, look for the citizens wearing red-and-white armbands, move to their location, and speak with them ([E]).
- **Ammo Carrier:** Check troops following you closely, as they are able to replenish some of your inventory during battle. Again, move toward them and speak to gather their ammo.
- **Shotgun, SMG, Pulse Rifle, RPG:** Troops carry these various weapons with them depending on the combat situation.

TACTICS

When the icons appear in the bottom-right corner of the HEV Suit display, you can gather up to four friendly troops to help you with combat. Moving them into position is simply a matter of aiming your target reticle and pressing [C]; the team will move to that position.

You have two basic tactics that work best. Order your team forward into combat, which helps you locate enemies instead of being surprised. Or, you can ambush enemies caught between you and your team by moving into a room while leaving troops behind.

Otherwise, the team acts independently, and don't need any instructions once combat begins.

INTRODUCTION

GETTING STARTED

HALF-LIFERS

WEAPONS DETAIL

THE BESTIARY

CHAPTER [1]

CHAPTER [2]

CHAPTER [3]

CHAPTER [4]

CHAPTER [5]

CHAPTER [6]

CHAPTER [7]

CHAPTER [8]

CHAPTER [9]

CHAPTER [10]

CHAPTER [11]

CHAPTER [12]

CHAPTER [13]

CHAPTER [14]

ANOMALOUS MATERIALS

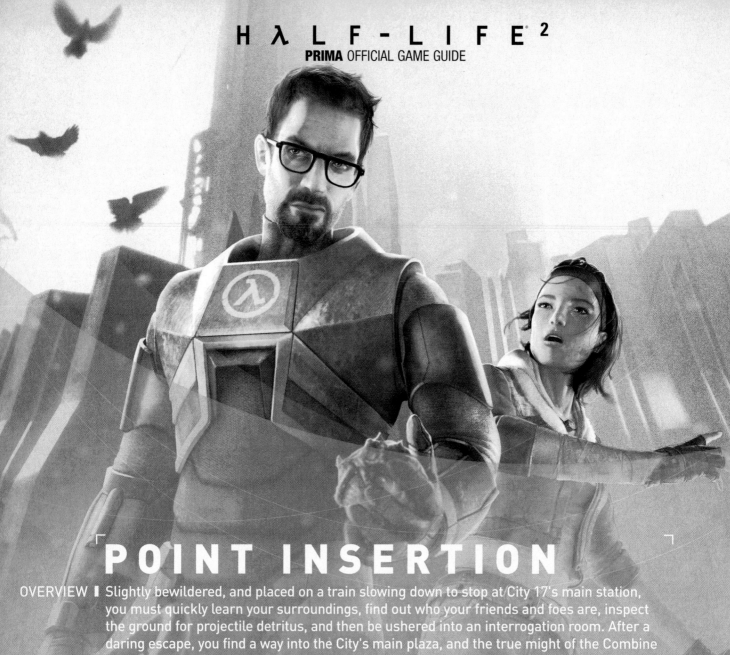

POINT INSERTION

OVERVIEW ▮ Slightly bewildered, and placed on a train slowing down to stop at City 17's main station, you must quickly learn your surroundings, find out who your friends and foes are, inspect the ground for projectile detritus, and then be ushered into an interrogation room. After a daring escape, you find a way into the City's main plaza, and the true might of the Combine is revealed. Remaining under cover, you must seek the help of the resistance force in a dilapidated tenement block, outrunning the Combine's police forces through the maze of corridors and apartment dwellings before a daring roof escape. Only then, and after a brush with the overzealous batons of the Metro Cops, do you meet the daughter of an old friend, who is determined to lead you to safety.

INVENTORY PICK-UP

- Scenic items only

ENTITY ENCOUNTER
FRIENDLIES

- City 17 Repatriation Citizens*
- Barney Calhoun*
- Doctor Issac Kleiner (via video feed)*
- Alyx Vance*

ENTITY ENCOUNTER
HOSTILES

- Metro Cops*
- Scanners*
- Dr. Wallace Breen (via video feed)*
- Combine Armored Personnel Carrier (Combine APC)*
- Strider*
- Combine Gunships*

* Indicates first exposure to entity

"WELCOME TO CITY 17. IT'S SAFER HERE."

| MAP 1 | **CITY 17: TRAIN STATION** |

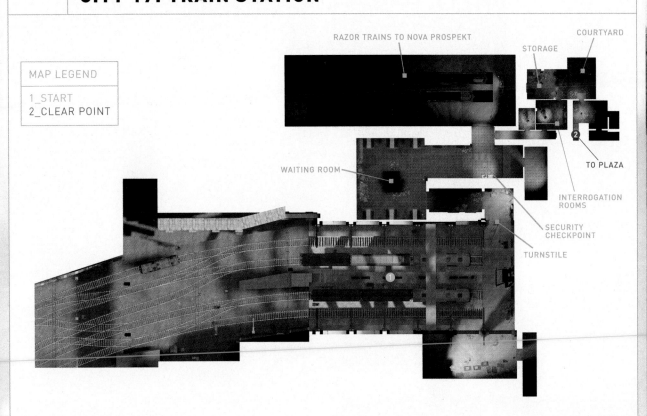

RAZOR TRAINS TO NOVA PROSPEKT

STORAGE

COURTYARD

MAP LEGEND

1_START
2_CLEAR POINT

TO PLAZA

WAITING ROOM

INTERROGATION ROOMS

SECURITY CHECKPOINT

TURNSTILE

Look out the train's window at the gloomy landscape passing by. The train is slowing down. There's a station in the distance. Welcome to City 17.

Walk out onto the train station platform. Above you, a hovering camera device known as a Scanner quietly buzzes around you, filming your moves. Ignore it and the area to the right (or behind you); a sturdy mesh gate prevents you from fleeing onto the tracks.

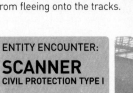

Move forward to chat with the passenger waiting at the door. He doesn't look too steady. He mumbles something about this being his third transfer this year.

Pass him and move to the car's far end. Talk to the bewildered sitting passenger; he never gets used to this "relocation." Hmm. Everyone seems to be dressed alike and carrying battered suitcases. The train is grinding to a halt. Face the door on the right.

ENTITY ENCOUNTER:

SCANNER
CIVIL PROTECTION TYPE I

These Scanners harass you from the moment you step onto the station platform. They constantly watch your movements, relaying a live feed to the Combine Civil Protection units in the field. Currently, they cannot be deactivated. Wait until you reach the rooftops to engage these in combat.

Instead, follow the two disembarking passengers as they round the corner and the front of the train, heading toward a turnstile. Above you looms the face of a white-bearded man. He looks familiar, but you can't place his face. He's welcoming you to City 17.

ADDITIONAL INVESTIGATIONS

Listening to the first of many Breencasts sends a chill up your spine: "Welcome. Welcome to City 17. You have chosen, or been chosen, to relocate to one of our finest remaining urban centers. I thought so much of City 17 that I elected to establish my Administration here, in the Citadel so thoughtfully provided by our benefactors. I have been proud to call City 17 my home. And so, whether you are here to stay, or passing through on your way to parts unknown, welcome to City 17. It's safer here."

When you've heard enough, you see a uniformed officer in an altercation with a man attempting to grab his luggage. You can't get involved, so pass it by.

At the turnstile is a young woman in the same drab uniform as the others. She's desperate for news on an incoming train; Overwatch has taken her husband in for "questioning." When you're ready to leave the station platform, pass through the turnstile and go around to the left.

ENTITY ENCOUNTER:
METRO POLICE
CIVIL PROTECTION

If you want to extend your stay on the platform, you can try hassling the officer. These are Metro Cops, and they police the city with an iron fist (actually, an electric stun baton). Currently, they have primed their batons to a light stun, but beware of their ruthless pursuit of resistance members. Combat must begin when a weapon of note is later secured.

INVENTORY ADAPTATION
SCENIC DEBRIS

Check around for an object, press E to pick it up, then throw it. The height at which you're looking influences how far the object will travel. Heavier objects cannot be thrown as far as lighter objects. Practice by throwing suitcases and cans until you are comfortable with the throwing behavior of different objects.

The Cop doesn't take kindly to thrown objects and will chase you for a moment, trying for a baton swipe. Don't worry, this is just a stun. But watch your throwing! You can also watch an alien slave sweeping while a Cop gives orders.

However, you cannot enter the area with the sweeping alien. Isn't that a Vortigaunt? Pass through the turnstile, optionally talking to the young lady again. Then inspect the lockers. You can open them by knocking yourself into them or pressing E.

There's little inside the lockers, so move to the drinks dispenser. This knocks out four cans of Dr. Breen's Private Reserve before the machine runs out. Practice throwing them if you want. Turn and walk through the small tunnel to the train station waiting area.

This looks like a waiting area for those expecting loved ones to arrive. Step into the room, look to the right, and you'll see a security checkpoint. Make your way over there in a moment. It's time to interview some citizens.

In front of you on a table is an older gentleman who reckons, "They put something in the water to make you forget. I don't even remember how I got here."

Over at the far end of the waiting room is a man pacing up and down, looking at the train departure times and babbling. It seems none of the trains from other nearby cities (numbered from 8 to 27) ever arrive on time.

The next man sitting down looks more than a little perturbed. "I see they took your suitcase too," he notes. "They can't get away with this much longer." The next seated man has a worried look etched across his face. "I'm working up the nerve to go on," he blusters.

These two are a little more upbeat. "Dr. Breen again? I was hoping I'd seen the last of him in City 14," the first man says. "I wouldn't say that too loud. This is his base of operations," the other retorts. When you've listened enough, move down the fenced area, snaking around to the security checkpoint.

Wait for the two citizens in front of you to be ushered off into different areas. While the man with the white beard, the Administrator of City 17, continues to speak, move forward toward the Metro Cops. Avoid attracting attention to yourself.

CAUTION

Don't mess with the Cops! If you must, grab a suitcase from the table to your right, and hurl it at a Cop. You'll feel the taste of his baton, but won't be wounded. Get too close to a Cop, and they'll push you back. Continue to hassle them, and they'll swat you away with their nightsticks.

The Metro Cop to the right won't let you through that gate, so step toward the other gate, passing between two guards. Notice the slender black camera tracking you through the station. Not a time for heroics.

Once you're through the gate, you see what looks like a giant, imposing train at a blocked-off platform with a sign reading Nova Prospekt. You're trying to remember: wasn't that the name of an old gulag?

Nova Prospekt isn't your destination though; the Cop is now blocking your path back to the checkpoint area, and the security door opens. Another Cop beckons you in. This doesn't look good. What are they trying to pin on you?

You have little choice but to follow the Cop down a narrow passageway with two cell doors to the left. Inside the first is a citizen valiantly trying to explain his security clearance. "This must be a mistake!" the man cries. "I got a standard relocation coupon, just like everybody else!" The Cop inside slams the peephole closed.

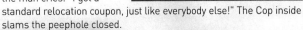

Try to ignore the shrieking, and continue to the end of the corridor and to the next cell door on your left. The Metro Cop bangs on the door loudly, a second Cop opens the door from the other side, and you're told to enter the room.

By the amount of blood in here, it seems the Metro Cops have been a little heavy-handed in their techniques. Ignore the objects in the room and listen to the Metro Cop while he deactivates the security cameras and babbles on about... a beer he owes you?!

It's a familiar face! Barney Calhoun, your drinking buddy from Black Mesa! He seems to have infiltrated the City 17 Metro Police Civil Protection program, and certainly looks the part. He then turns and taps into the computer terminal.

Barney introduces an old friend; Doctor Kleiner from the research laboratory. It seems Barney saved you from a one-way trip to Nova Prospekt! Kleiner seems most happy to see you, and agrees you should meet up with someone named Alyx. Now if only there was a way out of this interrogation chamber... did you hear a knock on the door?

The Metro Cops are on the other side of the door, waiting to know how your "chat" is going. You'd better depart, and Barney shows you the exit door. Perhaps you'll meet later. For now, head into the storage room, turn left, and pass through the gate.

Follow Barney's instructions on escaping this room by constructing some sort of elaborate box stack. Or, just climb the metal ladder. Make sure you're good at picking up and dropping objects before you head up the ladder.

At the top of the ladder, all you need to do to escape is place a crate under the left window, jump onto it, then up on the windowsill, and drop down to the small courtyard below. Once on the ground, look around.

TIP

A variety of objects here are great for throwing practice. You can only drop the heavy concrete bricks. The beer bottles, however, will fly through the window you just leapt from. This improves your aiming, so practice with a few bottles.

CHAPTER¹
ENCOUNTERS

INSTINCT MUST BE EXPUNGED

MAP 2 | ## CITY 17: TRAIN STATION PLAZA

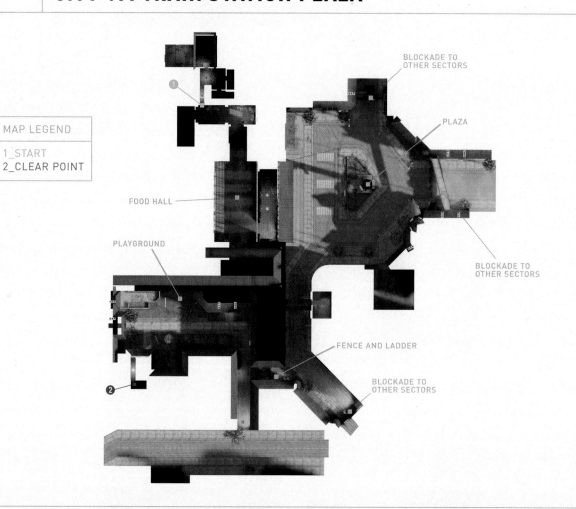

BLOCKADE TO OTHER SECTORS

PLAZA

MAP LEGEND

1_START
2_CLEAR POINT

FOOD HALL

BLOCKADE TO OTHER SECTORS

PLAYGROUND

FENCE AND LADDER

BLOCKADE TO OTHER SECTORS

When you've finished throwing practice, head through the door into a room; head up the stairs to the door. Go through to a slightly messy foyer. A Cop is at the entrance.

He flicks a can from the trash bin, and it drops at your feet. "Pick it up!" he says. Do as he says, depositing the can into the trash bin to the Cop's left, and he lets you through with a chuckle.

TIP

If you're not good with authority, you can also throw the can at the Cop, who takes a baton swing at you. Or, you can throw the can past the Cop into the courtyard, or ignore the can and barge into the Cop until he gets tired of swatting you and lets you through into a large open hallway. Even if you ignore the trash can, the Cop eventually lets you past.

The Administrator is again discussing the virtues of this enforced captivity. Is he mad? Or working for this junta? Move into this chamber. To the left is a surly Cop guarding a door. Ignore him, and check the citizens in line. They seem to be waiting for an automated device to dispense a sack of groceries. None want to talk to you. The food is less than palatable; "You gotta be damn hungry to wait in line for this crap," you're informed.

No point in spoiling the citizens' right to gruel, so head over to the Metro Cop guarding the gate at the far end of the hall. He's not letting you through here, so avoid a baton pummeling and head through the entrance to his left.

If you're craving a brew of mood-altering drugs and water, you can bang away at the vending machine here until five cans of Dr. Breen's Private Reserve fall out. When you're done, ignore the double doors at the far left end of the hall.

Instead, open the double doors in the middle of the right wall. This leads out to a spectacular plaza, with a large column in the center. Behind that, however, is a giant, towering structure taller than the clouds! This must be the Citadel Breen was talking about.

ADDITIONAL INVESTIGATIONS

Breen's continuing diatribe is unnerving. He reads aloud, "A letter I recently received: 'Dear Dr. Breen. Why has the Combine seen fit to suppress our reproductive cycle? Sincerely, a Concerned Citizen.'" Breen responds, "Let us consider the fact that for the first time ever, as a species, immortality is in our reach. This requires radical rethinking and revision of our genetic imperatives." He continues, "Our true enemy is instinct. Inseparable from instinct is its dark twin, superstition. It must be fought tooth and nail, beginning with the basest of human urges: the urge to reproduce." The Combine, apparently, must be thanked, for "giving us respite from this overpowering force. Let me assure you that the suppressing field will be shut off on the day that we have mastered ourselves... the day we can prove we no longer need it. And that day of transformation, I have it on good authority, is close at hand."

Let's hope you mount a full-scale assault on that skyscraper later. For now, inspect the courtyard, while the Administrator continues to placate the population who now, it seems, aren't even able to reproduce. No wonder they're grumpy.

Follow a citizen toward a security blockade, and you'll see them walk through a force field. It seems you're not welcome in the precinct the citizen has entered; a siren sounds, and your way is blocked. Again, the citizens don't want to talk and neither do the Cops.

After you finish inspecting the plaza, ignore the Scanners in the area and move right from the double doors, passing the aptly named Terminal Hotel on your left. There must be a way out of this zone.

As you head into the narrow road next to the Terminal Hotel, you'll see a door ajar. Beyond it looks like a Metro Cop interrogation, but you're not allowed to view the brutality going on behind the door. Continue on.

As you round the corner, something's wrong. Something eerie catches your eye. A huge sack of flesh with a form of heavy weapon attached to its underside is lolloping across the street on three giant but spindly legs. What fresh hell is this?

It disappears from view, flanked by Scanners. Blocking the road to another precinct is a Metro Cop Combine APC along with two Cops. They're as friendly as always. Back up before you're stunned by their prodding.

CHAPTER¹
ENCOUNTERS

COMBINE APC

STRIDER

ENTITY ENCOUNTER:
COMBINE APC

ENTITY ENCOUNTER:
STRIDER

The Strider's combat capabilities are yet to be tested, and you are currently in no shape to attack these lolloping synthetic life-forms. You'll get a chance later. The Combine APC is a well-armored troop carrier armed with a turret-mounted rocket launcher. You cannot enter APCs, and fortunately, this one isn't being aggressive.

You're looking for this alleyway. Go to this area. You have two choices: either climb up the metal ladder to the mesh walkway and drop down over the fence, or move the dumpster over to the fence, jump onto it, and then over.

Move along, there's nothing to see here. If you turn left, you'll be told in grunts to keep away from another police "interrogation." Just head down the alley to the right, rounding the left corner.

You enter a tenement block courtyard. To your right are two citizens moaning about the overzealous Cops raiding the building ahead of you. They certainly don't want to talk, so continue on into a children's play area, where you hear faint shouts of play.

You can mess around with the playground equipment if you want to.

The two Metro Cops at the far end of the chamber are certainly not in the mood to let you in, and the cement steps to the right lead to a sealed door. It seems your only way out is through the open doorway to your left, near the slide.

"KEEP MOVING, HEAD FOR THE ROOF!"

MAP 3 | ## CITY 17: TENEMENT BUILDINGS

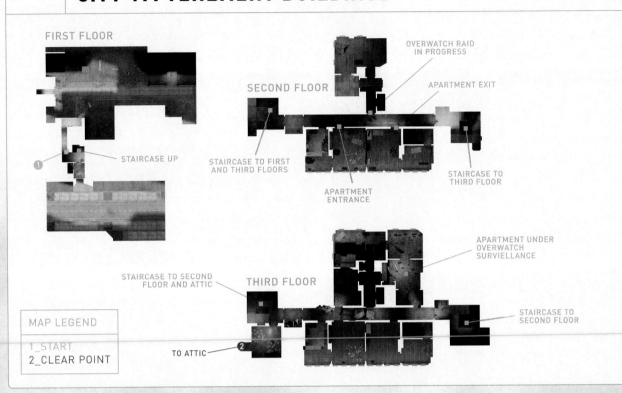

FIRST FLOOR

STAIRCASE UP

SECOND FLOOR

OVERWATCH RAID
IN PROGRESS

APARTMENT EXIT

STAIRCASE TO FIRST
AND THIRD FLOORS

APARTMENT
ENTRANCE

STAIRCASE TO
THIRD FLOOR

STAIRCASE TO SECOND
FLOOR AND ATTIC

THIRD FLOOR

APARTMENT UNDER
OVERWATCH
SURVIELLANCE

STAIRCASE TO
SECOND FLOOR

MAP LEGEND

1_START
2_CLEAR POINT

TO ATTIC

You're inside the tenement block. Head through the door to the entrance and check the elevator. It's locked. The door to the right isn't, but it leads to a small foyer with a locked door and a few items of little interest. Head up the stairwell.

Up on the next landing, there's some commotion. As a citizen peers around the right doorway, three Metro Cops break through into an apartment. The last one in refuses to let you see the new tactics the Cops have developed. But you can certainly hear them.

Don't go up the stairwell; a Metro Cop will stop you. Instead, enter the apartment you saw the citizen peer out of.

The grimy kitchen has a number of disgusting pots and pans to throw about and a dejected chap sitting at the table. Enter the adjacent room. Two citizens peer out the window.

When you've heard enough of the Administrator harping on, you can pick up the television (or any object around this size), and throw it out of the window. It allows a better view of an APC and Cops running in the street below. They seem to be swarming the base of the building you're in.

Head out of the glass doors and into the main apartment corridor, then into the next apartment where a weeping woman is comforted by her husband. That Administrator is on every television! Play with the furniture if you want.

Head out of the apartment around the left entrance, ignoring the dark bathroom. Head back onto the main landing, to the opposite stairwell, and head up the stairs. (If you go down, a Cop stops you).

Up on the next landing, a man beckons you forward into the doorway at right. This seems an obvious plan, because there's heavy furniture blocking the stairs going up. Be ready for the next set of maneuvers. Your life depends on it!

The citizens hiding from the Cops seem to be holed up here. As you enter the apartment, one screams, "They're coming!" and Metro Cops charge in. They don't discriminate; anyone who isn't wearing a white gas mask is whacked unconscious.

That includes you, so run past the sleeping guy on the sofa, out of the apartment, turn right on the landing, and run down the corridor. Four Cops chase you, and more are coming up the stairwell.

Head up the next stairwell without delay; don't dawdle or head downstairs, or you'll be battered unconscious; the Cops have turned up their stun batons a notch. When you reach the top floor, a man beckons you into a door. Follow him in; don't continue around as shown above!

CAUTION

Follow the stairs up without delay and run through the open door. Do not continue around the landing, or you'll be hemmed in and receive a fatal battering.

The citizen seems to know you need to flee, but that door he's pressed against won't hold the Metro Cops forever. He tells you to flee to the roof. That's a sound plan; head right, up the steps, and into the dilapidated attic structure.

"DR. FREEMAN, I PRESUME?"

| MAP 4 | **CITY 17: ROOFTOPS** |

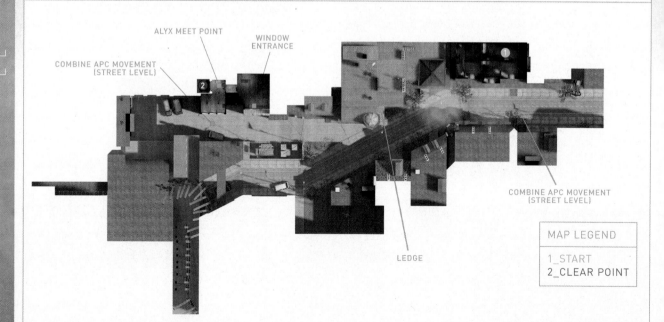

ALYX MEET POINT
WINDOW ENTRANCE
COMBINE APC MOVEMENT (STREET LEVEL)
COMBINE APC MOVEMENT (STREET LEVEL)
LEDGE

MAP LEGEND

1_START
2_CLEAR POINT

COMBINE GUNSHIP

ALYX VANCE

At the top of the attic stairs, turn left, run to the gaping hole in the roof structure, and drop down onto the rooftop ledge below. Move fast and don't return to the attic afterward; Metro Cops lie waiting. Instead, watch for flying objects ahead!

A Scanner has picked up your location already. Throwing heavy paint cans at it only delays the inevitable; it flashes a white beam of light that blinds you for a second. However, you can hit the Scanner with a well-aimed shot that destroys it; your first confirmed kill!

ENTITY ENCOUNTER:
COMBINE GUNSHIP

Combine Gunships constantly patrol the city, and you are ill-equipped to deal with them now. Fortunately, your small stature allows you to hide from their prowling sensors.

Ignore the Scanner and watch as two gigantic, biomorphic gunships whine above the rooftops. Did they spot you?

Face west and you'll see the terrifying Citadel tower structure in the distance and a small ledge that leads nowhere. To the right is a plinth around the yellow tenement block. As you move, you may see Metro Cops running along the street below. You can even hit them with small paint cans.

Head up the small roof ramp, then down the shingle roof to the turret ledge on the yellow tenement block. Cross the planks, and hug the windows as you maneuver around and to the right, along the ledge.

CAUTION

Don't move too quickly, or you may fall off the ledge to your death. Move slowly and with purpose.

Ignore the flapping pigeons and the two APCs driving toward the building ahead and below. Instead, concentrate on locating this open window, near the two red-and-white smokestacks. Hop over and into a small attic room.

Head down the narrow stairs and into a small T-shaped landing. It doesn't matter which door you choose; both are kicked in by Metro Cops. Back up! The stairs have collapsed. Where's the crowbar?! Ouch!

You're automatically battered into a state of unconsciousness and the screen goes white. Just before you're out, you hear a woman's voice yelling and agonized grunts from the Cops. You wake up a little later. A pretty young woman helps you to your feet. "I'm Alyx Vance," she says. "My father worked with you, back in Black Mesa. I'm sure you don't remember me though."

She certainly seems to be able to handle herself in a fight! If you wish, you can inspect the bodies of the Metro Cops she knocked out. Check the window; the APCs parked earlier had these Cops inside. Now head to the elevator before they wake up.

On the elevator trip down, the woman introduces herself as Alyx Vance. Her father was Doctor Eli Vance. Yes, he was one of the theoretical physicists from the Black Mesa laboratory. That seems such a long time ago. You step out of the elevator.

Alyx Vance introduces you to a propaganda poster of the droning Administrator you've been attempting to ignore: Dr. Breen. That name rings a bell—he's the old Black Mesa administrator! Flicking a switch, Alyx beckons you into a narrow passageway. Follow her. It's time for a reunion with an old friend and mentor.

HλLF-LIFE²

PRIMA OFFICIAL GAME GUIDE

"A RED LETTER DAY"

OVERVIEW Alyx Vance leads you into the makeshift laboratory of an old and trusted friend, Doctor Isaac Kleiner, and his pet Headcrab, Hedy Lamarr, which soon takes a fancy to Barney's cranium. After a joyous reunion, talk is quick and efficient. Kleiner has kept your Black Mesa HEV Suit and adapted it for Combine combat environments, but the main focus of his work is in the field of teleportation. Moving to his teleport chamber, Alyx bench-tests Kleiner's creation, and ends up at her father's laboratory at Black Mesa East. Alas, when you attempt to follow, a slight mishap forces you to seek an alternate route to Vance's hideout.

INVENTORY PICK-UP

- Crowbar

ENTITY ENCOUNTER
FRIENDLIES

- Alyx Vance
- Doctor Isaac Kleiner
- Barney Calhoun
- Hedy Lamarr*
- Doctor Eli Vance*
- Doctor Judith Mossman*
- Vortigaunt Ally*

ENTITY ENCOUNTER
HOSTILES

- Ichthyosaur*
- Dr. Wallace Breen
- Combine Overseer (via video feed)*
- Scanners
- Metro Cops

* Indicates first exposure to entity

"YOUR MIT EDUCATION REALLY PAYS FOR ITSELF"

MAP 5 | ## DOCTOR KLEINER'S LABORATORY

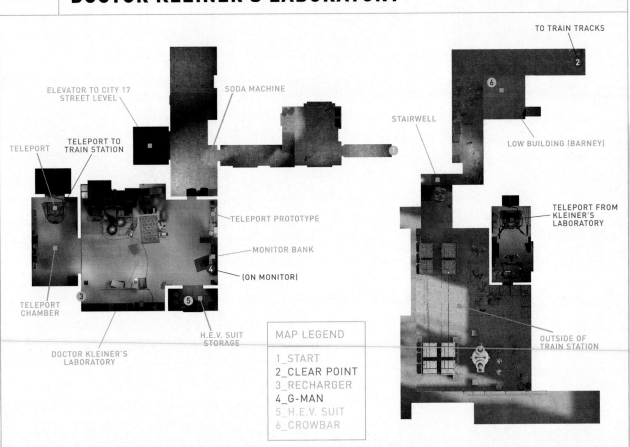

TO TRAIN TRACKS

ELEVATOR TO CITY 17
STREET LEVEL

SODA MACHINE

STAIRWELL

LOW BUILDING (BARNEY)

TELEPORT

TELEPORT TO
TRAIN STATION

TELEPORT PROTOTYPE

TELEPORT FROM
KLEINER'S
LABORATORY

MONITOR BANK

(ON MONITOR)

TELEPORT
CHAMBER

H.E.V. SUIT
STORAGE

OUTSIDE OF
TRAIN STATION

DOCTOR KLEINER'S
LABORATORY

MAP LEGEND

1_START
2_CLEAR POINT
3_RECHARGER
4_G-MAN
5_H.E.V. SUIT
6_CROWBAR

Alyx beckons you along a concrete hallway, informing you of an escape route she and the rest of the resistance have been planning for months now. The route on foot to her father's laboratory is plagued with Combine patrols. The resistance is on the verge of creating "a better way."

Look to your right before you follow Alyx as she vaults over a metal railing, and you'll spot a resistance poster. This gives you the first clue; the hand is clutching a Lambda symbol, an icon of the resistance. Alyx leads you to a small antechamber.

"Here, let me buy you a drink," she says, before tapping in a passcode to the vending machine, which creaks open to expose a fake wall with a reinforced entrance into a secret laboratory. Step on through.

LAMBDA
LOCATION

The information contained in this guide also shows the location of every Lambda marking. These are signs left by the resistance, such as the one on the wall next to the vending machine. Locate these, and helpful items are sure to be nearby, left by friends of the resistance.

CHAPTER²
ENCOUNTERS

DR KLEINER

HEDY LAMARR

G-MAN

Go through the opening to enter Doctor Kleiner's laboratory. The Doctor hasn't spotted you yet; he's banging on a cabinet and shouting at Lamarr. The good doctor takes a moment of cajoling to realize you have arrived. "It really is you, isn't it?" he says.

Kleiner says you've arrived at a most auspicious time, as Alyx has installed the last piece for a resurrected teleport. This must be the quicker route to Eli's lab that Alyx was talking about. Of course, the teleport hasn't actually been fully tested yet.

While the Doctor continues to tap away at his keyboard, Barney enters the room. He's on edge and checks the bank of security monitors to see if the Combine has spotted you. He urges the Doctor to hurry. "This is a red letter day!" the Doctor replies. "We'll inaugurate the new teleport with a double transmission!"

Barney is hopeful that the device will work this time, especially after the nightmares he still has about that cat. Alyx pricks up her ears, but her questions about the exact nature of a feline demise go unanswered. Because you're not taking the streets, Barney suggests you don a new outfit.

A garage door rises near the monitor bank to reveal a small dark chamber with an HEV Suit encased in its protective sheathing cabinet. Barney moves into the room, when suddenly he lets out a yell. He is being attacked!

Barney wrestles a seething mass of flesh and stumpy pincer arms to the ground. "Lamarr! There you are!" shouts the Doctor, as he dashes over to extricate Barney's head from Lamarr's gaping maw.

Lamarr leaps onto the metal cabinet and nestles closer to the Doctor. "Never fear, Gordon," remarks Kleiner, "she's de-beaked and completely harmless. The worst she might do is attempt to couple with your head. *Fruitlessly.*" Barney is

less enamored. Kleiner pats his bald head and ushers Lamarr onto it, but she has a different *modus operandi* and nimbly leaps to an upper balcony, knocks over a computer monitor, and disappears into an air duct.

INVENTORY ADAPTATION
THE MARK V HAZARDOUS ENVIRONMENT SUIT

This is a crucial body suit designed to constantly check the health of its wearer and administer morphine if you are wounded. It also provides an HUD in constant use. You can now check your health, suit protection, weapon inventory, and enemy direction if an enemy attack hits you. You can unlock the suit before Barney does if you press the release switch to the left while Barney is preoccupied with Lamarr.

G-MAN
ABOUT TOWN

Any time after Barney finishes checking the main monitor, move to it and flick through the various cameras by pressing E until you spot this view of the train-station containment area where Barney first met you. A mysterious suited man waits here for a moment, then leaves.

"Well, Gordon," Kleiner begins, "I see your HEV suit still fits you like a glove. At least the glove parts do." The Doctor begins to tout the improvements to the suit he has made since you last wore it but is stopped short by a loud klaxon blast. The outer perimeter has been breached. "We don't have time for this," Barney urges.

There's just enough time to juice up the suit, though. Head to the far end of the laboratory, under the balcony, to the Combine Charger, and then press E to increase your suit armor to 25 percent. Once this occurs, the Doctor straightens a picture on the same wall, revealing a retinal scanning device. Thrusting his head into the blue glow, the Doctor's eyes are recognized, and the wall of letters, historic documents, and blueprints pinned to a large corkboard slides open to reveal a teleportation room!

ADDITIONAL INVESTIGATIONS

Before you enter the teleportation chamber, a thorough inspection of the Doctor's laboratory is called for. There's the little things to notice, such as the starfield screensaver on one of the monitors and the names of the Doctor's two computers (Carmel and Black Mesa). You can read the clipboard for the HEV Suit after the Doctor discards it. Of more humorous interest is the Hawaiian hula doll by the monitors. Jostle the table to watch her dance.

To the left of the monitors is an interesting little device: a working teleporter prototype. There's a small cacti pot. Flip the switch to transport it from one point to the other. Now try it with any other item you can carry.

Of considerable interest is a group photograph of the Black Mesa research team taken in much happier times. You should recognize most of the people (including yourself). But who has had his face whited out? Note that if you adjust the picture (press E), the retinal scanner appears. If you attempt to unlock the door, it denies you access.

The Doctor's note-covered wall is also a smorgasbord of valuable information. It includes an old issue of *Popular Science* with a young Doctor Kleiner on the cover, Post-it notes including references such as "Field flux must self-limit," a newspaper cutting with the title "End is Nigh," various blueprints for teleport prototypes, a photograph of the New Mexico desert above the Black Mesa base, and even a drawing of the Doctor done by his nephew.

Once you're finished in the lab, enter the teleportation chamber. The monitor near Barney crackles to life, and the kind old face of Doctor Eli Vance can be seen peering in from his base. In the background, a female doctor is moving about. Alyx gingerly steps into the teleport itself.

"Let's see." The Doctor goes through the final teleportation checks. "The massless field flux should self-limit, and I've clamped the manifold parameters to... CY base and LG orbifold... Hilbert inclusive. Conditions could hardly be more ideal."

"About that cat," Alyx remarks, but it is too late. The teleport begins to rise, and then comes to a grinding, and rather embarrassing halt. "Fiddlesticks!" the Doctor curses. It seems the giant plug on the right wall has fallen out. Pick it up, and plug it in (you can try throwing it into the outlet if you're dexterous enough).

With the plug in, the large switch on the electrical charging unit still must be flipped. Using the breadth of MIT knowledge you gained, throw the switch, and Alyx disappears with a blinding flash, only to reappear moments later by her father's side. "Thank goodness," Kleiner sighs. "My relief is almost palpable."

Now it's your turn. Move into the teleport where Alyx stood, and wait for Kleiner to power up the system. Combine sirens are getting closer, so step in (the action waits for you). The teleport rises, and the displacement field begins to pick up speed. All is going well until a clanging thump can be heard. Over the whirling noise, Barney can be heard yelling, "It's your pet, the freakin' head-humper!"

CONSULAR BREEN

ICHTHYOSAUR

Lamarr appears out of the duct, and leaps at you, just as the teleport activates! Sparks fly everywhere, and your trajectory is knocked way off course! You appear swathed in a vortex of green light in a desert landscape. Lamarr bounds off, and a flock of crows flaps away in shock.

A moment later, you're warped back into the laboratory. Lamarr is gone, but a crow made the journey back with you and flaps erratically at Kleiner. A moment later, you're whisked away, appearing at the Black Mesa East teleport. Alyx, Eli, the female doctor, and the Vortigaunt wait with expectant worry for the event to finish. "What's going on, Judith?" Eli asks the doctor. "I'm not sure. Some kind of interference," she responds.

The vortex flickers out, and you instantly appear in a strange dark chamber with an ornate desk. Sitting at the desk is Breen the Administrator! He's just as startled to see you. He radios for security before you vanish again.

You're wrenched back into Kleiner's laboratory. Sparks are flying, and so are tempers. The noise of the protesting machine is deafening. Suddenly you're back in Eli's lab again. Then your resonance peters out.

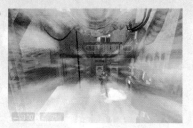

You're back in Breen's office. He is talking breathlessly with a Combine Overseer on his video screen. "That man I saw. I'm all but certain it was..." He turns to see you again. "Gordon Freeman!" You're gone.

You drop into a large primordial lake in the middle of a deserted landscape. Slowly sinking underwater, you catch the briefest glimpse of a most horrific creature: a giant Ichthyosaur lunging out of the darkness at you!

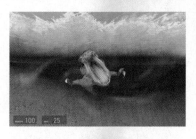

You're saved from a watery doom as the teleport warps you again, back to Kleiner's lab. Well, not exactly. You appear outside the window! Quickly shutting the machine down, Barney urges you to hide. Do it fast; the Combine is coming.

You're on a mesh walkway, and two Scanners take an interest in you. Turn left and run along the walkway, down the steps, and turn right, jogging around the side of the electrical substation. Ignore the Scanners.

You're searching for an exit, and this darkened stairwell is it. Bound up here, following the steps to a top floor, and follow the concrete ground past a group of crates and through a doorframe in a chain-link fence. It looks like you're making the trip to Eli's lab on foot!

"I THINK YOU DROPPED THIS BACK IN BLACK MESA"

| MAP 6 | **CITY 17: TRAIN STATION EXTERIOR** |

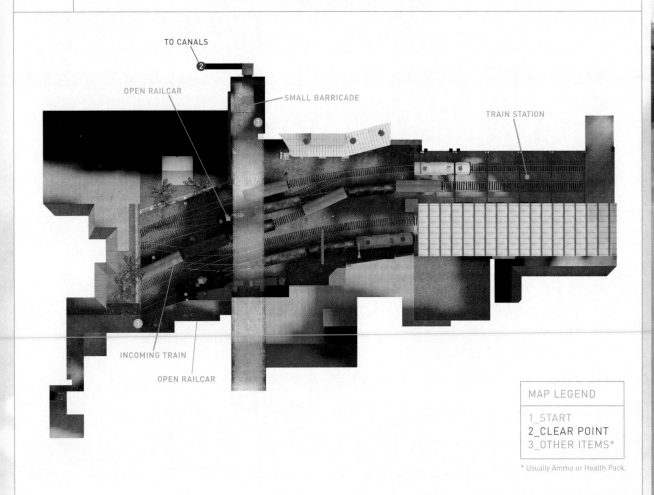

TO CANALS

OPEN RAILCAR

SMALL BARRICADE

TRAIN STATION

INCOMING TRAIN

OPEN RAILCAR

MAP LEGEND

1_START
2_CLEAR POINT
3_OTHER ITEMS*

* Usually Ammo or Health Pack.

As soon as you round the corner after the mesh fence, Barney appears on a rooftop to your right and beckons you. He points to the gigantic tower: "The Citadel is on full alert!" he shouts. "I've never seen it lit up like that."

Barney is correct. Use your HEV Suit's zoom capability (press Z) to peer at the pincerlike protrusions on the gigantic Citadel's super-structure and the hundreds of Scanners pouring out of the gaping vents along the east and west walls of the building. The time has come to seek cover.

HEALTH 100 SUIT 25

Barney tells you to take the route along the old Kanals; these eventually lead to Eli's lab. He reckons groups of refugees are likely to aid you along the way. Finally, he produces something from the back of his utility belt. "Good luck out there, buddy," he says with a wave. "You're gonna need it!"

CHAPTER ²
ENCOUNTERS

INVENTORY ADAPTATION
CROWBAR

This is the first time you have equipped an actual weapon. The Crowbar now remains with you. It can be swung quickly with a swift stabbing motion at any nearby enemies and is also extremely useful for breaking apart wooden barricades. But keep looking for a better weapon as soon as possible.

Ignore the crates in the zone you just came from, and instead continue to the mesh wall ahead of you. To the right is a hastily boarded-up doorway. Swing the Crowbar into the boards until they crack and splinter.

Clamber through the hole you made and step into a path with a train yard to your left. You are exposed, so find cover quickly. Head for the entrance directly before you.

Turn the immediate left corner, and if a Scanner attempts to blind you, attack it with your Crowbar in this cubby hole until the device explodes. Drop down to the ground below and quickly look right. Two Metro Cops send up a flare and begin to take pistol shots at you.

You have no offensive capabilities at this range, so back away from the two Cops and head left out of the entrance. Hug the left wall to avoid taking pistol fire. Use the crates as cover. You're looking for this red container car with the open door.

Jump into the train car, and you have no risk of being winged by the Cops. Turn left, and begin to demolish the stacks of crates in this area. They hold nothing; the crates just block your path to the exit on the opposite side of the car.

CAUTION

Watch out! A transport train is scraping along the rails to your left, and if you stay on the track, you will be hit and killed.

Drop down from the railcar and quickly run to the right until you can step left in front of a stationary car. Or, wait for the train to pass completely (it will grind to a halt), and walk around the left side of it.

NOTE

At either end of these train sidings are strange blue-colored electrical shields. These prevent you from escaping through the train tunnel or back to the station. You must find alternative methods of escape.

Whatever your method of escape, don't hang around in one place; a Scanner will spot you and relay your coordinates, and another Metro Cop will arrive and take additional pot-shots at you. Seek cover as you continue to cross the train tracks.

Head left, around the next stationary car, and turn left again. You're looking for an open railcar with two doors beckoning you in. You may come under fire as you reach this point, so sprint and dive in.

Once inside the car, quickly turn to your right and begin quickly swinging the Crowbar at the crates and boxes preventing your escape. Clear a path to a ladder leading up to the car's roof and climb up.

As pistol shots from the Cops zing around you, turn left so you're looking directly at the dimly lit alcove shown here. You must now leap from the railcar you're on, making sure you drop down on the far side of the chain-link fence.

CAUTION

As soon as you hit the ground on the far side of the chain-link fence, two new Metro Cops rappel from the bridge above you. They are both armed with pistols, and you cannot retrace your steps to fight them. Seek cover!

There is no other way to reach this escape route; maneuvering around the outer edge of the chain-link fence only results in you receiving more damage from the Cops. Dive for the health pack on your right, and use the upturned cart as cover.

While crouching behind the cart, jump up and quickly swing at the wooden barricade until you've beaten an entrance large enough to fit through. Quickly maneuver through this mesh fence.

Finally, move left to avoid fire and push the stack of crates and barrels into the indented steps to waylay the Cops. Then jump down the steps and into the passageway. There's an immediate left turn with a sign reading "Danger. Admittance to Authorized Personnel Only." Head down the steps.

ROUTE KANAL

OVERVIEW ▌ The adventure now begins! You must quickly find your bearings and a few new weapons as you progress through roving patrols of Metro Cops while locating the various stops along the underground railroad for rebels fleeing the confines of the Combine. React with cunning intelligence to a variety of traps laid both by the Cops and the indigenous fauna, now thriving years after the Black Mesa incident. Avoid the cannon of a Combine Hunter-Chopper, negotiate a maze of effluent inlets, and finally reach a shanty town—once a safe-haven, and now a place of despair and terror. Finally, commandeer the airboat and begin your journey to Eli Vance with haste.

INVENTORY PICK-UP

- Pistol
- SMG
- Grenade

ENTITY ENCOUNTER
FRIENDLIES

- Repatriated Citizens
- Pigeons*
- Vortigaunt
- BoxCar Joe*
- Resistance Citizens*
- Manhack Matt*

ENTITY ENCOUNTER
HOSTILES

- Metro Cops
- Scanners
- Barnacles*
- Combine APCs
- Combine Hunter-Chopper*
- Manhacks*
- Zombie Torso*
- Headcrabs*
- Zombies*

⌐ * Indicates first exposure to entity

"FOR GOD'S SAKE, THEY'RE KILLING US!"

MAP 7 | **CANAL ROUTE #1**

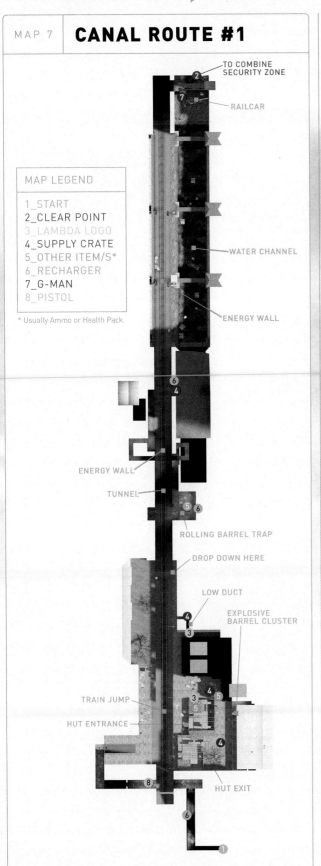

TO COMBINE SECURITY ZONE

RAILCAR

MAP LEGEND

1_START
2_CLEAR POINT
3_LAMBDA LOGO
4_SUPPLY CRATE
5_OTHER ITEM/S*
6_RECHARGER
7_G-MAN
8_PISTOL

* Usually Ammo or Health Pack.

WATER CHANNEL

ENERGY WALL

ENERGY WALL

TUNNEL

ROLLING BARREL TRAP

DROP DOWN HERE

LOW DUCT

EXPLOSIVE BARREL CLUSTER

TRAIN JUMP

HUT ENTRANCE

HUT EXIT

When you reach the bottom of the stairs (if you need the Flashlight, press F), stop and turn right. In the middle of the long narrow refuse-littered tunnel is a Health Recharger. Use this if you are low.

After you pass the Recharger, you hear the voice of a female citizen scream, "For God's sake, they're killing us!" It seems two Metro Cops are exhibiting some rough-housing tactics; time to step in. A male citizen goes down after a baton beating. When you step around the corner, the Cops get up and head your way.

Take them down with your Crowbar. Run at them, closing in quickly on the nearest and swinging at his head until he crumples. Shrug off a pistol round from the other, then strike him repeatedly with the Crowbar until he falls. If you back up into the tunnel, you'll be shot repeatedly as the Cops keep their distance. The Cop drops a Pistol during combat; don't bother switching to this weapon just yet.

The man lying prone on the ground is in bad shape. The woman looks up. "You'd better run!" she shouts. "There's nothing else you can do here! They'll be looking for you now!" With the Combine currently sending out Scanners to pinpoint your location, you must stay on the move.

INVENTORY ADAPTATION
PISTOL

Congratulations! Now you take down targets from a distance! Use the Pistol (with 18 shots per clip) for all combat from now on, changing to the Crowbar for tasks such as destroying barricades. Collect more ammunition from the fallen bodies of cops.

INTRODUCTION

GETTING STARTED

WEAPONS DETAIL

HALF-LIFERS

THE BESTIARY

CHAPTER 1

CHAPTER 2

CHAPTER 3
ROUTE KANAL

CHAPTER 4

CHAPTER 5

CHAPTER 6

CHAPTER 7

CHAPTER 8

CHAPTER 9

CHAPTER 10

CHAPTER 11

CHAPTER 12

CHAPTER 13

CHAPTER 14

ANOMALOUS MATERIALS

CHAPTER³
ENCOUNTERS

Use the Crowbar to smash through the boards blocking the doorway ahead. Quickly climb the stairs. A Metro Cop is descending. Shoot him while you climb, tagging him through the steps from below if you can.

Pick up the object he drops (usually Pistol ammo or a Health Vial), and reach the top of the gantry. Move across the landing to another set of steps on your right. As you make the turn, you may wish to strafe this corner, facing up the steps. Charge up and tag the Cop at the top.

At the top of the steps is a concrete path with various barrels strewn about and a flock of pigeons flapping away. Two good shots with your Pistol can actually down one of these birds, if you wish to practice your aim.

NOTE

The main item of interest here are the three red barrels, each marked "Explosive." There's a rather dangerous reason for this; shoot one once or twice with a Pistol, and it catches fire for three seconds before exploding. If you're caught in the blast, expect to take major damage.

It isn't wise to set fire to the barrels while standing anywhere near them. In fact, they shouldn't be touched; use them as a trap in a moment. Instead, inspect this concrete path area. A razor-wire fence blocks the far end. You cannot pass through here.

Instead, look for the mesh door on the right side of the path, overlooking a railway track below. As you move through the gap to the top of the steps, you hear a train's horn. A locomotive is

approaching! Stay at the top of the steps; heading down results in a dead end.

As the train approaches, jump onto the roof of a cargo or passenger railcar. Turn around, and jump across the railcar, and leap off just before the train reaches the bridge arch, landing on a small mesh platform with a ladder.

As soon as you land on this mesh platform, head up the small ladder to the top of the concrete wall on the other side. Shots ring out. Turn around immediately. Three Cops have appeared from the stairs you just came from. If you're fast, swivel around and plug the exploding barrel, and catch all of them in the blast.

If you already detonated the barrels, you can either stay on the opposite side (using the wooden planks nailed to the mesh wall as cover) and carefully plug away at the Cops, or you can hop across the now-stationary train, up the mesh steps, and engage the Cops at closer quarters. You may wish to return here for the ammo they drop too.

TIP

By now, you may be learning the Cops' combat worthiness; they tend to retreat and hide if they're wounded, and if they manage to shoot off a flare, expect another three to six additional Cops to arrive in this area. Therefore, make your Pistol shots quick and accurate.

When you have curtailed the Cop menace, move along the concrete wall's top to a derelict hut. The mesh fence to the left is impenetrable, although you can get a good look at the train track below. Bring out your Crowbar and break open the wood barricade at the door.

LAMBDA
LOCATION

Step inside this run-down hut and look left. This is an easy Lambda Location to spot; the wall is marked with the logo of the resistance, and some ammunition and health has been left for you. Grab it.

When you enter the building, you may hear the familiar whine of a Scanner. If the device is close, bring out your Crowbar and smash it until it explodes. If it is farther away, shoot it. With a couple of hits, it will smoke and lose control; then it will try to dive-bomb you. Step out of the way before it hits you.

TIP

Scanners usually drop Batteries when you destroy them. If you're running low, you know where to find some!

With the Scanner defeated, turn right (the door ahead is locked). In the next room is a stack of barrels blocking the exit from the building. Either lift each barrel out of the way, or blow them apart from a distance (from the previous room, ideally).

Step out into a small garden area and look left. There's a mesh fence with a door. Push the door open, but train your Pistol on the group of barrels above and to your right. Two Cops are waiting to ambush you around that upper-left corner near the barrels, so create your own diversion; destroy the far right barrel. This sets off a chain reaction that crushes and burns the Cops in their enclosed space. If you aim at the far left barrel, the explosion is more spectacular, but the Cops are more likely to survive.

INVENTORY ADAPTATION
SUPPLY CRATE

Before you continue, inspect the small crate near the mesh door. It is marked "supply," and any time you see one, immediately destroy it and grab the contents inside. These are randomly determined ammunition and health items. Be sure you smash each Supply Crate you see!

Now head through the mesh door, ignore the door to your left (this leads back into the hut, and is only useful if you're still fighting the Cops on the far side of the train track), pick up the items by the corner of the building, and then watch for further Cop incursions; leap up and over the collapsed chain-link fence to the right.

You're now on a very narrow concrete path with the train track on your left and a building wall on your right. If more Cops have been called, they appear in the gaps between the blue construction fencing. Tap your fire button quickly to plug Cops full of lead; they have less time to recoil and hide and a greater chance of falling down onto the track in a spectacular death crumple!

CHAPTER 3
ENCOUNTERS

VORTIGAUNT

BOXCAR JOE

LAMBDA
LOCATION

The next Lambda Location is also a route marker. Round the next corner, turning right, and seek cover from the Cops. You should spot the sign above a small duct opening. Crouch (press Ctrl) and enter the duct. Inside is an L-shaped duct with a Supply Crate.

Turn left, bring out your Crowbar, and make short work of the duct grating. Quickly switch back to your Pistol (Cops attack from the opposite side), climb out of the duct, and plug away at the Cops until they retreat or fall.

When the narrow concrete path is safe to walk along, and all the Cops opposite are defeated, walk to the end, turn left, and look down onto the tracks. Drop to ground level after lining yourself up with the pallet; this breaks your fall without you taking damage.

TIP

If any of the Cops you took down at the blue construction wall fell into the train tracks, head left to collect any items they may have dropped.

Be very careful as you begin your trek along the train tunnel. After you drop to the ground, turn right, and walk along the right side of the tunnel area. Two or three Cops are waiting to lay a trap; they roll a flaming barrel down the steps to your right, straight at you!

Be ready for this ambush; rapidly unload your Pistol into the barrel so it explodes halfway down the steps, killing the Cop hiding in the alcove to the stairs' left. Then move in to tag the barrel roller himself at the top. If a third Cop appears, it will be from behind the window and upper gantry. Blast him as you strafe facing left, up the stairs.

If you remain on the train track, prior to the barrel ambush, you may be able to coax a Cop out just as a large Combine Tren races by. Hug the right wall or face a messy death; the Cop can fall foul of the train too! Remember to inspect the alcove near the steps for a Battery.

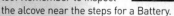

You may require patching up at the Health Recharger at the top of these steps. Then take a step or two back, and detonate the barrels in the corner, shattering the remaining windows; you don't want to retreat here and be hit by the barrels exploding from enemy gunfire. Head around the right corner with the windows on your left. There's a Cop at the end of the corridor; blow up the barrel up and take him down.

Walk to the end of the windowed corridor and look down and left. Two Metro Cops are dropping down from a concrete wall. Tag them immediately, backing up behind the window cover while you're taking them down. You may want to drop down at them, but you're more susceptible to gunfire.

TIP

You cannot pass through the energy shields the Combine has erected throughout the train tracks, just like before. However, the Combine forces can move through, so watch your step and take down enemies when they're on your side of the shield so you can collect items they drop.

Now continue up the narrow steps with the tiled walls and head around to a bridge to the other side of the train track. In front of you are a group of large crates and a Health Pack. Break out the Crowbar and demolish the crates, but watch your step: shots zing in from the left! Look down the tracks to see Cop reinforcements running in.

You can fight these thugs one of two ways. The first way is to crouch while smashing the crates, then head down the enclosed steps on the bridge's other side. Then wait. You'll hear them talking, but wait until they move single file over the bridge, and cut them down one by one without taking a hit.

The other way is to drop down from the bridge and charge back the way you came along the train tracks, blasting the trio of Cops with reckless abandonment. This results in a fearsome display of your bravery and also  results in a greater chance of getting severely wounded. Don't forget the Health Recharger after the battle.

When you're on the bridge's far side, you appear on a concrete balcony. Drop down to the tracks, this time on the other side of the shield gate, and face the three incoming goons along the tracks. Step to the alcove with Supply Crates and a Health Recharger for cover and combat supplies.

When the threat has passed, walk to the open area of the train tracks, until the shield gate prevents further progress. Ignore the buzzing Scanners, and look to your right. A broken gantry platform leads to a locked door.

The only way past the shield gate is to drop into the sewage overflow channel—a wide but shallow river of murky brown water with various floating debris.

Bring out your Crowbar and begin to swim. Note that your HEV Suit shows your air supply when you dive underwater. Press Spacebar (the jump button) to surface quickly when needed. Continue down the channel, smashing crates and squeezing through gaps in the bars. You can sit in the leaky boat and capsize it.

This watery effluent channel continues until you reach a patch of rubble and a red cargo railcar blocking your path. Move to the left side of it and climb the ladder to the roof. Move across the roof and drop through the hole to a mattress and a Health Pack below.

Check your instinct to fire, and watch as a Vortigaunt switches off the television it was watching, turns to face you, and lets his human companion, BoxCar Joe, do the talking. "Look," Joe explains, "we're just the lookout for the underground railroad. Main Station is right around the corner." The Vortigaunt rises, and begins to crackle with electrical discharge; he's powering up your HEV Suit!

Joe continues to talk in hushed tones. "We really can't afford to get noticed. Civil Protection catches you down here, it's bad news for the whole railroad." With that, he opens the side of the railcar and leaves you to drop into a mass of wreckage and rubble. It is time for you to leave.

When you first drop into the railcar, be sure you pay close attention to the television the Vortigaunt is watching—the G-Man appears on it for a brief moment. Also note the stylized poster of Breen and a map of the Kanal area ahead of you.

"THEY'RE FILLING THE UNDERGROUND WITH MANHACKS!"

MAP 8 | **CANAL ROUTE #2**

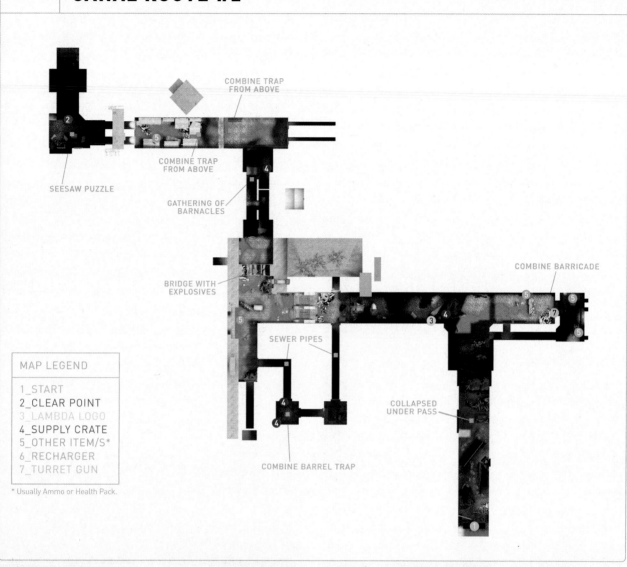

COMBINE TRAP FROM ABOVE

COMBINE TRAP FROM ABOVE

SEESAW PUZZLE

GATHERING OF BARNACLES

BRIDGE WITH EXPLOSIVES

COMBINE BARRICADE

SEWER PIPES

COLLAPSED UNDER PASS

COMBINE BARREL TRAP

MAP LEGEND

1_START
2_CLEAR POINT
3_LAMBDA LOGO
4_SUPPLY CRATE
5_OTHER ITEM/S*
6_RECHARGER
7_TURRET GUN

* Usually Ammo or Health Pack.

CHAPTER ³
ENCOUNTERS

BARNACLE

Follow Joe's instructions and hack your way through the wooden barricade to a group of crates near a fire, then turn and move to a barricade propping up a wrecked oil tanker railcar. The weakened barricade snaps and the tanker creaks, but the opening remains passable.

Turn right slightly and crouch to continue under the tanker, then move diagonally across to the opposite wall, turning left to appear out from the wreckage. You emerge under a bridge. Stay extremely still and do not move forward!

ENTITY ENCOUNTER:
BARNACLE

A crow, startled by your emergence, flies away and is grabbed by a long, sticky tonguelike protuberance and is rapidly pulled into a slobbering maw. This is a Barnacle, a dangerous creature that uses dark places to surprise its prey. Six shots defeat the barnacle, and it drops a disgusting array of partially decomposed body parts.

TIP

There are a few ways to avoid the Barnacle, the best of which is "Barnacle Baiting": Feed it by throwing or moving an object onto its tongue. After it slurps it up, run under it. This saves on ammo. Or, fire at it before it catches you. If you're grabbed, blast it immediately before your head is sucked apart!

Pass under the Barnacle and move around the right side of the green railcar and out to an open area of the sewage overflow. To the right is a barred tunnel and a large open area.

A trapped citizen on the other side of the tunnel bars shouts for help. It's too late, and a Cop inside the tunnel blasts both him and you with gunfire. Although you can tag the Cop from here, you can't get into the tunnel; seek an alternate route to avenge the citizen's death.

Round the right corner and prepare to take evasive action. A two-man sentry gun is in operation at the far end of this inlet area, and the Cops aren't afraid to paint the walls with your blood.

Dive behind the crates on the right wall and into the tunnel's side entrance. Turn on your Flashlight (press F) and then turn right after you're in the tunnel to tag the murderous Cop. Turn around and run forward, blasting a second incoming Cop.

TIP

Don't detonate the barrels you see against the left wall; these can be destroyed later in a spectacular ambush against opposing forces.

ADDITIONAL INVESTIGATIONS

You emerge in a small concrete alcove behind the sentry gun. A radio crackles on the opposite side of the chamber: "This is Station 8! We heard 12 go down and out. Surgical strike units are targeting railway stations. Repeat, Civil Protection is coming down on underground stations. We're already getting refugees from 9 and outlying! Looks like we're..." The radio cuts out abruptly. Another voice: "Station 8, are you there? We have confirmed reports of Manhacks. Repeat, they are filling the underground with Manhacks!"

While the chatter fades, pick up the items on the floor and mattress, and try not to worry too much about the "Manhacks" the radio voices mentioned. Instead, head up the ladder to the radio's left, and either step backward and blow up the barrel behind the two sentry gunners, or better yet, shoot them in the side of the head before they can react.

CAUTION

It is vital that you immediately turn and look up to the right, to a stack of explosive barrels on the top of the right wall. Shoot these quickly before combat begins. Otherwise, they will be used against you!

Now immediately man that sentry gun by pressing E; start strafing anything you see moving, including the two Scanners swooping around–they tend to blind you during the haphazard combat to come.

Metro Cops appear on the left upper wall sections, on the bridge ahead, on the right upper wall, and in the inlet area below. Wait until two Cops are standing on the wooden balcony to your upper left, then collapse it with gunfire. Shoot the barrel on the ground against the right wall to drop three more into an explosion that takes out the Cops on the ground. Also, shoot the barrel to the left of the upper bridge for more impressive blasting.

Your sentry gun escapade is halted with the arrival of a Combine APC. If you didn't deal with the stack of barrels above and right of you, the APC knocks them down and they explode, badly wounding you. Immediately back up to a corner until the smoke clears. The APC then launches homing rockets at you; these are dangerous, and the vehicle is parked out of weapon range. Time to leave.

Leave the sentry gun and run along the right wall's edge, quickly dropping any remaining Cops; then drop to the right of the tunnel wreckage to relative safety. Or you can dash along this route, straight to the tunnel, without stopping to fight the Cops, but you will be fired upon more.

At the end of the tunnel is a square overflow chamber with a couple of crates bobbing up and down. Look up to see two Cops. You can blast them through the grating, but this is tricky. It's better to turn right and leap to the inlet tunnel on the right. If you fall into the water, surface and climb up via the left wall as it is easier to climb up. You'll be shot at.

This opens to a second chamber with two Supply Crates in the water, but watch out for a deadly trap. Cops above have opened the ceiling grating and are shoving explosive barrels down into the water, the last of which is on fire. There's no time to shoot them before they explode. Dive, dive, dive!

LAMBDA
LOCATION

As soon as you enter the large tunnel, turn left and look behind you at the opposite wall to spot a Lambda logo. Climb over the car wreckage to a couple of Supply Crates, and then return to the tunnel.

Duck underwater so the barrels explode harmlessly on the surface. Then emerge, and tag both the Cops in retaliation for their deadly game. Plug them so they fall into the chamber with you for extra items. Then head right, to a final inlet tunnel.

Now watch your step as you gingerly maneuver through the tunnel. Two Barnacles are here, so either plug them from a distance, or feed them a piece of scenery and dash under them. Watch for the second Barnacle on the other side of the concrete tube you must crouch and walk through.

Emerge from the tunnel, instantly turn right, and dash for the green refuse bin and crouch for cover. Aim at the explosive barrel next to the Cop standing on the upper cement wall to the left, send him flying, and deal with his friend on the ground. Move forward and look right.

Another Cop drops onto the ground from the far corner, near an overhanging truck. Hug the other truck to your left, and plug the explosive barrel to catch the Cop as he heads toward you. Then finish him off, and move around the end of the truck, looking left.

Emerge from the tunnel to see that APC prowling along an upper road. Ignore it, and move across and turn left. A woman is on her knees hiding inside a concrete tube: "Keep going, friend!" she advises. "That station was raided, but there's others up ahead." Head through the gap in the bar and down a concrete inlet tunnel.

Three Cops dash onto the wooden bridge in front of you. Don't waste time plugging each one; instead, aim at the center explosive barrel under the bridge and bring the entire structure down, crushing the hapless police; watch for the truck on your right as it falls too.

Move to the bridge and pick a path under the collapse, over the Cops' dead bodies. Two more Cops drop from the cement-walled sides, one on each side. Take down each using the vertical support poles of the bridge as partial cover. Don't rush to the end of this area, or you'll be tagged in the back.

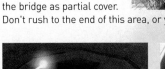

The way seems blocked, but there's a narrow gap at the top of a partially filled tunnel ahead and to the right. It is blocked by three barrels (nonexploding). Push (don't pick it up) the barrel forward. It slides on some sort of oily residue.

It is immediately picked up by two Barnacles. Watch your step; it is dangerous to slide around with these creatures clamped to the ceiling. Maneuver around the first two Barnacles and turn left. Carefully push an exploding barrel down the slope, taking care not to follow it. Backpedal if you slip, and shoot the barrel so it starts to burn. Don't detonate it.

The flaming barrel is picked up by one of a dozen Barnacles. Wait for the barrel to explode, sending offal chunks everywhere, and slide down to safety. Watch the ceiling; some Barnacles may remain (another explosive barrel

can be carried if you need it). Grab the items near the disgusting corpse, and exit this area.

Watch out for a vicious trap as you emerge into a waterlogged canal. Metro Cops on each side of the canal are dropping flaming barrels! Drop into the water and submerge, or you'll be caught in the blast as five or six barrels drop into the water.

Make a sharp left turn and head underwater, watching the bullets zing through the water at you. Head diagonally right as a barrel brings down a wooden platform, allowing you some protection as you dive under it.

Climb up the ladder fixed to the right wall, and stand on the platform under the bridge. Aim and blast the Cops on the far side, exploding their barrels before they can launch them. Then splash into the water on the other side of the bridge.

Swim underwater to the far end of the canal area, turn left, and clamber onto the wooden ramp with the Health Pack, taking cover behind the wooden barricade near the dead body. Slowly work your way along the wooden platform, aiming up and left, and blasting all enemies.

As you reach the bridge from the opposite end (there's a group of Cops on the left bank), detonate all their spare barrels, or you'll be shot and will suffer explosion damage!

Quickly move across to the platform on the other side, and run to the tunnel opening ahead on the right-hand side. Once inside, drop to a square-shaped chamber.

Use the plank of wood on a concrete tube to get over the wall. Dotted around the room are cement blocks. Pick one up and place it on the far edge of the wood plank, away from the exit tunnel. Continue this until the plank drops under the weight of the blocks (you'll need at least five). Then stand on the plank, run and jump across the gap, and into the exit tunnel.

HλLF-LIFE²
PRIMA OFFICIAL GAME GUIDE

| MAP 9 | **CANAL ROUTE #3** |

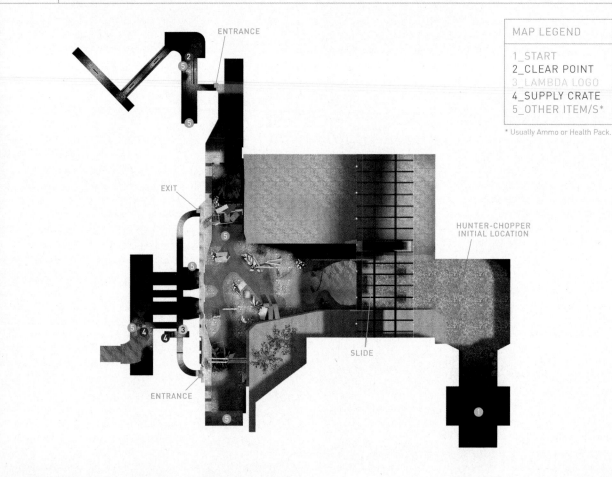

ENTRANCE

EXIT

ENTRANCE

HUNTER-CHOPPER
INITIAL LOCATION

SLIDE

MAP LEGEND

1_START
2_CLEAR POINT
3_LAMBDA LOGO
4_SUPPLY CRATE
5_OTHER ITEM/S*

* Usually Ammo or Health Pack.

CHAPTER³
ENCOUNTERS

HUNTER-CHOPPER

As you emerge from the tunnel, watch your footing and step back a little; you have been discovered by one of the Combine's attack helicopters, the Hunter-Chopper. This flying fiend hovers and sweeps left. Turn and follow it down a slippery slope; time to take evasive action.

Once you slide down the slope into a wreckage-strewn watery inlet area, you cannot retrace your steps. Furthermore, the Hunter-Chopper hovers before letting rip with a devastating salvo of autocannon fire. Quickly dash forward and crouch right, behind the temporary barricade shredded by the Chopper's first attack. Then dash out to the planks on the left side of the inlet near the junction, and hide there during the Chopper's second burst.

TIP

During your hide-and-seek bullet dodging, utilize your HEV Suit's Sprint function (hold down Shift) each time you run to a barricade so you aren't left wading in exposed water.

TIP

Remember the Chopper's attack pattern. It hovers in a stationary position firing off five-second autocannon bursts, then circles to another spot and fires again. Learn to dash just as the final shots hit the barricade you're hiding behind.

LAMBDA
LOCATION

As you move inside, run around the curved corridor, and spy a Lambda logo beneath the grating you're walking on. Before you continue, check the right wall for a gap and a ladder leading under the grating.

You can sprint to your third hiding spot–the barricade by the dead-end pool of water. You can collect items here, and you get a straight shot at running across the junction of the inlet area to your next shelter.

This cover is a little more substantial: a concrete piece of rubble protruding from the ground at the inlet junction. Depending on where the Chopper hovers, you can hide on either side of this rubble.

Here you find the putrid corpse of the citizen who placed the items here (in a small alcove opposite) and didn't make it out alive. Pick up the items, then use the ladder to return to the grating floor.

You're looking for an exit out of this trap. There are two methods to follow, both from the central rubble position. The first is to dash onto the bank and look left to see a blue door with barrels next to it. That's your exit. Run along the left lip of the wall, zip across the wooden plank, jump onto the railing, and drop to the left of the tin roof.

Now move to the end of the grating floor; bars block your way, but look through into the chambers to see Barnacles and the oil on the ground. There's also the ever-ready threat of Chopper attack. Head up the passage and break open the Supply Crate at the top.

The second option (which you can attempted by running along the top-left lip of the wall) is to reach the concrete steps at the far end of the inlet area. Dash around and hide behind the rubbish below the plank, then run under the plank, up the steps, and hug the sides so you miss being pulled up by the Barnacle. Then run around to the blue door.

Either method allows you to reach the stack of barrels and the blue door. There isn't time to move the barrels out of the way before another autocannon barrage, so duck behind the barrels, then pick up the barrel blocking the door and shove it out of the way. Quickly open and dive into the corridor behind the door.

CHAPTER³
ENCOUNTERS

Search the area at the top of the passage for explosive barrels; there's one to the left, near another dead body, and one near the oily slope on your right. Push a barrel down the slope, tagging it twice with your Pistol, and wait for the Barnacle to suck it down. Whooph! The barrel explodes, taking all the Barnacles in the ceiling indent with it, above the chambers you checked out earlier.

Push the second explosive barrel down the oily slope; when it's about halfway down, shoot it to set it on fire, and set fire to it around halfway down (remain at the top so you aren't caught in the blast or grabbed by the neck). This destroys the second group of Barnacles in this area. Now slide down to the arched grating, but don't get too close; the Chopper is still following and firing at you.

Turn left and maneuver into a second almost identical chamber that contains an oil patch and a drum to detonate once the Barnacles start slurping it. If you ignore or badly time the barrel-explosion method, slip down the slope along the left wall, look up, and blast the Barnacle just as it spots you, or use another piece of scenery to distract the Barnacle's tongue. A fourth and final set of Barnacles is at the base of this second slope; you can avoid them by staying left and leaping over the railing to the chamber's exit.

TIP

If you detonate a barrel too early when baiting a Barnacle, don't despair; just push the pieces of the barrel at the Barnacle so those are picked up, and run underneath.

This leads to a door and a low balcony behind the rubble you couldn't maneuver over. Open the door, peek your head out, and hide again as the Chopper blasts you; use the door as cover, then immediately turn left and sprint!

Cover as much ground as possible, following the low balcony all the way to the end of a tunnel. Ignore the effluent-filled water; it contains nothing of interest. Turn back and you'll still be targeted by the Hunter-Chopper, so make a left turn and escape it—for now.

The entrance soon narrows and splits at a T-junction. Head left to a dead end with a plank leaning against a wall. Move this out of the way for an item. Head right to see a burned corpse near some items. Grab the items, and move farther down the tunnel.

"SOUNDS LIKE THEY'RE CALLING IN EVERY CP UNIT IN CITY 17"

| MAP 10 | **CANAL ROUTE #4** |

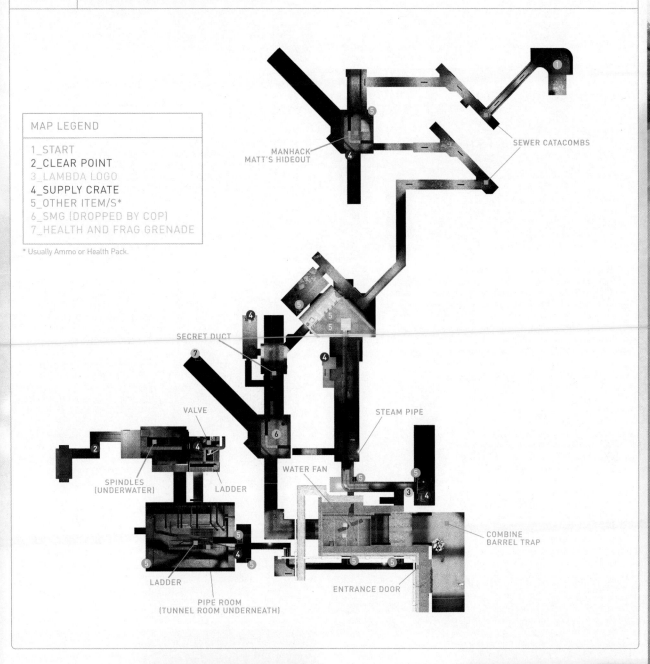

MAP LEGEND

1_START
2_CLEAR POINT
3_LAMBDA LOGO
4_SUPPLY CRATE
5_OTHER ITEM/S*
6_SMG (DROPPED BY COP)
7_HEALTH AND FRAG GRENADE

* Usually Ammo or Health Pack.

MANHACK
MATT'S HIDEOUT

SEWER CATACOMBS

SECRET DUCT

VALVE

STEAM PIPE

SPINDLES
(UNDERWATER)

LADDER

WATER FAN

COMBINE
BARREL TRAP

LADDER

PIPE ROOM
(TUNNEL ROOM UNDERNEATH)

ENTRANCE DOOR

Go on until you reach the continuation of the tunnel to your left. This is the only route, and it is blocked with an explosive barrel. There's a quick method and a slow method of maneuvering along this narrow passage. The quick (and easier)

method is to stand back and shoot the barrel; the barricade behind it explodes completely (but watch for a second barrel detonating at the far end). The slow method is to move the barrels by hand and Crowbar the wooden parts of the barricade.

Batter down the next barricade you see, and you end up in an inlet junction, complete with a resident named Matt. He quickly brings you up to speed on the happenings. He moves to the door in the opposite wall and opens the peephole. Uh-oh. Problems!

ENTITY ENCOUNTER:
MANHACK

These nasty robotic hovering devices have gyroscopic sensors to steady themselves in the air, and they tend to work in packs, charging you and savaging with rotating blades. Until you get other forms of weaponry, the best way to defeat a Manhack is by timing a Crowbar swing just as the Manhack zooms at you, before it connects. Then follow it with a second, killing blow, knocking the Manhack into a wall if you can. Pistols aren't the best choice, because you use too many bullets tagging them. Only use the Pistol if the Manhack is visible but unable to reach you.

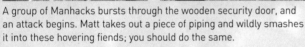

A group of Manhacks bursts through the wooden security door, and an attack begins. Matt takes out a piece of piping and wildly smashes it into these hovering fiends; you should do the same.

It is better to stay with your back to a wall (ideally in a corner) so that Manhacks can attack you from only one direction. Help Matt when you can and swipe at the Manhacks until all of them explode.

TIP

If you open a gate with a Manhack nearby, then close the gate and trap the Manhack between the mesh and the wall, the machine scrapes and fuses together, and then explodes.

Once combat ends, Matt tells you it really isn't safe here. You wholeheartedly agree with him. He offers some supplies, pointing to a ladder on the wall near the barricade you broke to enter this area. Climb it, grab the items from the Supply Crates on the raised bedding area, and cross the planks in the dark upper ledge.

Head through the remnants of Matt's security door and around the corner to a mesh door. Behind are three Manhacks, all attempting to attack, but the gate blocks them. This is an opportune moment to blast them with your Pistol, or you can ready your Crowbar and open the gate. Try hitting them through the gate with the Crowbar too.

Now wander to the end of the narrow corridor and turn left. Watch out! Manhacks have torn into an exploding barrel at the far end of the passage, and the barricade you're standing near is about to blow up. Immediately back up into the previous passage and wait for both exploding barrels to blow up. Then deal with remaining Manhacks.

Now, step through the smoking pile of debris, turn another corner, and spot two exits on the left wall. Ignore the chain-link door for the moment, and head left into a dark antechamber where you can grab a pile of supplies. Now return to the door and open it.

You appear in a meshed-in balcony outside. Look left to see a large pipe and tunnel. Look ahead to see a mesh door leading into darkness. Now look out: a couple of Cops run along a high parapet above and left of you. Tag them both quickly with your Pistol, using the planks on the mesh as cover.

You must take down the Cops immediately, because six or so Manhacks appear in the sky, dropping through the gap in the mesh roof to slice and dice you. Quickly move to a corner or backtrack into the passage; thwack them into submission. Remove the barrel blocking the opposite door and open it.

You appear in a dank and grimy sewer tunnel. An arched doorway with bars prevents you from entering and leads to a large stack of Supply Crates.

Look for another way in; stand on the pipe under the red light, above the tunnel channel. Draw your Crowbar and bash in a ventilation duct panel; then crouch and squeeze into the U-shaped duct corridor. Turn the corner, and beat apart a Manhack.

Make a second turn, and the ventilation duct ends with another panel to smash. Squeeze out into a small stone chamber, and run to the large stack of Supply Crates. Demolish them all, collect the items, and return to the duct.

Backtrack to the tunnel entrance. A Cop arrives to investigate the noise, standing at the entrance where you were. Plug the barrel to his left to send him flying into the dark. Then drop into the channel.

Head down the tunnel until the roof rises and you see a Metro Cop rappelling from a grating above. Immediately tag him with your Pistol; this Cop is armed with a brand-new weapon–one of the key items in the game. Search the water around the Cop's body for it!

INVENTORY ADAPTATION
SMG

The Submachine Gun, with 60 bullets per clip and a fantastic secondary Grenade-launch fire function (for which you have no ammunition yet), is a rapid-fire, all-purpose weapon. Begin using it by backing away from two more Cops splashing down the corridor. Shoot the barrel to the left so it explodes just as they reach this open chamber.

Collect more SMG ammo from their bodies, then turn around and switch back to the Pistol; shoot the barrel propped against a low arched grating (or move it out of the way); after it detonates, crouch and enter the hole.

TIP

When tagging barrels, holster your SMG and bring out the Pistol; the fast-firing nature of the SMG may detonate a barrel too quickly. Learn to lightly discharge SMG rounds (quick taps of the primary fire button (left click) before you go barrel-blasting.

ENTITY ENCOUNTER:
ZOMBIE TORSO

Crawl down this dead-end runoff channel; the remains of a citizen cradle a bunch of items. When you attempt to take them, however, something hideous moves toward you; it is the upper body of a corpse clamped and controlled by a Headcrab! Plug this Zombie Torso with pistol shots to the head until it gurgles its last.

INVENTORY ADAPTATION
GRENADE

There's another reason for daring to fight the Zombie Torso: it guards a Fragmentation Grenade. Although this isn't the optimal

time to use it (switch back to the SMG), this weapon is extremely useful later. Remember that [Alt] + Fire rolls the Grenade, while regular fire lobs it.

After you overcome the Zombie Torso (an entity usually encountered only when you've sliced the legs off a Zombie), exit the narrow tunnel and prepare your SMG for a firefight against another rappelling Cop. Bring him down, then continue along the large corridor.

After rounding the corner, you see a containment pool and a large archway that's barred. This is the continuation of your route, but you cannot reach that point yet. You must look elsewhere for a detour.

Jump into the pool on the left side. The large mixing fan slowly creaks counterclockwise, and you must quickly dart to the left into an underwater tunnel before the fan blade stops you. Swim down the tunnel. The first exit in the ceiling leads to a breathing area. Duck down again, follow the tunnel around, and climb up to an air-filled corridor.

Turn and look at the junction ahead. As you reach it, look left and right; a large steam pipe runs the length of this larger tunnel. Bring out your SMG and shoot the Scanner patrolling this area.

Work your way left, along the tunnel and underneath the steam pipe. Two more Cops rappel from the grassy area outside and ahead. Use the pipe as cover, and bring both of them down, ducking under the pipe and dodging each side.

TIP

You can stay left, move to the steps on the left wall, and shoot a Barnacle lying in wait. Stop by a Supply Crate near a locked door; use the left wall of this cubby-hole as protection, and force the Cops to expose themselves to your gunfire. Don't forget the items in the Supply Crate.

Venture into the grassy area; this is the open side of the mesh corridor you fought the Manhacks in earlier. Two Cops burst through into this area. Strafe and bring both of them down, or retreat if you wish; you can't grab the items they drop.

The "retreat" involves jumping onto the end of the steam pipe near the grass. Run along the top of the pipe, past the side passage you came from; watch the steam vent, making sure it doesn't damage you when you reach the corner. Avoid a Barnacle by leaping right, to an alcove. Feed the three Barnacles an exploding barrel, then look down and left for items strewn near a burnt corpse that a Barnacle tries to consume. Head along the pipe, stepping over the steam vents after they release.

LAMBDA
LOCATION

Bring down a Manhack in this area, and then peer down to the right side of the pipe. A logo is on the wall (signifying the presence of Supply Crates or item stashes), so drop down and crouch under the pipe, crawling under the bars to a Supply Crate. Retrace your steps, move into the tunnel opening, and drop into the water on the other side of the barred arch, near the containment pool.

Locate the ladder to the right of the water you're in, climb to the top, and wait. Use the zoom function to scan the grassy ground ahead. Two Cops wait on either side of a truck. This is a trap.

If you race forward, the Cops drop about six flaming barrels from the flatbed, and they roll down the grass toward you. You have two options: dive back into the water and submerge so all the barrels explode above you, or train your gun on the flatbed and shoot the first barrel before it even drops, taking out both Cops in a chain explosion.

Either method works, as long as you down both Cops before you turn right to check out two more Cops near a bridge. One drops in from the left wall; blast both him and the other Cop, then turn right and look for the mesh gate. Go through to enter another narrow tunnel.

A Manhack buzzes toward you in this space. Attack it with your Crowbar; when additional Manhacks arrive, watch their location so they don't swoop past and attack you from behind. The two right-side alcoves are good places to find items. At the far end, watch for the gate; five Manhacks are behind it. Close and open it to deal with one at a time.

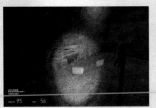 

The curved right exit leads to a gloomy tunnel with dim red lights. Flick on your Flashlight and peer toward a duct panel with ammunition in front of it. Look left in the darkened corner for more items.

Smash the panel, head down the duct, drop down, remove the floor duct, and you land in a water filtration area. Stay at the end where you dropped in, and look around the lower grating area you landed on. In the distance are stacks of explosive barrels.

A swarm of Manhacks descends from a duct on the far wall. Your options are to move to the small alcove on the opposite wall and seek partial shelter, then blast a barrel to set off a chain reaction that destroys a few of the Manhacks, or avoid hitting the barrels entirely, and whack each Manhack that charges you. There is a chance you'll receive blowback damage from the barrels, but combat ends more quickly.

TIP

A classic method of emerging from combat unscathed is to dash for the ladder, drop under the grating as the Manhacks arrive, then start the barrels exploding under the grating, keeping yourself out of the blast!

When combat ends, peer down by the ladder on the central support to see a chamber through the floor grating below. There's a large circular tube there, but it's too high to reach when you descend to this area. Instead, climb the ladder after checking the far corner of the room for items behind a regular barrel.

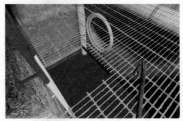

At the ceiling, step off the ladder backward onto a large pipe running across the top of the room. Follow it to the Manhack duct (which you cannot reach), crouch to crawl under a smaller pipe in the corner, and drop onto the upper balcony. You cannot reach this balcony from the bottom of the chamber.

Drop off the pipe and onto the balcony, and walk through a small adjoining corridor to a high platform above a water-logged chamber filled with pipes. To your left is a barred wall preventing access to an adjacent chamber. Below is a Supply Crate bobbing in the water. If you fall off this platform, swim to the ladder in the near right corner and move back up to this platform.

The water level needs to be raised. Time to find a suitable valve. Head right, to the jumble of pipes; drop down through the pipes, ducking so you land on the pair of small white pipes. Don't fall into the water. Spot the red-handled valve and use it.

The water level rises, allowing you to drop into the pool below, swim to the ladder, and climb it. Work your way back to the initial chamber, then keep your back to the wall as you're assaulted by five more Manhacks.

Defeat them, then drop from the balcony to the grated flooring. The area under the floor is now filled with water. Go down the ladder, press E to push yourself away, and turn around to swim through the tube tunnel.

Swim up to the surface and let the HEV Suit's air recharge. You're now on the other side of the bars, near the valve you used to fill the rooms with water. Unfortunately, you now cannot pull yourself up onto the exit path. Instead, dive to the bottom of this chamber and begin to hack the wood planks apart.

Concentrate only on the area of planks holding a large circular spindle underwater. Break the planks until the spindle is released, and stand on it as it ascends to the surface and floats.

From the spindle, leap to the far path (or hop across from the near path if you aren't standing on the spindle) and use it as a stepping stone. Ignore the crate as you head up three steps, and move along through a narrow arched passage.

TIP

You can smash more planks to release another spindle, then push them to make your route across easier.

MAP 11 | **CANAL ROUTE #5**

MAP LEGEND

1_START
2_CLEAR POINT
3_LAMBDA LOGO
4_SUPPLY CRATE
5_OTHER ITEM/S*
6_INFINITE AMMO
    CRATE

* Usually Ammo or Health Pack.

DRAINAGE DUCT

BARNACLE TRAP

UPPER LEVEL

RADIOACTIVE SLUDGE

SHANTY TOWN RADIO RECEIVER

"GOT THIS AIRBOAT ALL GASSED UP AND READY TO GO"

MAP 11 **CANAL ROUTE #5** (CONTINUED)

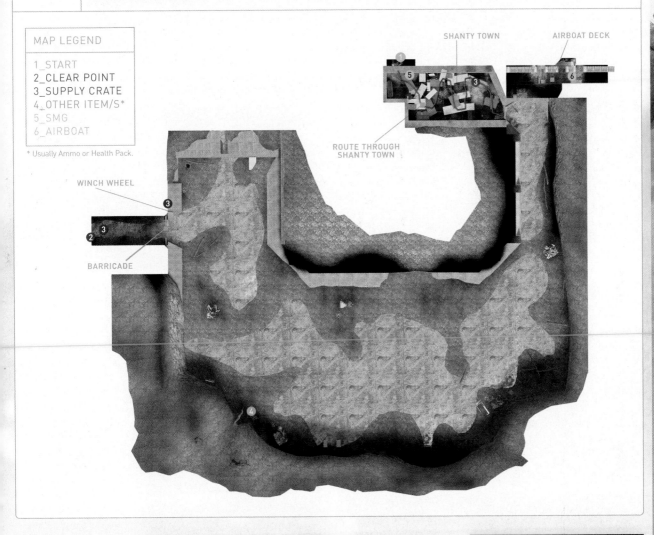

MAP LEGEND

1_START
2_CLEAR POINT
3_SUPPLY CRATE
4_OTHER ITEM/S*
5_SMG
6_AIRBOAT

* Usually Ammo or Health Pack.

WINCH WHEEL

BARRICADE

SHANTY TOWN

AIRBOAT DECK

ROUTE THROUGH
SHANTY TOWN

Move along the passage and round a left corner, up a ladder, and onto a pair of planks over a drop to a sewer overflow passage. The only way is down, so drop off from the planks to the water below and immediately look left.

The area behind you leads nowhere and it traps you, so run left, along the passage as two Cops rappel from the grating above. They release a Manhack; blast both Cops as you charge in, then deal with the Manhack.

After you neutralize the immediate threats, hop onto the barrel in the mire, then onto the ground, and check the corner for items. There's just enough time before a trio of Manhacks come buzzing in. Bring out your weapon of choice and down them.

Move down the corridor, hacking through debris until you reach a curved passage with an opening to your right. This is a sluice overflow area on two levels. Before you maneuver right, through the gap, follow the darkened passage.

CHAPTER³
ENCOUNTERS

HEADCRAB

ZOMBIE

Bring out the Flashlight and inspect the ceiling of this small antechamber; a group of festering Barnacles is ready to swallow your head. Use debris to feed them, head to the corner, and smash open a Supply Crate. Return to the sluice area.

The HEV Suit's radiation meter is picking up some severe readings in the form of a Geiger-counter crackle. Peer down to see a pool of radioactive water and gunk. Don't step in that, or you'll take some major damage. Instead, leap left to the sloping side, and step onto the corroding pipe.]

Clamber up the ladder, because a brick wall on the waterlogged ground area prevents progress. At the top, a series of planks in a long right-hand curve stretch across and through the wall that's blocked at ground level.

LAMBDA
LOCATION

Dash across the pipe to a stash of items hidden in an upper alcove near the pipe's end. Now drop down, avoid pools of radioactive water, and head toward the citizen.

LAMBDA
LOCATION

Up in this area, there's a stock of Supply Crates for you. When you reach the top of the ladder, look right to spot the first alcove behind you. Pick up the items here.

Shots ring out. The citizen is pointing his gun at two horrific-looking fleshy mounds with blubbery appendages as they shriek and twitch under a burst of bullets. "You got here at a bad time," he murmurs, before Alyx crackles through the radio. You're almost at a new mode of transportation: the air boat.

Bring out your Flashlight and carefully run around the curved plank pathway to a second sluice chamber, but don't fall down; check the dark alcove ahead for a second Lambda logo and more items.

INVENTORY ADAPTATION
INFINITE AMMO CRATE

Before you continue, inspect the large chest with the bullet emblem on it to your right. These are Infinite Ammo Crates and are constantly restocked with a particular ordnance, in this case SMG rounds. Bag as many as you need. You can come back to take more if you wish.

Don't backtrack thinking you've reached a dead end. From the upper planked plinth, fall down to the watery ground level. Look for the arched exit tunnel and follow it to the outside. Above, the Hunter-Chopper whirs by; fortunately, it doesn't spot you.

You are about to enter the shanty town (a home to citizens fleeing from Combine oppression and a once-major stronghold) on the way to Black Mesa East. Alas, no more. Walk carefully over the planks, stoop to head through the scenery, and then head out into the open.

Vapor trails fill the air and the ground shakes as a large metal rocket burrows partially into the ground, killing two citizens attempting to flee. The rocket clicks and a compartment releases, swinging open, and two disgusting Headcrabs plop out.

ENTITY ENCOUNTER: HEADCRAB

You can now get a good look at the parasitic pest responsible for changing the rebel citizens into cadavers: the Headcrab. Leaping up to scratch and tear, these whittle you down and then clamp onto your head. Brandish your Crowbar and destroy them both with a well-timed swing.

TIP

The best time to slaughter a Headcrab with gunfire is when they are emerging from the ground or from the rocket. Fire away!

Be on guard; more parasite rockets have landed nearby. Check left for some items, then move to an area covered by corrugated metal. Out of the ground burrow two more Headcrabs. Back up and start swinging.

As you reach the gate ahead, turn left (after you witness the horrific death of a citizen). There's nothing you can do (and you can't jump over to this area) except watch a shrieking man struggle to extricate a brain-sucking parasite from his head. He collapses and the fiend begins to feast.

Turn left around the corner and prepare for more Headcrabs to leap from the ground and from the scenery as the path winds around, and then move right. Two or three of these pests either burrow from the ground or are hiding in the refuse collecting in this godforsaken place.

ENTITY ENCOUNTER: ZOMBIE

As the path takes you under a tin roof again, watch out for the bodies slumped ahead. These are Zombies. One picks up a barrel and swats it at you. This hurts, so unload a Pistol clip to halt it from hitting you; or better yet, dodge to the left, behind the mesh. Use the SMG and shoot for the head until they drop.

With the shock over, turn left and watch for another crashed parasite rocket, still steaming, and another couple of flesh-hugging pests leaping out at you. Knock them away with Crowbar swings.

CHAPTER³
ENCOUNTERS

Now stop for a moment and watch your step; a live wire dangles and sways in the breeze, and this can seriously harm you if you're struck by it, so wait for it to swing out, then run past it. Bring out your SMG.

Another rocket lands as you move across the ground and out of the shanty town. As the rocket lands, detonate the barrel when you see the Headcrabs scurry out to toast them. Or flee the area.

Watch out! A Zombie smashes a piece of metal wall out toward you and lumbers in for a kill. Retaliate with accurate head shots to drop this beast, then turn right. The opening the Zombie came from leads you backward.

A tunnel is to your left and ominous radioactive sludge is on your right; the way is clear. Move into the tunnel, around the edge of the wooden walkway.

CAUTION

Use head shots on Zombies. If you aim for the stomach, when the host body dies, the Headcrab survives.

You meet a citizen tending to what looks like a collection of scrap metal masquerading as an airboat. This must be your ride. "You'll find more help up at Station 7, just a few bends up the river," the citizen informs you. "It's the old red barn."

Step into the electrified container, pausing to smack the Supply Crates, but don't let your HEV Suit brush against the sides, or you'll suffer heavy electrical damage.

INVENTORY ADAPTATION
AIRBOAT (AKA MUDSKIPPER)

Clamber into the seat on this boat and learn the rudimentary controls, especially the turning in reverse. Look with your mouse, and accelerate and turn with your regular movement controls. Let's ride!

Step out to another parasite rocket and aim carefully at another couple of Headcrabs. You can coax them so they leap at you, miss, and hit the electrified container.

Around the parasite rocket, another troublesome Zombie rises to his feet. This is the opportune moment for a killing, as the zombie is helpless until he's standing.

CAUTION

Heading back to the shanty town is a plan best left on the drawing board; more Headcrabs appear from the ground, infesting the place.

Speed out of the tunnel, and accelerate along a stretch of ooze to an open wasteland with various tenement blocks dotted around in the distance.

Turn your boat around for a view of the Citadel. Test the airboat's controls by zipping around this environment. Optionally, you can stop on the right bank, near a parasite rocket, and attack a Headcrab if you must eradicate them all.

The way forward is blocked, and the likely exit is obscured by a ramshackle barricade made from corrugated metal. Swing the airboat around to a parasite rocket embedded in the ground, park it, and move toward what looks like the barricade's raising mechanism.

Climb back into the boat, and take this the ramp (shown here) at top speed. It's almost impossible to overturn the boat, and it takes as much punishment as you can throw at it.

Walk up and onto the concrete raised area, taking care not to fall into any radiation pools. Move around the crates, but don't break the Supply Crate near a wheel winch; there's a Headcrab nearby. Blast it from a distance.

Bring the boat to a halt on the far left side, and check the debris here for an item scattered about, as well as another head-hugger. When you're done, head for the concrete walled area ahead and right.

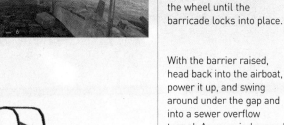

With the Headcrab squashed, turn and press E next to the wheel winch, which raises the barricade to a canal tunnel you couldn't previously pass through. Continue to turn the wheel until the barricade locks into place.

With the barrier raised, head back into the airboat, power it up, and swing around under the gap and into a sewer overflow tunnel. As you wind around debris, ram a Supply Crate to claim its contents. Do not get out to break this box.

WATER HAZARD

OVERVIEW ▌ Welcome to the canals, a winding series of concrete tunnels, channels, and overflow pipes designed to feed water and more unsavory substances in and out of City 17. Your plan is to quickly head away from City 17. However, the route is fraught with blockades, dead-end turns, and ramps to take with just the right amount of speed and talent. Naturally, the ever-present danger of the Combine is apparent, and a Hunter-Chopper doggedly chases you with a single-minded purpose: to destroy you. You must defeat this menace by cunning and violent means before finally reaching a dam and the entrance to Eli Vance's laboratory.

INVENTORY PICK-UP

- ▪ .357 Magnum
- ▪ Gauss Cannon (airboat only)

ENTITY ENCOUNTER
FRIENDLIES

- ▪ Resistance Citizens
- ▪ Crows
- ▪ Vortigaunt

ENTITY ENCOUNTER
HOSTILES

- ▪ Zombies
- ▪ Combine Hunter-Chopper
- ▪ Scanners
- ▪ Combine Dropships*
- ▪ Metro Cops
- ▪ Barnacles
- ▪ Combine APCs
- ▪ Headcrabs
- ▪ Manhacks

⌐ * Indicates first exposure to entity

"DIRECT CONFIRMATION OF A DISRUPTOR IN OUR MIDST"

MAP 13 | **CANAL ROUTE #6**

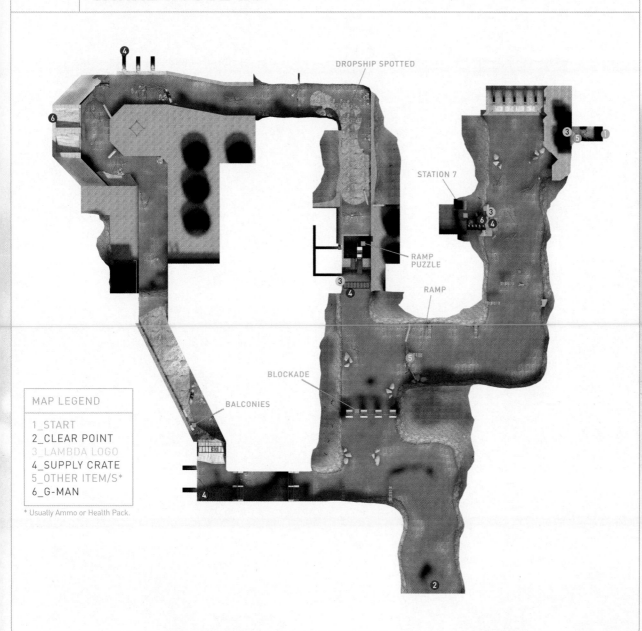

DROPSHIP SPOTTED

STATION 7

RAMP
PUZZLE

RAMP

BLOCKADE

BALCONIES

MAP LEGEND

1_START
2_CLEAR POINT
3_LAMBDA LOGO
4_SUPPLY CRATE
5_OTHER ITEM/S*
6_G-MAN

* Usually Ammo or Health Pack.

Accelerate through the tunnel, avoiding floating debris (but ramming a Supply Crate for items), and as you reach a sluice slope, open the throttle and drop the airboat down. There's no way back, so continue onward.

As the underpass tunnel turns to the left, there's a shaft of light on your right. Don't speed past this too quickly, or you may miss a sign on the concrete wall.

ADDITIONAL INVESTIGATIONS

Be vigilant! Rumor has it that someone, or something, has been placing human skulls in a variety of out-of-the-way locations throughout the canals. There's at least five to locate. Can you spot them all?

LAMBDA LOCATION

The sign is a Lambda logo. Step out of your airboat and look for a ladder on the wall to your right. Climb it, then jump the gap on the grating platform and acquire some ammunition. Then drop down.

Rev the airboat's engine and accelerate toward the opening at the end of the tunnel. You can slam into the planks of wood or into the channel markers they are attached to and not take damage. Ahead is the red structure of Station 7.

G-MAN ABOUT TOWN

As soon as you smash through the channel marker, use the zoom function (press Z) to check the upper entrance to Station 7. A gaunt man in a gray suit is watching you. He turns and enters the building before you arrive.

LAMBDA LOCATION

The time has come for a thorough building inspection. Pull up alongside the right wharf, and you'll spot another sign of the resistance. That means there are supplies somewhere. Perhaps dangling from that crane?

Get off the airboat and move up the steps onto the upper decking, facing into Station 7's main entrance where you spotted the G-Man. Watch out for flying barrels from two Zombies. Keep to the corner for cover.

After their barrels are gone, run in with guns blazing and neutralize both Zombies as efficiently as possible; headshots work best. Use the barrels to strafe around, and keep your distance from their rotting claws.

With both Zombies downed, you hear Alyx over the radio, attempting in vain to reach the remains of the radio technician at this station. Ignore his corpse, and keep your balance as you carefully step up along the left edge of the wrecked stairs, then turn around.

Do not walk forward onto the broken plank ahead; this cunning trap is loose and will drop you on the floor, followed by a crate on your head. Instead, work your way left and right; crack the crate with your Crowbar, turn left, and swat the Headcrab that drops in unannounced.

With the Headcrab removed, climb the ladder to the attic portion of Station 7 and inspect the winch mechanism. It is attached to a large metal container with supply crates inside. Bring your Crowbar out, and after the Hunter-Chopper flies by, check the barrel.

The barrel is jammed under a release cog, so smash it out of the way; the weight of the container drops it down into the water below. Jump down into the water after it and collect the items bobbing in the water.

After gathering the items you want (check underwater to see if any are jammed under the container), get in the airboat and continue through the canals.

You find a ramshackle barricade with a wooden ramp on it. Accelerate to full speed and zoom up and over the ramp.

Land on the other side in a large pool of still water. The way to the left is blocked, but the area to the right (with the channel markers) looks interesting. First check the ramshackle ramp area; return by accelerating up and over the left or right bank.

Exit the airboat and view the scenery: a water tower, various tenement blocks–and the hum of an incoming Scanner. Stand and blast it apart if you wish.

Now inspect the ramp thoroughly. Check under it for some ammunition. Then head back over the ramp.

TIP

The airboat can take some major punishment. Ram up and down the banked canal sides, spin around in the air, and try some jumping maneuvers until you're comfortable with the handling.

Although the wall with arched gratings is impassable, it does show the continuation of the canal. You'll reach there in a matter of minutes. For now, turn right and accelerate through the channel markers.

You may hear a voice above you as you pass under the bridge. This is a citizen dropping a Supply Crate into the water. He's then chased off by Scanners. Pick up the contents of his crate.

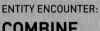

Park the airboat under the bridge and inspect the area. Ahead is a see-saw ramp blocking your progress. The far end of it appears to need raising to reach an upper bank on top of a concrete wall.

CHAPTER ⁴
ENCOUNTERS

COMBINE DROPSHIP

LAMBDA
LOCATION

Look to the left and shine your flashlight on a large circular effluent duct. There's a sign to the left of it, although this is the first time supplies aren't found; instead, the clue to raising the ramp is provided. Jump into the duct.

Run down the duct, turn right, and right again until you come to a second hole in the same large concrete wall. This overlooks a pit of water that the see-saw ramp partially rests in. There are a couple of blue plastic barrels up here.

The trick here is to push the blue barrels into the water, then drop in after them. Grab a barrel and submerge. Swim under the see-saw ramp to spot a metal catchment area. Place all the barrels you can find in this area.

The buoyancy of the plastic barrels raises the ramp. With no more blue barrels to place, return to the airboat, head back to the channel marker, then swing around and accelerate up the ramp, landing on the mud bank you couldn't previously reach.

ENTITY ENCOUNTER:
COMBINE DROPSHIP

As soon as you drive over the mud bank, a giant swooping thing, featuring eight massive spiderlike legs and holding a large metal container, drops out of the air and boosts forward. Is this organic or metal? Fortunately, it doesn't spot you.

Turn the left corner to see giant blue flames blasting out of the tail-end of this biomorphic Dropship as it carries its payload onward. Continue to follow it as you head over the rise.

Jump over the edge of a mud hill and down to a partially drained overflow system. Weave around either side of another mud bank in a slalom style as a second Dropship pulls away after depositing a group of Metro Cops.

The Cops are on the right side of your path. You don't have any long-range weapons (except if you step off the boat, which isn't advised), so hit two of the Cops at ramming speed with your boat as accurately as you can.

Then stop, get off, and finish any stragglers. The Dropships have disappeared over the horizon, so ignore them; focus instead on collecting items from the dead Cops. Now look to the right. A side pipe is missing its grating. Stand on a barrel to jump into it.

Dive into the waterlogged pipe and come out the other side into a small unpleasant cavern. Blast the Zombie and then collect the items at the back of the room. Return to the airboat.

Make a sharp right turn after the triple hit-and-run and quickly scan the canal ahead. There's a large blockade, and you may be stuck on it if you don't immediately swing to hug the left wall and keep your speed up.

G-MAN
ABOUT TOWN

As you get back on the boat, view the giant screen broadcasting to the oppressed tenement residents. The screen flickers through many images, one of which is the skeletal form of the gray-suited G-Man!

Boost up the ramp at high speed to ensure you make it over the barricade, and keep to the left as you land in a radioactive waste waterway. Drive the boat into the support strut for a side balcony, and watch it tumble into the acid.

Get on your boat, accelerate onward, and bank right onto the cement slope as three Cops rappel from the grassy bank. There's no need to stop and fire; run over them.

While continuing at speed, drive through balcony struts (knocking the balcony down) to the right side of the canal, shrugging off gunfire from two Cops; batter the support struts they're standing on. Both fall to their deaths in the acid, while you head under the bridge.

This part of the canals ends with a sharp left corner. Look to the right, though, and drive to the muddy bank and obtain supplies from the corner. Then drive around the two dangling Barnacles, to the left of the second bridge, and out into another open area.

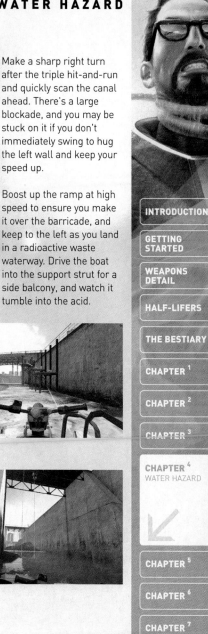

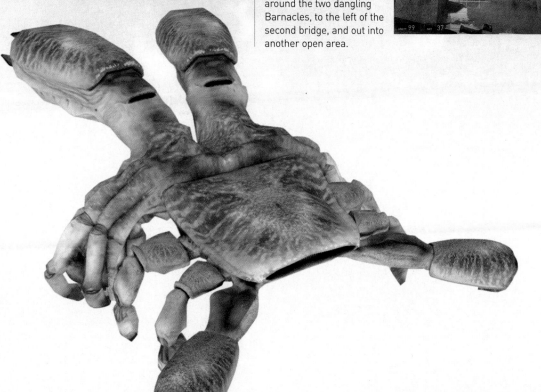

"THE LIBERATOR, THE ONE FREE MAN, THE OPENER OF THE WAY"

| MAP 14 | **CANAL ROUTE #7** |

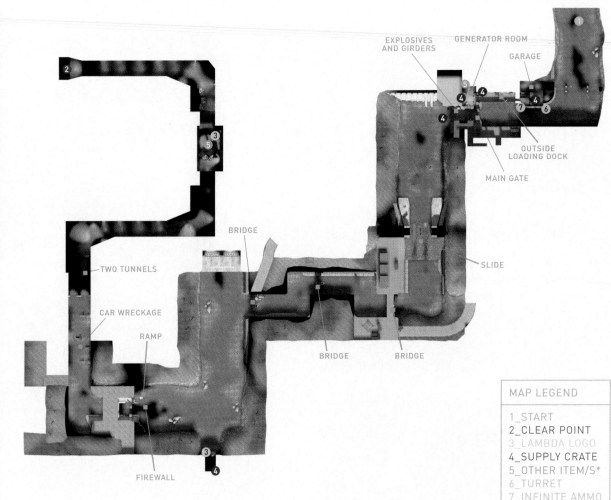

EXPLOSIVES AND GIRDERS

GENERATOR ROOM

GARAGE

OUTSIDE LOADING DOCK

MAIN GATE

SLIDE

BRIDGE

TWO TUNNELS

CAR WRECKAGE

RAMP

BRIDGE

BRIDGE

FIREWALL

MAP LEGEND

1_START
2_CLEAR POINT
3_LAMBDA LOGO
4_SUPPLY CRATE
5_OTHER ITEM/S*
6_TURRET
7_INFINITE AMMO

* Usually Ammo or Health Pack.

Pass a concrete wall to your left (this is the area where the citizen dropped a Supply Crate at you), and turn right, dashing toward a pier. A Metro Cop guards this area. You can cut across the gunfire splashing in the water by weaving around; then dispatch him.

To dispatch the Cop, get out on the bank and shoot him; or better yet, take out the pier's support struts and watch the end of the pier collapse. You can also swing the boat to the right, park on the right of the substation (co-opted by the Combine), climb the ladder, and tag him from the balcony. The way ahead is blocked by a large gate.

ADDITIONAL INVESTIGATIONS

With the guard taken out, you can hear the hated Breen rattling on with his diatribe, behind the metal door on the gantry. Open it, and listen to his talking head at the computer console.

Ignore Breen, or shoot out his screen, and move across the entrance room into a garage area. Don't shoot out the windows, or you'll attract attention. Open the door, and check out the garage. Two APCs are parked in this workshop.

Investigate the two doors on the opposite side of the workshop. Inside to the left is an interrogation room with a victim looking slightly worse for wear. The second is a storeroom with Supply Crates to break open.

Note the shelf attached to the ceiling near one of them. As you round this corner, face left and bring out your Fragmentation Grenade; two Cops hide behind and near the far APC. Don't stand under this shelf, or the Cops shoot out the supports and it crashes down, damaging you. Instead, shoot out the support struts and use it as a barricade.

Knock out or flush one of the Cops with a grenade throw, then dash behind the stack of tires and avoid the explosion reaction; in the confusion, cut down both the Cops, and then look to the windows on the left.

Five Manhacks swoop out from a room on the other side of a glass-paneled room. There's a Cop in there too. Back up so you aren't attacked through the window, and tackle each Manhack in the main garage with more room to move.

When you've destroyed all the Manhacks, use the wall under the windows as cover and bring your SMG to bear on the Cop in the room opposite. Don't worry about the camera; it doesn't affect the number of enemies, although you can destroy it.

Step through the smashed-window room, to the opposite chamber. Here you'll find a set of Manhack dispensers on the opposite wall, a Health Recharger behind the door, and most importantly, an Infinite Ammo Crate stocked with Fragmentation Grenades. Fill up!

You need Grenades for your forthcoming battle. Open the door to the right of the Infinite Ammo Crate, and you'll be outside in a courtyard with the canal and sealed gate to your left. Ahead is a Cop manning a sentry gun. You'll be cut down if you charge him.

Enact one of three cunning plans designed to deal with this long-range menace. The first is to pick up a barrel and carry it forward, using it to shield you. Then drop it and grenade the gunner. You can also sprint to the blue container area halfway along the courtyard to your right; that's a good Grenade range.

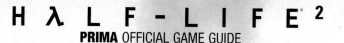

CHAPTER 4
ENCOUNTERS

Or, you can duck left immediately, arm yourself with a Grenade, and push the truck forward along the left side until you're in Grenade-throwing range; then step back (while crouching continuously) and lob a Grenade in there.

With the sentry gunner dealt a blow, inspect the blue container to the right of the sentry gun; a Supply Crate is on top. Now drop down, open the door to a warehouse, and lob a Grenade at the Cop behind the table on the far side.

Stay on the stairwell as you gun down both Cops you can see, and methodically work your way down using the SMG. At the base of the stairs, swing left, look up, and blast a third Cop on a balcony. There's another Infinite Ammo Crate holding Grenades behind the table, and if you climb on the generators to the right, you'll find your first SMG Grenade and other items.

Work up the stairs to the balcony where you blasted the third Cop, and inspect the gate controls. They've been tampered with. Open the door and step out into a canal-side balcony. Look left to spot the gate. Look right and take out a Scanner.

Look right to see an explosive barrel near a clump of debris attached to a bundle of heavy beams, which in turn are fastened to a crane. Set off a chain reaction by exploding the barrel, and the beams swing around and smash open the gate. As this happens, a Dropship swoops in and lands at the entrance to this substation.

Combine reinforcements have been called. Quickly backtrack through the warehouse, up the steps, and then out onto the sentry gun courtyard. Quickly man the gun, because about six Cops are trying to reach this position. Bring them down (and a Scanner before it blinds you) in a hail of sentry-gun fire.

During combat, the Dropship takes off. Don't waste ammunition firing at it; you cannot destroy this well-armored machine. Instead, concentrate on cutting down remaining Cop stragglers.

Move through the door and back into the blue-lit substation building. Fill up on health items and Grenades, then enter the garage and aim a well-lobbed Grenade at the Cop in the far left corner. This should send a tire stack flying.

Nimbly move around the first APC and watch for two Cops, one behind the barricade dropped from the ceiling earlier, and the other behind a sentry gun in the corner. Use a Grenade to force the gunner out, and cut down both with SMG fire.

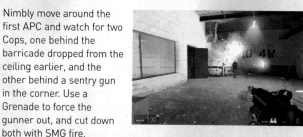

A final trio of Cops is behind the glass in the command room you first entered. Either lob a Grenade through the broken window, retreat from the blast, and enter to mop up stragglers, or dash for the sentry gun and use it on enemies entering through the door. Don't forget to backtrack to replenish your Grenade supply afterward!

You can now escape the substation, dropping down the ladder from the gantry to the airboat. Accelerate through the now-open gate, and ram the Supply Crate just after you exit the area. Turn left.

Ahead is a bridge, with two Cops strafing the water below. If you must take down every Combine force you see, park the airboat to the right, using the debris as cover, and cut down the Cops with SMG fire.

The easiest way through is to ignore the police and zoom under the bridge, as shown here. Launch into the channel markers and choose either archway, making a left turn as you drop into another canal channel.

As the next right turn nears, a Combine APC, parked on the canal bank ahead and left of you, begins to rain rockets down. Swerve left and right to avoid them, heading for the cover of the left bank, and swing around to face the bridge.

Ignore the empty red container and accelerate through the bridge. A rappelling Cop can slow you down, but not if you ram him as he lands.

The canal bends in an S-shape, and the rubble to the left of the next bridge forces you to maneuver around a Barnacle and under the right arch. Rappelling Cops should suffer the same fate as before: ram them!

The canal bends left and right once more, leading to a final bridge. Now a total of three Cops drop from above; none are necessary to fight. Slam into them, keeping to the left side of the bridge.

The Combine APCs are out in force as you swing left and then reach a right turn in the canal structure. Make a quick choice either to investigate the concrete drainage structure ahead or to continue on your way to the right.

LAMBDA
LOCATION

Stop at the edge of the drainage inlet, below the trajectory of the APC above you, and look for the sign to the right of the barred opening. Crouch and squeeze through, flick your Flashlight on, and check the far left corner for items. A Headcrab launches at you as you near, but keep the SMG primed, because two Cops rappel down to ambush you as you try to escape outside. Bring them down fast (there's nowhere to hide), and head back to the airboat.

Spraying gasoline over the canal ahead presents a new and deadly challenge. Firstly, ignore the Combine forces on the canal banks; stopping to shoot them will result in your death. Secondly, don't slow down; accelerate, but hug the right wall.

A corrugated ramp on the right side of the canal launches you up and over the wall of fire. If you slow down, you can miss the ramp and take fire and small-arms damage, so launch over the ramp at speed.

Head through either one of the narrow tunnels; when you're outside, swing right immediately. Rockets from a Combine APC on a bridge ahead have launched a car into the air, and it tumbles at you. Swing left to avoid it.

Now stay in the middle of the canal (there's more room to maneuver) avoiding the overhanging structure to the left. Rockets part two cars in the canal, so dash through the gap, and then blast through the channel markers and into either tunnel entrance.

The APC and Cops can no longer fire at you in this long inlet channel, so follow the tunnel at a more leisurely pace. Your slalom racing is over for the moment.

"BE WISE. BE SAFE. BEWARE."

MAP 15 | **CANAL ROUTE #8**

CHAPTER ⁴
ENCOUNTERS

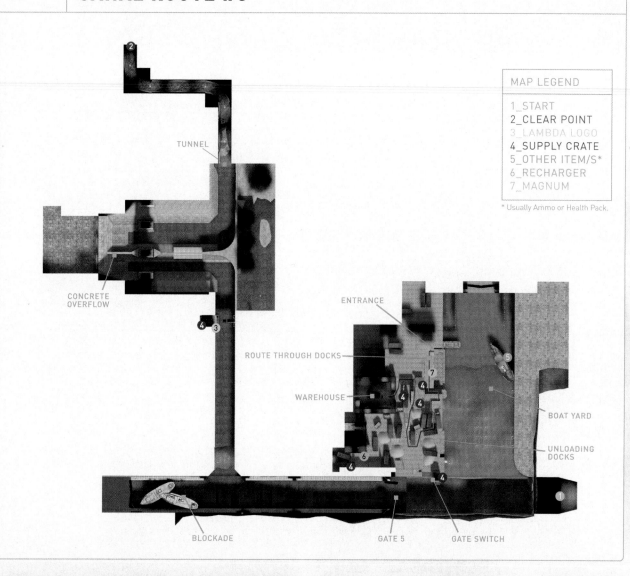

TUNNEL

CONCRETE
OVERFLOW

ENTRANCE

ROUTE THROUGH DOCKS

WAREHOUSE

BOAT YARD

UNLOADING
DOCKS

BLOCKADE

GATE 5

GATE SWITCH

MAP LEGEND

1_START
2_CLEAR POINT
3_LAMBDA LOGO
4_SUPPLY CRATE
5_OTHER ITEM/S*
6_RECHARGER
7_MAGNUM

* Usually Ammo or Health Pack.

Emerge from the long tunnel into a waterlogged area with fallen
masonry blocking your way. Swing right, avoiding the debris.

LAMBDA
LOCATION

Hug the right wall to spot a sign of the resistance ahead on a
concrete pillar. Exit the boat and look up to see a basket
suspended above you. Follow the rope back to a second basket
full of concrete bricks.
Pick up the bricks and
throw them away until the
first basket descends, and
claim the items.
Interestingly, one is
ammunition for a .357
Magnum.

Power up the airboat and drive it down the ramp and into an open canal lock area; drive toward a gated lock, which is slowly closing. In fact, it shuts before you can reach it. The facility appears to be a storage depot, and you've been spotted!

Alternatively, pull the airboat onto the pile of stones near an outflow tube, then tag the Cop firing wildly at you from the railed balcony on the edge of the facility. Take him down now to avoid dealing with him later.

You aren't able to gain entry to the base from this area; you must find the gate control to open the huge sluice gates and continue your progress. Head right, toward a beached boat. Dive down to the far side of the boat and look for a half-buried container of supplies.

Pilot your craft to a rickety jetty to the right of the concrete ground of the main base. Exit the airboat and search for a door. Produce your Crowbar and bash the lock off, then open the door and enter.

INVENTORY ADAPTATION
.357 MAGNUM

Walk around to the left, down an enclosed passage with pipes lining the walls, and check the table ahead for a brand-new weapon: the infamous .357 Magnum. Six shots, a lengthy reload time, and no secondary fire may dissuade you from using this, but ignore these shortcomings; the weapon takes down any pedestrian enemy with a single shot, even at range. Load up!

About a second after taking the Magnum from the table, the door ahead swings open, and a couple of Cops charge you. Stand your ground and blast the first one as soon as the door moves, sending him sprawling. To the left is a crate with more shells.

Walk forward and dish out an instant-kill headshot to the second Cop, and turn the left corner. Ahead, a third Cop appears. With the left corner wall protecting you, bring him down with a thud. Then head out onto the concrete walkway.

Turn right, negotiate some fallen barrels, and walk up the steps; turn left and train the Magnum on a Cop at the top of the steps. Bring him down before he has chance to fire. Now for the tricky part: avoiding the auto-cannon bursts of the Hunter-Chopper.

As the Cop goes down, run and hug the container until the Chopper shots stop, then dash left, between the container stacks. Quickly step out around the corner to the right, and blast a Manhack just as a Cop releases it. Then blast the Cop.

Run for the gray container the Cop stood next to, and take shelter from another round of chopper fire. Then dash out immediately, round the right corner (side-stepping in front of some crates to shield you from another Chopper burst from behind), and run straight for the Cop on a pile of stone chippings.

Bring the Cop down as you run over the pile and into the relative safety of an open container. The Chopper continues to buzz your location. Hug the door so you aren't strafed, then grab the items in the Supply Crate while the Chopper reloads. Finally, face the far end of the container and lob a Grenade, as shown here.

This panics two Cops waiting to ambush you; the explosion kills one or both of them and blows apart a Supply Crate under a wooden shelter to the right. Grab the items, then quickly head left, hiding against the red container.

With the Cop presence diminished, move to the area on the upper balcony where they came from: a short passage to a stock room. Watch the windows on the left, because they shatter as the Chopper spots you. Rush forward as it reloads.

CAUTION

If you didn't use the Grenade to take out the Cops and the Supply Crate, ignore the Crate; its contents aren't worth the exposure to Chopper fire.

Quickly step around a pillar, and then into the stock room; run hugging the left wall, out of gunfire range. Wait for the Chopper to strafe the stacks of boxes blocking your exit, then Crowbar through the rest.

Your plan now is to run into a large warehouse teeming with Cops. You'll be cut to ribbons in seconds if you dawdle or stay in the open once inside, so make a straight run into the warehouse and inside one of two open containers.

From here (ideally, the left one), stay in the middle and tag a few Manhacks–and the odd Cop who tries to flush you out. Deal with two Cops by the right side stairs by hiding, peeking out of the container, and tagging them.

Quickly switch to a gun and sidestep facing right, blasting a Cop against the far wall. Then, before two more Cops rush your position, stand at the top of the stairwell, drop a Grenade down the steps, and retreat. Shoot any Cops still alive, ideally from where the initial Cop blew apart.

Wait in the left container until two more Cops run inside the warehouse and try to hide in the far corner full of boxes, near the entrance. Plug them, then spend the rest of the time at the far end of the left container, shooting the Cops on the wooden balcony above.

Head down the steps to a Health Recharger and HEV Suit Recharge Station. Use the HEV Suit Recharger first, because the Chopper spots and shoots you when you use the Health Recharger. Quickly move to the side of the doorway, and when the Chopper stops firing, dash outside. If you need to, run right to an area filled with containers for a Supply Crate.

Whittle down the Cops to a couple of stragglers, then dash out and run to the right side of the warehouse, up the steps. Race to the top, and watch the balcony on the opposite side.

With one or two Cops left, you can tag them from long distance or rush them. Move over the tops of the containers and leap onto the balcony. Conduct a murderous hunt for all remaining Combine scum!

Now, using the containers as cover, head around the various gravel pits on the other side of this container yard until you reach a gate where a sign reads "Industrial Identification Required." Show the Cop here your I.D. in the form of a Magnum slug to the temple.

You're still under heavy fire from the Chopper, so run down the concrete walkway to a gate-control hut ahead of you. Before you climb into the control room, blast the Cop around the left corner on the main balcony if you didn't deal with him at the start of this bloodshed.

The control room is at the top of a ladder. There are two guards here, and it's sometimes difficult to blast both of them without taking major damage. Instead of climbing the ladder and half-hiding at the top while shooting both Cops, you can simply throw a Grenade up from the base of the ladder.

With the Cops down, grab stuff from the Supply Crates, but only after you grab the control room's sentry gun and bring it to bear on the pesky Chopper currently blasting your location. Shoot rapid-fire rounds at it from both gun emplacements until it catches fire and limps over the treetops and out of view.

Don't forget your main task here; press E by the gate control so the light changes color, and watch the gates swing open. You're free! Descend the steps, and swim back to the side entrance where you left the airboat.

Ride out and around the facility, then through gate #5. Directly ahead, rusting boats prevent you from heading forward, so swing right, just as another Hunter-Chopper arrives. This one is dropping water mines.

These knock your craft wildly about, and you take damage from the attack, so watch the trios of bombs the Chopper lays each time, keep your distance, and swerve around them. As you pass under the bridge, smash the Supply Crate in the water, and you'll get the items.

LAMBDA
LOCATION

Before you continue your merry dance with the Hunter-Chopper, take a moment to check the railway bridge. Look left, and you'll spot a sign. Get out of the airboat, run under the bridge, and smash open a couple of Supply Crates.

TIP

While avoiding the Hunter-Chopper's ordnance, observe these rules: If you stop or reverse (or retreat), it strafes you with cannon fire. If you continue forward, it drops water mines.

Turn left and accelerate hard under a bridge. Use the speed to slide up an embankment, making a long U-turn, and then drop down the other side and continue along the canal. Speed is the key here; slowpokes will be stuck!

Avoid some of the Chopper fire by moving under the wooden shelters before and after the U-turn. Then make a large left and speed up as you enter a long underground tube, away from the Chopper's guns and mines.

"GIVE 'EM HELL, DOC!"

MAP 16   **CANAL ROUTE #9**

CHAPTER ⁴
ENCOUNTERS

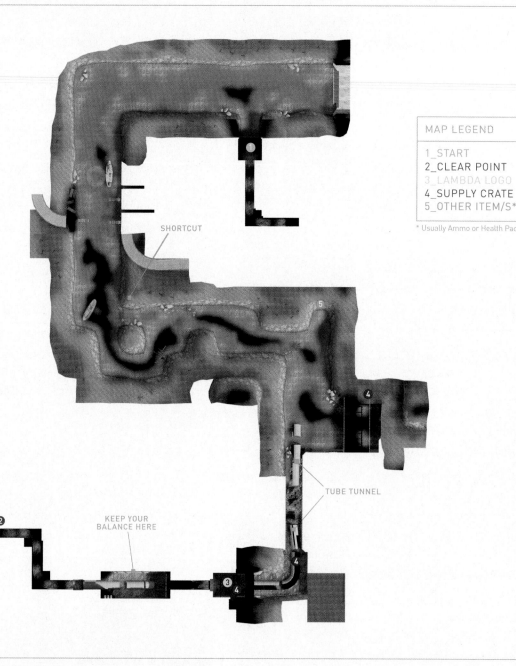

SHORTCUT

TUBE TUNNEL

KEEP YOUR
BALANCE HERE

As you emerge from the tube, another Hunter-Chopper arrives to intercept you. Swing left (the area to the right ends abruptly) and follow the Chopper as it weaves down a long and shallow canal channel.

The chopper is determined to blast you out of the water with a variety of well-laid mines; look ahead and react to the bobbing mines with effective swerving.

Try not to reach a position where the bombs are close together and the Chopper is very close to your position; hang back a little to improve your chances at avoiding a mine.

Haphazard progress continues apace as the Chopper continues its payload drop as you reach an abandoned ship on your left. Keep your eyes peeled; the route ahead becomes much trickier.

When you reach this area, you see that the canal continues onward and sweeps around in a large left turn. However, there's a shortcut on the left.

At full speed, hit the left bank to the left of a driftwood blockade, and you can drive up and over this area, cutting out the long corner and shortening the time you must play dodgeball with the Chopper.

Alternatively, you can swing around the long left bank, and use it to avoid the mines in the water below. Try banking your turns; proficient coordination with your craft is important for an upcoming fight.

The Chopper begins to drop more and more mines, so weave around them, using the left bank to avoid the balls as they roll into the water. Time your actions well, staying a little farther behind the Chopper than shown here.

As the Chopper turns around at the junction ahead, swing left, and boost your boat into a patch of grass and a curved dead-end bank; there's three Batteries to grab here. Accelerate down and make a sharp left.

Scoot under the low bridge, to the left of a partially constructed concrete tube, and stop near a bit of red graffiti on the cement wall. On the muddy floor is a Supply Crate.

Swing the boat around; the only way forward is up and through the partially constructed cement tube tunnel. The Chopper attacks from above, but ignore it and concentrate on keeping your speed up and not knocking into the openings as you make a long right turn. There's a floating Supply Crate to ram for items too.

LAMBDA
LOCATION

The tube becomes a tunnel, then pours out into a connecting chamber. The Chopper is nowhere to be seen, but a sign on the left wall indicates crates above. Ram the support posts, and the Supply Crates crash and shatter on top of you.

Continue through the next tunnel, and stay on the middle of a collapsed pipe section. This isn't easy, and you can slide off into a pool of radioactive waste. Return to the first pipe section, and try this precise control again until you reach the opposite tunnel.

"TEAR ON THROUGH TO ELI'S PLACE"

MAP 17 | ## CANAL ROUTE #10

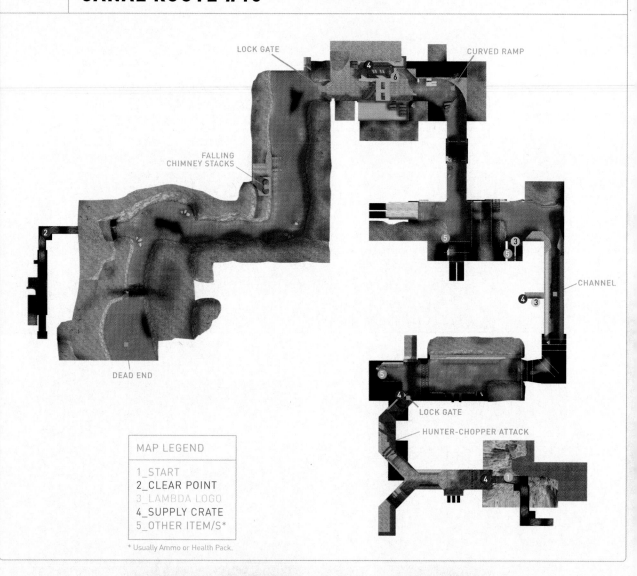

LOCK GATE

CURVED RAMP

FALLING CHIMNEY STACKS

DEAD END

CHANNEL

LOCK GATE

HUNTER-CHOPPER ATTACK

MAP LEGEND

1_START
2_CLEAR POINT
3_LAMBDA LOGO
4_SUPPLY CRATE
5_OTHER ITEM/S*

* Usually Ammo or Health Pack.

Careen into the tunnel; at the other end, slam into both the Supply Crates on the ground before you exit. The way ahead narrows into a large winding channel, and the Chopper has spotted you again!

The Chopper spins around and strafes your boat, and the barrels you slam into may knock you off into the water below. If this happens, simply exit the locks. If you manage to stay on the left shelf, follow it to the Supply Crate at the end.

Accelerate to the Y-shaped junction and take the right fork; the left is blocked. Stay on the left edge of the canal so you can go up some driftwood and onto a canal lock, staying to the left edge. Don't drop down.

Drop off the edge and continue to the right, along a large canal that takes you under a large bridge. The way behind is blocked, so keep swerving around the bombs the Chopper continues to drop. Note that the sun appears to be setting.

Night is near; creatures more horrific than those you've encountered may be prowling these watery inlets. Increase your speed, driving up the left side of a grassy bank to avoid the concrete dam ahead, and enter the tunnel.

Follow this around until you reach another steeply sloping channel. The Chopper swoops down again, determined to shoot you off your craft. Ignore its strafing, increase your speed to maximum, and gradually head up the left bank.

Now comes a spot of tricky weaving. While the Chopper attempts to pin you with cannon fire, make sure you're traveling at top speed before smashing through a channel marker and continuing your fast-paced escape.

At the second archway, watch for Barnacles, which can seriously impede your progress; they can grab you straight off your boat and begin to throttle you. If so, bring out the Pistol, tag them, then swim to your vessel.

After another turn, jet toward these channel markers and keep your speed up. As you emerge from under the bridge, stay to the extreme right; containers block the canal.

LAMBDA
LOCATION

Shoot up the left bank at a diagonal; otherwise, you won't have the power to maneuver up here to a gap in the channel. Exit the craft and sprint to a stash of Supply Crates at the dead end you've arrived at. Return to the airboat.

LAMBDA
LOCATION

When you exit this sluice channel, a concrete overflow structure appears on your left. Inspect the reeds in the right corner for Magnum shells, then move into the logo-adorned concrete structure to secure more items.

Head right at this point; you'll see a long, rising pile of mud and stones along the curve of the right-side wall. Don't try to ram and launch over the containers–only radiation lies past the containers.

Instead, speed up and launch your airboat off the edge of the ramp and over a gap. Below you is radioactive water, and behind you to the left is a dead end. You're heading for the warehouse building's top balcony, ahead.

Ahead are two large towers; you're headed here in a moment, but for now, park the airboat (ideally inside the warehouse). There's nothing outside except the incessant cannon-firing of the Chopper.

Step into the warehouse and check all the corners for Supply Crates and a pair of Rechargers. You won't be returning here, so suck all the juice from these machines. Mount the airboat again.

If you failed to reach the warehouse balcony, you'll land in the radioactive effluent. Your exit is to the right, around and underneath the warehouse.

Drop off the upper balcony, heading toward the huge dock gates. These are permanently open. When you pass them, ignore the area to your right, and swing left at top speed.

Loud, whistling bangs fill the air around you; parasite rockets are being fired from the city, and two land near you. One slams into the base of a large smoke-stack, which begins to topple. Full steam ahead!

Head to the right side of the collapsing chimney as it smashes into dozens of pieces. If you slow down and are in the middle of the canal, you'll be struck and severely damaged. Wait until the stack finishes falling, or gun the engine. Either way, head around the right side of the destruction.

Round the next corner and prepare for more punishment at the hands of the Chopper pilot, who strafes you repeatedly as you enter a long straight into a large tunnel ahead.

Inside the tunnel, it winds for a while, then brings you out at a strange little encampment.

"I ALWAYS LIKE TO BRING A LITTLE IRONY TO A FIREFIGHT"

MAP 18 | **CANAL ROUTE #11**

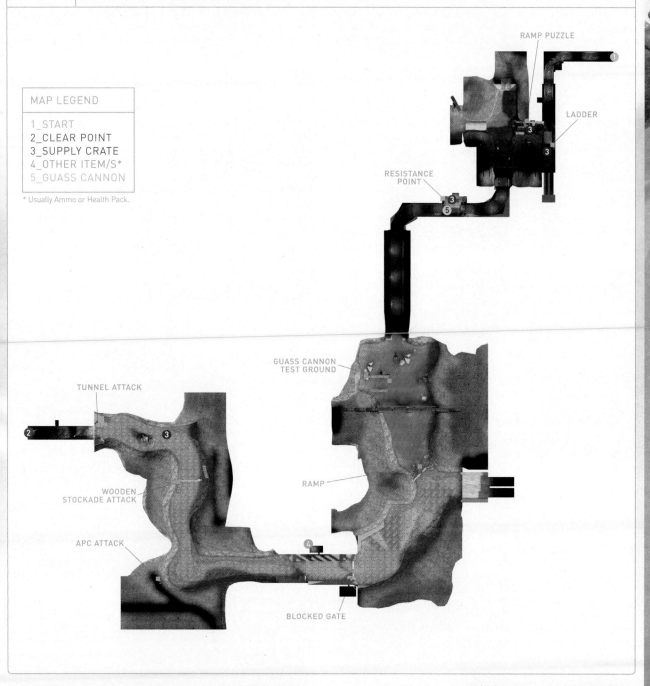

MAP LEGEND

1_START
2_CLEAR POINT
3_SUPPLY CRATE
4_OTHER ITEM/S*
5_GUASS CANNON

* Usually Ammo or Health Pack.

RAMP PUZZLE
LADDER
RESISTANCE POINT
GUASS CANNON TEST GROUND
TUNNEL ATTACK
WOODEN STOCKADE ATTACK
APC ATTACK
RAMP
BLOCKED GATE

NOTE

If you want to locate where escaped resistance citizens are attempting to hide out and thrive, look for windmills at the top of the usually spindly and dilapidated structures. This indicates that human resistance fighters have built the structure.

Exit the boat and look around. The Chopper hasn't spotted you and flies off to the left, leaving you to figure out how to maneuver your vessel to the other side of a large and immoveable barricade. Pick up a chair and throw it in the square metal basket. Collect the items from the Supply Crate, then release the lever.

What appears to be a ramp raises slightly, and the basket drops down. You'll need some extra weight to bring the ramp up to a height where you'll be able to launch over the barricade. Turn around and check the two pipe pieces for clues. Out pops a Zombie. Tag him, then look for items of interest.

A ladder is riveted to the far wall. Clamber up to the top, then jump and drop onto the top of the pipe. A makeshift ladder leads to a ramshackle balcony. Maneuver onto it.

Stand on the corrugated roof and drop down to the balcony almost directly above the basket. Up here is a very heavy washing machine. Push it forward until it falls into the basket with a clanging thud.

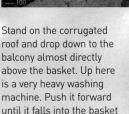

Now drop down and throw the switch. The basket drops, and the extra weight of the washer raises the rickety ramp up ahead with a splash. It looks to be just the right height.

Backtrack to the airboat; back it up so you have enough of a run-up, and then boost forward, up the ramp, and jet over the barricade, landing with a splash on the other side.

After a swift right turn, you'll enter another large cement pipe tunnel. This one is different, however; it is bathed in blue light and ends at a stockade. A female citizen peers at you, and a male walks across a gantry. "Well, I wouldn't believe it if I couldn't see it with my own eyes. Dr. Gordon Freeman himself," says the male.

It is good to be with friends, even if they're about to tear down the camp before the Combine picks them up. Park your boat and pass the Vortigaunt with the mean-looking Gauss Cannon. "Don't worry about the airboat," says the man, "Vort's gonna look after it for you."

The man beckons you into the hut. Note the Supply Crates to the right side. Break them open and enter. The man points to an accurate map of the canals area (which you can spend time checking), showing you a dam just up ahead.

"Eli's hideout is here, nestled in the old hydro plant," the man tells you. There's some rather encouraging news about your lack of firepower too: "The Vortigaunt's working his magic on your airboat." Step outside.

Move down to the boat. The Vortigaunt is finishing off a spot of welding on the front of your vehicle. You now have an exceptionally potent Gauss Cannon to fend off attackers. "The Freeman will accept this weapon, or suffer greatly on the road ahead," the Vortigaunt informs you.

After waving you off, start the boat, and bring your Gauss Cannon to bear on a Barnacle stuck to the tunnel ceiling. Make a sharp left turn and accelerate out of the camp. It's time to test your new toy!

INVENTORY ADAPTATION
HUNTER-CHOPPER GUASS CANNON

The front-mounted Gauss Cannon on the airboat is an exceptionally powerful weapon with infinite ammunition but a finite power supply. The energy of the weapon remains constant, but drains with repeated use, so watch the counter; the weapon needs recharging if it hits zero. Otherwise, fire at everything that moves!

Break out of the tunnel, slow down, and train your new weapon on the Chopper hovering at the exit, attempting to cut you down. Blast the structure of the helicopter until the machine begins to burn and limps off out of range.

TIP

In APC battles to come, you can shoot the APC's incoming rockets out of the sky with your cannon.

Spend a moment checking the empty lake area. Bring your weapon to bear on the train sitting on the bridge, the barrels on the wharf, and the struts supporting crates on a small balcony. Learn how destructive your weapon can be.

Make sure your weapon is at 100 percent strength as you near a rocky outcrop, then slow down and train your weapon on a Combine APC launching rockets from a distance. Swerve to avoid the rockets while training your weapon at the vehicle until it explodes.

When you've finished your destructive romp, quickly accelerate toward the ramp at the far end of the lake, on the other side of the bridge. Leap over the barricade, landing in radioactive goop, and continue to the right.

Watch the debris flying, wait for your weapon to replenish, then continue along the rocky canal basin to a wooden structure with two Cops guarding it. Bring out your weapon and strafe the explosive barrel to the right, demolishing the Cop. Then ram the left Cop from the ramp on the left.

Almost immediately, there's a corrugated barricade. You must drive your vehicle up onto a ramp, then down onto a walkway with Cops appearing on either side of a concrete facility. Bring your weapon to bear on the left side first and strafe barrels.

Round the corner and slow down; the next area is a little trickier. Run over the Supply Crate in the gunk to the right of the rocky island, then train all your firepower on the barrels in the water ahead and on the Cops standing to the right.

This destroys any Combine resistance on the left side. Now head through the right walkway, alternating between ramming and blasting the Cops in your way. Don't be shy about introducing them to your new gun! But don't leave this area yet.

Take care of every barrel and Cop, because more appear from side entrances as you reach the gate of this large tunnel. Stay focused on the right side, peppering the walls with Cop blood. Keep an eye on the Gauss Cannon's power.

Stop halfway along the walkway after you neutralize all the Combine troops, and head through the side door to a restocking room filled with items. Grab what you need, saddle up, and then drive off the right side of the walkway (the two gates are permanently closed).

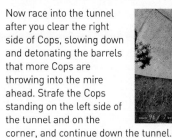

Now race into the tunnel after you clear the right side of Cops, slowing down and detonating the barrels that more Cops are throwing into the mire ahead. Strafe the Cops standing on the left side of the tunnel and on the corner, and continue down the tunnel.

"THE FREEMAN WILL ACCEPT THIS WEAPON"

MAP 19 | **CANAL ROUTE #12**

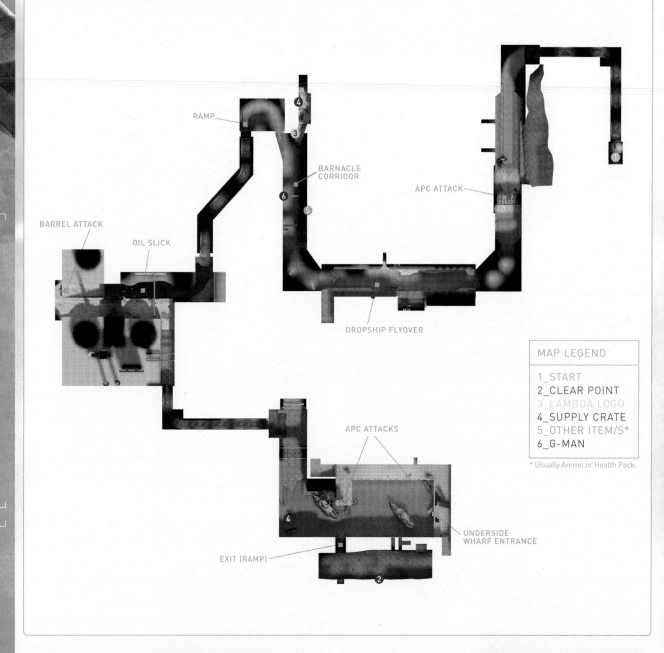

RAMP

BARNACLE
CORRIDOR

APC ATTACK

BARREL ATTACK

OIL SLICK

DROPSHIP FLYOVER

APC ATTACKS

UNDERSIDE
WHARF ENTRANCE

EXIT [RAMP]

CHAPTER ⁴
ENCOUNTERS

MAP LEGEND

1_START
2_CLEAR POINT
3_LAMBDA LOGO
4_SUPPLY CRATE
5_OTHER ITEM/S*
6_G-MAN

* Usually Ammo or Health Pack.

Out of the tunnel, you drop into a channel, turn a left corner, and boost up a long stretch of water with an APC at the far end. Weave to avoid the rockets, and tear the APC apart!

Drive over the cement ramp in the middle of the overflow channel, and optionally strafe the left wall to stop Metro Cops taking pot shots at you. An exploding barrel sorts them out. Continue under the bridge and around the right bend.

Moving to a long strait in a channel, power along until you spot a Dropship flying overhead. The ship itself cannot be downed in time, but the APC it carries can be destroyed before the Dropship disappears.

Before you tear down this stretch of canal, get out and run to the right around the large cylindrical vats, clicking on your Flashlight. Items are strewn around a corpse on the right side of this area. Return to the boat and continue.

Swing around another right turn, and the channel runs along side an old factory. Barnacles lie in wait, stuck to covered walkways. Weave between them, or shoot them before you pass to avoid being strangled. Hold on–who's that?

LAMBDA
LOCATION

As you reach the end of this channel, it splits. To the left is a banked corner leading to the next area. But first, check the logo in the center of the wall ahead, and mow down the Cop at the barricade on the right.

Exit the airboat and head to the makeshift hut of a citizen who was recently discovered by the Combine. A parasite rocket was dispatched. Headcrabs and the remains of the man flop down from the dark tunnel entrance ahead. Defeat them all! Check the upper floor of the hut to your left, and check the ground nearby for Supply Crates.

G-MAN
ABOUT TOWN

On a small gantry near the second covered bridge stands a gaunt, gray-suited man carrying a briefcase. At least, you think he's a man; he's impervious to your boat's weapon, and he stares at you intently, then walks off to the left.

Return to the boat and take the other route, hugging the right wall and riding it around, up a ramp, and into an upper overflow tunnel.

Don't slow down; ram the Zombies inside this winding tunnel, watch out for hanging Barnacle tongues, and then slow down as you exit.

You're now entering the refinery factory area, and the Combine is attempting to set fire to oil drums and stop your progress. Begin by strafing the middle section, bringing down enemies firing at you. Then drive straight through the fire.

CHAPTER ⁴
ENCOUNTERS

Weave up the concrete ramp, avoiding the exploding barrels thrown down at you. Keep your speed up, and reach the wall so the barrels pass over your head. Then swing the boat round and go down the other side of the ramp.

Swerve to the right as you pass under a bridge, avoiding the nasty Barnacle, then zoom forward, ramming the two Metro Cops as you swing right, around the corner. Boost forward into another tunnel.

Drop out of the other end of the tunnel, then slow down. This is a heavily guarded area, so be cautious. You want to launch up a ramp and into the tunnel in the right concrete wall you can see above. However, there are goods to grab in this area first.

Edge your craft around the beached boat to your left. Train your weapon on the APC on the wooden wharf and pepper it with gunfire. Don't edge forward any more; a second APC is on the wharf above and left of you.

As soon as the APC explodes, jet toward the boat at the far end of this wharf. Turn around, and use the boat to your right as a shield. Begin to blast the other APC as shown here. When you run out of power, recharge and spin your craft around the boat to hide from the rockets. Constantly move around the boat so you aren't hit.

As soon as the second APC is demolished, move to the container that's fallen into the edge of the wharf, and move on foot around it. On the other side, the container is open; inside are barrels at the other end.

Detonate the barrels, and the container doors fly apart. This hole allows you to maneuver your boat carefully through the container and under the wharf itself. Increase your speed slightly as you follow the path of the wharf around.

Continue in a counter-clockwise direction until you reach the first beached boat, then accelerate quickly up the ramp to its left. Fly through the air and land in the tunnel above the area where you sat and took down the first APC.

Fall out the other end of the tunnel, moving to the left, and take the square tunnel entrance along the right wall of the dock you've landed in. You're almost at Eli's place!

"TAKE THAT CHOPPER DOWN"

MAP 20 | **CANAL DAM**

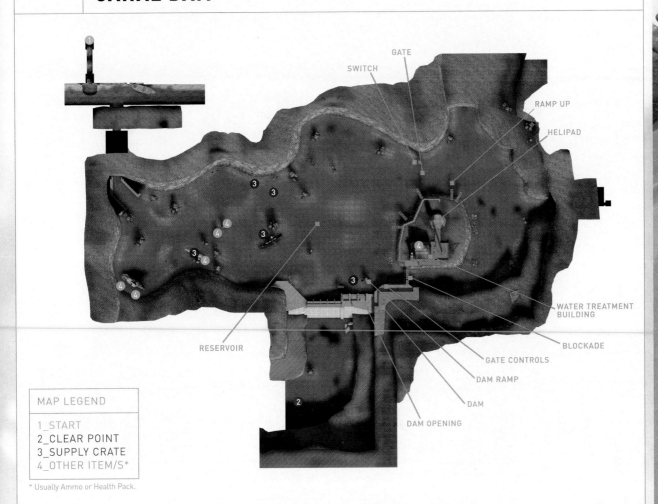

GATE

SWITCH

RAMP UP

HELIPAD

WATER TREATMENT BUILDING

BLOCKADE

GATE CONTROLS

DAM RAMP

DAM

DAM OPENING

RESERVOIR

MAP LEGEND

1_START
2_CLEAR POINT
3_SUPPLY CRATE
4_OTHER ITEM/S*

* Usually Ammo or Health Pack.

After you've maneuvered out of this last tunnel, you drop down a driftwood dam and find it almost impossible to return. Venture forward into the dam reservoir.

Use the banked turn to increase speed, and accelerate toward a wooden ramp, shown here. This is attached to a rock outcrop.

Continue slowly and to the right of the dam. Look for a red, rusting trawler and inspect the right side of it for some Supply Crates. Continue to work your way around the reservoir's right bank.

If you skim up the ramp perfectly, without falling even slightly to one side, you can "combo" your craft so it bounces on the tops of three rock outcroppings. A Supply Crate rests on the final rock top; it's one of the most difficult to obtain,

but the results are worth it: two SMG Grenades!

Until you hear the ominous sound of rotor blades, inspect the rest of the reservoir for items. Across from the rocky outcrops, on the opposite side of the lake is a piece of driftwood with a Supply Crate on it.

Backtrack to the entrance and to a stagnant pond with another Supply Crate near some wood.

Finally, look out for a piece of half-submerged cement pipe; it's under the rocks you combo off. Balance across this for a Supply Crate, then duck and crawl into the pipe for more items.

As soon as you hear the approach of the Hunter-Chopper, which rises from a dam building ahead, prepare for combat. For cover, use the rocky outcrops around the reservoir or use the beached boats. Shoot the Chopper as it passes overhead.

To begin, the Chopper either drops mines or shoots back with its weapon. Follow and shoot if the Chopper is using its gun, or remain stationary if it drops mines in your path. Keep unloading your weapon into the Chopper at all times.

More Supply Crates are in the middle of the reservoir, near a beached boat. Break these open at your leisure, after the battle. The wood propped against the other side of the boat makes a great ramp.

Keep up this devastating shooting from your boat until the Chopper starts to belch thick black smoke. It attempts to drop a vast array of bombs at this point. Continue with the pummeling, but move constantly to avoid the bombs.

Continue this strategy of hiding behind rocks, waiting for the Chopper to fly overhead, then demolishing it with your gun, until the vehicle splutters, grinds, and explodes in a shower of fire. A most impressive takedown.

Now move to the reservoir's far end. It is worth entering this area only after the battle, because explosive barrels are bobbing around, and you don't want to run over them accidentally. Shoot the barrels and then the distant Cop who's standing on the side of the dam building.

ADDITIONAL INVESTIGATIONS

Before the sun sets over the canals, locate an area of high ground and check the horizon while facing the general direction of the dam. The silhouetted outline of a gothic village can be seen against the glaze of the sunset. This has been visible since the ninth canal map. Perhaps you'll be headed there soon.

When you reach the gate to the dam building, climb up and turn the gate wheel to raise it; keep turning until the gate wheel clicks. Drop down, then move to the rickety ramp; this is the fastest way up and onto the top of the dam building.

Land your airboat expertly on the ground next to a helipad, and seek out a Cop patrolling the area. Use your boat or your own favorite weapon to take him out. Then move to the side of the building bathed in sunlight.

Here you find one or two Cops and a Manhack to tear apart. Your airboat's Gauss Cannon is excellent here. When you're done defeating the Combine, hop off the boat and open the door to the dam building interior.

Two Cops wait inside. Disrupt them by lobbing a Grenade a short way in, then follow up with SMG fire before advancing to the right and shooting the final Cop behind the shelving. Pick up the items and recharge yourself.

You're very close to Eli's place, but you need to find some way across the dam. This is achieved by crossing (in the airboat or on foot) the rickety bridge. Look for the sign reading "water control" and follow the arrow.

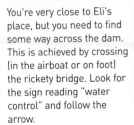

Over the bridge, turn right, move to the edge, and flick the switch. This drops a ladder to the ground, in case you fall off and want to return here quickly.

Drop onto the dam and run to the dam-control switch. The left one is short-circuiting, so move to the right side and pull the "gate override" switch. You'll hear a grinding sound. It appears as if the dam's gate has been opened.

Head back to your boat, and drop back down to the reservoir. Pilot the boat toward the dam, and you'll see an opening. In front of that is a stack of driftwood in what appears to be a ramp formation.

Floor it! Accelerate over the wood ramp, trying hard not to slip off course (or you'll come up short or slam into a wall and have to retry), and you'll pass through the gate. Drop down the dam in a spectacular descent! Next stop, Eli Vance!

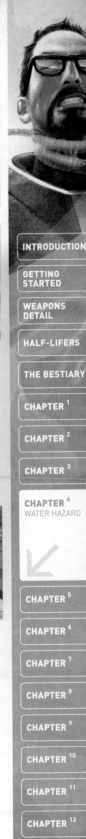

BLACK MESA EAST

OVERVIEW ▌ You've conquered the canals. Now you must locate the hidden entrance to Black Mesa East, which is a major resistance center, a test chamber for teleport technology, and the laboratory of Doctor Eli Vance. You'll meet Doctor Mossman and finally Eli himself; he's lost a little weight (and an appendage) since the Black Mesa Incident. After gaining further knowledge from the good doctors, your return to lab-coated experiments is cut short when Alyx offers to train you in the arts of Doctor Vance's latest creation: the Gravity Gun! You're joined by the cute-yet-fearsome Dog, Alyx's pet robot, for a spot of catch before the Combine sweeps through the facility and you flee for your life. The way to the doctor is blocked, and the only alternate route to the coast, and safety, is through an old abandoned mining town.

INVENTORY PICK-UP

- Zero Point Energy Field Manipulator (Gravity Gun)

ENTITY ENCOUNTER
FRIENDLIES

- Doctor Judith Mossman
- Vortigaunts
- Doctor Eli Vance
- Alyx Vance
- Dog*

ENTITY ENCOUNTER
HOSTILES

- Scanners
- Combine Hunter-Chopper

* Indicates first exposure to entity

"BACK INTO YOUR LAB COAT, WHERE YOU BELONG"

MAP 21	**BLACK MESA EAST (LABORATORY LEVEL)**

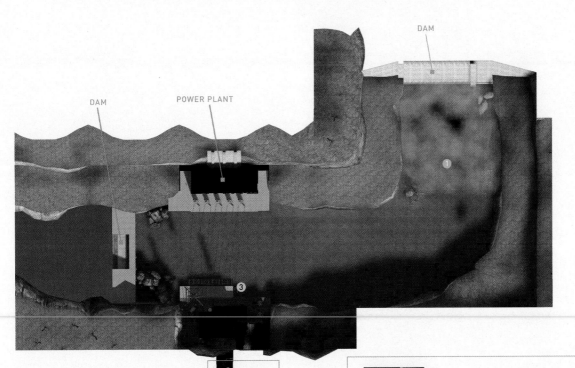

DAM

DAM

POWER PLANT

LABORATORY LEVEL

AIR LOCK SCANNER

ENTRANCE TO BLACK MESA EAST

ELEVATOR DOWN

MAP LEGEND

1_START
2_CLEAR POINT
3_LAMBDA LOGO

* Usually Ammo or Health Pack.

Once the airboat stops at the base of the dam, ease off the gas and float across to the left side of a power plant reservoir. To the right is the plant; ahead is a concrete wall you cannot access.

LAMBDA
LOCATION

You're looking for a concrete wharf with a wooden pier attached. Maneuver toward the Lambda logo near a ladder. Stop the boat and climb the ladder onto the wharf.

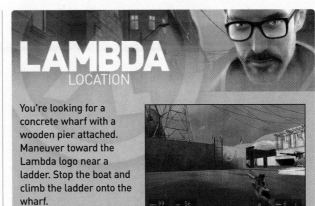

Look up at the hydro-electric power station on both sides of the water. Move along the wharf, looking for a flatbed with barrels scattered about. Move up the shallow ramp near these items.

Continue up the incline, turn left, and look for the white "Resist" poster. To the right of this is a trio of barrels. Push them out of the way and move through the mesh fencing, into an entrance chamber.

This looks to be some kind of airlock. You hear a woman's voice. The door behind you shuts, and a laser scanner slowly bathes you in red light as you're checked. Suddenly, the privacy screen flips open and you spot two figures. "Doctor Freeman? *Gordon* Freeman? Is that you?"

The female doctor introduces herself as Doctor Judith Mossman and beckons you to follow her out of the airlock.

She moves to an elevator shaft, talking quickly. Step into the elevator. The elevator drops down a level to a recreation room. A citizen lies on a mattress to the left, while a citizen and a Vortigaunt play a game of chess.

The next level is a corridor where a citizen watches a couple of Vortigaunts discharge electrical attacks in practice for a battle to come. The elevator continues to drop, and you arrive at Eli's lab.

ADDITIONAL INVESTIGATIONS

The Doctor's laboratory is a cornuCopia of information and interesting diversions. Check some of them out, like the "thing" in the jar.

A Vortigaunt is staring intently at a series of computer monitors and tapping in commands.

Next to the radio on a shelf is an old black-and-white picture showing a young Eli with his wife and Alyx as a young child.

Notice this pile of electrical junk and a number of well-thumbed books. Inspect the title of each. Also check the sweater Eli is wearing. He seems to have been an Ivy Leaguer.

The corkboard with the newspaper clippings tells of a horrific seven-day war and Earth's surrender to the Combine. Portal storms, the declaration of Wallace Breen, and some other interesting tidbits are gleaned from reading here.

The Doctor also shows you a small resonance cascade emulation that you can switch on or off with the two switches. This machine is called the Rotato.

After a few moments, Alyx appears from a side door. Eli suggests she take you to practice with the Gravity Gun.

Follow Alyx out into the connecting passageways. You both walk down a series of gray brick tunnels. She moves through a couple of passages, talking to you.

You pass a long corridor ending in a sealed door. Alyx points there and says, "We used to be able to go right up there to Ravenholm. It was an old mining town inhabited by some escapees from City 17. Believe me, that tunnel is sealed for a reason." She walks to an airlock. Step inside with her.

"LET ME CALL DOG. HE LOVES TO PLAY FETCH."

MAP 22	**BLACK MESA EAST (SCRAP YARD)**

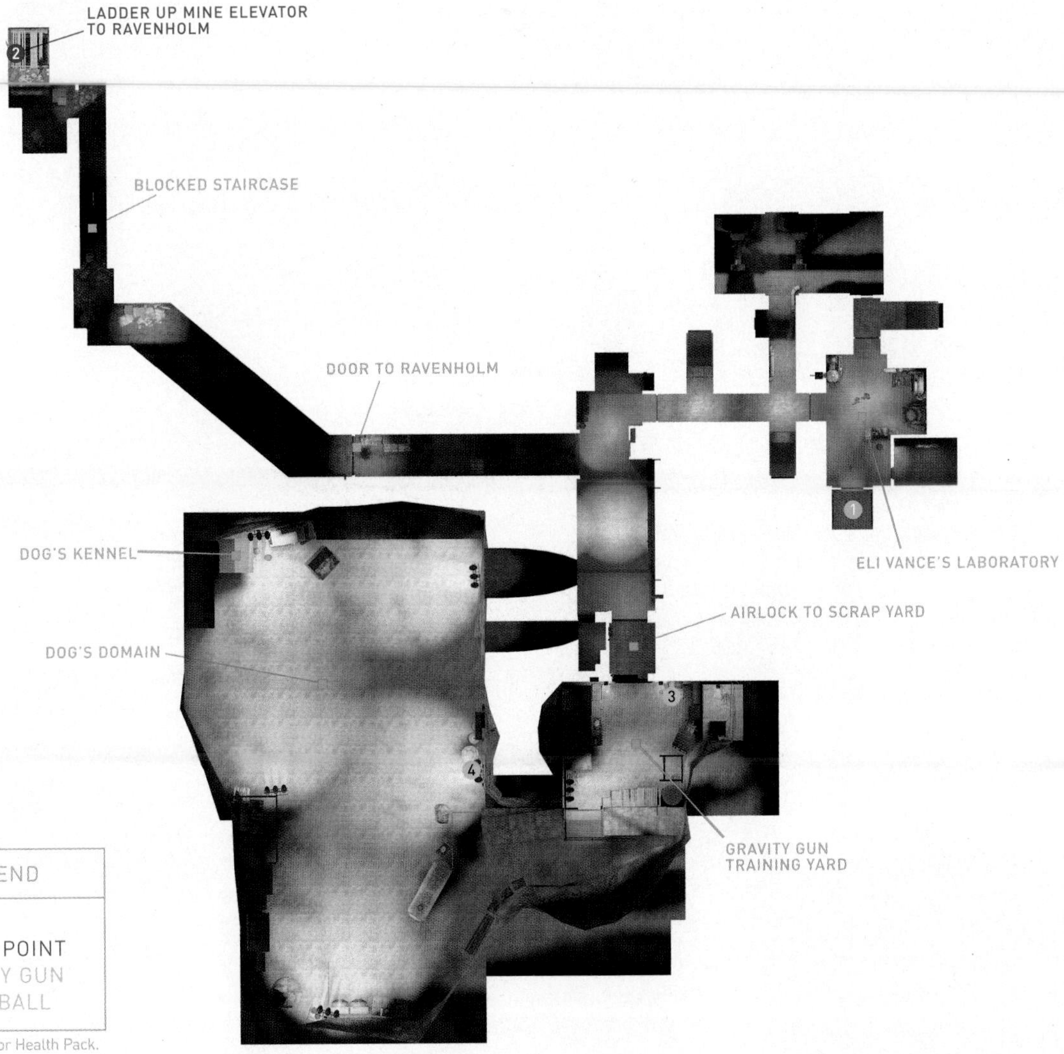

LADDER UP MINE ELEVATOR TO RAVENHOLM

BLOCKED STAIRCASE

DOOR TO RAVENHOLM

DOG'S KENNEL

DOG'S DOMAIN

ELI VANCE'S LABORATORY

AIRLOCK TO SCRAP YARD

GRAVITY GUN TRAINING YARD

MAP LEGEND

1_START
2_CLEAR POINT
3_GRAVITY GUN
4_DOG'S BALL

* Usually Ammo or Health Pack.

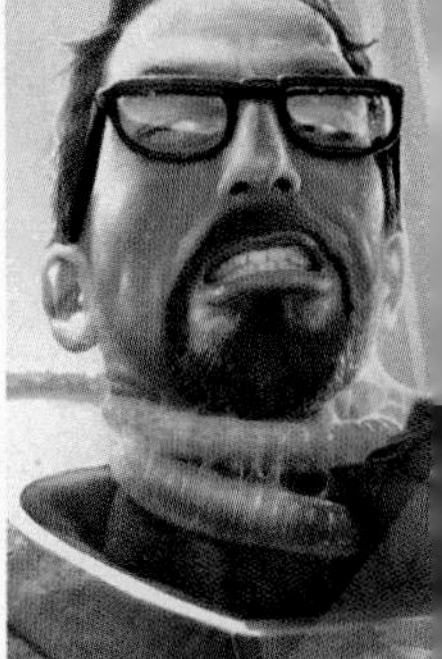

Alyx opens the airlock door and welcomes you to the scrap yard. Step out and wait for Alyx to unhook a cumbersome-looking weapon from its hook. She presents it to you; this is the Zero Point Energy Field Manipulator (Gravity Gun)!

INVENTORY ADAPTATION
ZERO POINT ENERGY FIELD MANIPULATOR (GRAVITY GUN)

Also known as the Physics Cannon and the Gravity Gun, the Manipulator is the most versatile, helpful, and sometimes devastating weapon you're ever likely to find. Refer to the weapons section of this guide for detailed information.

TIP

The best way to flick between the Gravity Gun and your favorite weapon is to press Ⓖ. That way, you can load your previous gun after you've used the Gravity Gun for a manual or noncombative task.

Alyx encourages you to play around with the weapon's abilities. Right click to suck up a lightweight item, such as this paint can. Press it again to drop it.

Left click to shoot the can forward after you have it floating in front of you. Or you can shove items out of the way by simply firing (left click) when you're close by; this is quicker than picking up and firing or depositing.

Now comes a spot of precision firing. Right click to suck up a larger item, such as a crate, and then take your finger off the button. The crate should still float until you release it.

Now fire it off (left click) and the crate flies off, landing on a balcony ahead (if you pointed your Gravity Gun at the correct angle). Try this again with a variety of items.

Alyx also wants you to learn the range of the sucking capabilities of this weapon. So stand away from the white cylinder and try to suck the crate on the balcony next to it. It moves slowly at first, then sucks right in!

You should also determine the type of item that makes a good weapon to fire against foes. The tire is a great example; when you shoot it, it flies off quickly, and is big enough to dish damage, but small enough for you to see what you're aiming at.

Alyx leaps onto the balcony ahead, and wants you to build a pile of items to reach her. This is easily achieved by turning left, sucking a barrel off a high ledge, and placing (not firing) it on the ground. Jump on it, then suck and place it again. Climb to Alyx.

You've graduated Gravity Gun Training 101. Now for more impressive techniques. Drop off the other side of the balcony and follow Alyx around to the quarry area. On the way is a sign: "Beware of Dog."

Crates are fun, but Dog really wants to play with his ball. This is in fact a deactivated Combine weapon called a Rollermine. Dog opens his "tin" to retrieve it.

"Now let me call Dog." Alyx says, "He loves to play fetch." She whistles, and a giant robotic bipedal robot gambols out of his kennel and excitedly rushes the both of you. She stops the large machine and pats it on the head.

She explains that Eli built this pet for her and has been constantly adding parts to him. He seems to be incredibly strong, and hopefully useful in the battles to come. For now, though, he just wants to play.

Dog holds the ball in an electrical field before lobbing it. Be sure you stand far enough away so you have time to catch the device. Then punt it back at Dog; try to land the ball on Dog's head to practice accuracy.

As the back-and-forth catch continues, stand in this general area, and try to shoot a few hoops with Dog. Rebounds are difficult, so increase the pitch of your throw so there's no banked shots before the ball drops through the ring!

Time to play catch! Stay where you are while Dog runs to the opposite end of the quarry, picks up a crate, and lobs it high into the air. As it descends, move under it, then right click at the last second to "catch" it.

If you mess up, Dog tries it again, and you have a number of opportunities to learn the timing needed to catch a falling object. Stand to the side of its impact spot, then suck it before it touches the ground; that works too!

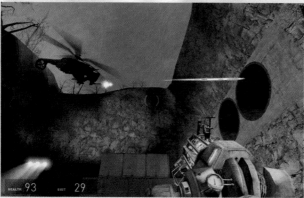

TIP

Vary your trajectory when firing items about; point your weapon straight up and you can throw and catch objects above your head, for example.

A terrible whistling sound echoes through the yard, as parasite rockets drop to earth with a bang. Scanners flock the skies, and a Hunter-Chopper appears. The Combine have found your location!

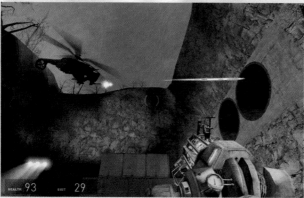

Back up; your weapons aren't a match for the Hunter-Chopper that begins strafing the facility's upper tunnels. Follow Alyx and Dog back to the airlock as quickly as you can.

On the way back, you may be tempted to challenge the Hunter-Chopper, but without the airboat's Gauss Cannon, this isn't a good idea. Waiting around only results in you being cut down.

"We're in the scrap yard airlock, stuck in a full autocycle!" Alyx is talking urgently to Eli on the door console. Eli begins to respond, urging you to head for the coast; then the console goes dead.

The airlock door won't open, so Alyx orders Dog to wrench it apart. Dog lumbers into position, and a second or two later, metal twists as the blockage is torn open. Alyx dashes through; follow her immediately.

Alyx heads down the corridor, turns right, and moves back to Eli's laboratory. She reaches the door when you hear a large rumbling sound. A second later, the corridor in front of you fills with rocks.

Your way forward is blocked. You're unable to reach Alyx, so follow the advice she shouts to her pet: "Dog, take Gordon to the Ravenholm tunnel, then circle around and try to meet up with me. Hurry!" Backtrack to the junction.

Dog lollops off toward the sealed airlock that leads to Ravenholm. Quickly follow him in toward the door, now bathed in red light from the emergency mechanisms the Combine attack triggered.

Dog picks up the base of the door and rips it up through its hinges. Quickly duck under the top of the door and run through. Dog retreats and attempts to rejoin his mistress.

Meanwhile, you're left in a junk-filled passageway with stairs at the end. Bring out the Gravity Gun and start to clear the stairs of the various large items; blast the wardrobe and barrels forward.

If you have problems maneuvering, pick up a large item, turn around, and fire it up the stairs behind you. Suck a barrel, then blast it over the "no entry" sign at the base of the stairs. Then head through the opening you created.

Trudge down the dimly lit corridor until you reach the base of an elevator shaft from an old mine. This must be the entrance to Ravenholm; there's certainly enough warnings here.

Stop to inspect your surroundings, and you're greeted by the skinned corpse of a hapless ex-miner and a bunch of crates scattered about that you can shove around. The Gravity Gun doesn't pick up organic matter though; the corpse stays put.

Ignore the two cameras on the wall to your left (they are surveillance from Black Mesa East) and try to climb the ladder inside the elevator shaft. A padlocked cage blocks your way.

Blast the padlock with your Gravity Gun until it shatters (or bring out the Crowbar for an old-fashioned smashing), and the cage swings open, allowing you to grab the ladder and go up.

Continue all the way to the top, pull yourself up onto a wooden-floored cabin, and move around into the darkness, turning right. What was it that Eli said back in the lab? "We don't go to Ravenholm?"

"WE DON'T GO TO RAVENHOLM..."

OVERVIEW ▌ Welcome to Ravenholm. It features all the delights you'd expect from a heavily Headcrab-bombed settlement; the walking undead, not to mention the running undead, and the poisonous undead, all with horrific Headcrab controllers to put down. Your task here is simply to survive, carefully negotiating a series of claustrophobic sheds, warehouses, and attics until you meet up with the village priest, Father Grigori. He's been driven a little mad, but his Shotgun skills match his righteousness! Heed his advice (and gifts), and fight your way to the church grounds, then through a pitched battle across a graveyard where the mad monk shows you the path to Shorepoint, a resistance outpost the other side of the mines. After you defeat snipers and Combine Soldiers, you can rendezvous with your compatriots.

INVENTORY PICK-UP

- Shotgun
- Overwatch Standard Issue Pulse Rifle (OSIPR)

ENTITY ENCOUNTER
FRIENDLIES

- Ravens*
- Father Grigori*
- Seagulls*
- Resistance Citizens
- Leon at Shorepoint*
- Alyx Vance (via video screen)
- Noriko at Shorepoint (via radio)*

ENTITY ENCOUNTER
HOSTILES

- Zombie
- Headcrab
- Poison Headcrab*
- Fast Headcrab*
- Zombie Torso
- Fast Zombie*
- Poison Zombie*
- Barnacle
- Combine Soldier*

* Indicates first exposure to entity

"IN RAVENHOLM, YOU DO WELL TO BE VIGILANT!"

| MAP 23 | **RAVENHOLM: DARK ENTRIES** |

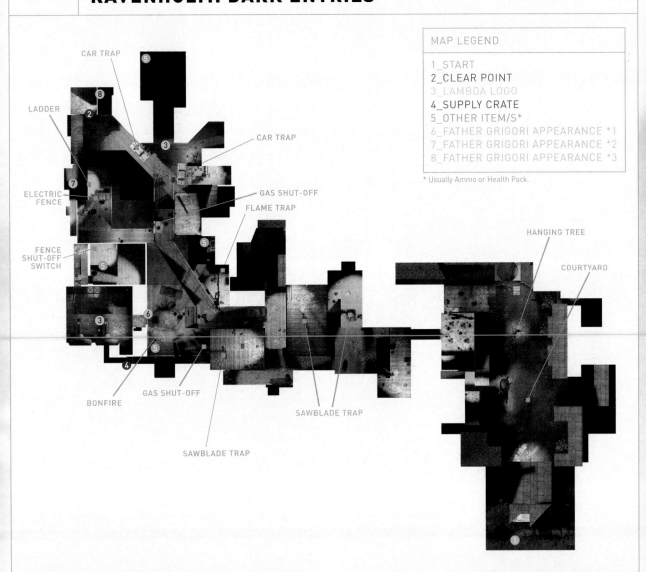

MAP LEGEND

1_START
2_CLEAR POINT
3_LAMBDA LOGO
4_SUPPLY CRATE
5_OTHER ITEM/S*
6_FATHER GRIGORI APPEARANCE *1
7_FATHER GRIGORI APPEARANCE *2
8_FATHER GRIGORI APPEARANCE *3

* Usually Ammo or Health Pack.

Map labels: CAR TRAP · LADDER · CAR TRAP · ELECTRIC FENCE · GAS SHUT-OFF · FLAME TRAP · HANGING TREE · FENCE SHUT-OFF SWITCH · COURTYARD · BONFIRE · GAS SHUT-OFF · SAWBLADE TRAP · SAWBLADE TRAP

TIP

One of the best ways to survive in this close-quarter Zombie combat hell is to ration your Health Packs. If you're healthy when you come across a pack, carry it with you and save it until you really need it.

After you trudge out of the wooden cabin from the ladder climb, you appear out in a grassy courtyard. A single dim street lamp is ahead, near a tree with *something* lashed to it.

As a flock of Ravens takes to the sky, begin methodically searching the area. The lack of light is a problem, so quickly flick your Flashlight on and off to check dark corners, but don't overuse it.

Sidebar navigation:
INTRODUCTION · GETTING STARTED · WEAPONS DETAIL · HALF-LIFERS · THE BESTIARY · CHAPTER 1 · CHAPTER 2 · CHAPTER 3 · CHAPTER 4 · CHAPTER 5 · CHAPTER 6 "WE DON'T GO TO RAVENHOLM..." · CHAPTER 7 · CHAPTER 8 · CHAPTER 9 · CHAPTER 10 · CHAPTER 11 · CHAPTER 12 · CHAPTER 13 · CHAPTER 14 · ANOMALOUS MATERIALS

The side streets to the left and right have dead bodies, and there's evidence of parasite rockets embedded in the ground, but nothing stirs until you reach the tree. A sickening pair of human legs dangles from a rope. A nearby Zombie wakes up too.

Deal with this prowling menace by using your Gravity Gun with skill; suck an explosive barrel from the stack ahead and fire it at the Zombie, burning it to death. Back up to avoid its death throes, then head into the shed, ripping off the wooden planks.

INVENTORY ADAPTATION
SCENIC DEBRIS

The shed has an interesting array of projectile weapons that can be employed, so look around. Top of the list are the circular saw blade, the paint pot, and the gas canister. Suck one of these items up, and practice blasting it at a wall.

CAUTION

Don't be too trigger-happy when firing gas canisters around enclosed spaces; these explode and trigger further reactions to nearby canisters and barrels, so keep your distance when launching!

Push any scenery blocking your way, pick up an item, and head around the doorway in the far left corner. A flesh-crazed ex-miner rises to his feet and attempts to tackle you. This screen shows the results of a saw blade aimed at his torso, slicing him in half.

It is always best to aim at the head, as Torso Zombies are sometimes created when the legs are removed, and these crawling terrors aren't what you need when being attacked from all sides. Step into the carnage-filled room; two more Zombies stir.

As you can see, the effects of launching a gas canister are spectacular. But make sure you're at this distance or farther from the explosion; back out of the room of bodies, then cut down Zombies as they shamble through the doorway.

Flaming Zombies are troublesome until they collapse and die. They can burn you, and Headcrabs can survive and leap at you while they burn, so a plan is to set fire to a group of Zombies, then slice any remaining ones that get too close.

Another method of attack is the paint-pot pummel. Pick up the enamel paint pot and fire it into a Zombie, and you'll discover the paint explodes, coating the creature in semigloss—more amusing than effective. Suck the pot back up and fire again, this time at the head.

TIP

Whenever a wooden barricade blocks a doorway, use the Gravity Gun to suck or blast the pieces apart; your Crowbar is now unnecessary for this task.

After you deal with the quartet of Zombies inside the shed (including coaxing a couple to the shelves of gas canisters and exploding them all in a firestorm), head into the body-filled room, take the right doorway, and drop out into another gloomy forecourt.

Various junk on the ground is available for the Gravity Gun, and a vicious-looking propeller trap lies ahead: a sharp blade is fixed to a car engine. Approach this, and two Zombies amble forward. Slice them up!

TIP

By switching the engine on (the lever is on the engine block) or blasting the blade in a clockwise direction in time with its revolutions, the trap can be activated. This is a great way to mangle multiple Zombies, but watch for crawling Zombie Torsos and Headcrabs falling off dead hosts!

Head around the left corner, up the steps, and into another dilapidated shed. The room is pretty quiet except for a couple of Headcrabs scuttling along the far wall. Some items are in the far right corner, under the table. Arm yourself, and watch for three Zombies trudging out of a cubbyhole to the left.

Pick up a large blade propped against the wall and sever all of them. Continue to suck and slice with the Gravity Gun. When all undead are downed, blast the wooden planks out of the doorway in the wall.

TIP

This room also has a propeller trap, but it isn't as effective, because Headcrabs leap at you and the Zombies can move around the sides of the blade. Stand with the trap directly between you and the Zombies, and they are more likely to be sliced.

You see further evidence of Combine parasite rocket attacks if you step out and turn right. Quickly pick up an explosive barrel and fire it at the Zombie trudging around. Do this before he spots you.

Walk to the end of the passage, turn right, and peer into another shed. Be vigilant, because three Zombies stagger to their feet, and one can shove a barrel or wardrobe at you. Catch it with your Gravity Gun, or dodge it by stepping back around the door frame.

Suck a barrel, and blast it into the Zombie along the far wall. Or use any scenic item to dish out death, including the propeller trap or saw blades. Clear the room of enemies; if flaming barrels roll your way, retreat into the passage. Then inspect the corner for supply crates.

Exit the doorway at the far end of the shed and step into a cobblestone street. The Zombie propped against the barrel is begging to be blown apart. Turn left and approach the Zombie-filled main street. Suddenly, one is cut down with a single shot from somewhere up ahead.

Watch as the remaining corpses are dropped by a heavyset bald man brandishing a Shotgun, and shouting on a balcony above a bonfire of crisping corpses.

He disappears from view, leaving you to watch the burning pyre in front of you. Move to the left, up the steps, and switch off the gas canister to extinguish the flame. Check the dark corner to the left; there are Health Packs and a Zombie shambles to life. Take it down.

The charcoal pyre left behind allows you to see an entrance into the building directly under the building this maverick Shotgun vigilante shot from. Go in. The upward-sloping path to the right ends in a dead end, and the building holds the key.

CAUTION

Don't switch to other weaponry; you need to perfect your Gravity Gun skills, and slamming scenery into the undead results in a more satisfactory victory. Save your other weapons for later.

CHAPTER ⁶
ENCOUNTERS

POISON HEADCRAB

CAUTION

Turning off the gas that powers the bonfire is an excellent plan, but switching it back on before entering the building is not; if you accidentally fire a shot near the escaping gas, it will ignite the bonfire. Because this is the building's only exit, you will have to leap through—and sustain severe burns.

When you're in the generator room, suck up a gas canister, spin around to the left, and fire the canister at the Zombies lumbering down the stairs to intercept you. This sets off a chain reaction with barrels, slaughtering most entities. Mop up any survivors by using available scenery items. Check the table for items.

There's no need to venture up onto the generator area at all, although you do spot a balcony up one floor. Back on ground level, turn right and look up the stairs blocked with debris. You can clear this with a single shot or by shooting the barrel with a sharp object from the Gravity Gun.

Dash up to the turn in the middle of the stairwell and blow apart the barrel at the top, taking down a Zombie. If he escapes the blast, backtrack and use wreckage to bring him down; shots to the head work best.

LAMBDA
LOCATION

At the top of the stairwell, sidestep right, then step out onto the balcony above the generators. Peer across, and you can spot a hastily sprayed Lambda logo on the pillar near the left generator.

Move across the balcony, then jump across to the far right corner, landing on top of the right generator. Stay at this level, leap across to the top of the left generator, then use the Gravity Gun to blow out the duct grating.

Behind the grating is a duct. Crawl through to a small, usually inaccessible alley with Supply Crates. When done, return to the top of the stairs.

At the top of the stairs, turn left. One of those Zombies, slumped against the left wall, isn't quite dead. Watch for his ambush. Suck a saw blade from the floor and finish the job.

There's a door to your left and a doorway ahead. The left doorway is blocked by a sofa. Move through the doorway ahead and wrench a radiator off the wall. Use it on anything twitching with a Headcrab stuck to it.

TIP

The radiator is a great weapon; it is easy to maneuver in tight spaces, but its heavy weight makes it ideal for slamming into the undead; you can knock more than one over, and the radiator doesn't break apart. Use radiators when you can.

ENTITY ENCOUNTER:
POISON HEADCRAB

Neutralize any Headcrabs and Zombies before you head through a doorway to the left. Ahead are two gigantic, spiderlike entities with dark gray mottled backs. They launch with a meaty maw opening. This is a poison Headcrab. If it connects, your health drops to 1!

However, Poison Headcrabs alone cannot kill you; other enemies striking you while you're reduced to critical health finish you off. This is why it is important to destroy these creatures quickly.

Your HEV Suit administers antitoxins, slowly rebuilding your health back to its original level. Slam furniture into these beasts.

The main area of interest is the window to the right. Flick the lever, and an electrical fence below deactivates. Below is a cobblestone street and a dead end. With the electricity off, you can climb the fence.

After you squash the Poison Headcrabs, check out the room. You can shift a wardrobe placed in a vain attempt to halt a past Zombie incursion. Doing this allows access to the door the sofa was blocking on the other side.

Time to leave. Head back down the stairs, or drop off the balcony into the generator room, and prepare for more scuttling Poison Headcrabs. Slam scenery items or the Crowbar at them. Exit through the bonfire location.

Now is the best time to investigate the sloping street to the right. Halfway up is a barricaded doorway, which a Zombie smashes through. Back up, then slam a piece of scenery into the Zombie.

After destroying the Zombie, enter the brick building. Inside is a butcher shop with an array of meat hooks, scenery, and a slumped Zombie inside a cage. Turn on the gas, and the Zombie staggers to life. Stand back and set fire to the cage with a gas canister or firearm.

It seems the villagers were experimenting with captured Zombies before the Headcrabs overran the hamlet. There's a variety of nasty implements to suck up and carry out of this building. Head up to the narrow street and switch off the gas to the right.

Follow the cobblestones to a dead-end area. Three Zombies slumped against walls rise to attack you. The electrical fence is to your right. Look up and left to see the window with the switch you just flipped to turn the fence off. If you haven't yet, backtrack and do this.

Back up if the Zombies are swamping you, and use the variety of weighty or sharp objects from the brick building to defeat the undead. When the area is secure, move to the ladder on the fence and climb over. Locate the ladder against the next building, and move up the exterior fire escapes to the roof.

CHAPTER ⁶
ENCOUNTERS

FATHER GRIGORI

FAST HEADCRAB

Jump across to the rooftop opposite the fire escape, then turn to view the building across from you with the hole in the roof. Through the hole, you see the man from earlier appear. He's wearing some sort of religious chain around his neck.

He shouts for you to look out, and then blasts a poison Headcrab behind you. He disappears. It is hard to determine whether he is an asset or a lunatic. Look down at a wooden plank leading across to an apartment window; then try out the man's traps.

Continue carefully across the planks on this improvised upper walkway. Peer off to the left, and you'll see a courtyard with some rusting cars suspended in the air. Move to the lit window and step inside.

Immediately suck a gas canister on the floor near you, and peer over the edge of a hole to the level below. Shoot the canister down, aiming at the Zombie trudging around. Don't shoot it as a Headcrab launches at you; you'll be hit by the explosion. Extra canisters are in the dark alcove on the same level as you. Switch to the Crowbar if you're being attacked by burning Headcrabs.

Then drop down, look for one of two holes in one of the walls, blast the planks, and pass through into the street. Turn left, and you'll see a winch attached to an old car suspended in the air. Wait until a pack of about four Zombies is under the car, then press Ⓔ at the winch to drop the car.

Use the shadow of the car to judge where the Zombies are, then slam the motor onto them. Switch to a weapon if a Zombie gets through. Then dash into the middle of the courtyard. You can flick a second winch, then quickly turn right and run, jumping on another car and riding it up, escaping the Zombies on the ground completely.

If you're too slow, fall off the car, or want to ensure a Zombie-free Ravenholm, wait at the second switch (you must have cleared the Zombies out of the initial area first), wait until two or three Zombies shambling in from a side street are under the car, then drop the car on them too.

CAUTION

Time is critical; with or without the traps positioned correctly, the Zombies will still maneuver around and swarm you. Use the car traps and follow up with gas canisters you suck down from the building you just dropped from.

LAMBDA
LOCATION

With all this Zombie carnage, you may be forgiven for missing another sign, this one on a wooden fence. You can't access it from here. When all Zombies are destroyed, drop the second car, then run and jump on its hood.

Ride the car as it ascends to roof level, then turn left and jump onto a wooden walkway. If you want the items behind the wooden fence, run and drop onto the first trap car.

After you're standing on the hood of this car, jump down, over the fence, and land in a darkened dead end. Search the far left corner for items, then look for a narrow support beam fixed against the right wall. This acts as a ramp to walk on, and drops down onto the courtyard again.

Ride the second car up again, and turn right this time, moving along a second walkway. Suddenly, a figure appears and introduces himself as Father Grigori. He disappears again with a manic laugh. At least you know the mad monk's last name. Follow the walkway to the open window.

"YOU'VE STIRRED UP HELL! A MAN AFTER MY OWN HEART!"

MAP 24	RAVENHOLM: CENTRAL THOROUGHFARE

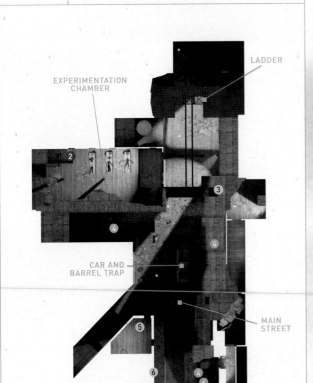

EXPERIMENTATION CHAMBER

LADDER

CAR AND BARREL TRAP

MAIN STREET

ATTIC ROOM

MAP LEGEND

1_START
2_CLEAR POINT
3_LAMBDA LOGO
4_OTHER ITEM/S*
5_FATHER GRIGORI APPEARANCE *4
6_FATHER GRIGORI APPEARANCE *5

* Usually Ammo or Health Pack.

Enter the open window and prepare for a nasty surprise behind the door ahead. Open it, and you'll see a stack of three barrels. At the end of the corridor is a Headcrab. It jumps directly at you. Arm yourself with the Crowbar and swat the Headcrab as it leaps. If you use the Gravity Gun to launch a barrel, the explosion sets fire to the rest of the stack, which explodes and wounds you.

ENTITY ENCOUNTER:

FAST HEADCRAB

A closer inspection of the Headcrab you just skewered reveals spindly elongated legs and a more streamlined, less lumpy appearance. This is your first encounter with a dreaded Fast Headcrab; they move more quickly and are more difficult to pin down. Shoot or throw objects from a distance as they close on you. Crowbar or Pistol shots at close range work well.

Move to the far end of the narrow corridor and open the door to your right. You're in a tiny upper tenement attic coated in filth. Suddenly, the window to your right shatters. Father Grigori is outside on an upper rooftop, blasting Headcrabs.

He's right; the outside balcony is teeming with Poison Headcrabs. Leave them to the good Father, and turn your attention to the wardrobe on your left. Slumped to its right is a Zombie. Use the Gravity Gun to blast the wardrobe into the Zombie; this kills it before it can awaken and ambush you. Now collect the goods from this attic room.

As the Father's Shotgun blasts echo around the street below, check the opposite balcony. Remain inside the attic until all the Poison Headcrabs have been destroyed, then step out (or blast them with gas canisters from the attic room). To begin, use debris to take out Zombies on your walkway. Grigori tags most of them for you.

Walk to the edge of the balcony to the right and look down. You can see barrels and the wandering undead below. Although blasting through these at ground level is an adrenaline-pumping proposition, a wiser Freeman should take stock of the enemy locations. Bring out your SMG.

Wait until a Zombie walks to the left of the car, then fire at the barrel to the right of the car. The barrel explodes, launching the car sideways into any Zombies and sets off a chain reaction that burns most of the other wandering deviants in the area.

TIP

If you fall off this walkway, try to suck a barrel to the spot where you're falling to break your plummet; this will save some health points.

The main Zombie force has been contained. Now move to the left end of the balcony and look down. A Zombie and some Fast Headcrabs scuttle around this area. You can tag a few Headcrabs from this upper vantage point.

Or, drop down on top of the barrels so the Zombie can't reach you, then finish off any remaining Headcrabs. Take care of the entities in this upper area before dropping to street level.

With minimal Zombie activity, thanks to your barrel chain reaction, you can move around to the right and check the main street. Clear away any remaining Zombie, then shoot the barrel behind these bars.

The grating flies out, and a trio of burning Fast Headcrabs shriek and scuttle out into the street. With some fancy strafing, you should contain and blast the Headcrabs until they're all put down. Then crawl into the tiny space; the remains of a citizen guards items inside.

Head down to the main street. By the car you shot across the ground using the barrel, there's a small gap to the left side of the main street; a dead body behind here yields items. Now move to the end. The ground level is blocked, so search for a long ladder pinned against the right wall. Climb up.

Now on a jutting gantry beam, walk across, above the wreckage of the car and the smoldering barrels, and stop at the T-junction. To the right is a window leading to an apartment building. You'll head there in a moment.

LAMBDA LOCATION

Turn left, turn on your Flashlight, and look into the attic opening on your left to spot a crude logo on the wall. Stoop to enter this attic.

Watch for a nasty Headcrab surprise as you enter this area. However, once you trawl the entire attic room, you'll discover a stash of grenades that makes this trip worthwhile. Now return to the gantry beam.

Look carefully at the building ahead, at the T-junction of the beam you're standing on, and you'll see Father Grigori engaged in some impressive close-quarter combat with two of his flock who fly out of a window!

Time to move into the open window on the right, into another old warehouse. Drop down with your Gravity Gun at the ready; A Zombie Torso stirs on the floor. Scoop up a cement block and use it to hammer the torso.

Open the door and enter a larger brick room with three operating tables to the right. Bodies in various states of decay look as if they've been experimented on. These are quite, quite dead. However, some other bodies are still in motion.

Grab a choice piece of scenery (in this case, a meat hook), and head for the stairwell in the far right corner. Go down and turn the corner to a corridor under the examination room.

There are about seven Zombies, all craving your fleshy bits. Blast that meat hook into the first couple, then suck it back and repeat. If you lose the hook, retreat.

If the Zombie culling isn't going well, you can always block the top of the steps with a table, or blast Zombies as they head up the stairs—before they can move into the room.

Don't forget you can back up! Try to take down as many Zombies as you can in the confines of the stairs, and any that escape can be struck down in the larger room that provides enough space to strafe around a foe.

When no more Headcrabs and Zombies roam this chamber, go down the stairs; have a sharp implement ready to fire from the Gravity Gun. A Zombie usually prowls the right corner.

Follow the corridor until you see the doorway ahead leading to a new area. Turn on your Flashlight and have a saw blade handy; you can take it through to the dark alcove ahead, where you can claim some items.

"MY ADVICE TO YOU IS... AIM FOR THE HEAD!"

MAP 25 | **RAVENHOLM: WAREHOUSE DISTRICT**

ELEVATOR

WATER TOWER

TRAIN TRACKS

CAR RAMP

WAREHOUSE

MAP LEGEND

1_START
2_CLEAR POINT
3_OTHER ITEM/S*
4_SHOTGUN
5_FATHER GRIGORI APPEARANCE *6

* Usually Ammo or Health Pack.

CHAPTER⁶
ENCOUNTERS

FAST ZOMBIE

Check for ammo on the ground before you step out into a gloomy exterior street. Look ahead and up slightly. Something is moving. Peer forward, and you can see a bony *thing* leaping from left to right, across the rooftops.

Don't stand around unarmed because this incredibly fast corpse is closing in on you. If you brought a saw blade from your previous location, slice this thing apart just before it reaches you. Otherwise, immediately arm the Magnum and plug the corpse with a slug.

ENTITY ENCOUNTER:
FAST ZOMBIE

↘

Perhaps the most frightening of the mutant undead, these Fast Zombies have been flayed, and their dripping corpses were commandeered by the fast Headcrab you witnessed earlier. Because they are so quick, stand your ground and fight; don't run. A sharp blade to the head or a single shot by a powerful weapon is the only real way to bring them down.

After defeating the Fast Zombie, inspect the grounds surrounding a large tenement block. To the left is a dark alley with a couple of Headcrabs to deal with. This leads to a gully. Look right to see a small fire.

You can also reach the gully by walking directly forward from the area entrance. Although this is a dead end, there are some items to pick up in this area. Step down the sloping path and into the gully and check under the water tower for goods.

Zombie welcoming committee staggers to life. Keep that saw blade handy (or use a cement block you can find in the area) and slice apart the Zombies. Standing on the far side of the fire allows you to coax them into the flames too.

When done snooping around outside, backtrack to the higher street and look for the large tenement block. Step inside, brandishing your floating saw blade, and inspect the washing machines.

TIP

The washing machines are too heavy to lift and float with the Gravity Gun. However, they can be dragged and blasted instead; their heavy weight means they really inflict nasty damage on a victim. The washing machine is a good alternate weapon to the radiator.

Step to the right, around the washing machines, and enter a dimly lit corridor. Cardboard boxes block your path. Either shepherd a washing machine through here and boost it through the boxes, or wait by the boxes for a Zombie to rise, and cut him.

The washing machine is a little too bulky, and the saw blade is easily lost on the ground once you fire it. The radiator, however, is just right. Snatch it from the wall, and fire it straight at the Zombie heading your way. Switch to a Pistol or Crowbar for Headcrabs.

Make a left turn and head up the stairs to the small landing area. You hear loud cracking noises as a Zombie smashes through a wooden barricade. Wait until he's through, then introduce him to the radiator.

Deal with any Headcrabs in the barricaded corridor, then return to the landing and open the opposite door. Inside this sparse room is a pile of boxes and a small pantry area with items to pick up, along with Magnum bullets and two Zombies. Dispatch them with a radiator or .357 justice.

Now move up the remaining stairs to another landing, turn left, and bring your Crowbar (or Pistol) out for a couple of annoying Headcrabs before you reach the door to the roof at the top of the stairs. Head through.

You spot Father Grigori taking potshots at the speedier members of his flock. Turn left and move to a case of Shotgun shells.

Pick up the shells as Father Grigori continues to blast the rooftops. He then gives you a Shotgun. Take the gun and follow the Father's orders: "Aim for the head!"

Father knows best: Those hellish Fast Zombies are approaching, so wait for them to appear near you, then blast them fully in the head, so the Headcrab dies and the corpse is no longer animated. Look to the left and blast the Fast Zombies 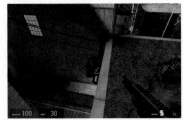 as they climb the building drainpipe; this ensures you're not wounded by claws.

INVENTORY ADAPTATION
SHOTGUN

An exceptional close-quarter weapon, Father Grigori's 12-gauge Shotgun carries six shells in the chamber, and you can carry a total of 20 cartridges in total. Look for the bright red boxes of ammo, and if you're out of chamber ammo, you can still load single shots instead of waiting for a full reload. Watch your damage at longer range; it tails off considerably; this is an essential weapon for blasting the Headcrabs off Zombies!

After the Zombie population has been driven from the rooftops, Father Grigori leaps out of sight again. "There is no rest in Ravenholm. Move on and I will meet you at the church!" That sounds like a fine plan. But where to go immediately? Sprint and drop off the roof, and land on top of a debris-filled water tower ahead and below you.

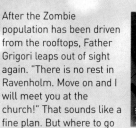

TIP

You can jump into the water tower and inspect the dangling corpse, but you don't need to leap into the water tank. Just land to the side, so you don't waste time climbing back out of it.

Immediately head up the ladder next to the water tower and onto the gantry, then to the square flat rooftop. Leave the items dotted around here until you really need them. Keep your eyes on the drainpipe on each side of the building. This is the route the Fast Zombies take to reach you.

More of these speedy fiends are incoming! Train your Shotgun on the Zombies and tag as many as you can on the drainpipe. Then back up against the wall and bring your Shotgun to bear on any Fast Zombies that make it onto the roof. And they will!

With about three Fast Zombies downed, collect the items you need, open the door in the wall behind you, and step into an attic. Immediately back up to the far wall as two more Fast Zombies crash through the skylights. Shotgun time!

Stay in the corner opposite the door. This way, you can see if any more of these crazed undead drop in, and you can see the additional Fast Zombies heading up the drainpipes. There's time to take careful aim before they maul you.

Or, you can risk a mauling by blocking the door and standing your ground. If you have time, block the door with a crate, stand behind the crate, and remove Headcrabs from Fast Zombie heads from just inside the attic. Continue until there's silence.

The horde of Fast Zombies has been temporarily halted. You'll face a new menace soon, so suck up a gas canister and bring it with you. Head right, to an elevator, and press the switch on the left to call it.

If Fast Zombies are still around, drop (don't blast!) the canister, and deal with these menaces first. As the elevator reaches ground level, look right and aim your canister at the *thing* shambling in the shadows.

Make sure you hit the creature full-on with the canister so it bursts apart and is engulfed in fire. Shrieking Poison Headcrabs jump off this entity and leap for you. Systematically retreat and blast all of them.

ENTITY ENCOUNTER:
POISON ZOMBIE

One car has a plank you can use climb over a chain-link fence. This is also a good escape route if the Poison Zombie combat overwhelms you. Move around the gap in the opposite chain-link fence.

A death too hideous to contemplate is being a host body for up to four Poison Zombies. Bent over double, the corpse moves slowly, but it takes colossal punishment (at least three Shotgun blasts to bring it down) and has a nasty close mauling attack. Back up and attempt to burn the host, then deal with the Headcrabs individually. No fire? Scenery items or Shotgun shells work well.

Wander down this alley; two Headcrabs leap out when you enter a small bedroom to the right. Stock up on goods (including some fine ammunition) and wrench a radiator off the wall, then move back into the alley and head for the opening.

With the hideous creature still twitching in the flames, check the rest of this courtyard. Down one alley is the ornate church Father Grigori told you about. But your way is blocked. Look over to the wrecked cars.

"THIS IS THE WRONG SIDE OF TOWN FOR YOU!"

MAP 26

RAVENHOLM: TOWN SQUARE

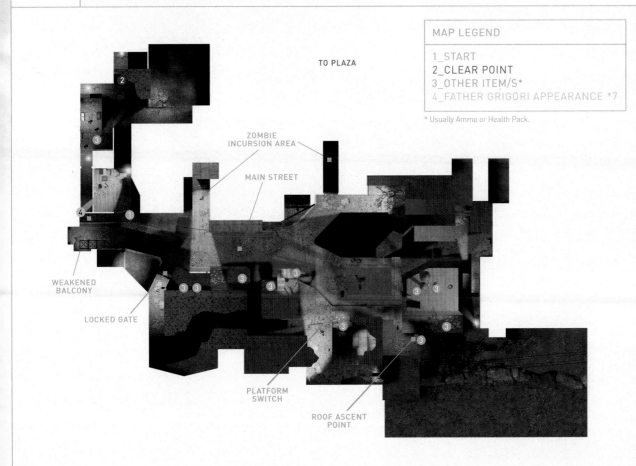

TO PLAZA

MAP LEGEND

1_START
2_CLEAR POINT
3_OTHER ITEM/S*
4_FATHER GRIGORI APPEARANCE *7

* Usually Ammo or Health Pack.

ZOMBIE INCURSION AREA

MAIN STREET

WEAKENED BALCONY

LOCKED GATE

PLATFORM SWITCH

ROOF ASCENT POINT

NOTE

This area contains an overabundance of Zombies and many dangerous dead ends. It is wise to escape with minimal combat experience. However, it is more pleasurable to cut down as many Zombie assaults as you possibly can before continuing. The choice of when to leave is up to you!

Step out into a slightly sloping main street that trails off to the left. To the right is a dead end and a small fire. You hear a clank as a couple of barrels come tumbling down, knocked off by fast Zombies prowling the rooftops. Use the radiator from the previous area if you carried it through. You'll need it!

If you're determined to deal with the overwhelming Zombie presence that's about to engulf you, go after all the Poison Zombies first. Run down the street to the alley on your left. Suck up a gas canister from the shadows of a grassy area and fire it at the Poison Zombie coming out of the dark doorway.

Back up and deal with all the burning Headcrabs before you retreat back up to the main street. As long as no Headcrabs are about, you can continue to fire gas canisters into Zombies, which are beginning to appear from the side alley near the entrance you came through.

The second Poison Zombie is across the town square with the propeller trap, in the earthy ground in the far right corner near a stack of crates. Quickly burn it to death and retreat; this is a dead-end.

By this time, as you enter the main square again, a third Poison Zombie lollops out of a side alley to the right. It starts from a yellow-lit passage, but he may trap you at the second Zombie's location, as shown here. Flee and regroup.

You can turn on the propeller trap the first time you enter the main square. Don't waste time spinning the blade with the Gravity Gun. A few seconds after spinning, the blade flies off the engine.

Pick up the blade; it can slaughter up to three Zombies at a time. This is useful when you're surrounded, so use the blade many times. When you lose the blade in the frenzy of combat, finish off as many Zombies with the gas canisters in the grassy area.

From the entrance, you can see a locked gate across the street. This leads to a passage that wraps around and links to the yellow-lit alley near the town square. This is the second Zombie incursion point.

You can scoop up the lock with your Gravity Gun and open the gate, or manually open it after running through a small, dark alley (usually oozing with undead). Although not necessary, this area can be used to "herd" Zombies out of alleys you need to run down.

There's no shortage of the gruesome undead to tear apart, and staying at the town square enables you to dodge a number of them thanks to the extra space. When you're feeling outmatched, run to the alley with the yellow light.

CHAPTER [6]
ENCOUNTERS

This is the area you should flee to. Above your head is a swinging noose and a pulley system. Avoid the steps to the right, which lead to the dark alley and the gate you can unlock. Dash forward and make a left.

Turn left and run to the end of the corridor. Even if a throng of Zombies lumbers behind you, don't stand your ground. Head up the steps as quickly as you can; you want to attempt this next plan as quickly as possible.

Turn left at the top of the steps and head into a small tower room with a lever on an outside balcony. Pull that lever at once! The pulley mechanism activates, and a platform trundles into place above you.

CAUTION

The platform provides you with the necessary ability to move across the rooftops. You must move the platform before you flee to the roof, or you'll fall down to the town square when you attempt the jump.

If you take your time in the tower, a Zombie posse begins swarming your area. You can leap out of the balcony and down to the town square (this hurts), or battle your way back down the steps to the alley.

One of the best items you can use to knock out Zombies–a gray plastic carton–is inside the tower. Aim it at each Zombie you see, then suck it back before it reaches the ground. Reuse it again and again. No scenery items? Use the Shotgun.

There comes a time when the Zombies continue pouring into the streets and there's nowhere else to run. Time to plan an escape. Make sure you pulled the lever in the small tower to bring the platform across, then locate this area: a group of boxes near where you found the second Poison Zombie.

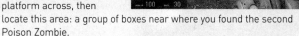

There may be Poison Headcrabs still in this zone, and Fast Zombies are jumping from gable to gable on the roofs. You need to be on higher ground. Climb to the corner (there's a Health Pack here), jump across to the small walkway, up the ladder, across the plank to the rooftop, and turn left.

You're almost at the rooftop overlooking the town square. Bring a gas canister, a barrel, or a Grenade with you and drop it on the fourth and final Poison Zombie to appear in this dead-end alley near where the first Poison Zombie popped out. This optional kill will make matters easier for you if you fall to the ground later.

HλLF-LIFE²
PRIMA OFFICIAL GAME GUIDE

Jump left onto the red-tiled rooftop where Father Grigori left a many items for you. Arm the Shotgun to deal with a couple of Fast Zombies.

Your progress from the red roof is stopped as you move three explosive barrels from a narrow walkway to your right. Suck them in, then blast them at the Zombies wandering the town square below.

TIP

You can suck down the explosive barrels from the ground level earlier or from the balcony by the lever.

Run to the end of the wooden walkway with the town square under you. Jump to the pulley platform you activated earlier; jump on top of it and to the rooftops on the other side. Ready your Shotgun.

Time to face more of the fearsome Fast Zombies! Cut down a couple at a time on the rooftop. There's health and ammo here to pick up. Head across the wooden planks to a second rooftop, working your way over the roofs.

At the far end of the roofs, peer over the edge to the ground below. You're actually across the street, and on the roof above the entrance to this section of town. After you get your bearings, catch another Fast Zombie in a midair leap. A figure appears on a rooftop to the left.

Blast another encroaching Fast Zombie in the cranium. Stay with your back to the wall and defeat all four remaining Fast Zombies.

Now comes the most important jump of your adventure so far. Father Grigori disappears, and while there's a lull in Zombie activity, make a long jump (optionally holding [Shift]) across to the walkway on the opposite building.

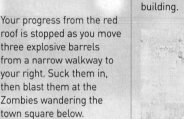

It is *vital* that you land on the walkway next to the door. Otherwise, jump on the left part, and the walkway collapses partially, sending you tumbling to the beginning of this nightmarish street. Retrace your steps, and when you're inside the well-lit room, suck as many saw blades as you can; fire them into the doorway to your left.

Head through the doorway, turn right, and watch as about seven shambling Zombies smell your blood and lumber forward. Grab your saw blades and fire them at the door frame so they stick in it. Then move to the door frame, and locate the Zombies. Pull the blades from the frame, and shoot them at the Zombies. If you don't aim your saw blades at the doorway, you're forced back into the room and combat will be messy and frantic.

Move across the interior landing, optionally blasting a gas canister down the stairs to your right and lighting up any remaining Zombies on the prowl. Then step down the stairs and into a connecting room with a ladder up a floor. Ready that Crowbar!

"A SHEPHERD MUST TEND TO HIS FLOCK."

| MAP 27 | **RAVENHOLM: CHURCH GROUNDS** |

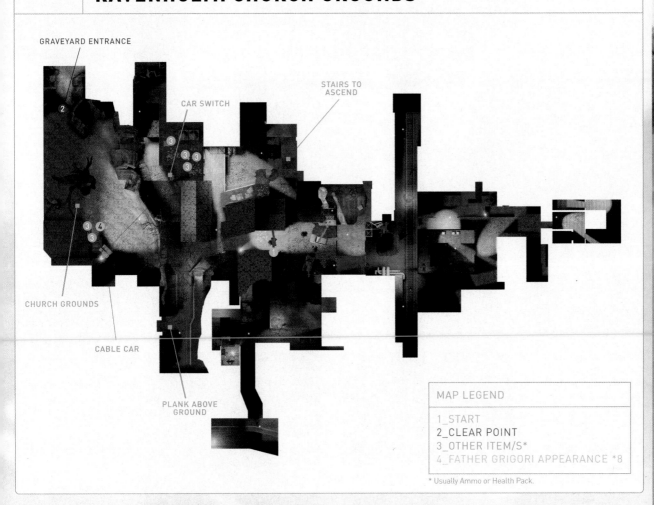

GRAVEYARD ENTRANCE

STAIRS TO ASCEND

CAR SWITCH

CHURCH GROUNDS

CABLE CAR

PLANK ABOVE GROUND

MAP LEGEND

1_START
2_CLEAR POINT
3_OTHER ITEM/S*
4_FATHER GRIGORI APPEARANCE *8

*Usually Ammo or Health Pack.

At the top of the ladder, step up into a junk room filled with decomposing boxes and a trio of ravenous Headcrabs. Defeat them, check the room for items, then head through the only door.

You appear out on a roof gable, and looking right, you can see the wrecked cars you stepped over earlier. However, train your eyes on the ghastly *thing* bounding over the roof toward you. Blast it immediately!

This is another Fast Zombie, so cut it down with Shotgun fire as quickly as possible, and don't fall from your vantage point. Head across the planks and up and over a roof to an industrial building and small courtyard.

You can spend a few moments on the ground blasting apart a Poison Zombie and his parasites (optional). Locate the metal stairs in the corner and quickly bound up them. You're almost at the church.

At the first corner of the steps, turn around with your back to the corner and watch another Fast Zombie intercept you. Bring out the Shotgun and liberate the Headcrab from the fleshy victim before continuing along the walkway.

HΛLF-LIFE ²
PRIMA OFFICIAL GAME GUIDE

The walkway is a great place to fight from: you have a good view of any incoming Fast Zombies, you can hear them clanking up the stairs to the left, and there's a narrow angle for combat. Great for you and problematic for the undead.

This is the location of the second drainpipe, overlooking the church grounds. Your flashlight makes spotting Fast Zombies easier. Don't sidestep off this vantage point; the plummet will kill you.

When you're done on the walkway, head through the door, into the warehouse, pick up the bullets, and look for a ladder up. Choose either your Magnum or Shotgun before you climb.

Keep on culling! Although you can retreat down to the metal walkway, it is better to stay up here and guard both drainpipes, pausing to run over the items to refill your inventory. After 12 Fast Zombies, the cart finally locks into the cradle.

Clamber up to the roof. Turn right to Father Grigori waving at you. He says he's sending a cart across from the church grounds.

Leap into it at once, turn around, and pull the lever. The cart slowly moves across the rooftops, over the fence, and into the church grounds. Don't drop out on the way!

The cart is slow moving and takes a couple of minutes to reach the cradle platform you're standing near. Until it arrives, you'll be swarmed with Fast Zombies. Dust off your Magnum and sidestep between two locations: drainpipes to either side of the cradle.

As you progress, you'll see Father Grigori on the grass below, beckoning you to a table filled with ammunition. When the cart finishes moving, jump out and find the priest.

TIP

Use the Magnum until you're out of bullets, then switch to the Shotgun. You can tag Fast Zombies coming from the ground up the drainpipe with more accuracy and range using the Magnum.

You have successfully negotiated Father's traps, and he now aims to help you: "I suspect you have little wish to remain in Ravenholm, so I will show you to the mines," he says. Pursue the pastor as he heads toward a rocky glade.

Should any Fast Zombies reach the top of the drainpipe, blast him in the head with a single shot, then run to the edge of the building and slam more bullets into the other Zombies climbing up.

"MAY THE LIGHT OF LIGHTS ILLUMINATE YOUR PATH"

| MAP 28 | **RAVENHOLM: GRAVEYARD** |

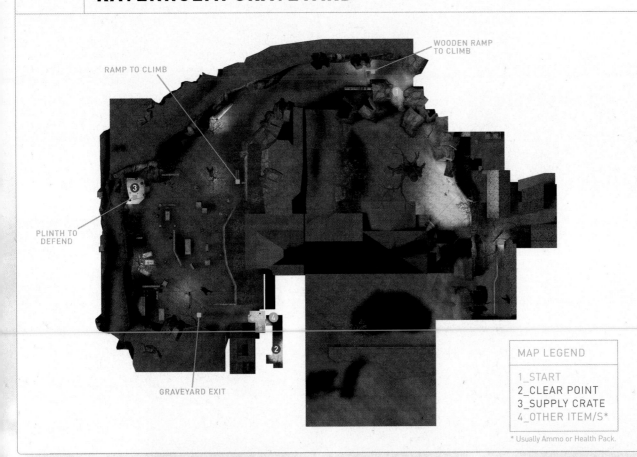

WOODEN RAMP
TO CLIMB

RAMP TO CLIMB

PLINTH TO
DEFEND

GRAVEYARD EXIT

MAP LEGEND

1_START
2_CLEAR POINT
3_SUPPLY CRATE
4_OTHER ITEM/S*

* Usually Ammo or Health Pack.

Follow Father Grigori across the grass and over the chain-link fence. Father Grigori now slows a little, and you should do the same.

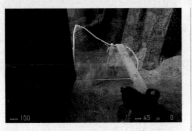

TIP

Father Grigori is a man with a mission, and Zombie mauling doesn't get in the way of his path to righteousness. As long as you keep an eye on him, you can let the Father deal with all of his "flock" without wasting any ammo at all. However, helping him is more honorable!

Hang back, or you'll attract the attention of more slavering undead. As you near a large propane tank to the right, you see shadows skipping across the rocky outcrop above. Incoming Fast Zombies! Father's Shotgun echoes around the canyon.

Back up Father Grigori with Magnum blasts to the heads of any Zombies presenting a challenge to the priest. Stay close to him, tagging enemies he isn't aiming at, and slowly advance through several Fast Zombie attacks.

Hop over another fence and drop to the ground of the graveyard. Stand side by side with the Father as he dispenses divine justice at the shambling masses ahead. You can use up ammo or switch to the Gravity Gun.

CHAPTER⁶
ENCOUNTERS

Slowly follow the path past the gravestones and blast a saw blade into a couple of Zombies to help the priest. There's a steady stream coming, so slice any that venture too near you or Grigori.

At the first right corner turn, you can drop an extra saw blade over the fence and use it later. Then turn to the right and continue a slow-but-steady path around the graveyard, demolishing Zombies in your way.

When you reach the crypts and mausoleum area, you can suck the saw blades you left earlier, and deal with yet more undead menaces. You're almost at the end of the graveyard now, so clear the path for the priest.

Keep this up until you reach a plinth in the graveyard's far left corner. You should have cleared this of explosive barrels right before you reach here. While Grigori blasts away in the darkness, prevent Zombies from sneaking up from the side.

At the crypt, Father takes a defensive position behind a gravestone. Be sure you have an explosive barrel, and shoot it at the Poison Zombie who tries to slowly ambush you from the left side of the mausoleum.

TIP

If you're using explosive barrels to defeat Zombies, locate an enemy, then pick up the barrel with the Gravity Gun, and fire it at the Zombie.

Just after the Poison Zombie succumbs to the fire, you can spot the gates of the graveyard. Run up the slope to the lighted doorway. Pick up the Health Pack and leave.

Use the barrels to set fire to the ground in front of the plinth, then make sure no flaming Zombies make it through the fire to Father's location.

Father Grigori startles an ex-parishioner as you head through the middle of the graveyard. There's no end of Zombies in sight, so keep your chin up and Grigori's back covered.

If you turn around, you'll see Father Grigori waving you off. Head to the mines.

The door ahead is open, and you see a gloomy corridor with a light at the far end. Head through the doorway, and ready yourself for a drop into the mines.

"ONWARD TO THE MINES! LOOK TO YOUR OWN SALVATION!"

MAP 29 | **RAVENHOLM: THE MINES**

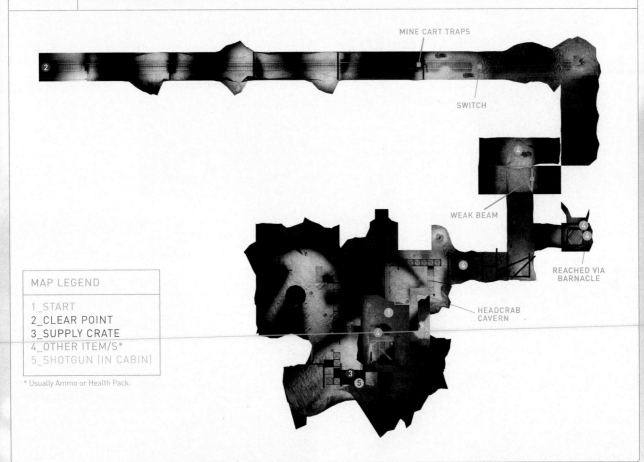

MINE CART TRAPS

SWITCH

WEAK BEAM

REACHED VIA BARNACLE

HEADCRAB CAVERN

MAP LEGEND

1_START
2_CLEAR POINT
3_SUPPLY CRATE
4_OTHER ITEM/S*
5_SHOTGUN (IN CABIN)

* Usually Ammo or Health Pack.

Head to the corner of the dimly lit room and inspect the large mine shaft. Peer off the edge. Knock a barrel off to gauge the distance of your calculated fall (an uncontrolled fall will result in a deadly plummet).

The explosive barrel is also at the top of the shaft for a reason; nudge it off without lighting it, then stand on the same edge as the barrels, look down, and step off the edge.

Force yourself against the wall as you fall, landing on the wooden edge. This is likely to give way, so steer yourself against a perpendicular edge to another narrow wooden support ledge. Stop for a moment and look down again.

Slide down this same edge to the base of the shaft, and you'll see the cavernous chamber below. Small beasts are moving in shadows. It seems the entire floor is covered in Headcrabs. Check the barrel's location.

Don't worry if you can't find it. You must stay on this wooden support and move to the edge of the jutting beam. Jump to the walkway, near the Health Packs (don't land on the cavern floor or Headcrabs will tear you apart).

Run to the small hut at the other end of the walkway, and stock up on provisions from the Supply Crates there. Now peer downward. The Headcrabs only notice you if you appear on the ground. Time to make a move.

Time to raise the temperature down on the cavern floor. Begin by standing at this position, overlooking another part of the broken walkway. Your exit is the cavern tunnel ahead, but it is fenced in. You need a distraction.

Stay on the walkway and shoot all the explosive barrels possible. Pieces of Headcrab go flying as many are consumed by the chain-reaction explosion. Sprint to the base of these stairs right now.

Quickly move to the walkway at the top. Crouch down and wait for the inevitable rampage of scuttling entities. They can attack only one at a time and from one direction, saving you health and sanity. Bring out the SMG and fire away!

TIP

Crouching at the top of the stairs is the most proficient method of dealing with the Headcrab menace down here. If you wander around the cavern floor, you'll be attacked from all angles.

In a lull before more Headcrabs assault the walkway, run forward toward the cavern tunnel, leap over the fence, and land on top a beam. From here, you can snipe the couple of Headcrabs in this area.

Drop to the tunnel floor and arm the Crowbar to save ammunition on the last couple of Headcrabs.

Turn the corner, avoiding an explosive barrel detonation near you, and peer over into another mine shaft. This leads down to water. On the other side is a corpse. Use the Gravity Gun to suck the items near it across to you.

This is the only way to grab all of them unless you make a Sprint Jump across. If you try to stand on the wooden support at the top of the shaft, it gives way, sending you plummeting into the water.

You must dive into the water anyway, so stand on the wooden support so it gives way under you (or jump down) and swim across to a wooden support and to the end of a Barnacle tongue. Swim to the surface here, but keep your weapon in check.

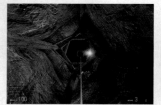 

Switch to your Pistol and snag yourself onto the Barnacle tongue. Ride the tongue up to the top of an otherwise inaccessible shaft, keeping the Barnacle alive until you're a few feet from its maw.

Just before you're bitten, shoot the Barnacle, then land on a tiny upper ledge; you have only one chance to do this. Here you can claim the full array of items left by the Barnacle's previous victim. Then fall back to the water.

TIP

Instead of using the Barnacle to claim the items, you can use the Gravity Gun from the water's surface to suck some (but not all) of the corpse's items.

Swim between the wooden underwater support, diving into a subsequent murky mine shaft, then turn a corner and rise to the surface. You appear at the bottom end of a tunnel with a mine shaft to your left. This leads to the surface.

Naturally, there's a mine cart and a lever to pull. This is optional, but once it starts, you cannot stop it. Press the lever, and the cart, with an attached propeller blade, trundles up and down the rails of the shaft.

Anything (including you) caught in these spinning blades is damaged severely and usually cut in half. You can avoid this simply by ducking.

Start the cart, then follow it to the first indent on the left or right wall. Two Zombies appear on the left. Maneuver so they are in the cart's path.

The cart slices and dices the two Zombies and then three more at the second alcove up the shaft. Stay to one side, between the Zombies and the path of the cart for best results.

With your Magnum at the ready, bring it to bear on two final Zombies at the tunnel's surface (or you can elect to outrun them), and move into the light, just as Father Grigori predicted.

"THEY'VE TAKEN MY FATHER!"

MAP 30

RAVENHOLM: RAILWAY SIDINGS

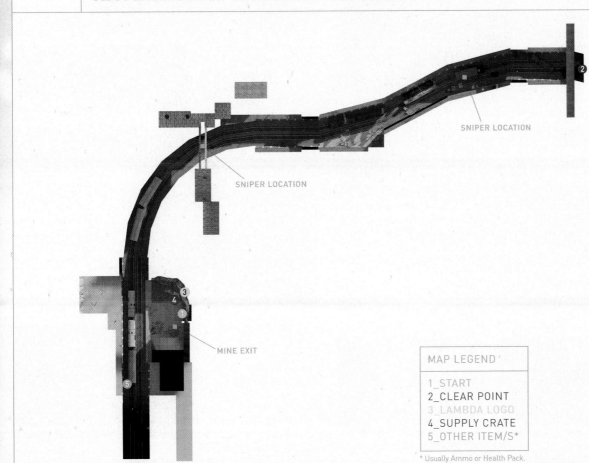

SNIPER LOCATION

SNIPER LOCATION

MINE EXIT

3
4
1

5

2

MAP LEGEND

1_START
2_CLEAR POINT
3_LAMBDA LOGO
4_SUPPLY CRATE
5_OTHER ITEM/S*

* Usually Ammo or Health Pack.

| MAP 31 | **RAVENHOLM: SHOREPOINT ENTRANCE** |

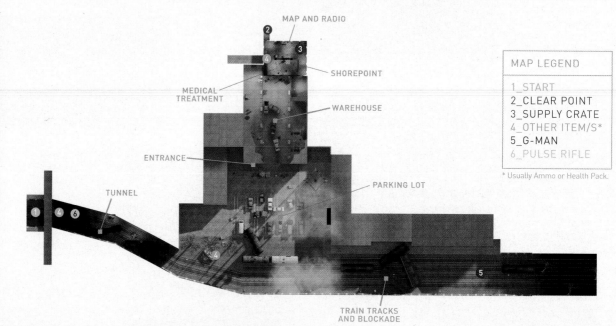

MAP AND RADIO

SHOREPOINT

MEDICAL TREATMENT

WAREHOUSE

ENTRANCE

PARKING LOT

TUNNEL

TRAIN TRACKS AND BLOCKADE

MAP LEGEND
1_START
2_CLEAR POINT
3_SUPPLY CRATE
4_OTHER ITEM/S*
5_G-MAN
6_PULSE RIFLE

* Usually Ammo or Health Pack.

CHAPTER⁶
ENCOUNTERS

COMBINE SOLDIER

As your eyes adjust to the sunlight, step out onto the mine entrance as the sun breaks. Dawn on the outskirts of Ravenholm is still a dangerous place. Begin by heading left, around a rusting railcar for a Health Pack.

LAMBDA LOCATION

Before you continue along the train track, check the tunnel entrance behind you. A Lambda symbol adorns the arch, and a stack of Supply Crates provides items for you to the left of the logo.

Return to the junction where the mine shaft is and scare a small flock of seagulls away. You can perfect your aim by shooting them with the Pistol if you want.

Advance to the green railcar. A Fast Zombie dances across the roof in a fit of glee and leaps down at your throat. Greet it with a Shotgun blast to the head. Now advance down the train track, to the right of the railcar.

Peer down the track and you'll see a blue laser beam hone in on a couple of marauding Zombies, cutting them down expertly. When you reach the Supply Crate and open it, the sniper, who's in the covered bridge up ahead, begins to train his weapon on you.

Pass under the connecting bridge where the sniper is, look up and around at the open window, and throw a grenade into it. The sniper is blown out of the window.

He looks like a heavily armed version of the Metro Cops. He is a Combine Soldier, and you'll engage with him more in a moment. For now, sprint along the train tracks; when a blue laser hones in on you from a bridge ahead, quickly sidestep left.

For obvious reasons, don't hide behind the explosive barrels. Move quickly around to the low railcar as the sniper continues to aim at you; before he blows up barrels on the flatbed railcar, stoop and crawl under the left side. Blow up a Headcrab at the far end.

Crawl out of the railcar, then sprint to the left side of the next sleeper car. With partial cover, look up through the gap in the car, and toss another grenade into a second corrugated covered bridge. A second later, another sniper falls out.

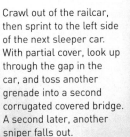

Collect the Grenades and other supplies from the crates inside the car, and then bring out a close-assault weapon. Head for the open railcar, toss a Grenade through to the other side, and dash forward after the explosion.

Zombies and a Combine Soldier are engaged in close-quarter fighting; aim your weapon at the head of the Combine Soldier and shoot him until he drops. Back up, because he has a shotgun and can whip you with it if you get too close. Check for another guard, then deal with the undead.

ENTITY ENCOUNTER:
COMBINE SOLDIER

The shock troops of the hated Combine, the Soldier is an intelligent infantryman who works well in a team and has multiple methods of attack, depending on the combat situation. Learn their traits in the Bestiary chapter of this book. For now, bring rapid-fire weapons to their heads as a matter of urgency.

Check the area near the campfire for hostiles. If you find none, head into the nearby railcar ahead, and stock up on Supply Crate goods. There's an interesting-looking weapon in here too: the Overwatch Standard Issue Pulse Rifle.

INVENTORY ADAPTATION
OVERWATCH STANDARD ISSUE PULSE RIFLE

An exceptional rapid-fire variant to your SMG, the Overwatch Pulse Rifle is an impressive piece of Combine manufacturing issued to some of its Soldier classes. Featuring extremely hard-hitting pulses, a quick reload, and a secondary fire that's second to none (but not yet available), this is a viciously powerful weapon.

Head out of the tunnel and into the outskirts of a scrapyard and train sidings. You'll hear radio chatter between Overwatch forces. Head directly to the wrecked van for cover and take the goods inside. Then view your foes.

Step out to the fence on your left and use a quick Pulse Rifle burst to bring down the Combine Soldier efficiently. Dart back behind cover, and move to the right of the railcar on the tracks.

Step through the wrecked vehicles and train your weapon at the warehouse entrance, lobbing another exploding barrel at it to down another couple of Soldiers. Then race over to the entrance and remove any nearby exploding barrels.

By now, a Soldier has been dispatched to outflank you on the tracks, so ignore the Soldiers in the scrapyard grounds and bring down the Soldier near the railcar. Keep moving, because more are coming.

Step inside and immediately cut down another Combine Soldier before he can react. You hear gunfire in the warehouse ahead. It seems a recon Combine team is under fire from refugees. Time to win one for the team.

G-MAN
ABOUT TOWN

This is the hardest opportunity to witness the odd behavior of a gray-suited individual. If you remain calm under Combine fire, jump up onto a railcar, and zoom ahead to the railcars blocking your way, you'll just have time to see the gray man stride off into a tunnel.

Cut down the nearest Soldier you can see, then roll a Grenade over to the far side of the warehouse, away from the refugees, near a couple of soldiers hiding out near some machinery. Dash over after the grenade explodes.

Arm a rapid-fire weapon and pepper the Soldier, then continue until all threats are neutralized. Keep your combat to this area, and you'll halt any more refugee casualties.

Step around the railcar and onto the grounds of the scrapyard. If you have the skill, suck in an explosive barrel, and before you're shot, fire it at one of the Soldiers appearing at the warehouse entrance ahead. Grenades aren't quite as effective, because the Soldiers can scatter.

The refugees are taking stock of the wounded. The medic tells the commander that Winston's been hit. The commander, named Leon, notices you.

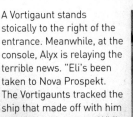

Leon beckons you to a door and raps on it. The door opens, and a female medic breaks the news to you: "I've been on the line with Alyx. Her father's been captured." Leon moves quickly to an old television that doubles as a monitor. Follow him in.

A Vortigaunt stands stoically to the right of the entrance. Meanwhile, at the console, Alyx is relaying the terrible news. "Eli's been taken to Nova Prospekt. The Vortigaunts tracked the ship that made off with him and Judith Mossman. While the trains are still running, I'm going to hitch a ride."

"Here's where you come in, Gordon." Alyx continues, "I need you to make your way along the coast until you get to Nova Prospekt." Alyx requests a scout car that Eli rigged with a Tau Cannon.

Leon orders the buggy out and Noriko duly obliges. Alyx tells you to meet her at the train unloading dock inside the prison. Leon gestures you to look around the base.

ADDITIONAL INVESTIGATIONS

Of particular interest is this map. Leon tells you it's out of date and says, "but you can still see more or less the route to Nova Prospekt ..." Check your location marked with the red Lambda symbol. Leon also cryptically advises you to "stay with the car, make use of the thumpers."

Welcome to Shorepoint. Grab all the ammo and Health Packs you need, and head through this door when you're ready to ride. Leon is trying to radio the next resistance outpost, New Little Odessa, as you leave.

HλLF-LIFE²
PRIMA OFFICIAL GAME GUIDE

HIGHWAY 17

OVERVIEW ▍ You are hereby entrusted with one of the resistance forces' main offensive vehicles. It might be pieces of scrap metal welded onto a dune-buggy frame, but the Tau Cannon and hardiness of the Scout Car can't be underestimated. Use it to jump gaps, run over new and vicious giant insectoid mutants called Antlions, and flee to the coastal road. You'll encounter various settlements, including New Little Odessa where Colonel Cubbage resides—who refuses to come out to fight. Learning how to down a horrifying Combine Gunship is your first major task, after which the cruise continues all the way to a variety of crumbling rural settlements crawling with Combine Soldiers. After you acquire the Crossbow, there's a final tricky task of maneuvering across the underside of a suspension bridge before you can escape.

INVENTORY PICK-UP

- Tau Cannon (Scout Car)
- Rocket-Propelled Grenade Launcher
- Crossbow

ENTITY ENCOUNTER
FRIENDLIES

- Noriko (crane operator)
- Resistance Citizens
- Vortigaunts
- Colonel Odessa Cubbage*

ENTITY ENCOUNTER
HOSTILES

- Antlions*
- Carnivorous Leeches*
- Poison Zombie
- Poison Headcrabs
- Combine Soldiers
- Combine Armored Personnel Carriers
- Combine Gunships
- Rollermines*
- Combine Dropship

* Indicates first exposure to entity

"DAMN MAGNET'S FAILING... HOLD ON!"

MAP 32 | **SHOREPOINT BEACHHEAD**

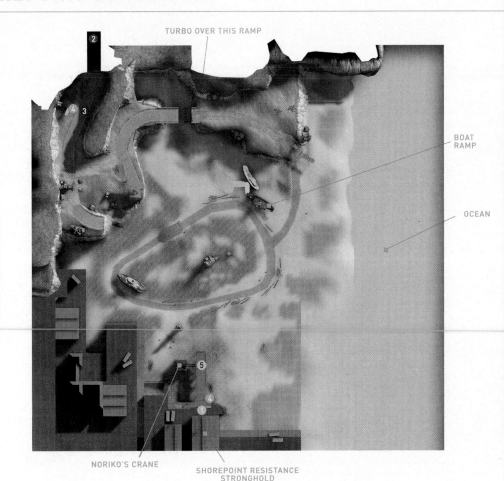

TURBO OVER THIS RAMP

BOAT RAMP

OCEAN

MAP LEGEND

1_START
2_CLEAR POINT
3_SUPPLY CRATE
4_OTHER ITEM/S*
5_SCOUT CAR

* Usually Ammo or Health Pack.

NORIKO'S CRANE

SHOREPOINT RESISTANCE STRONGHOLD

Step onto Pier 87, and listen to the instructions Noriko is radioing to you from the crane. Look around, and you'll spot some items on to the right and the Scout Car up ahead. Rapid-fire shots are going off at the end of the pier.

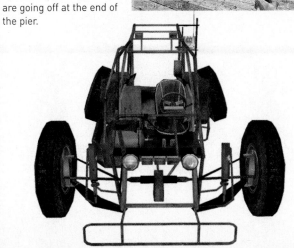

INVENTORY ADAPTATION
SCOUT CAR

Based on a dune-buggy frame, Eli Vance's travels across the dangerous coastal zone is this Scout Car. Robust, and usually able to land on all four wheels, it is controlled in a similar manner to the airboat (use your mouse to look, and movement keys to steer).

The Scout Car features a turbo to give you a boost up sharp inclines and over jumps (press Shift), and it has a handbrake turn (press Spacebar) to stop suddenly or skid and slide. Try out these special moves, and also inspect the rear: There's infinite SMG ammo in the case; use it!

INVENTORY ADAPTATION
TAU CANNON

Firing this weapon evokes memories of a device you used during the Black Mesa Incident. However, this Tau Cannon is bolted firmly to the right front end of your car. Tap the left mouse button to fire a stream of beam fire, great for knocking back Antlions and firing faster than your regular Handgun. Secondary fire is a charged beam (hold right mouse button, then release) that pulls apart anything up to the size of an Antlion with a concentrated blast.

Before you get in the car, you can walk over to the far end of the pier to a citizen manning a gun turret, shooting as many strange, insectoid beasts as she can. These are Antlions, and they are vicious.

If you fall off the pier, you'll feel the full force of an Antlion's powerful mandibles as you're swarmed on all sides. Retreat, while firing, to the ladder under the citizen manning the turret, and climb to safety.

Sit in the Scout Car and wait for Noriko to winch you across and down to the ground below. The citizens are laying down suppressing fire, covering your escape.

"Damn magnet's failing; hold on!" shouts Noriko as the crane drops you onto the beach below. Naturally, you land upside down, in the middle of an Antlion colony. Evacuate!

As a throng of Antlions rushes you, bring out the Gravity Gun and shoot the nearest beast. It falls and lands on its back, temporarily immobilized.

ENTITY ENCOUNTER:
ANTLION

Vicious predators that hunt in herds of around six, Antlions attack with giant sharp mandibles that skewer and rend flesh, and they have savage mouths that knock you back and severely damage you. Twice as fast as a human and able to fly before pouncing, these fiends can easily overwhelm you. Retreat, run them over, shoot them with the Gravity Gun, and escape. Antlions attack in waves, so after you cull about five or so, you have a moment to escape before more arrive.

TIP

You can use the Gravity Gun to temporarily hold off the Antlions—it doesn't waste any ammunition. Alternatively, use the SMG and then restock later from the crate on the Scout Car.

As the Antlions regroup, they fire a charge at your car, flipping it onto its tires. Jump into the driver's seat and accelerate away from the pier. Now is the time to practice your driving skills.

Start your Scout Car driving school with a quick tour of the beach, driving around the tarmac path in a circle. You can achieve skids by tapping or holding the handbrake and turning. Note the traction your tires have on tarmac. Stay off the sand if you have that choice.

You can also drive into the ocean, although this is definitely not recommended. If your car gets stuck (about half-submerged), you must hop out and blast it onto dry land—while fending off Antlion attacks.

ENTITY ENCOUNTER:
CARNIVOROUS LEECH

Shoals of nasty Carnivorous Leeches provide a good reason for staying out of the water. If they appear, back out of the water. Their continuous attacks will make short work of both you and any Antlions.

You can also test your vehicle's off-road capabilities or, more specifically, its off-the-wall abilities. Drive to the right of the hill along the beach front, then hit your turbo just before you reach the rock wall; turn left. You can drive up the wall and land on the upper ground to the left.

There's a tarmac path running around a beached boat in this area. Use it to check out the turbo and the handbrake. Practice blasting the Tau Cannon's barrels at high speed too.

Look for natural and man-made ramps to fly up and over. When you're comfortable, try zigzagging around the beach, weaving through pier posts, and learning the width of your vehicle. Launch up over the boat's deck.

When you've finished your beachcombing, follow the tarmac road around and up to the raised ground. Ignore the small pier to your right, instead swinging the car left and continuing along the road.

Up ahead is a bridge with a gap in it. Launch yourself over the ramp, hitting the turbo just before the ramp and keeping your car straight. If you fail, you fall to the sand below. Flip the car over and try again.

Assuming you have the mettle to make it across the gap, ease off the turbo and climb the stone and tarmac rise, around the large rock and onto the beginning of the coast road. Make a right, as the left area is completely cut off.

Accelerate toward the tunnel, but before you smash the warning signs and head through, stop at the small shed. Get out and head inside; there's a good supply of items in here. Retrieve them before heading into the tunnel.

"A PRIZE WORTHY OF ANY MANTELPIECE!"

MAP 33 | **NEW LITTLE ODESSA**

CHAPTER⁷
ENCOUNTERS

Labels on map:
THUMPER
EXIT ROUTE
NEW LITTLE ODESSA (RESISTANCE STRONGHOLD)
COMBINE BINOCULARS
PROMONTARY
BOAT RAMP
ENTRANCE
OCEAN
THUMPER
PROMONTARY
CELLAR ENTRANCE

MAP LEGEND

1_START
2_CLEAR POINT
3_SUPPLY CRATE
4_OTHER ITEM/S*
5_INFINITE AMMO CRATE
6_COLONEL ODESSA CUBBAGE
   ROCKET-PROPELLED GRENADE
   CRATE AND HEALTH

* Usually Ammo or Health Pack.

Accelerate out of the tunnel, pointing your car directly between the flimsy warning barricades up ahead. There's a slight drop as the entire road drops away. A landslide forces you down to the beach. Continue straight ahead.

Keep your speed up—you're on sand now, and slowing down means you won't have as much tire grip. Use the Tau Cannon to tear apart any Antlions scrabbling out of the ground, and head left to the inner side of a promontory.

Take the Scout Car up the steep hill, and onto the tarmac atop the promontory. Head for the long black device protruding from the ground. Use the Tau Cannon on any Antlions, then step up to the device.

Back at Shorepoint, Leon mentioned Thumpers—this device is one. Press the switch to activate it. The piece of Combine equipment, appropriated throughout the coast by resistance and enemy forces, starts to pound the ground.

CAUTION

The Thumper is the key to remaining safe from Antlions while you're on foot. When the Thumper is activated, Antlions will avoid a large area around the device, and the seismic vibrations stop them from heading at you if you're near the Thumper. Remember to switch them on!

Look back at the area you came from, to see another Antlion nest. Even with the Thumper on, these Antlions can attack as you move along the promontory to the small house. Speed and good shooting are key.

When there's a lull in Antlion incursions, step up to the small house. A skull and crossbones adorn the walls. The front door is sealed. Look for an alternate entrance. Blast the storm cellar doors apart with the Gravity Gun, or break the window above and throw in a grenade.

Bring out your fast-firing SMG, and enter the decaying cottage. A couple of Poison Zombies prowl the grounds. Tag them, then run over to an Infinite Ammo Crate full of grenades. Prop up items to reach the collapsed floor above. Then hurl a grenade at the door opening above the cellar entrance.

Watch out! The reason for the skull-and-crossbones sign is now apparent: a Poison Zombie is using this as a lair. Quick bursts of SMG fire are best (resupply at the car); then grab the magnum and ammo the beast was guarding. Remember to use grenades to soften him up first.

Venture across the broken floor, and break the wood sealing the front door. Sprint back to the car near the Thumper, turn and accelerate down the other side of the promontory. You can drive or shoot through the wooden fencing (but not the support posts).

Bounce down to sea level, and accelerate across the coast again. Any Antlions are simply fodder for your Tau Cannon or front bumper. Shorten your time to the next objective by launching over the right deck of the beached boat.

Once on the other side of the boat, look ahead to spot two buildings on another promontory. As you reach a patch of tarmac near both buildings, notice that the Antlions aren't appearing as frequently because the sand is farther away.

Slow down slightly as you drive up to a tarmac yard, next to a barn. Step out of the car and immediately activate the Thumper if it isn't already working. Then inspect the barn to the left. Stock up on the items.

Run up the ramp to the shack at the top. Listen. Three Soldiers are using it as a lookout post. There are various ways of defeating them; be ready to fight two inside the building, and one on the balcony overlooking the ocean.

Storm the right side of the building, using a gas can to douse the enemy in petroleum, rendering him flammable, but mostly harmless. After all the Soldiers are dead, finish off the others with close-assault ordnance.

Take your newly christened car, and drive it off the far side of the promontory, following the slope down to the sand dunes; stay along the left wall. Shoot or slam into any Antlions as you pass another nest.

TIP

Avoid Antlions by standing on grass, gravel or stone; more will appear when you're standing on sand. Watch your step!

CHAPTER 7
ENCOUNTERS

COL. CUBBAGE

ADDITIONAL INVESTIGATIONS

If you hear a Soldier radio "Outbreak! Outbreak!" during a battle, take note. This is a code to let others know he's the only remaining squad member; adjust your tactics accordingly when you know he's the only one left.

Stay away from the edge of this building because Antlions will appear. In fact, they sometimes are fired on by and attack the Soldiers. Let the two sides fight it out. Afterward, strike the tire swing and watch it go flying.

Your main reason for securing this objective is to pick up the Batteries and other items inside, and then step up to the binocular tripod on one of the windows. Peer through with E, and the device scans a resistance settlement ahead. This must be New Little Odessa.

Leave the building, run down the ramp, and head back to the Scout Car. A seagull has "done its business" all over your car! Shoot it as it flies away. This happens if you leave your vehicle for extended periods of time. The mess washes off in the water.

In the distance is a boat house that is under Combine control; an APC and three Soldiers are staking it out. Don't be shy; introduce yourself by accelerating around the left side of the APC, and ram one (or two!) Soldiers standing to the right of the Thumper.

Dive out of the car as the remaining Soldiers run for the shed, and move back to the APC, using it as cover. The APC isn't armed, so don't worry about it. You have several options for defeating the remaining Soldiers. You could toss a grenade into the shed...

...or steam in with the SMG blazing. Or, you could switch off the Thumper and watch as the Soldiers are overwhelmed by Antlions! When the Soldiers are dead, turn on the Thumper and enter the boathouse. Check the crates near the door and on a boat. Take the Supply Crates off the boat, but don't stand on the boat–it's a trap. To avoid it, stand inside the boathouse, on the deck next to the boat, and suck the crates from the boat you're rocking. If you stand on the boat, it will collapse, dropping you into the sand, and a swarm of Antlions will appear. Fight your way back to the Thumper if you fall.

TIP

If you spot an enemy in your path, drive straight through it; this saves on ammo and provides endless entertainment.

Enter the Scout Car (the APC is sealed), and continue around the coast. You'll spot a larger set of structures up on higher ground, but the only way to drive up is to move around the beach, looking for an entrance.

It's located between two rock outcrops, near a rickety windmill. Drive up onto the tarmac, which the Antlions can't burrow through, and park your car near the van ahead. Welcome to New Little Odessa!

Get out of your car and greet the inhabitants. They seem to be slightly on edge. Three or four are wandering among the various buildings. Speak to one. "Gordon Freeman!" he exclaims. "Hurry and get in the basement! We're expecting Gunships at any moment."

That can't be good news. There's another resistance fighter, near the large barn with the items inside. "Colonel Cubbage will be glad to see you made it. He's in the basement, Dr. Freeman." Cubbage? That must be the fellow Leon was attempting to raise back at Shorepoint.

Use the ladder to reach the lookout on the high post. The resistance citizen up there doesn't appreciate your ladder-climbing exploits.

It might be prudent to head down into the basement. Across from the locked gates is a shell of a large house. You can inspect it, and the entire base, at your leisure. Learn where every item crate is (including locations of rockets); you'll need them for a battle to come.

Head through the doorway to the right of the main building, and follow the steps down to a basement where an older man holding a lethal-looking weapon is instructing his troops. This dandy chap is Colonel Odessa Cubbage. He's talking about a rocket launcher.

"Using the laser guide, you can steer your rocket past the Gunship's defenses and prevent it from shooting down your rocket. After several direct hits, you'll be rewarded with a prize worthy of any mantelpiece! Now... who's going to be the lucky one to carry it into combat?" He spies you, and hands over the weapon. Suddenly, you hear a roaring whine. The Gunship is here!

Exit via either the stairs to the first floor or out the door. This door is particularly excellent in this battle, as it protects you from Gunship cannon fire, and it is a good place to stand and wait for supplies from your team.

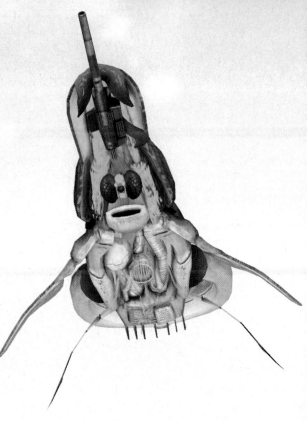

CHAPTER 7
ENCOUNTERS

Or, you can continue up to the top floor, using the crumbling walls as cover. The Gunship is preoccupied with the small-arms fire the resistance fighters are using. It concentrates on you only after your first shot hits.

INVENTORY ADAPTATION
ROCKET-PROPELLED GRENADE LAUNCHER

With only three shots before the ammo is depleted, the RPG's single-shot strikes can't be wasted, but they are devastating. Rockets are launched with the primary attack only; fire once to launch. The rocket is heat seeking, but not very intelligent, and it's easily cut down by intelligent enemy Gunships. After firing, press and hold the left mouse button to bring out a laser that you can use to guide the rocket to your target. Use this weapon at range.

As soon as the first rocket strikes, find cover and ammunition; you may run out after constantly missing your target. Wait until the Gunship finishes a volley of cannon shots, then step out of cover and fire.

Note the smoke trail above. This corkscrew technique is how you fire a rocket. With the laser out (left mouse button pressed), execute a circle with your mouse, ending with you manually targeting the Gunship. The rocket follows this route. If you elongate the circle, the Gunship's weapons won't have time to shoot down the rocket.

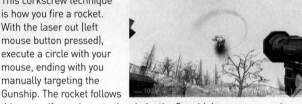

Vary your location. Higher ground is always best, so stay away from the many tarmac areas and any explosive barrels. To get more rockets, back up into the shed, the small outbuilding, or the second floor of the main building.

The resistance fighters are here to help. Keep them close, and move toward them when you're low on health or rocket ammo—they'll hand you supplies. Do this under cover, or your team may be cut down.

After three, five, or seven successful strikes (depending on whether your adventure has been rated "easy," "medium," or "hard"), the Gunship wobbles, bursts into flames, and explodes. Pieces rain down on the camp.

Perhaps this place should be renamed New Little Freeman, as Cubbage was decidedly absent from the fracas. Head down to the basement (there's health there). Cubbage has been sending a message to the lighthouse. He congratulates you on your victory.

Leave this tactician to his maps, but remember his advice about a forthcoming area of coast: the bridge appears to be under Combine control. Now exit New Little Odessa, drive up the road, and swing down a grassy opening between the rocks.

"HOLD ONTO THAT LAUNCHER, DR. FREEMAN."

| MAP 34 | **NORTHERN PETROL FACILITY: 137 DOCK** |

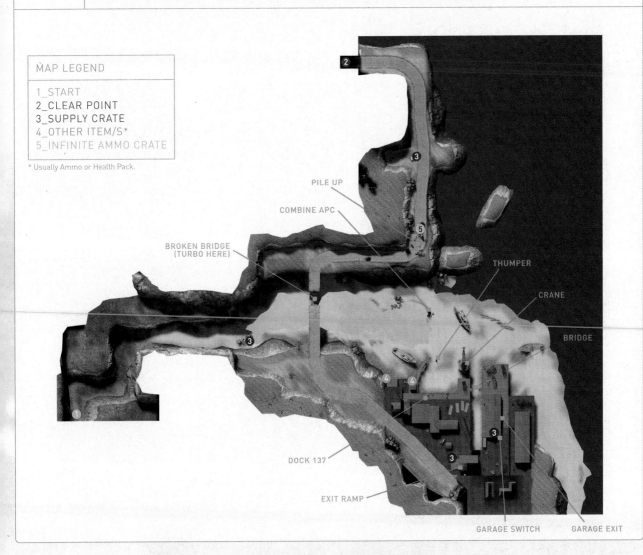

MAP LEGEND

1_START
2_CLEAR POINT
3_SUPPLY CRATE
4_OTHER ITEM/S*
5_INFINITE AMMO CRATE

* Usually Ammo or Health Pack.

PILE UP

COMBINE APC

BROKEN BRIDGE
(TURBO HERE)

THUMPER

CRANE

BRIDGE

DOCK 137

EXIT RAMP

GARAGE SWITCH   GARAGE EXIT

Follow the grassy path between the rocks down to a sandy area and a sharp right turn. Swing the car around to spot a small clump of rocks ahead and a viaduct beyond that. Slow down as you reach the clump of rocks, shooting any Antlions you see.

Step out onto the rocks and inspect this small outcrop. An escapee seems to have driven off the rock above, and the remains of him and his vehicle lie here along with some Supply Crates. Grab what you can, and retreat to the car before you're swamped by Antlions.

Go under the viaduct. You can choose either side of the small shallow lake, but the left side is preferable. To the right and ahead is Pier 137. Maintain your speed.

Go around the left side of an APC that's flipped over. The Soldiers are braving Antlions to reach the pier nearby. Run them over. Taking the left-hand route means you won't be attacked by these Soldiers.

Accelerate and stop in front of (or crash into) the Thumper to the left of the ramped pier. Hop out, and immediately switch on the Thumper. Otherwise, you'll be attacked by the Combine and the Antlions. Run to the pier.

NOTE

Park to the left side of the Thumper, near the crane. If you park next to the pier, you won't be able to pick the car up with the magnet later.

With the Thumper on, only a few Antlions appear, leaving you to launch an attack up the ramp. Bring out a rapid-fire weapon and cut down the Soldiers holding out at the edge of the pier.

Go around the right side of the white shed, and toss a grenade up at the two Soldiers on the upper pier. Watch out—they may return it or throw grenades themselves. Take a defensive position behind the shed, and pick off each one.

TIP

Are the Soldiers throwing grenades at you? Switch to the Gravity Gun, suck up the grenade, then blast it back at the target. That should foil your enemies' plans.

After you defeat the nearest two Soldiers, open the white shed's Supply Creates. Use the Gravity Gun to suck items from a tiny alcove at the back of the red shed near the "137" pier number. Then go up to the upper deck. The Soldier standing by the crane in the distance is begging to be shot with the RPG.

With your preferred offensive weapon ready, move to the far end of the pier. Remember that if a Soldier is hiding behind a barrel, the Gravity Gun can turn it against him, and you can use the barrel as a shield too.

Move to the edge of the giant pier, and check the bridge to the petroleum warehouse. It's raised, and you can't drive your car up here anyway. There's another way through—head up the crane, then up a second ladder and into the seat.

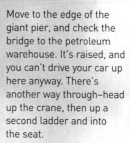

When you enter the crane, learn the controls: The crane arm pivots around in a circle and moves in and out. W and S extend and retract, A and D turn, and left-click drops the magnet on a target and releases it. Lift a container on the far dock.

Now slide or drop the container into the Soldiers firing at you. With some swing, you can really send them flying. Play with the magnet; slam it into Soldiers, drop explosive barrels, and even drop your own car on the enemy. This is where the car parking comes into play; make sure the car is within the arm's range, and line up the magnet's shadow with the car. Drop the car on the left side of the bridge or anywhere on the deck. Finally, and most importantly, knock the bridge into place!

TIP

The APC may seem too far away to grab with the magnet, but if you ram the APC with your car (instead of striking the Soldiers) and push it into crane range, it can be used as another toy to drop on your foes.

INTRODUCTION

GETTING STARTED

WEAPONS DETAIL

HALF-LIFERS

THE BESTIARY

CHAPTER 1

CHAPTER 2

CHAPTER 3

CHAPTER 4

CHAPTER 5

CHAPTER 6

CHAPTER 7
HIGHWAY 17

CHAPTER 8

CHAPTER 9

CHAPTER 10

CHAPTER 11

CHAPTER 12

CHAPTER 13

CHAPTER 14

ANOMALOUS MATERIALS

TIP

If the car is outside of the crane's range, hop out of the crane, climb down the ladder, and release the switch on the far side of the deck to get a ladder. Climb down, run to the Thumper, and repark the car, then dash back to the ladder before you're mauled by Antlions.

When you're in the car and over the lowered bridge, swing right, driving into the large warehouse. Use a mixture of Tau Cannon and ramming to deal with Combine forces. Get out and use the machine gun on the rest.

Move to the far end of the warehouse and into a small corrugated hut. Look for the switch that opens a garage door in the left wall (or right as you're coming out of the hut). It's your only exit. Bag the items from the Supply Crates too.

Head out the garage door, turn right, and go up the ramp. Ram and gun the waiting Combine guards, then speed up and run over two more Soldiers as you near an open warehouse ahead and right.

The warehouse is empty except for a ramp and a large window. Speed up or use the turbo to ram through the window. You've escaped! Head right, up the road. If you want, stop for the crate on the other side of the warehouse.

A low rumbling sound and quivering telegraph wires announce another Gunship hunting you. It swoops under the viaduct, and then flies off and around, hovering over the beach. Follow the road, and jump the viaduct using the turbo. Keep that car straight—dropping off the bridge means mission failure.

Follow the road after the bridge as it bends right and then left around a cliff side. Ahead is a jumbled mass of cars, charred from a multiple pileup weeks ago. Park your car, and switch to the RPG. Time for a little payback.

Your biggest concern may be running out of rockets. Fortunately, the white van in the middle of this mess has an Infinite Ammo Crate filled with them. Load up, then look to the skies for the Gunship.

Remember the attack plan you learned back at New Little Odessa. If you fire the rocket straight at the Gunship, the missile will be blasted before it can strike.

Corkscrewing your rockets after using the car wrecks as cover to avoid the ship's cannons is the only plan. Use the wrecked cars as cover to avoid the ship's cannons. Although circular motions work best when controlling your homing, flicks left and right produce interesting results.

CAUTION

After three, five, or seven rocket strikes, the Gunship drops out of the sky. Normally this is not a problem, as the pieces disintegrate over the beach below. However, if you destroy the Gunship when it's above the road, it could come crashing down on you. Dash for cover to the left side, away from the cliff edge.

With the Gunship down, it's time to continue through this winding road of traps. Bring out the Gravity Gun and shove the car wrecks out of the way, creating a path for your car. Then ride up the road.

The road rises and turns slightly left. If the road barrier on the right side is missing, don't investigate the edge unless you want to fall off! A better plan is to stop by the blue van on the left; supplies are available here.

After you pick the blue van clean, head back to the road, around the bend, and into another mountain tunnel.

"OUTBREAK, OUTBREAK, OUTBREAK!"

MAP 35	**MOUNTAIN ROADS AND PETROLEUM STATION**

APC POWERING
COMBINE WALL

PETROLEUM STATION

MAP LEGEND

1_START
2_CLEAR POINT
3_SUPPLY CRATE
4_OTHER ITEM/S*
5_GRASSY KNOLL
   WITH CROSSBOW

* Usually Ammo or Health Pack.

COMBINE
AMBUSH

MOUNTAIN
DWELLING

GARAGE

After you're through the tunnel, swerve right to avoid a wrecked car, and then accelerate down the road. As you pass the car, you see a glowing blue ball of energy. How curious. Drive closer.

A strange humming device latches on to your Scout Car and pulses every few seconds, buffeting your vehicle. The device can make you lose control of the vehicle, so hop out, grab the Gravity Gun, and suck the limpetlike device off.

ENTITY ENCOUNTER:
ROLLERMINE

The pulsing orb is a Rollermine; a Combine creation that steadfastly refuses to power down. These balls appear on roads or in buildings, then home in on you, buffeting you and causing nasty electrical damage.

If you're in the Scout Car, the mines buffet it; and more than one can cause severe control loss. Bring out the Gravity Gun, suck up each mine, then punt it over a nearby cliff into water, where it will short-circuit. Note that explosions (from barrels or gas cans) also destroy Rollermines.

The Rollermines continue to be a hassle as you continue down a curving road. Watch the sharp left corner on the way down—the mines could nudge you off the cliff edge here. Slow down if you don't want to pry the mines off.

At the end of the downhill stretch, you find a banked corner and a telegraph wire collapsed near two ramshackle buildings. The crackle of Combine radio chatter fills the air. There are hostiles in the area. Step out of the vehicle and seek cover.

NOTE
There are several methods for securing this area; Combine battles are never the same twice, and you may find other ways of completing this objective. The way shown here results in victory with minimal self-harm.

Begin by creating a diversion. There are four Soldiers, and reinforcements are ready to arrive from farther up the road. Throw a grenade at the Soldier near the left outbuilding, and then run to the right, into the cover of the shed.

This area has one or two Soldiers attempting to flush you out with grenades and Rollermines. Switch to the Gravity Gun, punt both back into a Soldier's face, and seek cover. When wrestling with mines, be sure you have cover.

Now secure the outside perimeter of the main concrete dwelling. Hunt down Soldiers in the grounds, but stay near the building so you aren't targeted from inside. Drop anyone in the grassy garden outside and keep moving.

Time to spring a trap of your own. Shoot out a window near the front door, and throw in a grenade.

The Soldiers on the ground floor are forced to run out the front door or out the door in the back. Ambush and cut them down.

Now head into the building, secure items from the main floor, and hole yourself up in the attic. To view incoming Soldiers, peer through the window at the opposite end of the room from the stairs. Offer some resistance, but stay away from the windows.

Let the Soldiers come to you. Wait at the top of the stairwell, listening for the enemy footfalls to determine their location. Use the Gravity Gun to suck up any grenades they toss and throw them back. When the Soldiers climb the stairs, cut them down from behind the stairwell.

When the last Soldier shouts "Outbreak!", hunt him down and drop him. Return to your vehicle, remove any Rollermines, and skid around the corner and up the mountain road. An oil truck explodes ahead, and the cab slips off the sides.

This trap shouldn't faze you. Accelerate and bring the Tau Cannon or the front of your car to bear on the two Soldiers. Don't fall off the cliff to the right. Halt the car and grab the Supply Crates' contents.

Head around the corner, then slow down as you reach a burnt-out oil tanker at another corner. Take a moment to disembark and recon the immediate area.

You must clear the clump of metal girders and the wrecked car. Use the Gravity Gun to cut a path, but stay behind the rock outcrop to your right. Head up here for a vantage point.

A Supply Crate next to a burned corpse holds items, and nearby is a new weapon: a Crossbow with the latest in sight-zoom technology. There's a view of a petroleum station. Start using the Crossbow by aiming at and tagging the Soldier on the billboard sign.

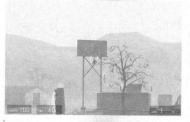

INVENTORY ADAPTATION
CROSSBOW

The Crossbow is the ultimate in stealth-sniper weaponry. Although the available ammunition is loaded singly, and you may carry only a maximum of 20, the results are impressive. Primary attack fires, while secondary zooms in on a target at a greater range than your suit. When you want to view potential ambush points ahead and can spot an enemy at extreme range, use this hard-hitting, single-strike takedown armament.

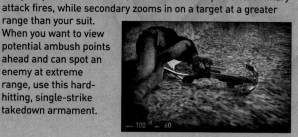

Taking out the Combine lookout prevents him from radioing the other troops in this set of buildings. You can see an energy wall blocking your path. This must be deactivated. Clear the corner road and drive on.

Drive across the bridge and stop by the energy wall. Step out of your vehicle, head around the gap to the right of the wall, and prepare for combat.

NOTE

Don't leave the Scout Car behind and continue on foot—trudging along the miles of coastline takes an incredible amount of time on foot, you'll run out of ammo, you aren't protected, and there are gaps to jump that only a car with a turbo can complete.

Plan your combat efficiently. To stay covered, move to the large shed to your right. There are two outbuildings on the left (one is a garage with two Rollermines) to watch out for. Punt the mines away before continuing.

Step out of the cover of the main shed, and check the gas pumps and the outbuilding ahead. Bring out your preferred weapon and create a diversion by blowing up the pumps. This explosion (don't forget to back up) creates confusion among the Soldiers, who appear from the building and begin to throw grenades. Step back behind cover.

TIP

When the Soldiers throw grenades, you can pull out the Magnum and try to blast the grenade back at the throwers. This is a very difficult but possible method of returning an incoming pineapple.

Stay at the gas pump area, watching for explosive barrels that haven't ruptured (stand away from them), and slowly work your way up to the outbuilding, cutting down any Soldiers who stand their ground. Note that the APC isn't operational.

Watch for more grenade throwing as the Soldiers become frantic. Sidle around the back building, and give anything with a respirator a final burst of justice. Secure the back side of the building so you aren't attacked from behind.

The old "flush 'em and crush 'em" technique is another great way to enter the building after softening up your foes. Smash a window, lob in a grenade, listen for excited chatter, and waltz through the door after the explosion.

Go into the building and take down the Soldiers inside this structure. A Flashlight may be required. Use the walls as cover, and press the Soldiers with a charge. Come back for any items after combat ends.

The grenade attack may have driven the remaining Soldiers out the front door, so quickly maneuver around the cliff-side rear of the building, and around the other side; then charge and bring down the final two Soldiers.

Now you need to figure out how to deactivate the energy wall. Trace the telegraph wires from the wall, and you'll see the APC is powering it. Either fire a Gravity Gun burst at the APC, or knock the blocks away from the front tires. Let the vehicle roll off the cliff, into the ocean. The telegraph cable snaps, and the wall deactivates. Hop in the Scout Car and continue up the road.

HλLF-LIFE²
PRIMA OFFICIAL GAME GUIDE

"USE EXTREME CAUTION WHEN APPROACHING THE BRIDGE!"

MAP 36

CLIFF-TOP LOOKOUT AND BRIDGE

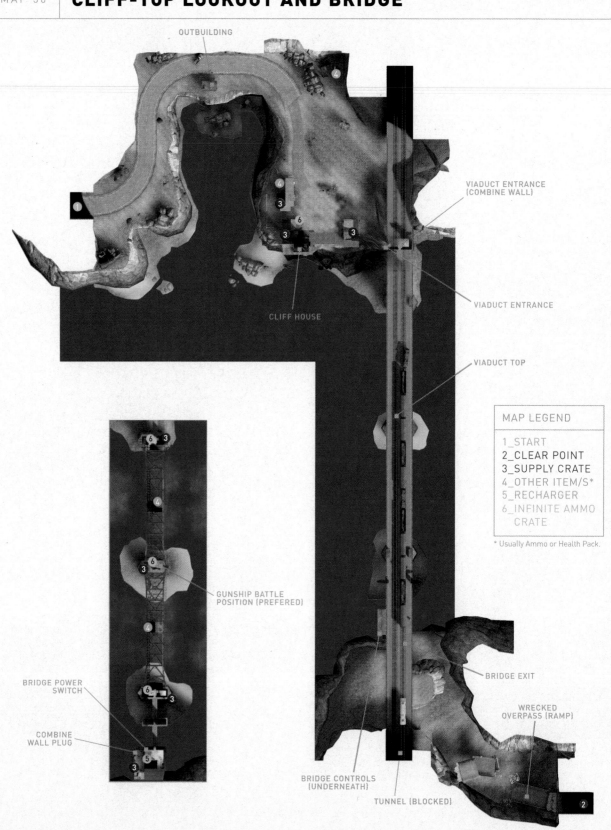

OUTBUILDING

VIADUCT ENTRANCE
(COMBINE WALL)

VIADUCT ENTRANCE

CLIFF HOUSE

VIADUCT TOP

MAP LEGEND

1_START
2_CLEAR POINT
3_SUPPLY CRATE
4_OTHER ITEM/S*
5_RECHARGER
6_INFINITE AMMO
   CRATE

* Usually Ammo or Health Pack.

GUNSHIP BATTLE
POSITION (PREFERED)

BRIDGE POWER
SWITCH

COMBINE
WALL PLUG

BRIDGE EXIT

WRECKED
OVERPASS (RAMP)

BRIDGE CONTROLS
(UNDERNEATH)

TUNNEL (BLOCKED)

When you arrive at this corner, slow down a little, and watch as a Combine Dropship takes off from a small settlement of houses near a huge suspension bridge. It appears Cubbage was correct; the Combine controls this area.

As it departs, the Dropship may spot you and rain cannon fire on your vehicle. There's no point in responding as the ship cruises off over the hillside. The container it's carrying indicates it has just made a troop drop.

Skid right, around the bend, and accelerate along the road. Ahead and to your right is a small building, and a Soldier is standing on the road. Run him down, and don't stop. The building houses little of interest.

NOTE

Again, the combat with the Combine in this area is different, depending on your actions. The techniques shown allow minimal damage to you and maximum harm to enemies.

TIP

There are around six Soldiers to take out, and you need to pay attention to their weapons. Shotgun-toting Soldiers are very dangerous at close range; unload on them with a full clip because they can charge and pistol-whip you.

Park the car so it's facing the rise up to the bridge and use it as partial cover. Get out, make a dash for the nearest large building exterior, and take cover. There are enemies in the nearby buildings.

By the garage, step out into the open, and check the forecourt. You're a sitting duck if you head into this area, so stay close to the right-side buildings, and bring the pain down on a Soldier nearby.

When it's quiet, throw a grenade through a broken window to flush out the enemy. This building should be secured next.

After the grenade explodes, check the rear door on the right side, or burst through the front door facing the garage, and cut down the enemies in here. Search the room for items (the corpses of the Soldiers have ammo), and exit.

The second takedown area to be wary of is the shed next to the cliff-top house. Soldiers can throw grenades at you from here, and there's a line of sight across the forecourt to the white outbuilding on the other side. Blast the Combine apart.

Search the barn for goods or hiding Soldiers, and then clear out all the enemies. An RPG launched inside tears everything apart. There's an Infinite Ammo Crate next to you, so fire away!

If you enter the barn, check the flooring; there are some major structural defects because the building is slowly falling into the ocean. You can drop to a narrow cliff path that wraps around the side of the buildings, and back to the shed across the forecourt.

CHAPTER ⁷
ENCOUNTERS

Step out onto the balcony, and look left to see a green maintenance door at the base of the suspension bridge. This may be the only way to go if the bridge has been sealed by Combine control. Now check the main house.

Using your turbo, scramble up the gravel bank to the railway line running across the bridge. The tunnel to the left and the bridge span itself are both blocked by an energy wall. There appears to be no way forward.

Head up the steps on the deck, and listen for sounds of the enemy. You should have defeated them, but if any remain, break the windows with rapid-fire guns, and throw in grenades. Then dash for the front door.

Drop to the cliff path on the underside of the buildings, or walk around the path leading down from the shed. Under the buildings lurks a Poison Zombie. Attack with vigor, and watch your strafing steps!

Inside is a messy array of furniture. Check for items. The steps up to the second floor have collapsed. If you wish to investigate the upper level of this house, drag a table over to the steps, jump, and go up.

Continue along the cliff path, or if you're at the energy wall above, go down along another path to this point. Move toward the metal door ahead. Deactivate that energy wall. The answer to doing this lies somewhere under the bridge.

Amid the wreckage on the top floor are two separate ways into either a small or large room. Whatever route you take, a Poison Zombie appears behind you, so head around in a circle and cut the beast down, using the doorway as cover from the Headcrabs. Supply Crates are your reward.

NOTE

The following route is the easiest to take while crossing the underside of the bridge. You are free to attempt other routes, but watch your step; it's a long plummet down!

Back outside, don't be surprised by a couple of Headcrabs crawling about the area. The Soldiers may have been defeated, but your progress is halted. You need to figure out a way over the bridge.

Head through the metal door, into the support structure of the bridge. Pick up the items in the small rooms, go up the steps to check the other level, then head for the exit, moving out onto the bridge's span.

If you want, hop back in your Scout Car, and drive it up the gravel area to the left of the buildings. Swing the car around on the way up, and check the rotting wooden-fenced area. Amid the Poison Headcrabs are supplies.

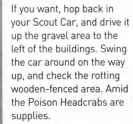

More infinite crates: Perhaps a portent of enemies to come? Step out onto the upper catwalk. You now must negotiate the maintenance platforms under the bridge. Check the ladder and side platforms for goods before continuing.

Switch to the machine gun (or the RPG) and blast a Barnacle on the bridge roof. Your first plan is to try to make it across to the first maintenance hut. Stand on the broken platform, and jump to the other side of it on the support girders on the right side of the span.

Then follow the girders to the hut and stand on the sturdy platform. Tear apart a Headcrab or two in the hut before scavenging any items of interest. Now check the next part of the crossing. You must head to the hut in the middle of the underside of the bridge. Step onto the broken catwalk, then maneuver across the diagonal girders.

Find the creaking platform on the left. It looks unsafe but will take your weight. Jump on it, dash to the top, and follow it around to a ladder above the central concrete support, and then to the hut on top of that. Go down the ladder.

The hut contains a rather messy victim of a recent attack, and a stack of items, including more Infinite Ammo Crates for the rocket. Load up your rocket and turn left. There are a couple of Combine forces on the next maintenance hut. Shoot off a rocket, tracing it into the hut or into the Soldier standing near it, and continue until both fall. Then rocket the Barnacle on the roof. This may be overkill, but you have rockets aplenty.

Now comes the tricky part; scaling the windswept girders to the hut you just hit with rockets. Begin by carefully walking up the diagonal girders until you reach the remains of a catwalk to the right. Jump to it, then run up, and jump into the hut. Bring your SMG out before the climb so you can deal with any Headcrabs that may have survived your shelling.

The rest of the bridge span is easily accessed. Simply exit the hut via the right doorway, and jump onto a catwalk that leads to the far end of the bridge underside. You've made it! Now check the room inside the concrete support for supplies, check the Supply Crate on the top floor outside the balcony, and take the ladder down to the base platform. When you're done, exit via the doorway on the lower level.

Step out along the concrete balcony between the bridge supports, and immediately turn and engage two Soldiers spotting you from a two-level catwalk to your right. Don't waste time blasting them with anything other than rockets. Now switch to a close-assault weapon and get ready for Soldiers appearing from the doorway ahead of you. Bring any down you see.

Step forward into a storage room within the bridge support, and watch for a few Soldiers to begin attack strategies. If you're quick and can aim at the barrel on the upper balcony, you can bring the whole platform down on the Soldiers. Mop up survivors, and open up any Supply Crates.

Follow the path around the storage room to the outside catwalk where you just launched rockets at the two Soldiers. Quickly look right and up at the lookout post on the far end of the bridge. Bring down the Soldier with RPG rounds or the Crossbow.

Swiftly ascend the ladder, and head around the upper catwalk. Pause at the doorway to the right of a window. There are about three Soldiers, and it's safer to wait until the first heads out, then shoot him (ideally so he flips over the railing and plummets to his death).

Strafe and bring down the remaining Soldiers, then force your way into the small brick lookout building and around into another storeroom. Head up the stairs, armed with whatever weapon you wish; for example, a paint pot for the two Soldiers at the top of the stairs.

With Soldiers in your path, take a small breather and inspect the bridge control room. The interesting machinery is blocked by an energy wall. Unhook the large plug on the left generator with the Gravity Gun. Then use the chargers to replenish your suit. Finally, check the computer console. Press the switch to the left to deactivate the bridge energy wall.

TIP

Be *very* sure you've deactivated the energy wall; you don't want to retrace your steps!

As the energy wall deactivates, you hear a Combine Gunship on its way to intercept you. It starts peppering the window with bullets. Flee the control room, retracing your steps to the concrete balcony. Shoot the two Soldiers ahead of you, and then watch as the Gunship detonates a fuel tank strapped to the bridge. This prevents you from taking a risky route back onto the structure.

Run to the top of the bridge underside; you must fight the Gunship in an area where you can see it, and there's a plentiful supply of rockets. Jump the gap in the catwalk, and head into the first maintenance hut.

Think you've mastered your suit? Then try maneuvering to the lower hut with the rocket ammo. Instead of gingerly descending the broken catwalk to the left, stand at this point, hold down Sprint and run!

CHAPTER 7
ENCOUNTERS

TIP

Your speed allows you to dash over the diagonal girders and drop onto the lower hut area. If you're too slow, you'll fall to your death.

When you're at the lower middle hut, the Combine Gunship starts to circle around you. This is the chance you've been waiting for. Stand between the Gunship's cannon fire at a girder so you aren't hit; then when the fire stops, launch and aim a rocket at the ship. You don't really need to corkscrew the rockets in. Your finest plan is to continue this combat until the ship is destroyed.

Or, you can dash back to the cliff-top house area. You'll need to return here anyway, so follow the diagonal girders up to the initial underside point, across the first maintenance hut, and back down to the concrete balcony. Take any remaining items from the yellow-lit rooms, and exit via that metal door you first came through.

Walk along the cliff-top path, under the buildings, around and up to the right, and onto the main forecourt area. There may be a Poison Zombie and a couple of Antlions to fight through on the way, as well as the Gunship if you failed to strike it down.

The Soldiers are back! There are around three to watch out for, so make a quick sweep of the area, don't get out-flanked, and bring them down quickly if the Gunship is still alive. Use the tactics described earlier to ensure all Soldiers are dropped. Check all the shed areas and sides of the buildings, trotting around the left side of the buildings and garage to ensure you aren't going to be ambushed.

Then, if the Gunship wasn't defeated on the bridge, refill your rockets at the ammo point, and corkscrew enough ordnance to bring the beast down. Another Combine synth that won't be self-replicating!

Go back to your car. With the energy wall deactivated, drive through the now-open bridge entrance. There are a few rusting carriages to your left, forcing you to drive on the right train tracks.

Watch out! A Combine train is speeding toward you, and your bridge crossing turns into an impromptu (and possibly deadly) game of chicken. There are two ways to safely cross the bridge. If you meet the train at this point (above), you're slammed and crushed to death and the car is ruined.

The first way to avoid the oncoming train is to drive past the rusting carriage until you see the train, then execute a handbrake turn and turbo back the way you came, skidding onto the right side of the track (facing the start of the bridge), and letting the train pass to your left.

The second method is to cross the bridge before the train blocks your path. Straighten your car up on the right tracks, use the turbo, speed past the stopped carriages on your left, and swerve left as the left track opens up, just missing the oncoming train.

After you've crossed the suspension bridge, you have no need to investigate the tunnel or outcrop overlooking the bridge. Instead, bounce down the rocks to the left side, landing on a grassy area near an area of segmented road bridge parts.

This bumpy area is difficult to drive around at speed, so concentrate on steering under the partially collapsed bridge arch, swing left, and speed up the final part of the bridge, which acts as a ramp into another long tunnel.

SANDTRAPS

OVERVIEW Your coastal excursion continues into the twilight as you battle through a tunnel full of the frothing undead. You negotiate a Combine checkpoint and a small encampment overrun by enemy troops, and you meet up with a human resistance at Lighthouse Point. The citizens' joy is short-lived as you buckle down for a Combine onslaught; four Dropships deposit Soldiers for you to defeat, after which a Gunship needs its wings clipped. With the car no longer available, alternate means to Nova Prospekt are needed. You'll have to cross an Antlion beach using nimble feet. This foray ends in combat with a new and horrific foe—the powerful fiend known as the Antlion Guard. Out of his defeat comes a lucky break as a Vortigaunt creates a powerful Pheropod that drives Antlions wild, effectively making them obey your commands (as long as those commands are "kill" or "regroup"). With your new Antlion pride, it's time for a final beach assault against Combine sentry gun emplacements and an ascent of the cliff wall. Then, in the prison yard, you'll wage a final and terrifying battle against Soldiers and two Gunships before infiltrating the prison.

INVENTORY PICK-UP

- Pheropod (bugbait)
- Sentry gun (emplacement)

ENTITY ENCOUNTER
FRIENDLIES

- Resistance Citizens
- Sandy
- Laszlo
- Vortigaunts

ENTITY ENCOUNTER
HOSTILES

- Zombies/Fast Zombies
- Headcrabs/Fast Headcrabs
- Combine Soldiers
- Rollermines
- Combine APC
- Combine Gunships
- Combine Dropships
- Antlions
- Antlion Guard*
- Manhacks

* Indicates first exposure to entity

"HERE COME THE DROPSHIPS!"

MAP 37 | **COASTAL WILDERNESS**

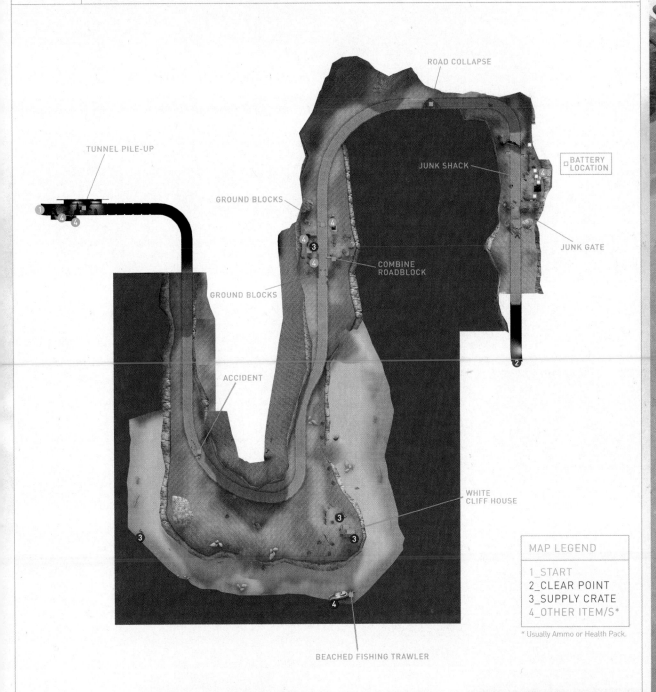

ROAD COLLAPSE

TUNNEL PILE-UP

GROUND BLOCKS

JUNK SHACK

BATTERY LOCATION

JUNK GATE

COMBINE ROADBLOCK

GROUND BLOCKS

ACCIDENT

WHITE CLIFF HOUSE

BEACHED FISHING TRAWLER

MAP LEGEND

1_START
2_CLEAR POINT
3_SUPPLY CRATE
4_OTHER ITEM/S*

* Usually Ammo or Health Pack.

Once you're in the tunnel, the eerie lighting blinks out. As you round a corner and peer into the gloom ahead, you see the remains of a multi-vehicle crash. Shorepoint hadn't heard from contacts in this area for 28 days.

Piles of burned cars, refuse, and explosive barrels are everywhere, and the path around them is too narrow to ram with your vehicle. Clear a path with the Gravity Gun. Exit the vehicle. The door to the right is firmly sealed.

This place is a deathtrap! Scuttling sounds and scraping footfalls precede a rush of Fast Zombies! There are a couple of Fast Zombies on the raised pavement to the left. Back up and tag them using the fence to ensure you're only attacked from the front.

Down on the tunnel highway, the scenery shifts and more Zombies appear, attempting to swarm you with vicious swiping attacks. Back up and burn them with a barrel explosion, but keep your distance! You need to find a safe spot to hide.

Shrug off the unwanted Zombie advances and run to the raised pavement area to the right of the blue door. Check the wall on the left for health and a cubby hole. Dive in; the Zombies are too large to follow you.

From here, break out the SMG (as there's limitless ammo on the back of your car), and strafe the storage room of Headcrabs. Pick up the items in this room, ignore the rotting corpses in the corner, and step back to the cubby hole, ignoring the blue door. Now take down the Zombies gurgling in this region. Poke your head out to coax them toward the hole, then step back before they slash you.

When there are no more Fast Zombies, step back out into the main tunnel. From here, move back to the Scout Car, and look for additional undead to tackle. There's usually a few on the higher pavement.

When the entire tunnel is silent, switch to the Gravity Gun, and blast the car wreckage blocking your path. Create a path along the left wall—it's quickest to drive around. Get into the car and speed out of this tunnel of terror.

You'll come out onto another windswept beach road. Slow to avoid a recent two-vehicle pile-up, swing around the scattered boxes, and check the promontory to your right. As you make a long left turn, there's a lone white house. If you want, drive over and inspect it.

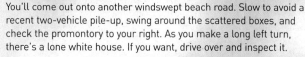

Your first plan should be to rid yourself of Combine danger. There are two Soldiers who have just finished burning the bodies of Resistance Citizens in a central pyre. Use the Tau Cannon or ram them. The parked APC is inaccessible, but use the nearby crates as cover and check them for items.

Carefully maneuver into the large hole the APC blew out of the house. Bring out the Gravity Gun, and enter the living room. Head to the stairs, and ascend to the second floor, and then up to the third floor. There's an eerie silence. Peer out of a window facing the beach, and you'll spot a rusting trawler banked on the sand.

There's a barricade at the far side of the third floor room, with a couple of Health Packs to snag. As you reach this area, you're ambushed by two Rollermines. Retaliate by immediately sucking

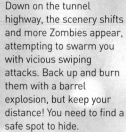

them up with the Gravity Gun, and then blasting them out a window. Stand near the window to ensure the glass shatters. Head for the second floor.

The hole to the right of the fireplace is a second ambush point. Be ready to clamp a Rollermine with your Gravity Gun, then spit it out into the ocean, via a window. Fight your way to the ground level, watching for breaking windows and more Rollermines near the entrance hole. Punt them out into the ocean before escaping.

NOTE

Don't blast a Rollermine into the fireplace while on the second floor—it'll appear in the ground floor fireplace area and attack you again!

Before you continue along the main coastal road, inspect the beached boat you saw from the house. Accelerate off the promontory and down to the beach. On the side of the boat nearest the ocean are supply crates. There's  another crate farther up the beach, toward the tunnel.

Head in the opposite direction, back to the road. Ease off the accelerator as you reach a Combine checkpoint. Rocks to the right block your path, and there's movement on a lookout post.

Stop the car by the roadside sign, bring out your Crossbow, and take careful aim at the Soldier atop the turret. Bring him down with a single shot, then continue on foot, heading left around the checkpoint entrance.

A second Soldier is patrolling a balcony; surprise him from this side. Bring him down, but don't head up the ladder or into the center of the road yet; there are more Soldiers to tackle.

Sidle down the rocky area to the left of the main, single-story building. By now you should be familiar with the "frag-'em-and-tag-'em" technique; shoot the window to the left of the doorway, throw a grenade in, and wait for it to detonate. You'll hear shuffling movements and loud exclamations. In the confusion, burst in, and use a rapid-fire weapon to finish off a couple of Combine Soldiers.

The Soldiers may try to escape via the front door on the opposite wall. Step out onto the coastal road and blast any that appear with your preferred weapon. Or stay inside the main warehouse, checking the far end for another Soldier (close combat single-blast weapons work well here, like the Shotgun). After you secure the entire area, return to the warehouse for multiple items.

The last place you'll find Combine Soldiers is in the shed at the opposite side of the road from the warehouse. Stealthily creep to the front door and gun them down, or simply fire on them with the RPG. Check the remains for items. The checkpoint is now secure.

Return to your vehicle and drive it carefully over the set of two ground barriers (don't try this at speed; you'll be buffeted severely and lose control), and around the wooden and ground barriers at the far end of the checkpoint.

CAUTION

It is possible to avoid combat and drive like a madman, straight over the barriers, through the checkpoint, and around the far barriers, but you'll come under fire and lose the element of surprise.

The coastal road curves right in a long arc. You should check out the human settlement and large windmill in the distance. Don't ignore the fissure in the ground as you near the place. Drive left and around it; if you don't, you tip into the ocean and suffer an embarrassing demise.

As you reach the encampment, you'll find an overturned tanker truck blocking the road. Exit your car, and listen for a whine of combat engines. Dropships! Two are taking off from the other side of this encampment. They've already dropped their payloads–about six Combine Soldiers who are taking defensive positions behind the junk that lies around this area. Step around the tanker after the Dropships depart and take apart this squad.

Once you've finished them off, look at the gate on the far side of the encampment. It is firmly closed, with electrical wires running to the main shed.

There's around six Combine Soldiers that scatter from the Dropship deposit, and move around the ramshackle gate at the far end of the road. Systematically take them down with whatever weapon you deem necessary. A barrel works well; you can use it with your Gravity Gun as cover, then blast your victim. Stay in the area around the caravan to take down the first two foes.

Go into the shed and find the set of generator coils that operate the gate. The current is incomplete–two batteries separate the coils. An impromptu treasure hunt is in order. There are five batteries, the first of which is already connected to the generator.

The second is on the bed frame near the corpse inside the shed, just to your right.

The third is positioned under a bathtub in the outside "lawn" area near the outhouse. Blast the bath with your Gravity Gun to reveal it.

The fourth is difficult to spot; look up at the windmill and zoom in on the small platform. Resting on it is the battery, as well as some counterweights. Use the Gravity Gun to pull the objects off and claim the battery when it falls.

The final battery is in the engine of a car. Suck it out of the car on cement blocks to the left of the main shed.

Bring two of the last four batteries back to the main shed, and slot them into place to create a current. Grab the battery, flick the switch, and exit the building. The gate should be rising, allowing you to easily drive your vehicle through once you've negotiated the tanker and the debris on the road. Speed away from the encampment, pausing only to suck and blast a Rollermine into the water.

"THEY'RE LOOKING FOR YOUR CAR."

MAP 38 | **LIGHTHOUSE POINT**

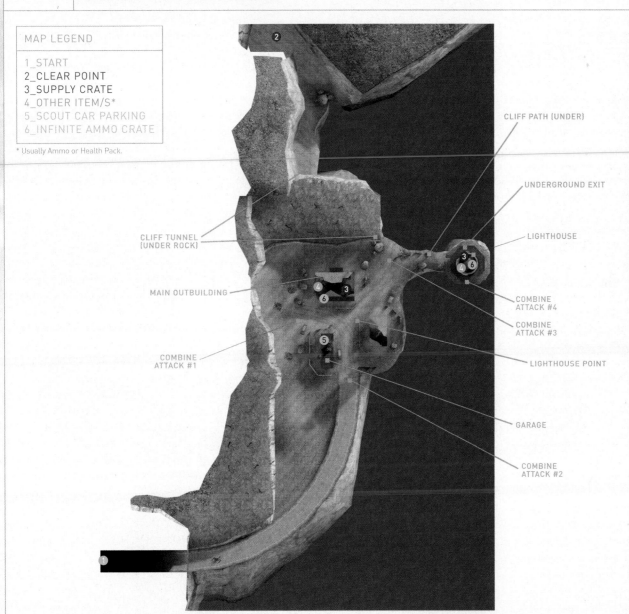

MAP LEGEND
1_START
2_CLEAR POINT
3_SUPPLY CRATE
4_OTHER ITEM/S*
5_SCOUT CAR PARKING
6_INFINITE AMMO CRATE

Usually Ammo or Health Pack.

CLIFF PATH (UNDER)

UNDERGROUND EXIT

LIGHTHOUSE

CLIFF TUNNEL
(UNDER ROCK)

MAIN OUTBUILDING

COMBINE
ATTACK #4

COMBINE
ATTACK #3

COMBINE
ATTACK #1

LIGHTHOUSE POINT

GARAGE

COMBINE
ATTACK #2

By late afternoon, you come out of a final tunnel, to the last part of the coastal road leading to a lighthouse and lookout point. This is the final resistance hotspot that Leon attempted to reach via radio.

Drive into the small settlement, and you're beckoned quickly over by a member of the resistance. "You're gonna have to ditch the car, Freeman. They're looking for it now," the man remarks. Pull into the open garage on the left.

CHAPTER ⁸
ENCOUNTERS

Once you've parked and exited the garage, the team jogs over to say hello. There's little time for pleasantries, however; "Dropship! Over the field!" one of the team yells. The next few minutes is a constant series of combat opportunities as the Combine tries to take you out by depositing four squads of Soldiers onto the ground near you and the rebels. Take cover as the first Dropship descends, landing in the small field behind the garage.

NOTE

The following combat can be attempted in any manner you wish. The tactics we suggest leave you with more survivors, with the least amount of damage. There are other methods of attack, but none as effective as the plan that follows.

CAUTION

When you're watching Combine troops leaving the Dropship containers, don't bother throwing a grenade to take them down in one fell swoop; the up-jets from the Dropship create a wind effect that blows grenades back at you!

TIP

There's no need to worry about your team; they can look after themselves. However, you can get help from your side by remembering the two uniform types–the medic with the white armbands can patch you up during or after combat and the dark-blue suited citizen can re-supply you.

Bring down the quartet of Soldiers departing from the first Dropship. The SMG grenade doesn't suffer blowback problems like the Frag Grenade, so bury one into the container. Make sure you're also firing from behind cover, dodging the Dropship's covering salvos.

Stick close to a colleague and fan out a little. Attacking from the fence and wall around the left side of the garage is a good plan, or from the front door of the house to the right. Cut down the Soldiers before they have chance to find cover.

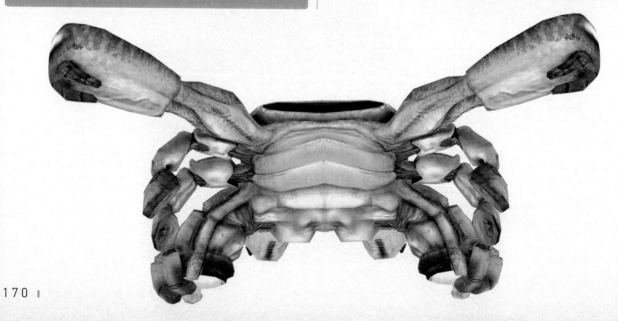

NOTE

The second Dropship arrives a minute after the first leaves, so use that time wisely and violently. The third Dropship descends when a single Soldier from the previous squad remains. Bring this straggler down immediately, then concentrate on the new threat.

The second Dropship arrives and lands on the road near the garage you just drove into. Prepare for combat by staying back, crouching behind a low wall, or at the corner of the garage. If your team members are near the garage door, move left to the other building near the cliff to provide supporting fire. This time, attacking from two sides with your team is a good way to flummox your foe. Pick up several items in the house, and then check out the window to find the incoming enemy.

The enemy usually heads to the cliff-top house, and then tries to charge the main building where your team is milling about. Watch for accurately thrown grenades; remember to punt them back with the Gravity Gun. Stay at the doorway, and don't forget there's an Infinite Ammo Crate at the main building, too. Fall back to the main building, and look for enemies as they cross the road to your location. A good plan is to stop them from outflanking you and rushing in from the building's back entrance; so head out there yourself, staying at the corner facing the lighthouse, and cutting down enemies from this area. This spot provides excellent maneuvering and shooting capabilities.

The third Dropship deposits its cargo of Soldiers from the promontory to the left of the lighthouse. This isn't the best spot for your enemy to exit, but it's great for you. Hole up in the main building, wait for the Dropship cannons to stop, and then check the enemy from the window and the rear entrance while your friends guard the front. Dashing around the back and front of the building after locating the enemy works well here.

CAUTION

If you have the opportunity, tag the Soldiers armed with shotguns first—they are most devastating at close range and are responsible for most of your own team's deaths.

The final Dropship attempts to deposit its Soldiers at the base of the lighthouse. This is another flawed strategy for the Combine; bring out the RPG and burn the Soldiers alive as they exit the container. Your teammates sense victory and follow you up the path to the lighthouse. Use the fence and rocks as cover, and continue to batter the Soldiers as they emerge. Switch to rapid-fire ordnance and drop the remaining forces as they round the base of the lighthouse. You can even use your team as cover, or watch them finish the job for you!

TIP

If your loyalty extends only to your own personal safety, when you park your car in the garage, ignore the yells of the resistance fighters and rush immediately to the lighthouse. Enter it and, from the base or top, begin an RPG assault on the enemy. This way, you won't be street-fighting, but rather playing the role of artillery launcher. Although the Dropships can't be downed, the Combine Soldiers don't stand a chance!

Once the Dropships are done, there's a new threat. "Oh man...now what?" a weary rebel asks. "It's a Gunship!" The team scatters, and points you in the direction of the lighthouse, where there's a large collection of rockets. One of the resistance fighters brokers a deal: "I'll take you out on the cliff-side path as soon as you kill that Gunship. There's no way we can make it with that thing harassing us." Sounds like a deal. Enter the lighthouse, and climb the stairs.

CHAPTER ⁸
ENCOUNTERS

Dash up to the top of the lighthouse (although there's health if you descend to the basement). The Gunship shoots out the windows as you head up, so duck and avoid it, or run up between volleys. Grab RPG rounds near the top steps and more health.

The deal with the resistance is now complete; leave the area via a secret exit beneath the lighthouse. One of the citizens leads you down to the basement and opens a hidden doorway. Remember to refill on health, items, and rockets before you leave.

At the top of the lighthouse, on the enclosed circular balcony outside the light, prepare for combat. Wait for the Gunship to finish a volley, then corkscrew in a rocket.

You emerge on a very narrow cliff ledge. Turn left and look up and down to spot another Combine Soldier attack force. Strafe the Soldier on the edge above you, and watch him plummet to his death on the rocks below. Maneuver across the jutting ledges, grabbing the items from the supply crate and lashing out at the Headcrab. As you move along, a Dropship swoops past. It has the Scout Car coupled to its base! The Combine has appropriated your vehicle!

Don't worry about the lack of room; the other side of the light can be used as cover, as can the steps leading down to the Infinite Ammo Crate. Peek out, and the Gunship usually hits the railing instead of you for some of the cannon volley. Then send out another controlled rocket launch.

With the Scout Car stolen, there's only one way onward, and that's to leap (or sprint-jump) across the gaps in the ledges, and head for the relative safety of a narrow natural tunnel up ahead. Time for some rock climbing.

Drop the Gunship out of the air after three, five, or seven direct hits (depending on the difficulty of your adventure) by refilling your rockets downstairs, heading back to the top, waiting for the cannon fire to cease, and then quickly firing a laser-guided shot into the hide of the Gunship. It eventually breaks apart, and the final Combine menace is floored.

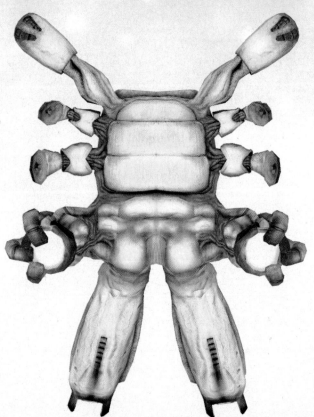

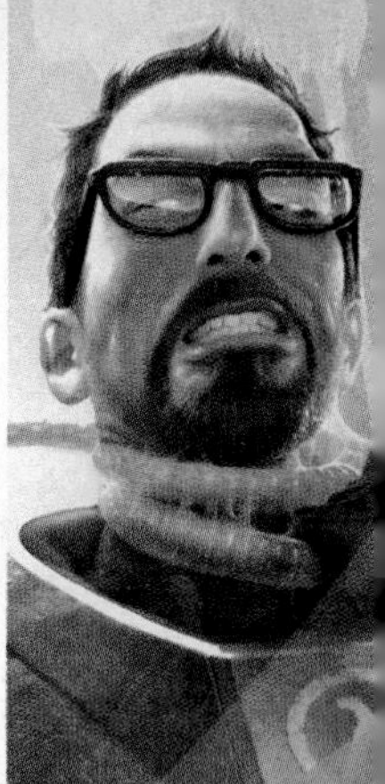

"WE WERE HEADING TO THE VORTIGAUNT CAMP."

MAP 39 | **VORTIGAUNT CAMP**

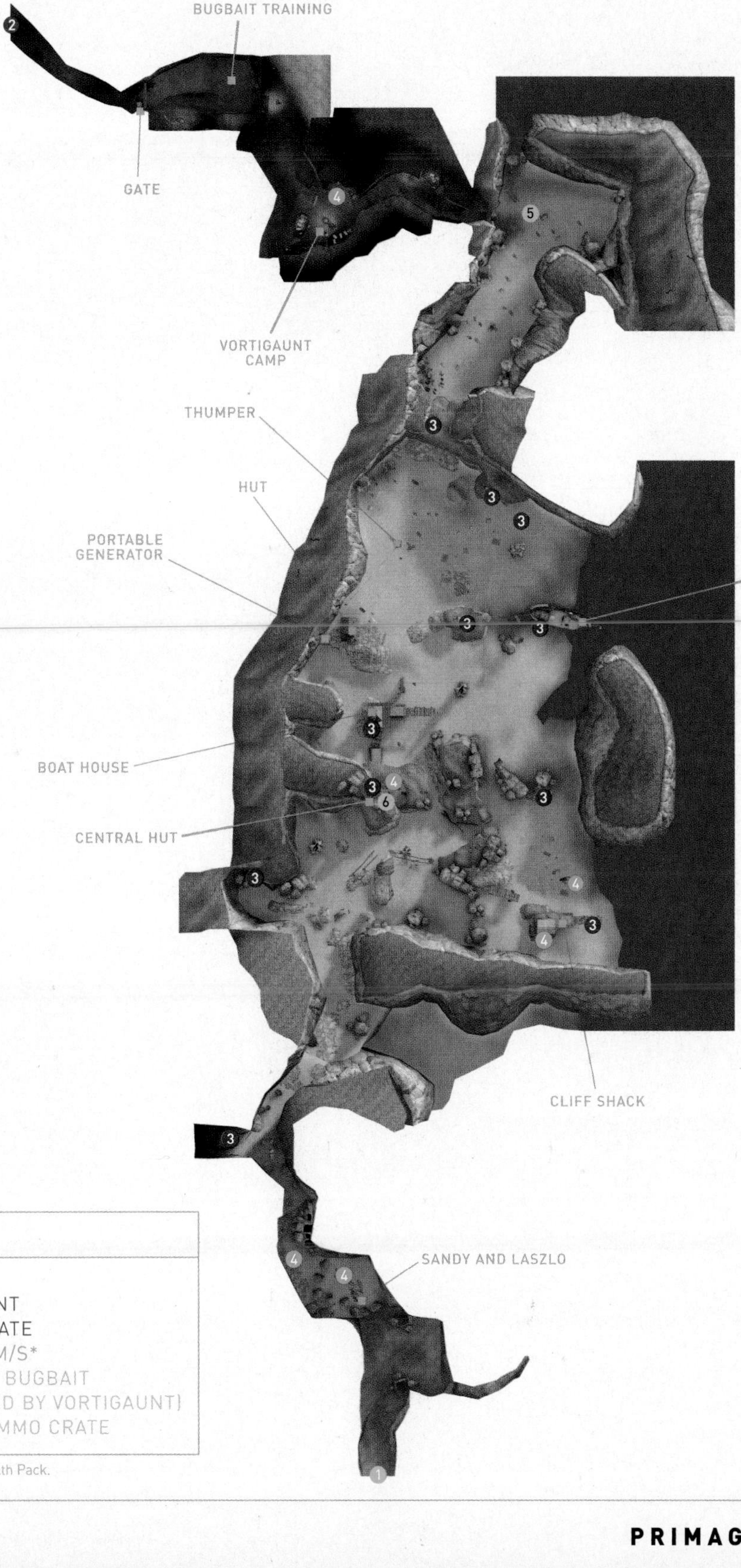

BUGBAIT TRAINING

GATE

VORTIGAUNT CAMP

THUMPER

HUT

PORTABLE GENERATOR

BOAT HOUSE

CENTRAL HUT

BEACHED BOAT

CLIFF SHACK

SANDY AND LASZLO

INTRODUCTION
GETTING STARTED
WEAPONS DETAIL
HALF-LIFERS
THE BESTIARY
CHAPTER 1
CHAPTER 2
CHAPTER 3
CHAPTER 4
CHAPTER 5
CHAPTER 6
CHAPTER 7
CHAPTER 8 SANDTRAPS
CHAPTER 9
CHAPTER 10
CHAPTER 11
CHAPTER 12
CHAPTER 13
CHAPTER 14
ANOMALOUS MATERIALS

MAP LEGEND

1_START
2_CLEAR POINT
3_SUPPLY CRATE
4_OTHER ITEM/S*
5_PHEROPOD BUGBAIT (EXTRICATED BY VORTIGAUNT)
6_INFINITE AMMO CRATE

* Usually Ammo or Health Pack.

Trudge through the tunnel as the sun sinks lower in the sky. You appear in a small natural valley as the cliff top path opens up, with steep rocks surrounding you. Remember that Antlions are still hunting in this area! Head straight then left.

"Hold still, Laszlo! Someone's coming!" A citizen is kneeling on a rock near the bloodied body of his friend. "Don't step on the sand! It makes the Antlions crazy!" This is Sandy and his friend, Laszlo. The ground erupts with Antlions. Fire at them to help Sandy stave off the attack. Stay on the rocks so more Antlions don't arrive. If you're proficient, Sandy survives. If you're too slow, both citizens are sliced to death by Antlion mandibles.

ADDITIONAL
INVESTIGATIONS

Assuming Sandy survives the Antlion assault, it's still curtains for Laszlo. A sorrowful Sandy is there for Laszlo's lament: "Dear God...poor Laszlo...the finest mind of his generation...to come to such an end...."

Perhaps it would have been better to let Sandy die than listen to this? The eulogy finishes; "We were heading to the Vortigaunt camp–hoping to pick up some bugbait so these damn things would leave us alone. But without Laszlo...what's the point?" You aren't blamed for the demise of Laszlo, though. "I know you tried to help," says Sandy. "I'll stay with him a while...there's something I have to do."

If Sandy isn't dead, he gives you a final piece of advice: remain off the sand. Heed this plan. Leave Sandy and Laszlo, bring out your Gravity Gun, and drag the supply crate and a wooden palette. Smash the crate, pick up its contents, and jump across to the rocks ahead.

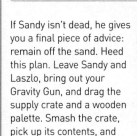

TIP

You'll be using the Gravity Gun almost exclusively in this area, but remember to use Ⓖ to quickly switch from this to your favored close-combat weapon, ideally the SMG or Shotgun. Reach for real ordnance if you disturb the sand.

Reaching this point presents little in the way of problems, but the distance between rocks requires a small run up and a sprint-jump to ensure you don't drop short of the rocks ahead. When you fail a jump, expect at least two, and possibly as many as four, Antlions to swarm you. Attack with your back to a rock wall if possible, and don't step back on the sand! You are free to continue once this wave of Antlions is culled, and you remain on the rocks.

When you reach this area, there's another jump that can be tried with a sprint. After this is a much longer gap between rocky outcrops. This is the time where your Gravity Gun comes in handy. Drag and drop a palette in the middle of the gap, then drop onto the palette and to the desired rock area. Or, use two pieces of scenery and create your own stepping stones. These can be placed in a continuous to-and-fro path to your desired location. Remember the supply crates in the alcove to the left can be sucked from a distance; there's no point in traveling to them.

The protruding rocks along this next narrow section present their own problem; your landing must be exceptional to avoid sliding off and into the sand. If you slip, run forward to the flat rock ahead and engage the Antlions that appear.

CAUTION

When you're using wooden scenic pieces (such as palettes) as stepping stones across the sand, be wary of their fragile nature. The palettes can be damaged by one accidental blast instead of a drop, or if you release them too high off the ground. A broken palette is much trickier to stand on. Be sure to gently drop wooden objects.

Once you've negotiated the treacherous alley of rock and sand, the area opens up into a multitude of stepping stones, rocks, and debris. There is no immediate pathway, and the rocks continue into the far distance (with an Antlion nest visible on the horizon). However, the main route to take is toward the long wooden seesaw up ahead.

Before you reach the seesaw, find a couple of corpses and several items in the second alcove on the left side of the rock wall. Grab the items from afar by using the Gravity Gun.

Move quickly back to the main upper rocky path and to the seesaw. This is the only way to reach the upper rocks you're facing, but there's a specific method to follow. First, walk to the middle of the seesaw, and suck the large crate off the  far end, so the seesaw rises slightly. Do *not* smash the crate. Drop it on the opposite side of the seesaw so it remains pointing up to the rock as you run and jump off it. Otherwise, it falls down under your weight, dropping you into the sand.

The way through this beach-combing exercise is to the left, but if you want more items, investigate the small hut on the rocky promontory and pier ahead and right of you. Run across and enter the hut, scaring off the Seagulls. Grab more goods from the crates at the end of the pier, then look down on the beach front to spot another crate. Don't go to it, as the pain you'll suffer at the mandibles of the Antlions outweighs the crate's usefulness. Use the Gravity Gun to safely suck up the items.

Back on the main rocky outcrop, negotiate the grassy outcrops and gaps,–don't fall. Continue until you reach the edge of the outcrop and look left to spot a shanty and a barn. To your right is a boat house. There are no signs of human life anywhere.

The Gravity Gun comes in very handy here. Suck the large plank of wood at the foot of the shed, and drop it to bridge the gap in front of you. To ensure the plank straddles both rocks, drop it on the area where you're standing, move so the length of the plank is directly in front of you, then pick it up again; that way the plank is at an angle that makes it easier to place. Once at the other side, place the plank against the shed and run up it onto the roof.

Before you reach the roof, clear the shed of supply crates and refill from the Infinite Ammo Crate. There are more crates and explosive barrels at the hut you can only reach via the plank. Drop the barrels or punt them into the distance. From this vantage point, plan your next series of jumps; you're heading for a Thumper. For the moment, drop to the rickety wooden deck leading to the boathouse. Bring that long plank with you.

Place the plank from the deck up to the boathouse, and climb up into the building to secure goods from another crate. Run to the beach-front end of the pier to get more explosive barrels and another supply crate. When you're done, look across to a beached boat and to the left to spot another rocky outcrop with more supply crates. Don't attempt the boat and outcrop yet. It's time to activate the Thumper.

Use the plank or an expert jump to reach the small white stone hut with the red shingle roof. This is the key to activating the Thumper up ahead. Step through the hole in the building's side and grab more goods from the crate inside. Exit via the hole in the opposite wall and step to an orange mobile generator. If you follow the electrical wires, they run from the generator to the Thumper. Press the switch on the generator, and it splutters to life.

The Thumper pounds the ground allowing you to step on the sand for the first time in this area and not get savaged by Antlions. The beasts still appear, but as long as you're near the Thumper, they don't attack. You can now get the items from the boat and the crates from the outcrop, and then flee back to the Thumper before you're attacked.

When you're finished grabbing crates, locate the rocks near the left side of the rock wall, leading to the upper ledge ahead of you past the Thumper. From the Thumper location, punt explosive barrels into any nearby Antlions, then flee to the ledge. Turn and blast any remaining Antlions from here.

Look over the ledge to see a mass of twisted bodies, blood oozing into the sand, and pieces of wood, supply crates, and other materials scattered about. There's no way forward, except down and onto the sand itself.

When you land on the sand, the ground shakes and something surfaces from an underground warren. The creature is about five times the size of an Antlion, but retains certain traits from its greener brethren. It is the feared Antlion Guard!

ENTITY ENCOUNTER:
ANTLION GUARD

One of the most feared creatures outside of the Combine Citadel is the Antlion Guard, also known as a Myrmidont. It is an enlarged genus of the Antlion family, sporting more earthy tones and a larger elongated head. It scuttles quickly across any surface and relies on a thick sinewy head to smash into targets, creating horrific blunt trauma damage. You can kill this beast if you shoot heavy objects into it, use high-explosive weapons or barrels, or enlist resistance citizens to help fire on it from multiple sources.

The Antlion Guard taps the ground and three Antlions appear. Don't lose your nerve just yet; flee to the far edge of this sandy arena, laying down suppressing fire on the Antlions as you go.

At the far end of this area is a barricade, and at the top is a resistance fighter with a gun turret. He peppers the Antlion Guard with rounds, affording you time to regroup. The first plan is to constantly circle-strafe; you need to remove yourself from the Antlion Guard's head butt and charge. Step away and around, and back up. The second plan is to bring this hideous creature down by sucking up an explosive barrel and launching it toward him.

If you cut down the Antlions, then concentrate on the Guard, it summons more to attack you. Time your barrel launch so that it explodes at the point the Antlions emerge, catching all the creatures in the explosion and saving ammunition. Next, try a grenade, or RPG rockets. Slam them into the Antlion Guard's hide. Stay close to the barricade so the gunner helps slaughter the Guard, too.

After hits from a few rockets, barrels, and some rapid-fire machine gun or Pulse Rifle rounds, the Antlion Guard lets out a piercing moan and drops. A moment later, a Vortigaunt appears from the doorway at the base of the barricade and speaks with haste: "The Freeman will do wise to heed our extraction of the Myrmidont's aromatic Pheropods. The process is not entirely hygienic. Therefore, stand aside." The Vortigaunt bathes the dead Antlion Guard in green electrical sparks. Several Pheropods fall out of the carcass. "The Freeman will have need of these Pheropods on the paths ahead. Gather them now." Heed this advice, then follow the Vortigaunt into the doorway.

INVENTORY ADAPTATION
PHEROPODS (BUGBAIT)

Before you follow the Vortigaunt into the camp, make sure you scoop up several Pheropods from the slowly dissolving remains of the Antlion Guard. The Pheropods allow you to control Antlions from this point onward; they never attack you again. The Vortigaunts show you how to use the Pheropods in a moment. Claim any crates that remain in the sandy area, then enter the camp.

With a sense of relief, you find yourself among friends in a Vortigaunt encampment deep inside a rock fissure. Campfires burn as humans and Vortigaunts converse. Take the items and health you wish, then listen in on the conversations. "Well, Dr. Freeman, you're a regular Antlion now!" one remarks. "I swear by the Pheropods myself," confirms another. "The Antlions won't bother you now, Doc," a third concurs.

Follow the Vortigaunt shepherd up the hill to another barricade. A citizen waits at the top and opens a gate for a Vortigaunt to pass through into a large stone chamber. "Get going, Dr. Freeman," the

man urges you. "Nova Prospekt is just ahead. One man alone wouldn't stand much chance going in there. But a man and a pack of Antlions...well that's a different story." The Vortigaunt beckons you to follow him down a slope into a natural concave area. "The Freeman will now be instructed in the use of Pheropods," he informs you.

INVENTORY ADAPTATION
PHEROPODS (BUGBAIT) TRAINING

Floodlights fill the cave with bright illumination. Follow the Vortigaunt's instructions: "The Freeman will now break out his Pheropods and toss one into yonder pit." Do so with, and a couple of Antlions immediately swarm to the haze of pheromones filling the air above the pod's impact point.

The Vortigaunt commends you, then states; "The Freeman can also coax his Antlions to attack specific targets. Observe the training manikin, and mark it well with another Pheropod." Check out the dangling remains of a Soldier, step back, and throw another Pheropod so it lands on or very near the mannequin. The Antlions immediately attack it.

This pleases the Vortigaunt. "The Freeman again excels at all tasks!" he states. He then gives a final set of instructions. "Now, attend well. Apply pressure to your Pheropod, to signal the Antlions in your command to follow you." This is

easily achieved by pressing; any nearby Antlions immediately arrive at your location, ready for herding. Your training is over.

The Vortigaunt moves to a giant log barrier and opens it. "And now this one must bid the Freeman farewell," he says. "Nova Prospekt lies just beyond. Remember well what you have learned here. The Eli Vance has greatest confidence in you." Squeeze the bugbait, and move up into a long tunnel-like fissure with your new Antlion friends following you.

"HEED OUR EXTRACTION OF MYRMIDONT'S AROMATIC PHEROPODS."

MAP 40 | **NOVA PROSPEKT: WATCHTOWERS**

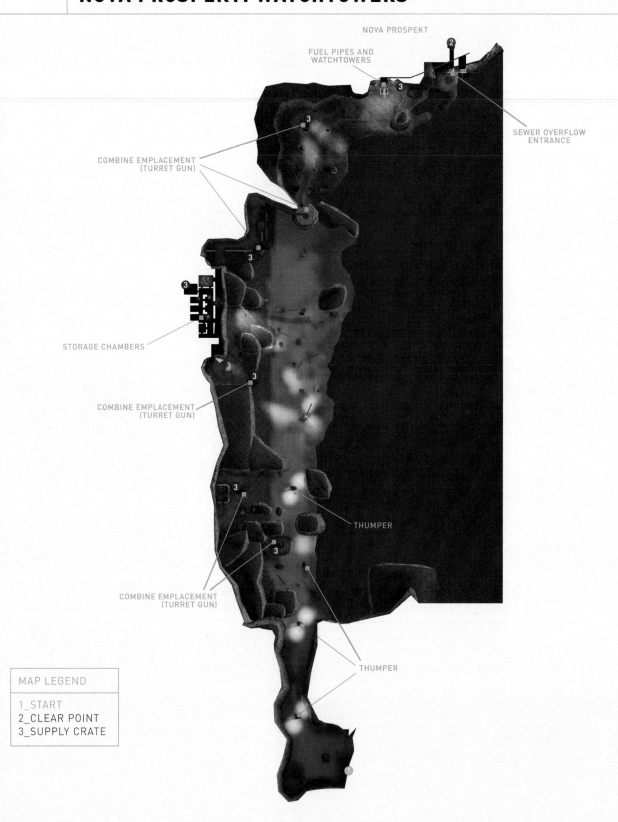

NOVA PROSPEKT

FUEL PIPES AND
WATCHTOWERS

SEWER OVERFLOW
ENTRANCE

COMBINE EMPLACEMENT
(TURRET GUN)

STORAGE CHAMBERS

COMBINE EMPLACEMENT
(TURRET GUN)

THUMPER

COMBINE EMPLACEMENT
(TURRET GUN)

THUMPER

MAP LEGEND

1_START
2_CLEAR POINT
3_SUPPLY CRATE

As you emerge from the tunnel, give your bugbait a squeeze; you need to round up an Antlion posse for a series of Combine Soldier takedowns, and you'll let your newly acquired monstrous friends take most of the damage. The only problem is the Thumper in front of you; it is activated. Run to its base, climb the ladder, and switch it off. Hop down and beckon your Antlions to your location.

The same problem occurs when you move through to the next open area. The rocky outcrops of the Vortigaunt base diminish and a much wider series of warrens appears, stretching out in front of you. Climb up to the switch on the second Thumper and switch it off. A third Thumper and a sentry gun emplacement are up ahead. That's where you'll need to send your Antlion crew.

TIP

Antlions are expendable. If a few dozen die in your assault on Nova Prospekt's exterior, then so be it. Remember, these critters are only reacting to the pheromones given off by your bugbait; they should be used and abused as cannon fodder.

Silently move up the beach with the water almost lapping against your ankles; attacking from this area is okay, as you aren't engaging a large number of Combine just yet. About three or four Soldiers spot your progress and investigate.

Engage! You're going to be moving up the slope now, between the rocks, and throwing bugbait directly at the Combine Soldier giving you the most problems. Land the shot into or at the feet of the Soldier. You'll see the cloud of pheromones as it partially chokes and completely incapacitates the Soldier for about six seconds. Squeeze

the bait, just in case the Antlions aren't all arriving, and keep peppering the ground with bugbait. The Antlions make short work of the Soldier.

TIP

The distance you throw the Pheropod isn't measured by the length of time you hold the 🖱 button. Line up the target with your reticule and then throw. It may come up shorter than expected at long range, but usually where you aim is where the bugbait lands.

TIP

Bugbait is an excellent weapon to use on Combine humanoid forces (but not monstrous hosts, such as Zombies). When the bugbait bursts near a Soldier, he is immobilized for a few seconds. Usually, that's when the Antlions pounce. Even when you don't control any Antlions, the Soldier is rendered immobile—meaning you can finish him off with another weapon at your leisure.

Head up to the rock edge on your left, and run for the rear of the sentry gun emplacement. The remaining Soldiers are on the beach; throw bugbait to immobilize the nearest two of them, then leave the Antlions to do the rest while you run into the emplacement. Make sure it's empty of Soldiers and grab the sentry gun. Strafe any remaining Soldiers in the weapon's line of sight.

Squeeze the Pheropods, and assemble your Antlion group in front of the first emplacement. You must now breach a second emplacement. It's slightly more difficult to reach because there's a Thumper on the beach that the Antlions won't go near. Combine Soldiers are using this to their advantage, and a couple of them are holding out here. Head through the narrow gap between the rocks, and force your Antlions left and up the slope.

Antlions are dead meat if they head toward the Thumper. Throw the bugbait at the approaching Soldiers in the concrete bunker area near the emplacement, behind the gun's trajectory. There aren't enough Soldiers to repel your assault, so let the Antlions devour the Soldiers, then clean out the emplacement. Meanwhile, you should follow behind, cracking open crates and keeping a lookout for the Combine.

TIP

During your beach assault, send your Antlions ahead while you follow. You'll be able to spot enemies as they attack, and the Antlions are the bait instead of you.

The fight continues at the back side of the emplacement. Some wayward Antlions need a close rein kept on them; they need to stay away from that Thumper and polish off the Soldiers still near the emplacement. Take out the Soldiers straggling by the Thumper with a long-range RPG, Crossbow, or sentry gun shot. Alternatively, launch a charge straight at them, bound up the Thumper ladder, and turn the machine off. Seconds later, they're swamped by your carapace-coated friends.

The third emplacement is the trickiest so far—it's above the beach level, a long way back, and the gunner spots you almost immediately. Stay low, head along the beach, and go past the emplacement.

When you reach this area of rocks, use them as cover. Coax your Antlions along and around the rocks, then up this space to the top of the beach, onto the grassy area to the right side of the boulders. On the way up, you have numerous opportunities to immobilize and then lacerate the Combine Soldiers. Push up, toward the crates.

Stay low and to the right side of the boulders; it really annoys the gunner, who can't get a shot on you. You'll lose a couple of Antlions as you continue the assault, but as long as you keep moving swiftly up to the supply crates and grass, you'll step behind the emplacement, effectively making the sentry gun useless. Throw more bugbait into the emplacement and watch the Antlions tear up the gunner inside. With no Soldiers left standing, regroup.

Once you've ransacked the third emplacement, turn around, and check the indented concrete bunker to your left. Ahead of you is an opening in the rock wall; it leads to a small warren containing various storage rooms. This is the only way to reach the next emplacement with the majority of your forces intact, so enter through the door, step to the right side, and throw bugbait ahead of you. Let the Antlions deal with a few Manhacks that are loose in this confined space.

A couple of long corridors in this chamber are lit by flares the Soldiers used in an attempt to spot you. This area is extremely dangerous; the far end is filled with explosive barrels and a quartet of guards, so send the Antlions in and wait for combat to begin. Detonate any barrels out of harm's way as you continue along the corridor, wiping out any Soldiers you see attacking the Antlions. You'll lose a couple of your forces in the battle, so call more to your aid.

Assemble your motley crew in the gloomy red glare of the flares, and search the warrens. A couple of side doors lead to small antechambers with crates inside. Emerge from the far end of the warrens.

Your next two gun emplacement opportunities are simple, but require you to move forcefully forward. Emerge, turn right, and throw bugbait into the first emplacement, running to secure it and any items inside. Combine forces have seen your prowess and are wisely backing up along a cliff path. They are trying to waylay you with grenade and gun fire. Dart forward to the corner, and come within range of the next emplacement. Once you take out the Soldiers on the path, throw bugbait into the emplacement.

NOTE

Stay on the path and watch the emplacement ahead as a Soldier falls to his death in a spectacular plummet!

The final emplacement is the trickiest of all and requires immediate action. Grab the sentry gun, and aim it at the troops trying to reach the unmanned emplacement across the valley from you. They are running right to left. Drop them all!

INVENTORY ADAPTATION
SENTRY GUN (EMPLACEMENT)

First accessible at the first emplacement along the beach, this weapon is identical to the one you fired back at the beginning of your adventure as you engaged the Metro police in the start of the canals. Shoot rapid-fire pulses directly into the enemy.

If the gun is manned, it makes the assault a little more troublesome. But, whatever the outcome, step out of the emplacement and sprint down the left side of the valley, throwing bugbait to halt the Soldiers on the right side.

The emplacement gunner attempts to cut down your Antlions, giving you a host of problems if you let him continue. Throw a grenade at the group of Soldiers guarding the emplacement and storm it. Use the Pheropod to call in more Antlion replacements. Take out the gunner, and hold the emplacement, using it as cover for the additional Combine troops deposited by the Dropship. Peek out, locate any stragglers, choke them with bait, and finish the assault.

At the top of the first platform, watch your step, as you don't want to follow the Soldiers. Step off, going down and right to a grassy ledge with crates to restock your supplies.

Run to the concrete landing spot, and look up and left. The looming menace of Nova Prospekt's outer wall can be seen stretching toward the dirt-filled skies. Your plan is to ascend this extremely steep cliff and gain entrance to the prison. There's a cliff-top path to follow around and to the right. Watch your step; you need to run onto a jutting tree stump and leap a gap. Failure isn't an option, unless you prefer to end your mission now. Follow the path up to a small campfire.

The camper who was hiding out in this alcove fell afoul of a Headcrab, and the Zombie struggles to his feet. This is an ideal opportunity to load up your SMG and shoot the gas canister under the shelter. It explodes, destroying the Zombie and creating an impromptu ramp for you to climb. Alternatively, you can let your Antlions do the killing.

Continue up the pathway, looking up and left every few steps until you spot an upper platform. Send a herd of Antlions up there to wreak havoc on the look-outs. There's another platform farther along, near a sewer outflow tunnel, and the Soldiers up here need to suffer the same fate.

Switch to the Shotgun as you near a sewage outflow pipe; there's a nasty Fast Zombie ready to bound out and ambush you. Of course, if you followed the main strategy and sent the Antlions ahead, they'd soak up the damage. Strike down the undead, and enter the pipe.

Continue along the narrow cliff path to a pipeline embedded in the rock wall, similar to the one you encountered back in the Black Mesa escapade. Atop platforms are Combine Soldiers. Immediately stop and throw bugbait onto the underside of the platforms. A frothing mass of Antlion body parts and screaming Soldiers bounce off the cliff as they fall to their deaths. When the gantry is Combine-free, climb the ladder in the rock to the left of the pipes.

"THE ELI VANCE HAS CONFIDENCE IN YOU."

| MAP 41 | **NOVA PROSPEKT: ENTRANCE YARD** |

WATCHTOWER

CORNER ROOM

ENTRANCE AFTER EXPLOSION

LOWER YARD

UPPER YARD

WATCHTOWER

SEWER GRATING (UNDERNEATH)

SEWER (FROM OUTSIDE)

SEWER GRATING (UNDERNEATH)

WATCHTOWER

MAP LEGEND

1_START
2_CLEAR POINT
3_SUPPLY CRATE
4_OTHER ITEM/S*
5_RECHARGER
6_INFINITE AMMO
　CRATE

* Usually Ammo or Health Pack.

Crawl through the concrete overflow tunnel, making sure you stop and gaze up at the grates for an interesting view of the outskirts of Nova Prospekt you normally wouldn't see. When you reach the small pool of water, smash the supply crate, then climb out of the area to the prison yard.

Survey the scenery. Ahead and to the left are two watchtowers overlooking the outer wall you infiltrated. There are no other enemies nearby to worry about; just the Soldiers patrolling atop the towers.

Break open the bugbait, and let it fly! Run down to the yard area. When you reach the spot shown in the first picture, throw several Pheropods at the platform atop the tower so the Antlions swarm and destroy the guards at the top. Move on to the next tower after all the guards are destroyed. Apply the same technique here; aim a little farther up than the target reticule, let the bugbait fly, and watch the carnage with a sense of satisfaction. Beware of falling Soldiers!

Once the second tower is secure, turn and study the layout of the prison yard. There are steps to run up and a couple of large containers to hide behind. Run up the steps into the main yard. Time is of the essence here because there are a couple of Soldiers behind the container on the left. Let the Antlions make quick work of them, and collect the items by the wall. Then take a deep breath. You've been spotted!

The whine of a Gunship fills the air, and the twilight is drenched in cannon fire as the ship closes. You now have the double menace of an airborne foe and Soldiers on the roof to the right and above you. The best technique there is to throw bugbait up on the roof, as shown, and let the Antlions deal with all the Soldiers up here. You need to get rid of the foes on the ground before you fight those in the air.

While the Antlions are removing the threats on the roof, step to the right corner of the yard as the Gunship circles clockwise and out of sight. A couple of Soldiers are in the small room in the corner of the building. They usually shoot; when this happens, lob a grenade through the open window and step back to wait for the explosion. Mop up any survivors with gunfire. If you want, enter the room and grab the items (including rockets). Use the rechargers if you are wounded badly. If not, save them until the end of the fight. Then move out of this small room, along the courtyard. Shoot out a window at the control room ahead, and lob a grenade in there.

Reach the corner of the building on your left, and hug the wall so you aren't cut down by the Gunship. Clear the roof of Soldiers by summoning more Antlions before flipping around and throwing more bugbait at the control room you just hit with the grenade. You need to take down all the Soldiers so no one is firing at you. Run to the open container for health; it's also an excellent spot to hide as you attempt to take down the Gunship.

Go around the side of the open container, up some steps, and to the upper yard area. By this time, there's a second Gunship arriving to back up the first! Don't waver from your plan to remove the Soldiers, though; throw bugbait at the last control room to the right of the Nova Prospekt sign, and make sure they all die. Then turn around, and bring the rocket launcher out. It's Gunship punishment time!

First, fill your rocket launcher to maximum capacity. There's an Infinite Ammo Crate on the wall in the upper balcony, which is a great place to stay, darting behind the central container when the need arises. Keep your back to the wall so you aren't shot at from behind, and begin the Gunship takedowns. As usual, the plan is simple; corkscrew in your rockets so they can strike the Gunship before it can shoot them down.

It doesn't matter which Gunship you destroy first, and it's difficult to continuously aim at a single one. Shoot whichever one is in your sights, rather than concentrating on a particular ship. Keep moving, running to the rechargers or items along the upper courtyard if need be. The Gunships fly in a large circle around the central building of the yard. The best time to fire is just as the ship finishes firing its cannon and passes around the outer wall area—there's more room for your rocket here.

When you enter the facility, the Antlions refuse to follow. A large fire is burning in this area. Look for the valve to the right, and twist it to turn off the fire, and a second patch burning around a corner. Stoop under the pipes.

Gunning down both Gunships takes a few good hits (as many as 14 direct strikes to rid yourself of both on Hard difficulty), but it's important to succeed in this battle. The pieces of the second Gunship strike a gas cylinder on the upper balcony near the control room, blowing a large chunk of wall clean away and allowing you inside the prison. Stock up on items in the control room before you enter.

Head around the corner, out of the hot pipes, and wait for the Antlions to catch up now that the fire is out. Unfortunately, a violent rumble sounds through the corridor and pieces of the prison ceiling rain down behind you. This blocks the Antlions from following, and your exit is also blocked, forcing you to head down a darkened corridor. Welcome to Nova Prospekt Prison Level A3.

TIP

During combat, keep Antlions close; use them to soak up cannon fire from the Gunships by crouching near them, in partial cover.

HλLF-LIFE²
PRIMA OFFICIAL GAME GUIDE

NOVA PROSPEKT

OVERVIEW ▌ The feared gulag, where some of humanity's most hated killers and ne'er-do-wells spent their final days, has become an even more horrific place since the Combine took over. The Combine is slowly rebuilding the facility into its own prison of death and torture. Featuring a train track directly from the station where you first disembarked, Nova Prospekt is a gloomy, desperate, and deadly place. Your task here is to wind through the corridors, engaging any Combine forces you encounter and using your new-found Antlions in close combat or shock troops to soak up enemy fire. Fight through the various cellblocks to your final destination: a meeting with Alyx Vance.

INVENTORY PICK-UP

- Sentry Gun (hostile)

ENTITY ENCOUNTER
FRIENDLIES

- Antlions
- Alyx Vance

ENTITY ENCOUNTER
HOSTILES

- Headcrabs
- Sentry Guns*
- Barnacles
- Fast Headcrabs
- Antlion Guards
- Combine Soldiers
- Manhacks
- Dr. Breen (via video feed)
- Stalkers (via video feed)*
- Combine Elite (via video feed)*

ENTITY ENCOUNTER
HOSTILES (continued)

- Poison Headcrabs
- Poison Zombie
- Zombie

* Indicates first exposure to entity

"THE CAPTURE OF ELI VANCE IS OF MAJOR SIGNIFICANCE, MAKE NO MISTAKE."

| MAP 42 | **NOVA PROSPEKT CELLBLOCK A LEVEL** |

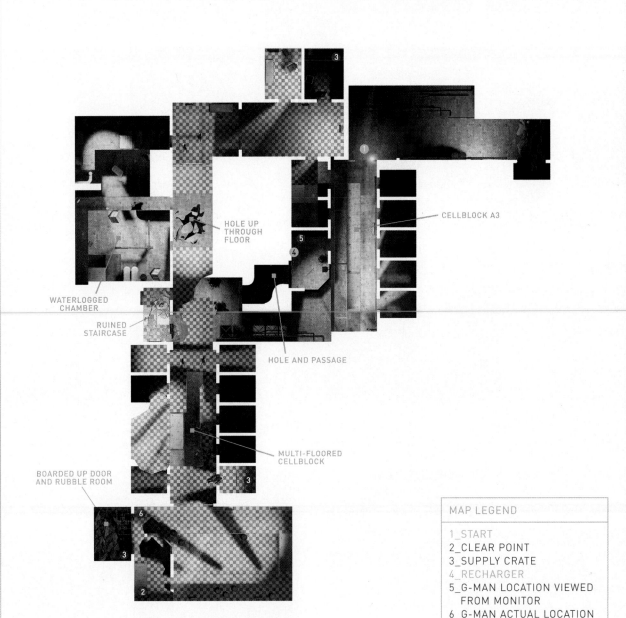

HOLE UP THROUGH FLOOR

CELLBLOCK A3

WATERLOGGED CHAMBER

RUINED STAIRCASE

HOLE AND PASSAGE

MULTI-FLOORED CELLBLOCK

BOARDED UP DOOR AND RUBBLE ROOM

MAP LEGEND

1_START
2_CLEAR POINT
3_SUPPLY CRATE
4_RECHARGER
5_G-MAN LOCATION VIEWED FROM MONITOR
6_G-MAN ACTUAL LOCATION

Go forward through the unlocked door. Move into the main cellblock for area A3 of the prison.

Move to the far end of the balcony and look across. There's a control room with a monitor displayed on it, and what looks like a stairwell. However, the area is fenced in.

Head down the stairs and inspect the cell under the control room on the left wall. A hole in the back of this cell is your only escape. Crouch-jump into the hole and arm the Crowbar to destroy the Headcrab. Use the Flashlight.

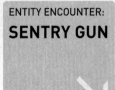

Scramble out of this hole and inspect it a little more closely. It appears to have been made by digging mandibles, not unlike an Antlion's. Drop into the control room, where you find blood on the walls and corpses on the floor: signs of a recent fight between a Combine Soldier and an unknown force. Follow the "exit" sign and step into a corridor.

As you move along this corridor, check the barred gate to one side to spot a small sentry gun device, not unlike those in the original Black Mesa Incident. Antlions prowling this area knock over the gun, and it unleashes a burst.

ENTITY ENCOUNTER:
SENTRY GUN

These tripod-mounted sentry guns have a 90-degree field of fire facing forward. These weapons are motion-sensitive; when they detect movement from organic beings, the machine guns atop the sentry mounting activate. Fortunately, you can topple them easily.

When facing such a device, use Antlions as fodder to soak up the gunfire, or use a barrel or radiator as a shield. Move to the side or around the back of the sentry gun and run into it to knock it over. Or, you can blast it with a shotgun, or pick it up and drop it. Make sure to pick it up with the gun pointing away from you! Once pushed over, a sentry gun fires a burst and deactivates until placed right-side up. You can also knock over sentry guns by using well-placed grenades or thrown objects. You can even carry sentry guns and use them to destroy non-Combine forces (but watch your Antlions!).

With the knowledge that your Antlion friends managed to tunnel into this complex, locate the stairwell and head up until the rubble and fallen ceiling make it too rough to walk. Leap up and through a bent mesh fence.

As you pass another cellblock balcony, you spot another sentry gun firing as a swarm of Antlions pounce on it and begin to clatter around the cellblock area.

Pass this barred gate, and look ahead; you're on the other side of the fence you saw when you entered cellblock A3, and you can now investigate the control room with the monitor. Check the control room for items, then fill up at the Health and HEV Rechargers.

TIP

When viewing the monitor, press E to flick between cameras, indicated by the green LEDs on the bottom right of the monitor.

G-MAN
ABOUT TOWN

View the monitor in the control room. Amid the other activity, a man walks to a side window near the double doors, adjusts his tie, and strides off to the right.

This man on the monitor is close by, but there's no chance of locating him. Continue to where you saw him by moving to the stairwell and climbing.

This checkered-floor corridor leads to a number of cells used for storage. Look for Supply Crates; the store room with the door on the floor is of particular interest. After resupplying, go through the barred gateway at the end of the corridor.

Two sentry guns are facing left as you step into this area. They fire at you only if you step in front of them. Run into them to push them over, or blast them with the Shotgun.

The only way to advance is to open the door on the opposite wall and head down to the basement area. Look at the ceiling to reveal a couple of Barnacles.

Save ammo by bringing out the Gravity Gun. Toss a crate or a barrel toward their tongues. When they pull it up, run under them to avoid the confrontation. Move up to the walkway across the flooded chamber, feed the other Barnacle, and exit via the doorway. Look for the rubble and climb up it through the ceiling to another part of the prison.

As you step out of the crumbling floor onto the upper level, watch for falling masonry from a skylight above as Fast Headcrabs (about four) drop to attack.

Step through the only available gate exit to the top of a three-tier prison corridor. If you run around this balcony, the way is blocked by a gate, and beyond is a balcony and two sentry guns that begin to fire. Drop to the second floor, ignoring the Antlions who pose no threat; these are usually cut down by the sentry guns in the room ahead.

There are signs everywhere of recent combat between Antlions and Combine Soldiers, including the remains of the trans-human forces scattered about the floor. There's nothing of real worth to collect on this floor or the lower cellblocks. Head to the mid level and exit via the open gate.

The best way to deal with this threat is to throw a radiator up into the balcony to knock over a gun. Repeat this for the second gun.

Climb the steps to the mid-level balcony and walk past a sentry gun disabled earlier. At the end of this walkway is a locked door; this is where you saw the G-Man on the monitor. Break open the planks to the left of the door and jump through the opening to a tight chamber of fallen concrete. Grab the items behind the door before returning through the window.

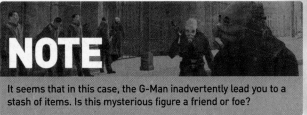

NOTE

It seems that in this case, the G-Man inadvertently lead you to a stash of items. Is this mysterious figure a friend or foe?

The only possible way to go is through a store-room door. As you step into the next area of the prison, a Headcrab leaps out to attack. Be ready for it, then throw the stack of crates blocking your exit out of the way.

"TURN HIM OUT, TURN HIM OVER TO OUR CAUSE!"

MAP 43	**NOVA PROSPEKT SHOWERS AND INTERROGATION CHAMBERS**

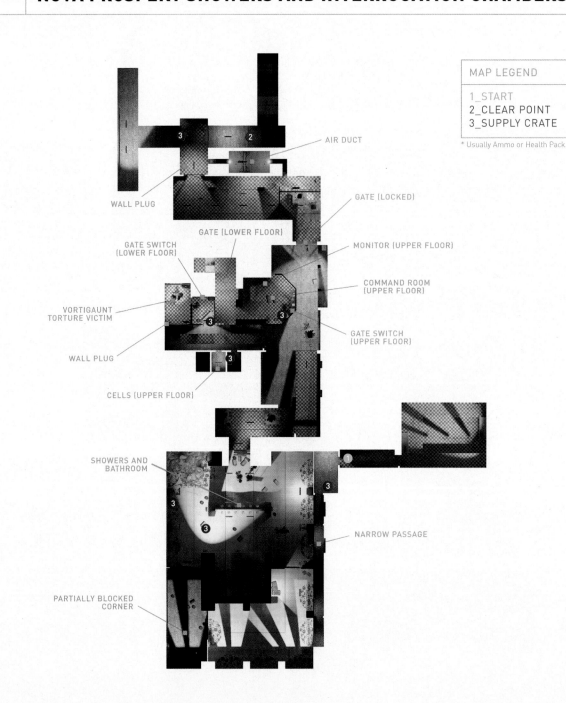

MAP LEGEND

1_START
2_CLEAR POINT
3_SUPPLY CRATE

* Usually Ammo or Health Pack.

AIR DUCT

WALL PLUG

GATE (LOCKED)

GATE (LOWER FLOOR)

GATE SWITCH
(LOWER FLOOR)

MONITOR (UPPER FLOOR)

COMMAND ROOM
(UPPER FLOOR)

VORTIGAUNT
TORTURE VICTIM

GATE SWITCH
(UPPER FLOOR)

WALL PLUG

CELLS (UPPER FLOOR)

SHOWERS AND
BATHROOM

NARROW PASSAGE

PARTIALLY BLOCKED
CORNER

Once you've battered through the boxes and crates, move along the walkway with the mesh wall on your right. Check the large washroom and shower facility to your right. Signs of a recent and bloody conflict stain the walls and floors. Be cautious as you zoom in using your suit, checking the floor for the remains of Combine Soldiers.

At the end of the upper walkway, drop onto the ground level at the corner of the large two-room shower. You have a second to react to a large lumbering entity lolloping in from the adjacent chamber (you can see it through the window of the door it smashes through). Time to run; an Antlion Guard is ready to buffet you with its gigantic sinewy head.

Flee to an area where there's partial cover, rip a radiator off the wall, and throw it into the beast's hide.

Combat can be frantic as you attempt to outrun this behemoth. Sprint to reach an area of partial cover. Keep moving, suck up exploding barrels after the beast finishes a charge, then blast them into your foe.

CAUTION

The explosive barrels are a fine plan when facing this foe, but don't forget that you'll be harmed if the explosion is too close. Don't suck up this item if you're about to be charged, or if the Antlion is nearby when you release the barrel.

To the far side of the shower room is a piece of broken wall leading to a storage room, which contains a few more exploding barrels. The Antlion Guard smashes through the opening and follows you in here; check the other hole in an adjacent wall and flee before becoming trapped here. Don't linger here.

Keep the fight around the wash basins, circling while keeping an eye on your foe. If you blindly run around, the Antlion Guard circles back to meet you; it's important to see it at all times. The radiators, wash basins, and toilets are all great for smashing into the beast and reusing. Continue this porcelain barrage, and after a dozen direct hits, the Antlion Guard falls.

After the combat, stagger to the double doors blocked by a variety of laundry carts, benches, and other items. Quickly remove them, open the doors, and escape this area.

HλLF-LIFE²
PRIMA OFFICIAL GAME GUIDE

TIP

You could have cleared this exit door of debris while dodging the Antlion Guard, but you would have been chased and trapped in the subsequent corridors, making it impossible to continue. Finish off the Antlion Guard in the wash rooms.

In the next corridor, pull out the bugbait. An Antlion hole is nearby, so call out a full compliment of them to do your bidding, and move to the gated entrance. Movement has been detected.

Ahead, Combine troops have placed two sentry guns at the far end, and a couple of Soldiers on the ground near the open gate near where you're standing. Another Soldier is on the side balcony on the right. Launch your Antlions by throwing bugbait at the Soldiers near the gate, then keep the Antlions occupied with the Soldiers and the Manhacks down a corridor to your left.

While the Antlions devour the Soldier on the side balcony, pick up a barrel (press E–don't use the Gravity Gun) and dash along the left covered passage. Step to the side of the sentry guns, then drop the barrel to knock them over. A third sentry gun is behind the barred gate, but you can't reach it yet. Avoid its fire as you run to the ladder leading up to the side balcony. Check this area for items.

With this initial corridor secure, it's time to finish the Soldiers down the side corridor. Keep summoning Antlions with bugbait as you incapacitate the Soldiers, letting the Antlions bare the brunt of the enemy forces and Manhacks. Use the Gravity Gun to suck Manhacks out of the air and toss them into walls or enemies. When the Soldiers at the energy wall are defeated, inspect the area.

You and your Antlions can continue once the energy wall has been deactivated. Suck the large plug off the left wall, and the energy wall vanishes. Step through into a small room on the right.

Check the wall of this small security room for three switches. Press the one under the red light, and a gate next to the security room unlocks, allowing access upstairs. Head out, around the security room, and through the open gate. At the foot of the stairs, turn to check on your Antlions; summon more and go up.

At the top, a short corridor leads to the gate control on your left. Step to the left side corner and throw bugbait to the end of the corridor. The first Antlion will cross a faint red laser line coming from a laser trip-mine planted on the left wall. Be sure your Antlion activates it, and not you! Then stay in this corridor and let the Soldiers inside the gate control room come to you, incapacitate them with bugbait, and let the Antlions do the rest.

TIP

There is no need to ever be caught by one of these laser trip-mines. Simply stay back, throw bugbait across the beam, and let an Antlion cross the beam, taking one for the team.

When there's one or two Soldiers left, dash in, and cover them in Pheropod matter. While the Antlions are savaging them, move to the window and press the button, changing the switch's color to green. The gate below you, in the first corridor chamber, slides open.

CHAPTER⁹
ENCOUNTERS

ADDITIONAL INVESTIGATIONS

Before you leave the gate control room, be sure to flick through the available cameras linked to the monitor in this chamber. It seems that a number of Antlion Guards are roaming this facility, and the Combine Soldiers are having a difficult time subduing them!

Exit the gate control room, head through the adjacent door, and investigate the top corridor above the torture room. Check the darkened cells for Supply Crates before dropping to the ground and moving to the now open gate.

The Combine has set up a rather unpleasant trap using three sentry guns. The first is ahead, in the far-right corner. As you step toward it, ideally using the Antlions as cover, you'll see more gunfire cutting down your crew from the left. Two more guns are firing from behind an energy wall. With Antlions taking the damage, pick up a radiator and rush around the left corner, then throw it into a sentry gun behind the energy wall. Suck it back and use it on the other.

The first of the three sentry guns can't fire at you from the energy wall, so deal with it when you please. However, there's no way past this energy wall. Smash open a duct on the ground in the right wall and crawl inside. Step out into an enclosed area with a huge ventilation fan.

The fan spins at high speed and will slice you if you attempt to crawl under it. Various cleaning implements are scattered above. Jam a bucket or broom handle into the middle mechanism of the fan until it stops. Then quickly crawl through the gap and into another duct. Bring out the Shotgun and blast the Soldier at the opening once the duct connects back to the main corridor.

Move out of the duct and suck the plug off the opposite wall. The energy wall you couldn't deactivate (now to your left) vanishes, allowing you to rendezvous with your Antlion posse. Bring them down the corridor, past a gate, into a side passage, and to the base of some stairs. Cellblock B3 is just around the corner.

"THE MAN YOU HAVE CONSISTENTLY FAILED TO SLOW, LET ALONE CAPTURE, IS AN ORDINARY MAN!"

MAP 44	NOVA PROSPEKT SHOWERS, CELLBLOCK B LEVEL

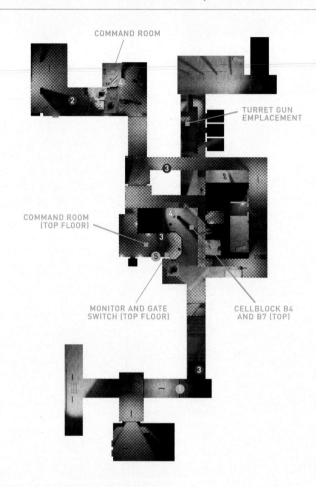

COMMAND ROOM

TURRET GUN EMPLACEMENT

COMMAND ROOM (TOP FLOOR)

MONITOR AND GATE SWITCH (TOP FLOOR)

CELLBLOCK B4 AND B7 (TOP)

MAP LEGEND

1_START
2_CLEAR POINT
3_SUPPLY CRATE
4_OTHER ITEM/S*
5_RECHARGER

* Usually Ammo or Health Pack.

Prepare to enter the maximum-security wing of Nova Prospekt. A zone the Combine hasn't brought its architecture to yet, but still a maze of corridors with danger at every turn. Follow your flock up the stairs.

grenade, and throw a second bugbait up to the balcony, where another Soldier is attacking you. Subdue him, summon more Antlions, and let them finish the Soldier upstairs.

At the top of the stairs, survey the cellblock ahead and make two fast maneuvers. First, subdue the Soldiers on the ground ahead. Land a well-placed bugbait spore at their feet and let the Antlions do the rest. Second, step back to the left, behind partial cover away from the

There's danger up ahead, but if you can, ignore the Soldier manning the turret and stay along the left wall, throwing bugbait into the right side corridor and letting the Antlions deal with the waiting Soldiers.

Step back from the tripwire on the ground by the side corridor, and instead send an Antlion to detonate it. Then, throw bugbait at the gunner on the balcony above, at the end of this ground-level corridor. Antlions should swarm him, although you can switch to a Grenade and get the job done that way.

TIP

At this point, you can diversify your tactics. The preferred method is to minimize self-harm by sending Antlions to attack, but you have other impressive methods to use against groups enemies, such as the Pulse Rifle's secondary fire, a bouncing orb of energy that completely demolishes a foe. Try it here, if you haven't already.

With the gunner out of commission, summon more Antlions and head down the side corridor, watching your step at the end. Two sentry guns fire at you from this area. Step into cover, suck in an explosive barrel, then throw it down so it explodes and knocks over both guns.

At the end of the corridor, turn right and listen for the buzzing sound: Manhacks have been released. Switch to the Gravity Gun, and while the Antlions engage the Manhacks, suck in a Manhack, climb to the next floor balcony, rush the Soldier guarding the corner, and split him apart using the Manhack chainsaw technique. Wait for all Manhacks to be destroyed before continuing.

The gun emplacement at the corridor's far end has been recovered by the Combine. You're now on the second floor balcony, looking over

the ground you just covered. Begin your assault by stepping forward in front of the Antlions and picking up a barrel to use as cover. Throw it with the Gravity Gun at the Soldiers on the balcony itself, and dive right, into cover away from the gunner. Then emerge, and use another object to launch an attack on the gunner, knocking him out. Grenades also work well here.

Rush the gun emplacement, looking up past it to the top of the stairs and the next floor balcony. There's two Soldiers here, and before they can react, incapacitate them with bugbait. As the Antlions swarm them, throw more bugbait across the upper balcony you haven't reached yet, as Combine Soldiers appear from the right, across a walkway. As the Antlions fight them, hang back, or offer fire support from the turret.

Now you're on level B4. Avoid the walkway in the middle to your right for now; it leads to a closed gate dead-end with a sentry gun down a corridor to your right. This gate must be opened from a control room. Instead, spin around and take the open mesh door route, along a side corridor, sending an Antlion in first to set off the tripwire.

When you reach the end of the side corridor, turn right and check the barricades ahead. The Combine has been preparing for you. Create havoc by lobbing a Grenade down to the far end of this corridor, causing the Soldiers at the far end to flee. Switch to bugbait and launch an Antlion attack, paying special attention to the enemies appearing from the darkened cells to your right. Slaughter the four or five Soldiers using your Antlions and close-assault weapons if the Antlions are getting killed.

Round the right corner, moving into area B7, and head across the balcony staying at this level, then turn the corner. Across from you is the control room. Breen is rambling on the PA system. Go around, then head left, across the catwalk to the right of the control room.

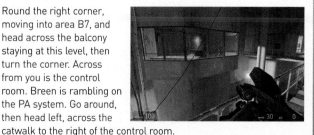

Watch your step as you round the corner. You're parallel to a gated area you can't reach. To open the gate, head down a path to the left, toward an open door. Sentry guns fire from it. Either send in Antlions to act as cover, or use a barrel, then slam the door shut—another way to stop a sentry gun.

Throughout your battles in the prison, Breen's voice echoes through the command rooms. Once the tirade has passed, use both Rechargers on the wall, check the area for items, and then press the control switch on the wall next to the monitor to open the gate area. Move to the balcony and deal with the Combine reinforcements.

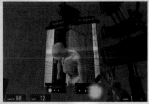

Now inspect the monitor. You're seeing the Combine Stalker and Elite for the first time!

With Combine forces in decline, return to the gate area and send in your Antlions to knock over the sentry gun. Then follow your swarm through the corridor to another control room.

CHAPTER '
ENCOUNTERS

"THE ALTERNATIVE, IF YOU CAN CALL IT THAT, IS TOTAL EXTINCTION!"

MAP 45 **NOVA PROSPEKT SHOWERS CELLBLOCK B LEVEL**

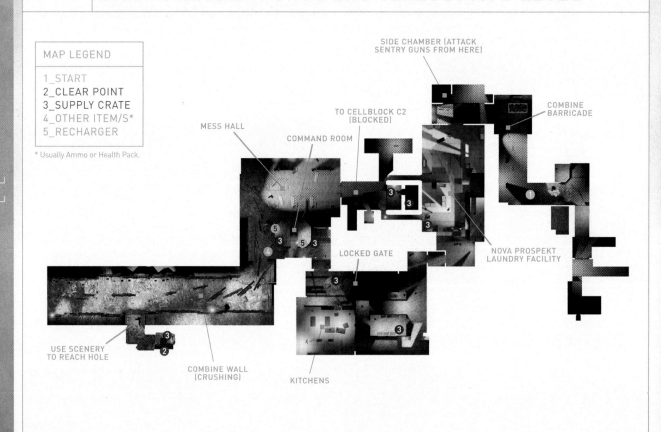

MAP LEGEND

1_START
2_CLEAR POINT
3_SUPPLY CRATE
4_OTHER ITEM/S*
5_RECHARGER

* Usually Ammo or Health Pack.

SIDE CHAMBER (ATTACK SENTRY GUNS FROM HERE)

COMBINE BARRICADE

TO CELLBLOCK C2 (BLOCKED)

MESS HALL

COMMAND ROOM

NOVA PROSPEKT LAUNDRY FACILITY

LOCKED GATE

USE SCENERY TO REACH HOLE

COMBINE WALL (CRUSHING)

KITCHENS

With your Antlion team assembled, check the control room to your right for signs of items, and while you're there, flick through the channels on the monitor. Study the movement in a laundry room up ahead; that's your next destination.

With your Antlions in front, head down the corridor and round the right turn, throwing out bugbait to immobilize the Soldier behind the bedding barricade. After the Antlions tear through any enemies, check the doorway to the left.

At the end of this long narrow corridor are two sentry guns. Avoid rushing or lobbing Grenades at these guns. Instead, throw bugbait at the sentry guns, let four or five Antlions rush in, then follow them in, letting them take the brunt of the sentry gun attack. Quickly sidestep to the right into a parallel corridor. Run to a small store room, open the door to the left, and you're behind both guns. Knock them over, then summon more Antlions.

The opening left of the sentry guns allows access to the prison's large laundry facilities. The Combine has considerable presence here, and it is important to deal with problems as you meet them, rather than charging in.

CAUTION

Your main concerns in the laundry room are Combine Soldiers on upper walkways at the far end of the room, and the sentry gun at the far area. The following tactics allow you to tackle these problems while sustaining minimum damage.

To minimize your pain, stay on the left upper area rather than the main lower laundry room. Throw bugbait at the Combine Soldier on this walkway, and let the Antlions devour him as you take cover behind a washing machine. Use Antlions to absorb the sentry gun bullets, then run to the gun, knocking it over quickly.

On the way, incapacitate the Soldiers to your right, near the large washing machines, and let the Antlions overpower them. Now under the upper balcony, look for shots coming from any remaining Soldiers on this level firing at the Antlions below. Turn around and fling bugbait at them.

When you've finished tearing apart the Combine Soldiers, check out the room to locate two narrow corridor entrances along the right wall. Enter this area, to encounter a small connecting chamber with a tiny store room stocked with Supply Crates. As you reach the crates, spin around and cut down the Poison Zombie ambushing you from a dark corner; defeat him and his parasite Headcrabs, then return to the laundry chamber.

After defeating the Poison Zombie, climb up the steps to the far end of the room. Make sure your Antlions enter the open door first. They clear a path and burst apart after treading on the laser trip-wire mine cunningly placed left of the exit. You're now in the main corridor to the kitchens; prepare for combat.

CHAPTER 9
ENCOUNTERS

Engage the enemy swiftly, but move past the first right-hand corridor, which ends at a gate with a sentry gun behind it. Instead, pull your Antlions into the lit corridor, so they charge and overwhelm the room with the soldiers. Forcefully charge in here, as the Combine forces will retreat once the area is overrun. Don't be caught at the initial dark area; press forward.

Remain in this well-lit corridor, and wait for further Antlion replacements to arrive. Force your way down the corridor to a darkened area, and check the windows as you go; two Combine Soldiers in a room to your left have spotted you, but the thick glass doesn't allow you to strike them. Push through to the end of the corridor.

Once through this door, the combat continues with you heading right, then into the room you saw Soldiers in. Antlions, quick Grenades, or Shotgun blasts do the trick here.

With the area devoid of Combine Soldiers, locate this doorway and enter it, following the corridor to the prison's main kitchens. Use the Antlions at your command to swarm in and overwhelm the two sentry guns. If they start firing, throw in bugbait and duck under the window.

Gas is escaping in these kitchens, and it is best to light the gas from behind partial cover of the windows than from in the kitchen itself. As the fire begins to spread, the Antlions may not be able to reach the far sentry gun. Lob a Grenade, or a secondary-fire Grenade from your SMG to sort out this problem. Leave through the hole in the wall.

As you emerge, ignore the laser trip-mine to your left and step into the courtyard area. Lob a Grenade to force the Combine Soldiers at the base of the stairs back up into a corridor you're about to breach. Send an Antlion to detonate the laser trip-mine, then move in toward the stairs, taking down Soldiers with your favorite ordnance or Antlions. At the top of the steps is a corridor to the left and a barred gate to a mess hall ahead.

The gate is locked, so move to the side corridor. The steps immediately to your right lead to a control room where the remaining Combine Soldiers are making a final stand. Send a few Antlions up there to even the score, then head up the stairs and finish off any remaining Combine Soldiers. Finally, look for items.

There's no way forward except through the open window to the right side of the control room. Drop down to see a squad of Combine Soldiers burst through the mess hall doors. Hold your fire, because they don't seem interested in you. Their frantic radio chatter indicates they're in the middle of fighting a larger foe. Soldiers go flying through the doors a split-second later.

An Antlion Guard bursts through the doors, and a Combine Soldier unloads his Shotgun into it. The beast lets out an ear-splitting roar and butts the Soldier into the wall, killing him instantly. It then turns and starts to engage the Combine Soldiers, about three of which are taking up defensive positions at the left end of the mess hall.

TIP

In this specific battle, the Combine Soldiers are actually more of an asset to you. Let them try to wound the Antlion Guard while you stay out of combat until all the enemies fall.

When the Antlion Guard has finally defeated the Soldiers (which can happen quickly), be ready to attack with one of the two main pieces of scenery in this hall: a radiator or an explosive barrel. Stay in this area, with the low wall between the support struts, and run around it so you aren't in the open while facing the creature.

The beast's incredibly tough skull is the most obvious attack to worry about; make sure you circle-strafe around its bony head so you aren't crippled by a connecting strike. Stay inside the mess hall. Don't venture down the corridor from where the Soldiers fled; this is a dead end (literally). Continue throwing items, like the radiator.

Keep the relentless barrage of radiator parts thudding into the Antlion Guard until it topples to the ground. Check the Soldiers' bodies and the concrete wreckage for items.

When you've finished gathering your goods, go through the open gate and maneuver carefully to what appears to be a half-destroyed wing of the prison. A gigantic Combine wall of metal is chewing and smashing the prison slowly and resculpting the area in its own darkened image. Head down the twisted steps, pausing only to blow apart a Zombie slumped at the base of the stairs.

This next part requires timing and accurate Gravity Gun use. Pick up a table from the concrete wreckage and throw it forward, then move to the middle of a rapidly thinning corridor with the Combine's harvester pincers to your right. As they slam down, shaking the ground around you, place the upright table (or a crate) below the opening above and left of you. Immediately leap up and into the hole as the Combine wall grinds your previous location into dust.

CAUTION

If you fail to place an object near the left side hole and clamber up and inside, you will enjoy a messy and extremely lethal death as you are squashed under the advancing wall.

Once inside the hole, bring out your Headcrab-killing tool of choice to deal with one that tries to scare you in the fiery rubble. Next, drop down among the broken pieces of cement and look for an opening in the wall leading to a darkened passage area. Head through this gap.

It looks like the Combine has constructed a gigantic prison. Up ahead, you see a figure at a computer terminal. Is that Alyx?

HλLF-LIFE²
PRIMA OFFICIAL GAME GUIDE

ENTANGLEMENT

OVERVIEW In the lower levels of the prison, you finally meet up with Alyx. She is proficient in close-quarter fighting, as you'll discover after battling through a series of control rooms. Alyx locates Eli, her father, sealed inside a frightful coffin-like pod. She programs the pod to move to the Combine's teleport room. The only other problem is getting you and Alyx there. Brace yourself for three hold-out battles where the placement of re-programmed sentry guns is just as important as a good aim. In the process, a traitor is revealed, and when the final teleportation chamber is breached, you're left behind! You must make a final stand and teleport back to City 17 to untie yourself from this entanglement.

INVENTORY PICK-UP

- Sentry Gun (friendly)*
- Sentry Gun (hostile)

ENTITY ENCOUNTER
FRIENDLIES

- Alyx Vance
- Doctor Eli Vance
- Doctor Judith Mossman?

ENTITY ENCOUNTER
HOSTILES

- Combine Soldiers
- Manhacks
- Headcrabs
- Fast Headcrabs
- Zombies
- Barnacles
- Combine Elite*

* Indicates first exposure to entity

"I CAN RECALIBRATE THE COMBINE PORTAL TO GET US OUT OF HERE."

MAP 46 | **NOVA PROSPEKT CELLBLOCKS**

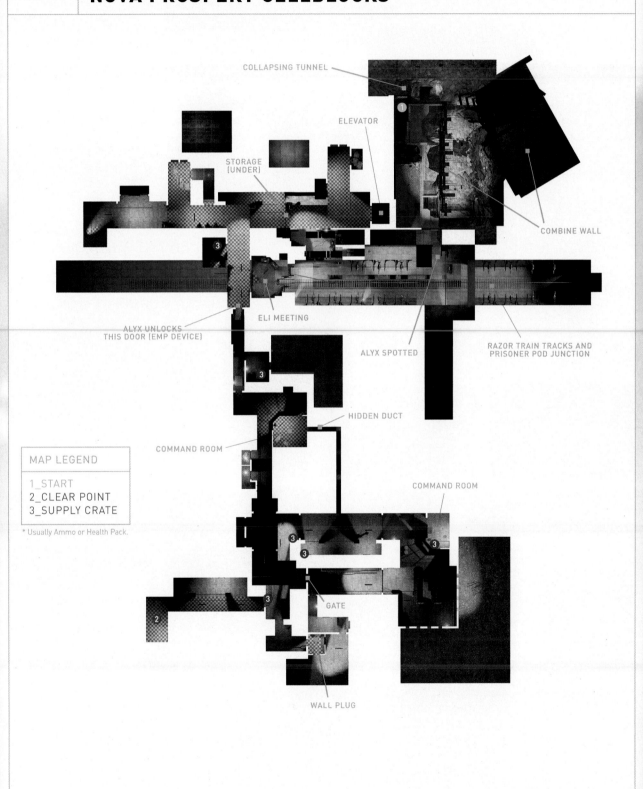

COLLAPSING TUNNEL

ELEVATOR

STORAGE
(UNDER)

COMBINE WALL

ELI MEETING

ALYX UNLOCKS
THIS DOOR (EMP DEVICE)

ALYX SPOTTED

RAZOR TRAIN TRACKS AND
PRISONER POD JUNCTION

HIDDEN DUCT

COMMAND ROOM

COMMAND ROOM

GATE

WALL PLUG

MAP LEGEND

1_START
2_CLEAR POINT
3_SUPPLY CRATE

* Usually Ammo or Health Pack.

CHAPTER ¹⁰
ENCOUNTERS

Walk to the end of the crumbling tunnel, and watch as Alyx finishes at the computer terminal and runs down the tracks. A giant train rumbles by. Jump to a small maintenance duct under the tracks.

Follow the duct along the underside of the tracks until you hear sounds of a scuffle. A second later, the crumpled body of a Combine Soldier falls through a gap in the grating above you. Alyx is dealing with threats above.

Clamber out of the duct via the ladder, checking above as you emerge onto the train track area. Follow Alyx as she leaps to a balcony and reaches a Combine lock and door. "My Dad's up there somewhere, in that holding area." She zaps the lock with an electrical scrambler and the shell-like door opens. Go inside.

You enter a storage room with little in the way of items. Alyx walks around to the right, heading for a freight elevator. She calls it down and steps inside, waiting for you. Draw a rapid-fire weapon of your choice. There are Soldiers to cut down as soon as you ascend a couple of floors. Look directly ahead as the elevator doors grind open.

CAUTION

Alyx Vance is a commendable ally, and an exceptional shot with her pistol. But don't forget she can fall under fire; make sure you're backing her up, and stay together (or clear the way ahead for her) in combat situations.

There's a couple of Soldiers to rampage through as you step onto the checkerboard corridor. Ignore the area to your right—it's free of enemies (but check it for supply crates after the battle). Instead, roll a grenade at the advancing enemies, then strafe them with SMG bullets, and bring them down while covering Alyx. Your objective is to cut down the Soldiers just inside the hole in the left wall. Another grenade, or rapid-fire shooting, is called for here.

Alyx steps into the hole and moves to a Combine computer terminal in a processing room. She hacks into the computer and cycles through the prisoners awaiting transportation. She spots the sleeping face of her father

and continues to fiddle with the terminal controls. A cell pod detaches from the main waiting wall and begins to move along a conveyor belt.

Check the tiny storage rooms for supply crates. An energy wall blocks your path when you return to Alyx's side, but she disables it and runs to the next corridor. Go up the staircase, looking left as you reach the top.

A Combine force greets you at the next energy wall to your left, at the corridor junction, and a wild firefight erupts. You can't seek cover and leave Alyx open to attack. Instead, rush the command post and bring down the quartet of Soldiers with a combination of your rapid-fire (or Shotgun) assaults and Alyx's single shots from her pistol. Move away from Alyx so the Soldiers have two targets to aim at, and catch them all in the crossfire.

You can't breach the energy wall the Soldiers were guarding, so the way forward is dictated by available exits. There's an opening behind you. Follow Alyx to a Combine door. Go in after you've checked the side doorways for supply crates.

Alyx is busy at the interrogation room computer terminal, guiding in her father's pod. Moments later, a black metallic sarcophagus arrives at the window, and opens. Inside is Eli Vance, trapped in some kind of restraining device. The Doctor is both thankful and annoyed at his rescue.

Before Alyx sends Eli to the teleportation room, he tells you that Doctor Mossman is in this facility, too.

While Alyx patches through to your suit via the prison security radio and maneuvers her father as close to the teleportation chamber as she can, locate Judith Mossman. Alyx unlocks the metal door back in the corridor. Move through, then blast the crates and other items blocking the stairwell in front of you. At the top of the steps, Alyx cuts through and appears on the monitor. You're at the first security post.

The area is disturbingly empty. Run along the corridor to the right of the post to secure supply crates and items from some of the side rooms, then return and enter the post room. There appears to be no way out, until Alyx mentions an alternate exit. Use the Gravity Gun to blast the two bookcases off the wall behind you and locate a hidden air duct. Break off the grating, crouch, and enter the duct with your Flashlight on, and your Crowbar swinging at the Headcrab duo inside.

Crawl through the air duct, dropping to a lower duct area and continuing until you reach a grate and a dark storage room. There's a laser trip-mine on the wall directly below you, so be incredibly careful not to fall. Use the Gravity Gun to grab a barrel, and drop it to activate the mine, backing up into the duct so you aren't caught in the explosion. Bring out the Crowbar and pummel the Fast Headcrabs from here–it's easier than dancing around on the ground looking for them.

Drop to the ground, making sure you aren't near any remaining Headcrabs. Look for any items in the room, then study the barricaded door to your right. Peer through, and you'll see two sentry guns pointing down a corridor you haven't reached. Lob a grenade through the open window and topple them.

NOTE

Taking out these sentry guns now means you don't have to deal with them when you reach this corridor later.

Go left around a corner to a second security post. Alyx cuts through the ether, and you can spot her patching a video feed into the monitors above the supply crate inside the post. Combine Soldiers are coming! Arm yourself for a confrontation. Try the Pulse Rifle's epic secondary fire if you want to impressively demolish your foes. Step into the dark generator room beyond to prevent the Soldiers from moving in here for an easy ambush.

Once you've taken out the four or five Soldiers, fight your way through the open gate and head along the corridor. At the first junction, execute the Soldiers you can see, but don't step into the junction until the way ahead is cleared of foes. To your left are another Soldier and two sentry guns. Lob a grenade to pitch both guns forward and then back up, blasting the remaining enemies.

Locate the narrow passageway shown here. Before the Soldiers around the left corner can ambush you, lob a grenade off the wall and around the corner.

Go around the corner, past the cover the Soldiers were using, and step through a doorway to the right, into an L-shaped room. An energy wall prevents you from moving too far into the chamber, but the Soldiers aren't affected by this problem, and promptly open fire. Take cover behind the wall to your right, and bring down the Soldiers one at a time with rapid-fire ordnance. Toss a grenade whenever a Soldier backs into the room beyond.

The energy wall is troublesome, but if you peer through the bullet-proof window, you can see the plug to unhook the generator powering the device. The problem is that you can't get a proper pull with the Gravity Gun. Instead, toss a grenade in there to dislodge the cable and pull the plug. Once you're inside the room, lob a grenade into the tiny pass-through chamber so it bounces off the far wall heading right, landing at the feet of a sentry gun. Roll the grenade if you're unsure of your lobbing prowess.

Ahead is a lengthy corridor with two sentry guns at the far end. This is the area you saw after you emerged from the duct. If you lobbed a grenade earlier, both guns should be out of commission. If so, simply leave via the left corridor. If you did not take out the guns earlier, pick up a large object to use it as cover. Dash forward and go into the narrow alcove, out of firing range. Punt the item you used as cover at the guns or lob a grenade to upend them both.

When both the guns are neutralized, stop at the entrance corridor to your left and smash open another supply crate. Walk to the gate, moving to the base the steps. You've battled your way to the first command security post.

CHAPTER [10]
ENCOUNTERS

"YOU WOULD HAVE HAD FREEMAN IF YOU'D JUST BEEN PATIENT AND WAITED FOR MY SIGNAL."

| MAP 47 | **NOVA PROSPEKT: COMMAND SECURITY POST** |

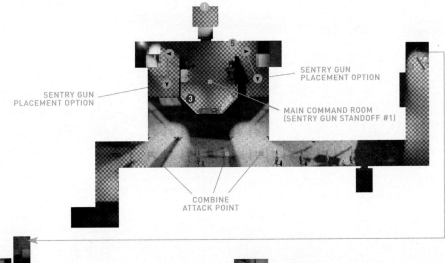

SENTRY GUN
PLACEMENT OPTION

SENTRY GUN
PLACEMENT OPTION

MAIN COMMAND ROOM
(SENTRY GUN STANDOFF #1)

COMBINE
ATTACK POINT

FLOODED
CHAMBER

COMBINE
ATTACK POINT

COMBINE
ATTACK POINT

SENTRY GUN
PLACEMENT
OPTION

COMBINE
ATTACK POINT

CELLBLOCK 08

COMBINE
ATTACK POINT

GATE (CLOSED UNTIL
END OF COMBAT)

SENTRY GUN
PLACEMENT OPTION

COMBINE
ATTACK POINT

MAP LEGEND

1_START
2_CLEAR POINT
3_SUPPLY CRATE
4_OTHER ITEM/S*
5_RECHARGER
●_SENTRY GUN
  DIRECTION

* Usually Ammo or Health Pack.

Force your way into the command post by throwing a grenade up the steps at the two Soldiers at the terminal, and drop them with quick-firing armaments as they try to escape. Check the left side of the post for a retreating Soldier, and bring him down, too.

Alyx radios in, letting you know a Combine attack force is heading your way. An energy wall is blocking your escape, so you have little choice but to repel the force. Use the two sentry guns in the cabinet to the right after Alyx re-programs them. Place them as shown in the following screen shots.

45-Degree Angle from the Wall, Pointing across the Right Stairwell

Overlooking the Right Side of the Command Post

45-Degree Angle from the Wall, Pointing across the Left Stairwell

Overlooking the Left Side of the Command Post

TIP

You only have two sentry guns, so the four recommended spots to place them are options. If you place the guns to the side of the command post, you can cut down Soldiers coming in from the energy wall and corridors behind it. However, some may make it to the stairwell, so you must physically guard the stairwell yourself.

INVENTORY ADAPTATION
SENTRY GUN

The sentry gun, although it has an unstable tripod base, is a definite bonus to have working for you. The key to placing sentry guns is to make sure there's a long line of sight, and to use its 90-degree swivel to cover the widest open area your foes will be maneuvering into. Always pick up a sentry gun with E, not the Gravity Gun. Otherwise, you won't have a weapon when you drop the sentry gun. You'll need that weapon to open fire on the targets the gun spots. Remember that enemy weapons (especially the shotgun) can knock the gun out of alignment. Accomplished players can shoot around corners carrying this weapon without being tagged.

Soldiers attack from the left corner (above) and the right corner of the corridor behind the energy field. Concentrate your fire on these two places. Flit between the two sides constantly to make sure your guns haven't been overrun.

If your weapon is placed too close to a stairwell or balcony and a Soldier manages to reach the top, he can knock the weapon down or off the balcony itself. Don't waste time rushing for it; suck it up with the Gravity Gun and replace it.

Play with the position of your stairwell sentry gun. Make sure it can aim at Soldiers as they ascend, but isn't so close to the railing that it can be easily swatted away.

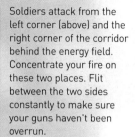

A few minutes into combat, look for a Soldier appearing on the far balcony, across from your position. He releases Manhacks into the fray. Take him down manually while the sentry guns concentrate on the Soldiers that refuse to retreat.

TIP

When a gun falls, pick it up from behind so the gun nozzle is facing forward. Grabbing it from the side or front means you must move to the side before placing it if you want it to face a certain direction.

Manhacks can knock over a sentry gun in seconds, so you need to deal with them quickly. Suck them in, blast them against the wall, or use them as impromptu chainsaws against Soldiers moving past a downed sentry gun. Keep this up until all Soldiers are defeated.

ADDITIONAL INVESTIGATIONS

Mossman appears to be in the middle of a conversation. Alyx's elation turns to shock as she listens in; Mossman's speaking with Breen!

Alyx must prevent Mossman from delivering Eli to Breen. She stays and attempts to disrupt the next level of security for you. Grab a sentry gun (use E to carry it), and pick the command post clean of items. Enter through the deactivated energy wall, and go left.

TIP

Although it's slightly unwieldy, make sure you bring a sentry gun for the rest of the prison investigation. There's bound to be a place where this extra firepower comes in handy.

At the end of the long left corridor is a door, partially obscured by a barricade of beds and boxes. Blast these away with the Gravity Gun and open the door, stepping through into a stairwell. Fire the sentry gun to the bottom of the stairs (don't worry, it's sturdy), and then rampage down to the bottom, knocking away all obstacles.

After untangling yourself at the base of the steps, use the Crowbar to batter the Headcrabs lurking in the storage room to your right. The confined space makes striking them difficult, so you may want to barge into the room and let the sentry gun do its job while you swat at any Headcrabs invading your personal space.

Check the storage room for items, then head out to a balcony overlooking a generator room. The ground level is knee-deep in water, the machinery on the left wall is sparking, and electrified cables dance across the water. Step or fall into this water, and you'll suffer nasty electrical damage; you can only survive for a few seconds. Before you descend the steps, use the Gravity Gun to shoot the sentry gun all the way to the far side of the room.

Move down the steps, but keep an eye (and your Flashlight) trained to the ceiling; there's a Barnacle to avoid. It's nestled on the path you'll need to take as you jump across the gap to a walkway on the right side of the room. Shoot the Barnacle, then position yourself over the gap and make a sprint-jump to land on the walkway.

Immediately start hunting for Headcrabs. A couple will leap out from the pile of boxes on the walkway; plug them with whatever weapon you wish (the crate makes an excellent killing tool as it blocks the Headcrabs when they try to jump at you). Head down to the base of the walkway and the water's edge. Don't fall in! Suck up the blue barrels from the corner of the walkway and the water, and start placing them in the gap between the walkway and the exit steps.

Drop the first barrel into the water near you, and jump onto it. Grab another nearby barrel with the Gravity Gun, and drop it in front of the first barrel. You can then either pick up a third barrel, or turn around and suck up the first barrel, flip around, and place this in the water in front of you. Do this until you can comfortably reach the exit steps. Use the Gravity Gun to reclaim the sentry gun.

HλLF-LIFE ²
PRIMA OFFICIAL GAME GUIDE

TIP

When standing on the blue barrels, jump and land on the very middle part of the barrel so you don't slide off, lose your balance, or start the barrel rolling.

The way forward is fraught with danger. As you open the door, you're about to be swamped by Zombies. Place the sentry gun on the ground first so it soaks up some of the attacks and cuts down Zombies. Then back up and start firing. By using the sentry gun, you might be able to survive the two chambers here without lifting a finger to your trigger. If you lose the sentry gun, bring out the Shotgun, and aim for the Zombies' heads at short range. Bring them all down efficiently.

Maneuver down the next stairwell with the sentry gun still carried in front of you. Get through the barricaded doorway by shooting the planks away with the Gravity Gun, and step through to a large cellblock.

Welcome to Cellblock D8, which now contains a new type of reprobate—the Combine Elite. There are two giant cellblock corridors, and a security station between them on the lower level. Stay on the upper balcony, listening for Alyx's instructions, and set the sentry gun to blast away at the few Soldiers on the upper balcony ahead and left of you. Inspect the security center for items, and then drop to the lower level. Combine forces are coming, and you must hold them off for a total of six minutes.

TIP

The gun placements shown below will ensure your success in this battle. Although this is the preferred method of completing this section of the prison, there are other (less cunning) methods that aren't explained here.

First, drop to the ground floor and check the sentry gun delivery pod area. There are two Rechargers to head to if you need them. Set up the sentry guns at the right side of the cellblock. The reason is simple—the left side has a balcony above the main corridor and you can easily be attacked and overrun from above. Not the case on this side.

The placement of the sentry guns is vital, and the optimum position is shown above. Be sure to bring the sentry gun from the previous confrontation with you, so you have four guns. Grab the three new sentry guns from storage, and set them up with one pointing at the energy wall at the end of the corridor, and the other covering the connecting passage to the other cellblock corridor.

Did you ignore the earlier advice to bring a sentry gun with you? Then place two sentry guns as shown, and the third at a 45-degree angle covering both the energy wall and connecting corridor; pay special attention to it.

About a minute after you place the guns, the Soldiers arrive in waves for a six-minute struggle. Arm the Gravity Gun, and side-step between both sentry gun sets. As soon as the Soldiers arrive, let the guns cut them down. Move the guns farther toward the middle of the corridor if the Soldiers manage to reach and knock one over. Grab it immediately and right it.

As you can see from the screen shot, the Soldiers love to knock the sentry gun slightly out of alignment. The right gun in this case is pointing to the left, enabling the Soldiers to head up through the connecting corridor. Adjust the aim immediately.

The two guns on the right side of the corridor fare a little better than the one on the left. They are farther from the energy wall at the far right end, meaning that most of the Soldiers are cut down before they reach the guns. They can still topple the sentry guns with shotgun blasts, so keep an eye on those guns. If a gun falls, pick it up and reposition it, making sure it's firing at the enemies even when you're carrying it.

As expected, the hated Manhacks appear during combat, and this is where the Gravity Gun comes in handy. Suck them in, and blast them into a nearby wall. Guard your sentry guns from these infernal devices; you're dead meat if those guns are out of operation for more than a few seconds!

After the six minutes of combat, the Combine literally has no more forces in the immediate vicinity to throw at you. Alyx arrives, dropping from the guard rail. Head through the open gate near the Recharger.

The two of you descend the steps to a long storage corridor with dim lights that flick off, one by one. The entire area is plunged into darkness. It's a trap! Grab your favorite weapon, and have at it.

"THE COMBINE USES A PECULIAR PULSE-FORMING NETWORK WITH A VERY LONG RISE-TIME..."

MAP 48 | **NOVA PROSPEKT: TELEPORTATION CHAMBER**

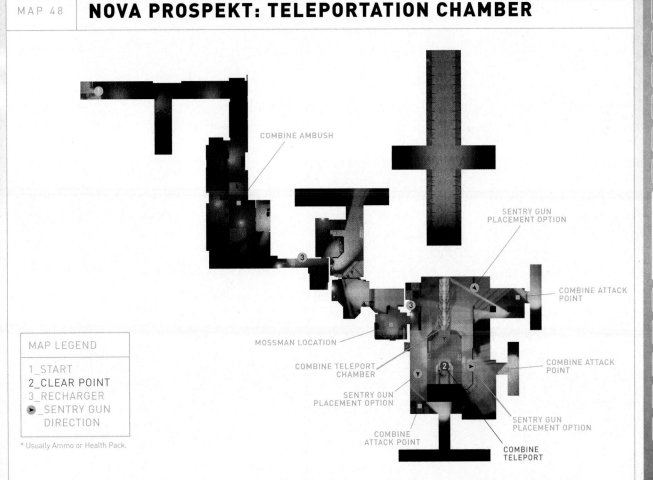

COMBINE AMBUSH

SENTRY GUN PLACEMENT OPTION

COMBINE ATTACK POINT

MOSSMAN LOCATION

COMBINE TELEPORT CHAMBER

COMBINE ATTACK POINT

SENTRY GUN PLACEMENT OPTION

SENTRY GUN PLACEMENT OPTION

COMBINE ATTACK POINT

COMBINE TELEPORT

MAP LEGEND

1_START
2_CLEAR POINT
3_RECHARGER
▶_SENTRY GUN DIRECTION

* Usually Ammo or Health Pack.

CHAPTER ¹⁰
ENCOUNTERS

ADDITIONAL INVESTIGATIONS

Mossman is working with Breen. Mossman tries to argue the opposite, but Alyx ignores her. "Shut up and be glad you're still some use to us," Alyx growls. "We're going to reconfigure this teleport and get the hell out of here!" Mossman reveals that she's already done that. She enters the coordinates for Dr. Kleiner's lab.

As red flares illuminate the ground, start hunting down and destroying those responsible. You won't need to look far. About a dozen Soldiers, in waves of four, are hidden in the packing hut to the left, the storage corridor to the right, and the area ahead and around the right corner. Blast them with any close-combat weapon, or throw an SMG grenade at a group when they are close together. The Pulse Rifle ricochet is another fine plan, as long as you aim it directly at an enemy to ensure a hit.

Eli's pod arrives, and Alyx runs to greet him. Alyx patches through on another terminal to Doctor Kleiner back in City 17. "We're in Nova Prospekt, and we're running the Xen emulation for the first time. Are you ready for us?" Alyx shouts into the terminal's microphone.

This next section of the prison is where Alyx and Judith Mossman finally meet up. Follow Alyx up some steps.

Alyx plans to send Eli through first, but Mossman slips into the teleport. Alyx radios Kleiner in panic. Kleiner hasn't received either of the doctors. "Oh my God!" she says with dismay. "What coordinates are these?"

Alyx remotely slams down security doors. Follow her as she takes off running.

After a ruthless double-cross, Mossman has left you and Alyx to deal with the incoming forces! Your only escape is via the teleporter, but the device requires minutes of recharging before you can leave. It's time to hold off the Combine one last time; start by placing the sentry guns.

When you both reach a huge blast door, run through it. Alyx stops on the other side, turns, and seals it. She leads you to the door of a control room. Inside the room, behind a viewing window, Mossman stands trapped, looking a little flustered.

NOTE

Unlike in Cellblock D8, it isn't imperative to have extra sentry guns for the combat to come. The three provided are all you need.

Place the first turret across from the main chamber, behind the glass window wall, in the corner near the junction. Place it so the gun fires at enemies coming in from both corridor areas left and ahead.

This screen shot shows the teleport's energy bank building back up. It takes a few minutes for the bank to fill with green material. As you move around the chamber, check its progress to determine how long you have left to fight.

Place the second gun between the steps (or even up behind the guard rail), between the two sets of low steps, facing the Soldier infiltration point (the door is closed in this picture).

The Soldiers are more likely to knock down your guns this time, usually with shotguns or grenades. Throw the grenades back with the Gravity Gun. Running around with a sentry gun firing is good only when you're picking it up; otherwise, use your arsenal of weapons to lay into the Soldiers. Keep control of the main corridor; that's your main objective.

Position the third gun near the energy wall opening to the right of the main teleportation chamber. Drop it a few feet away so the Soldiers are cut down before they can topple it.

TIP

You can try varying the location of the sentry guns, placing a few behind or on top of the guard rail.

Incoming! Stand at this junction, ready for combat. This corridor area is the busiest of the three. Make sure you've placed the first turret at an angle that allows it to cut down enemies appearing from this entrance, as shown.

Remember to pick up a turret with E, not the Gravity Gun, so it's easier to manage and switch back to a regular gun. With the sentry gun at this point, try placing it around the glass window, still pointed at the enemies. The Soldiers will attack from the now-open door and the passageway behind the teleport. This area is the most important to watch.

Run to the open teleport and step inside next to Alyx. The Combine forces break through your sentry guns as the teleport platform ascends, and a new, fearsome troop type clad in all-white attempts to shoot you down. They fail, and the teleport roars into life. Everything goes white.

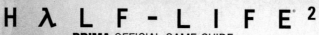

HλLF-LIFE²
PRIMA OFFICIAL GAME GUIDE

ANTICITIZEN ONE

OVERVIEW ▌ After discovering your teleportation ride has taken much longer than expected, a meeting with Doctor Kleiner reveals the Nova Prospekt escape has galvanized the resistance into an all-out rebellion across City 17. Barney Calhoun is in the thick of it, and while Alyx and the Doctor find shelter, you have the unenviable task of battling through the city streets to his rendezvous point.

Although Dog accompanies you, he is preoccupied with larger Combine forces and leaves your side early. You must then meet up with likeminded citizens, fight pitched battles through many tenement blocks and war-torn streets, and eventually meet up with Alyx, who needs protection while she powers down a Combine sector generator. After that, the rendezvous point is changed because of heavy Combine fire, and you disappear into the city's sewers. Welcome to the Street War.

INVENTORY PICK-UP

- Hoppers*
- Sentry gun turrets (hostile)

ENTITY ENCOUNTER
FRIENDLIES

- Alyx Vance
- Doctor Isaac Kleiner
- Dog
- Barney Calhoun (via video feed)
- Resistance Citizens
- Resistance Citizens (squads)*

ENTITY ENCOUNTER
HOSTILES

- Combine Soldiers
- Combine APCs
- Combine Dropships
- Scanners Type II*
- Metro Cops
- Striders
- Headcrabs
- Zombies

ENTITY ENCOUNTER
HOSTILES (CONT.)

- Sentry gun turrets (hostile)
- Manhacks
- Zombie Torsos
- Fast Headcrabs
- Fast Zombies
- Combine Elite*
- Dr. Breen (video feed)

* Indicates first exposure to entity

"WE'RE PLANNING TO TAKE CONTROL OF AN OVERWATCH NEXUS."

MAP 49 | **CITY 17: SLIDE THOROUGHFARE**

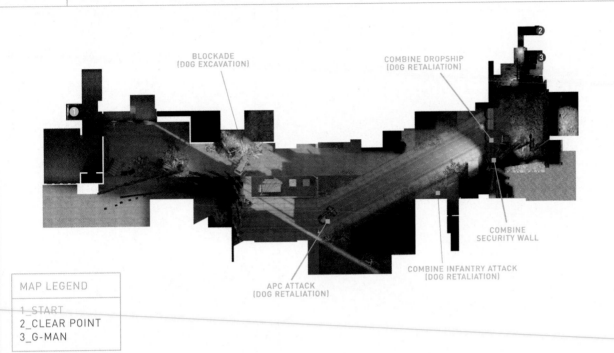

BLOCKADE
(DOG EXCAVATION)

COMBINE DROPSHIP
(DOG RETALIATION)

COMBINE
SECURITY WALL

COMBINE INFANTRY ATTACK
(DOG RETALIATION)

APC ATTACK
(DOG RETALIATION)

MAP LEGEND

1_START
2_CLEAR POINT
3_G-MAN

ADDITIONAL INVESTIGATIONS

The blinding white light of the teleport fades. Shockingly, the process was a success; you're back in Kleiner's laboratory. The greeting isn't the warmest you've encountered; the Doctor appears at the secret door brandishing a Shotgun! "My dear," Kleiner stammers, "I–I had given up hope of ever seeing you again." Alyx agrees telling him the Combine teleport exploded as you left, and Kleiner informs her of some shocking news:

"Indeed it did...and the repercussions were felt far and wide, but.... That was over a week ago! Fascinating." Kleiner muses, "We seem to have developed a very slow teleport." Alyx is more interested in the repercussions of your actions. "The blow you struck at Nova Prospekt was taken as a signal to begin the uprising!" the doctor informs her.

More troubling is the news of Eli. "According to the Vortigaunts, he is a prisoner at the Citadel, " Kleiner states. "Wallace Breen has undoubtedly been trying to extract information from him. And Dr. Mossman, I'm afraid...well, you were right about her." Hope isn't lost, though.

"The revolution is no longer a secret enterprise. Barney has been leading a push," the doctor tells her, "with her father's rescue in mind." Another friend of Alyx's has also arrived. Kleiner releases the storeroom door switch, and Dog rolls out.

Alyx makes a gleeful yelp. "I sent him here when I headed for Nova Prospekt," she tells Kleiner. "If we didn't make it through, he was supposed to help protect you."

Continued...

ADDITIONAL INVESTIGATIONS

At that moment, Barney appears on the main monitor bank. "Hey, Doc? Are you there?" he shouts.

"Yes, Barney," Kleiner responds, "and I'm no longer alone. Alyx and Gordon have just arrived. I believe they'll want to join your advance."

Barney sounds pleased, but a little frantic: "I'll take all the help I can get. We're planning to take control of an Overwatch Nexus and set up a staging area for attacking the Citadel."

"Gordon and Dog can head your way," Alyx tells Barney. "I want to get Dr. Kleiner somewhere safer, then I'll meet up with you."

Kleiner protests, then Barney cuts in: "If you head toward the Citadel from Dr. Kleiner's lab, there should be plenty of citizens who'll steer you toward our position." Suddenly, the screen crackles. "Oh crap... incoming!"

The monitor fades, and Alyx turns to you: "Okay, Gordon, you heard him. I'll catch up with you as soon as I've got Dr. Kleiner settled."

"Just a minute," Kleiner retorts. "I can't leave without Lamarr. Now where did she get to?"

NOTE

The Combine teleport explosion registered on Kleiner's seismographic printout, next to his computer. Check the huge anomalous reading!

Follow Alyx's advice, as the Doctor won't find Lamarr while you're in there (the Headcrab fears your Crowbar, as the doctor will tell you if you stay in his lab), so head out of the exit door, stopping to smash open Supply Crates on your right. Then drop down the elevator shaft.

Dog follows you down with a tremendous thud, unravels itself, and waits patiently. Step into the open street. You're now at ground level facing a pile of junked and burning cars blocking your way. Dog follows you, remaining at a respectful distance.

NOTE

You're now on the streets below the narrow rooftops ledges—the same ledges from the beginning of this adventure, after you escaped through the attic.

Dog picks up a wrecked van effortlessly, and pitches it forward about 50 feet at a couple of Combine Soldiers. Although Dog can handle himself, follow him up at a safe distance, dropping any stragglers your new bodyguard may have missed with his van toss.

Remain by the bodies of the slain Soldiers and watch as a Combine APC skids toward Dog, launches a rocket attack, and tries to escape. Dog lands on the vehicle's roof, flipping it over and raising it above its head. Dog lobs the APC into a second squad of Soldiers near the corner of a warehouse, crushing them all, and collapsing the building's corner.

G-MAN
ABOUT TOWN

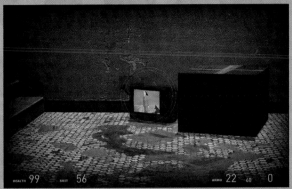

In the tenement foyer, zoom in on the television. A special program shows the gaunt gray-suited man who's been stalking you since the Black Mesa Incident.

If Dog is helping battle the Combine forces, your trek to the Combine Nexus should be straightforward and impressive to view! Dog moves to a Combine security barricade, twists the metal back, and creates a doorway for you.

The foyer is almost completely blocked with fallen masonry, a parasite rocket, and rubble. The only way forward is along a concrete-filled corridor to the right.

A Combine Dropship is zeroing in on you and Dog. Dog slams the wall back into place as the Dropship lands on the other side, trapping Dog with the Dropship and its cargo of Soldiers. Watch the top of the wall and you'll see Dog mauling the troops. Seconds later, Dog latches onto the Dropship's superstructure and begins to pound on it! The ship takes off, wobbling slightly, over the main Combine wall with Dog still attached!

Dog is gone, and the remainder of this trek occurs without the benefit of his help. Look to the left at the partially collapsed mesh fence. Try a running jump over the gap. Drop onto the tiny patch of earth and locate the large hole in the tenement block to your right. Step through the rubble to the entrance foyer.

"THE REVOLUTION IS NO LONGER A SECRET ENTERPRISE."

MAP 50	**CITY 17: MAIN PLAZA (REVISITED)**

MAP LEGEND

1_START
2_CLEAR POINT

CHAPTER ¹¹
ENCOUNTERS

SCANNER TYPE II

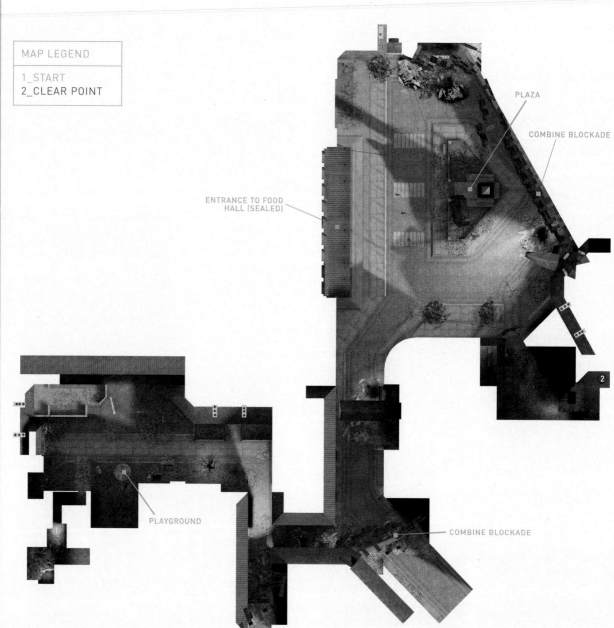

PLAZA

COMBINE BLOCKADE

ENTRANCE TO FOOD
HALL (SEALED)

PLAYGROUND

COMBINE BLOCKADE

Step out into a courtyard familiar from the start of your adventure. For now, swing right and look up; two floating Scanner are trying to cut down a citizen. Shoot down the objects so they explode, then run to the wounded citizen. Welcome to the street war!

ENTITY ENCOUNTER:
SCANNER
CIVIL PROTECTION TYPE II

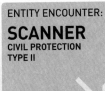

The Scanner features a quick-firing machine gun and the usual blinding searchlight. They have multiple purposes: attacking citizens, carrying mobile mines known as Hoppers, or simply searching for undesirables. Shoot these out of the sky before they can drop any cargo. Scanners drop batteries; check the debris for batteries for your HEV suit.

Retrace your steps to the train station. The streets are more chaotic, with the Combine fighting human insurgents at almost every turn. The way forward is blocked, so take a left, then another left under the connecting bridge, now fallen under heavy gunfire.

Step out into the main plaza. A few citizens are attempting to topple the large Breen monitor from its moorings on the central column. They succeed, and the screen comes crashing into the plaza, shrouding the area in dust. They immediately greet you, and join your cause! Point them (with ⓒ) at the small Combine gate ahead and right of the column. When two Metro Cops investigate the disturbance, have the team bring them down.

ADDITIONAL INVESTIGATIONS

During the uprising, Breen's rambling on the monitors around town is short-lived because citizens are silencing him. Listen to it if you find a television playing the message.

Shoot or punt the televisions with the manipulator to silence this blathering madness.

INVENTORY ADAPTATION
CITIZEN TEAMATES

Throughout your assault on City 17, dozens of citizens are willing to join and fight with you. They automatically join you, up to a maximum of four, and unpleasant as it might be, they are mainly useful for scouting ahead and absorbing fire.

There isn't a complicated scheme for ordering your team about; just aim your target reticle at the location you want the team to move to, and press ⓒ. Once there, they attack and act independently of you until you call them back. Use them to scout areas so you don't come under fire or take damage in an ambush. Finally, remember to read up on the "pincer" maneuver you can attempt with them later in this chapter. Medics and ammo-carriers can give you items when you talk to them, just like before in New Little Odessa.

HλLF-LIFE²
PRIMA OFFICIAL GAME GUIDE

"REFUSAL TO COLLABORATE IS A REFUSAL TO GROW..."

| MAP 51 | CITY 17: STREET WAR (TENEMENT ALLEYWAYS) |

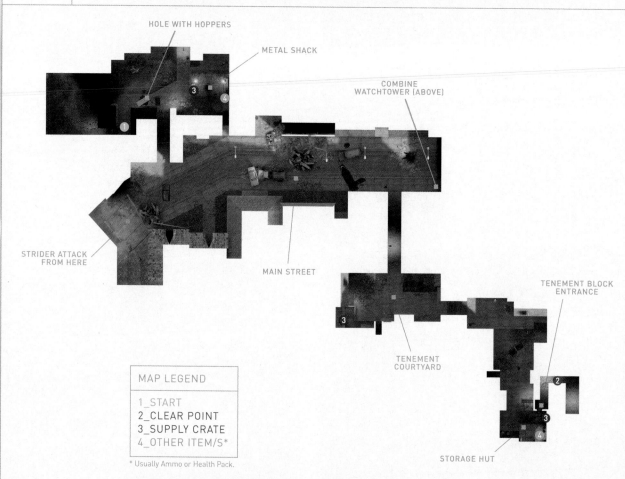

HOLE WITH HOPPERS

METAL SHACK

COMBINE
WATCHTOWER (ABOVE)

STRIDER ATTACK
FROM HERE

MAIN STREET

TENEMENT BLOCK
ENTRANCE

TENEMENT
COURTYARD

STORAGE HUT

MAP LEGEND

1_START
2_CLEAR POINT
3_SUPPLY CRATE
4_OTHER ITEM/S*

* Usually Ammo or Health Pack.

CHAPTER 11
ENCOUNTERS

Once the Metro Cops have opened the gate for you, rush up some steps and left around the side of a tenement block. Turn right and head out onto an upper walkway next to a lower grassy area. You're told by a nearby citizen to watch out for the Hoppers.

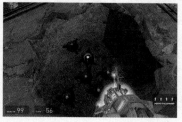

Remove the corrugated sheet metal to find Hoppers, a cluster of strange, minelike devices. They are used for and against you during this attack. Suck them up one at a time, then punt them away so they explode.

INVENTORY ADAPTATION
HOPPER

Hoppers take their name from their proximity attack, which is to "hop" toward a target and then explode. These mobile mines are usually concealed by Combine forces, but can be appropriated for your use against them. The color of the device is most important; red Hoppers are active, and will hop and attack you. Yellow hoppers are primed and ready to launch, so be extremely careful around these; suck them from the ground, and with your Gravity Gun handy, use them as grenades to launch at enemies. Blue Hoppers are "friendly" models, which you can set by dropping on the ground. Finally, green Hoppers are friendly mines set by you or your team. Watch your step; always clear away Hoppers before securing an area.

Drop into the hole after removing all the Hoppers, and move across the yard. Watch for more Hoppers, punting them away from you. Go up around a shed, pausing to detach a television so the hated Breen cannot be heard. Exit the shed.

Step through a narrow alley to a cobblestone street. Before you reach the end of the alley, a huge explosion rocks the area. Watch as two Striders maneuver around a city block, cutting down resistance forces. Ignore these entities; you can't fight them right now.

With the powerful Strider still fresh in your memory, turn left and quickly tag a Combine Soldier on a lookout post with a crossbow bolt.

Look up at the incoming Scanners carrying Hoppers to reseed the battlefield and rain down on your team. Shoot them from the sky and collect the batteries they drop. Suck up the Hoppers to punt them into enemy Hoppers lying on the ground ahead or Headcrabs lurking at the far end of this street. Clear the area of these pests, and with your team in tow, head down the alley to your right. Punt a Hopper into the alley to clear debris and an enemy Hopper before you enter.

The end of this alley leads to a small courtyard surrounded by tenement blocks. While your team deals with any Cops coming in from the ground level on the left, punt a Hopper up to the tenement window ahead, taking out a Cop.

Send another Hopper or explosive barrel (or Grenade) into the shed to the right; a Cop is hiding in there, along with some items.

Finally, if your team hasn't dealt with another Cop in the open window on the left tenement block, send an explosive barrel or Grenade up there to finish the job. Now walk left, down a set of steps.

At the base of the steps, turn right and immediately secure the Hopper that was about to leap and detonate the barrels. Then step out onto the open walkway and turn right.

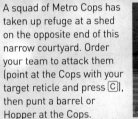

A squad of Metro Cops has taken up refuge at a shed on the opposite end of this narrow courtyard. Order your team to attack them (point at the Cops with your target reticle and press C), then punt a barrel or Hopper at the Cops.

When one or two Cops are left, rush the shed and gun them down, taking care to watch for Hoppers in the yard. Search the shed for ammunition, then load up with a Shotgun and enter the tenement building door in the left wall.

MAP 52   **CITY 17: STREET WAR II (COMBINE BARRICADE)**

TENEMENT BLOCK
(LOWER FLOOR)

ITEMS IN
BASEMENT LEVEL

TENEMENT BLOCK
(UPPER FLOOR)

TENEMENT
ENTRANCE (UPPER)

MAP LEGEND

1_START
2_CLEAR POINT
3_SUPPLY CRATE
4_OTHER ITEM/S*
5_RECHARGER
6_MAGNUM
7_SMG'S

* Usually Ammo or Health Pack.

COMBINE
SECURITY WALL

SWITCH

EXIT FROM
BUILDING (ABOVE)

INSIDE BUILDING
(UPPER FLOOR)

MAIN STREET

INSIDE BUILDING
(LOWER FLOOR)

TENEMENT BLOCK

UNDERPASS   STRIDER SIGHTING

When you enter the tenement block, head up the main stairs for items or citizens to help the cause. There's one at the first landing, watching television!

Ack! He appears to be decomposing! In the kitchen, a Zombie has been waiting to ambush you. Using your Shotgun, or the watermelon on the kitchen counter, destroy the Zombie and check the room for items. Then move into the other room, prepped for another Zombie to drop. Collect the ammunition, and then return to ground level and the street.

Use this exit, and carefully peek outside to survey the destruction. To the left is a large Combine barricade and a large hole in the ground; that way is blocked, and it would be suicidal to run in that direction. Ahead and right, a Strider maneuvers in another part of the city, cutting down unseen citizens. Ignore this monster; it's too far away.

Instead, look up at the floating Scanner about to drop a Hopper in your lap. Blast it out of the sky, then punt the Hopper away from your team. It isn't wise to carry it with you where you're going. Step out into the street, turn right, and run quickly to the area beneath the partially collapsed freeway overpass. Look for the small campfire where citizens tend to a wounded member. Grab the Health Pack here.

Once you've finished checking the underpass, check out the building ahead. The front is sealed with Combine metal. Check the doorway on the side. Head down the steps, turn left, and check out the

basement storage room. Amid the debris are some Supply Crates to feed your inventory appetite.

When you're done in the basement, head back out with your team, and instead of returning outside, look for the stairs leading up the right wall. Continue upward, because the ground level leads nowhere. Stop at this landing.

The Combine is active in this building, and the Cops are using it as a base. Use the "pincer" maneuver to catch Cops in a crossfire. To attempt this, leave your team outside the landing, run to the end of the first corridor, and blast the Cop opening the door once you turn around. Then summon your crew; Cops are coming in from a side corridor, and you can blast them from behind while they concentrate on your citizens. Or, you can always roll in a Grenade as you enter, into the room behind the glass doors.

With the firefight over, check each room carefully, including the bathroom and torture chair, for Supply Crates. Use the Flashlight to make sure you don't miss any in the dark. Then head through the exit.

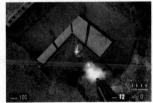

Step out onto the upper room that's been partially demolished in countless firefights. Look out on the street below; the Combine barricade is to your right. Bring down the Cop emerging on the opposite side of the street, then peer down the hole in the corner of the room. This is where you're heading next. However, there's an explosive barrel and two hidden sentry guns waiting to trap you in a massive explosion of crossfire. Shoot the barrel. This shatters the windows and knocks over both guns.

Drop onto the ground level, and if any sentry guns remain, quickly knock them down. Then step out and focus on the barricade to your right. The longer you remain here, the more enemy gunfire you'll attract. Stay in cover near the car frames, and perhaps tag one or two Cops, but then you must dash to the opposite side of the street. The plan is to ambush the barricade guards from behind their cover.

The barricade is yours. Check the street you just came from, and if any citizens are stuck on this side, use the switch on the barricade to open the doors and let them in. Refill at the Health Recharger, then step up onto the barricade ledge. Swing left, plug any Cops waiting in this area, and then enter the yellow building.

Step around the wreckage of a half-destroyed building and into a burned room. Immediately bring down a Cop on the opposite side of the chamber, then deactivate the Hopper before it explodes. Check the area for items.

Execute a sweep of the floor in this building's interior, using your team to help you blast the Cops in the rooms. Bring each one of them down, search the room for items, and continue to the next. Pay special attention to the Cop behind the table cover, as he can drop a couple of your teammates if you don't back them up. Don't rush through this Cop-flushing task; methodically check each room.

Move toward the location of the slain officer and turn left into a landing of another tenement block. Destroy the Hopper at the base of the stairwell, or it wounds you and your team. Head up a floor, bringing vigilante justice to another Cop on the way.

TIP

Another good tactic is to send in your Shotgun-wielding teammates first, then run down the main corridor right to the end, turn around, and catch enemies in crossfire while you retrace your steps. Use this plan in all the tenement corridor confrontations.

On the next floor are some Supply Crates. Refill, then look to the floor for means of escape. Drop through the hole to ground level, but on the Combine barricade side of the building.

Payback time! Exit through the doorway and immediately look up. A Cop is on the roof of the opposite building. Drop him with SMG fire or a Crossbow bolt. Then step out into the open, turning right, and gun down the Cops on the barricade. Bring out your team and slaughter the Combine now that they aren't in cover.

At the end of the corridor, steps lead up to a sentry gun. This nasty trap can cut down your entire team. If it activates, quickly launch a piece of scenery at it, or run up and push it over.

Instead, head downstairs to another corridor filled with Metro Cops. These don't stand a chance if you use Magnum or Shotgun blasts. Pay special attention to each room, making sure you aren't attacked from both sides, and take one room at a time. There's another Cop hiding behind a table. Save Grenades for later.

Go down one more floor to a basement corridor, where the Cops have the most troops deployed. This is a vicious firefight, and you will lose most of your team. In fact, if you're worried about self-preservation, order them into the corridor first. As you head down the stairs, blast the Cop behind the cover of the low wall, then roll a Grenade down the corridor.

At least three Cops attempt to stop you. If the action gets out of hand, use a side room and wait for the Cops to come to you, especially when they release Manhacks at your team. The Manhacks are an obvious weapon to use against the Cops. Suck one in, then either use it as a chainsaw, or punt it back at the Cops; the explosion kills an officer and the Manhack. Watch for Cops in ambush at every side room.

After defeating the Cops, inspect each room for goods, then exit to a sub-basement. There's a Health Recharger here. There is also a Supply Crate, along with two sentry guns facing right at the far end. Watch out; this is a trap. A third sentry gun sits in an alcove to your left, which activates as soon as you head in. Knock it over with your Gravity Gun, or dash left around its circle of fire and push it over. Then open the crate and use one of the two remaining sentry guns to open fire on a disgusting Zombie Torso that's devoured some citizens in the far area.

Go outside to a small area of roadway blocked by a gigantic Combine wall. Over on the opposite side of the street is something interesting to check out before you proceed.

LAMBDA
LOCATION

The citizens haven't forgotten your heroism, and have begun to place stacks of items for you around the city. These are behind a

sturdy fence, and you can grab them only by sucking and smashing the boxes with your Gravity Gun.

With a full complement of goods, return to the main road and locate the passageway leading underground to an underpass and a series of tunnels beneath the city. Look for the "Danger" sign; these stairs lead downward.

"LOOKS NASTY IN THERE."

MAP 53	**CITY 17: STREET WAR III (UNDERPASS TUNNELS)**

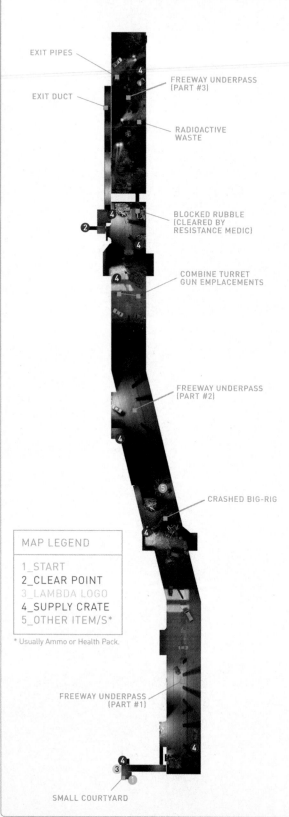

EXIT PIPES

FREEWAY UNDERPASS
(PART #3)

EXIT DUCT

RADIOACTIVE
WASTE

BLOCKED RUBBLE
(CLEARED BY
RESISTANCE MEDIC)

COMBINE TURRET
GUN EMPLACEMENTS

FREEWAY UNDERPASS
(PART #2)

CRASHED BIG-RIG

CHAPTER ¹¹
ENCOUNTERS

MAP LEGEND

1_START
2_CLEAR POINT
3_LAMBDA LOGO
4_SUPPLY CRATE
5_OTHER ITEM/S*

* Usually Ammo or Health Pack.

FREEWAY UNDERPASS
(PART #1)

SMALL COURTYARD

Follow the passage down and into a large, freeway tunnel. This is an excellent way of maneuvering across to Barney's position without overland combat. Turn right as you enter the tunnel, and you'll discover another team of fighters. Head down the tunnel.

Take point, and move first along either side of the tunnel. Use the Zoom function if you wish and check the distance; it appears to be devoid of enemies. This is good news. Hold on though; a Manhack has appeared!

As you reach the opening in the tunnel's roof, Manhacks pour in from the upper buildings, attacking you and your team. Quickly switch to your Gravity Gun and begin immediate combat with these devices. Suck in one and punt it directly into a wall, then repeat the process to subdue this invasion. Help your team out first; if they are being attacked, suck a Manhack away from them and finish the job yourself.

TIP

When attacking, stand with your back against the wall so you aren't sliced from behind, and you can quickly spin and slam the Manhack into the wall to quicken combat takedowns.

The Manhacks continue to fly until you've destroyed at least 24 of them, then the tunnel goes silent once more. With your remaining forces, trudge along to the remains of an accident involving an oil tanker and other vehicles, and wind your way through the refuse.

The only available exit is via a mesh door, but it is firmly locked. Unlock it from the ground with a Gravity Gun blast. Don't forget to let your team in.

The mesh fence area ends at a door. Go through into a narrow passage with a window to the right. Continue into a second tunnel. A few scattered Manhacks buzz about. Back up to the near end of the collapsed tunnel and deal with them. A sizable Combine force waits at the far end of this area.

LAMBDA
LOCATION

No sign indicates this area, so it is easy to miss; check the rickety barricade near the collapsed end of the tunnel for some badly needed supplies. Return here after the next fight if required.

Keep your team under control, or you'll lose them all in the tunnel with a full complement of Combine troops at the far end. Rush to cover behind the yellow car, and bring your weapon to bear on a couple of Combine Cops before they defeat your crew. Then step to the right side of the tunnel and peer ahead with the Zoom function. Use the central columns as cover if you're shot at.

From this extreme distance, you can see two turret guns manned by soldiers. These will severely injure your teammates, so have them stay back. Use a Crossbow headshot to pick off the soldier on the left, then charge forward and blast the explosive barrels stocked near the right-side turret gun, and take care of the second soldier.

As you run forward to secure the turret area at the end of another tunnel section, check the area above for another view of a massive Strider taking care of your comrades above ground. Again, your ability is limited, so ignore this beast.

In a moment, Combine reinforcements will arrive, but for now, check the fallen freeway blocking your path. A medic on the other side recognizes you, and says he'll blow a hole for you to enter. Hold off the enemy until then.

A squad of Manhacks approaches backed up by a few Combine Soldiers, attempting to defeat you and any of your remaining team. Prevent the Manhacks from overrunning you by manning one of the turrets and blasting all Manhacks that swoop in. If you're attacked from behind, switch to your Gravity Gun and back up to the partial cover behind the gun, near the Supply Crates.

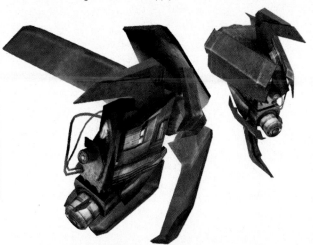

CHAPTER ¹¹
ENCOUNTERS

All that remains is to secure the area, and that involves flushing any Combine Soldiers you didn't cut down with the sentry gun. Flick on your Flashlight and demolish any hiding Soldiers, then return to the medic's location. He's removed enough debris for you to maneuver into a subsequent chamber. However, he tells you that the door is firmly locked to the outside, and can only be opened from the other side via an expedition to the next tunnel area.

Even if you're high on health and ammo, you still need to leave quickly. Look for the half-submerged car and jump onto its hood.

Head through the tunnel. A tanker has spilled its load, filling this section with knee-deep slime that destroys you in moments if you land in it. The only option is to step along the objects floating in this mire. Watch your footing; the car roof sinks into the ooze as you step on it. Quickly jump right, onto the crates. Then jump onto a spindle.

From this car hood, leap onto the side of an upturned truck, and remain up here. Look down to see more Zombies clawing out of the ooze. They can't climb, but they can hurt you if they swat a barrel at you. Now tag them at will. Then check the left wall for the exit.

NOTE

Look to the walls, and you'll see a tally of Combine Cop kills a past citizen has scrawled on the wall. Alas, he's certain to have died in this disaster!

Although pointless, you may find yourself at the far end of this tunnel stretch, surrounded by nothing except rubble and Zombies. Watch out for ooze, too. Reach the white car's roof quickly.

Leap from the spindle to a small area of sturdy ground. Then leap to the center of the tunnel, onto firm ground between two support pillars. As expected, the ooze parts and Zombies begin to swarm you. Bring out your boomstick and cut down any foes near your location. The Zombies continuously appear, so if you're low on ammo, use the Gravity Gun to slam the car axle against Zombies.

From the white car's roof, look for the rusting pipe sloping down to your location. Run to the top of it and stoop, then crawl to one of the three duct gratings on the right side and break one open. Drop down, landing in a blue corridor that's safe from the hordes on the other side. Run to the far end, open the door, and free your team. Lead them up the steps to street level.

"WHAT'S THE PASSWORD?"

MAP 54	**CITY 17: STREET WAR IV (TENEMENT BATTLE)**

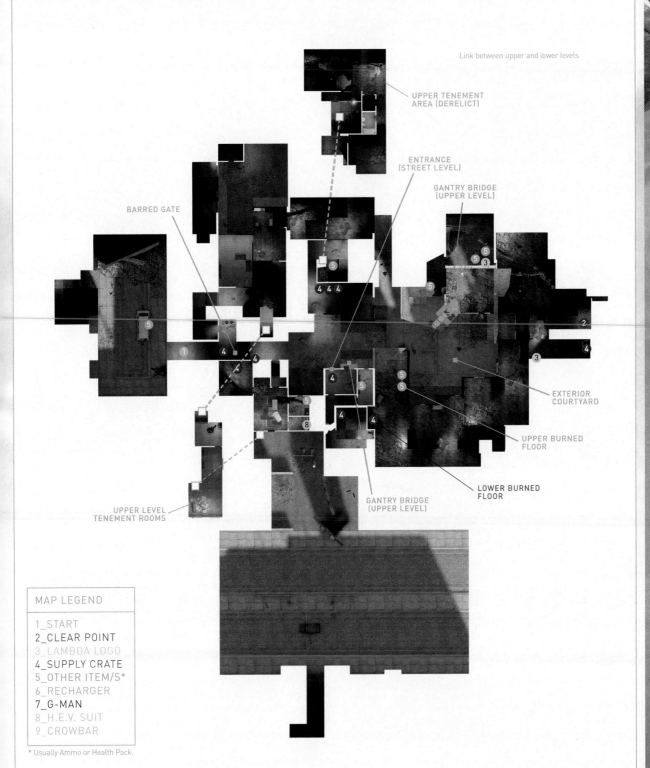

Link between upper and lower levels

UPPER TENEMENT AREA (DERELICT)

ENTRANCE (STREET LEVEL)

GANTRY BRIDGE (UPPER LEVEL)

BARRED GATE

EXTERIOR COURTYARD

UPPER BURNED FLOOR

LOWER BURNED FLOOR

GANTRY BRIDGE (UPPER LEVEL)

UPPER LEVEL TENEMENT ROOMS

MAP LEGEND

1_START
2_CLEAR POINT
3_LAMBDA LOGO
4_SUPPLY CRATE
5_OTHER ITEM/S*
6_RECHARGER
7_G-MAN
8_H.E.V. SUIT
9_CROWBAR

* Usually Ammo or Health Pack.

At the top of the stairs, there's barely time to move into the small courtyard before parasite rockets explode around you. Fast Headcrabs pour out; deal with them at once.

Continue through this second apartment, checking the kitchen for goods, until you locate the room with missing flooring. Immediately drop onto the Supply Crates. A Combine wall greets you. Head out and down, then across to another apartment, where two citizens huddle together. They may be little help, but their kitchen is well stocked; grab the Grenades in here!

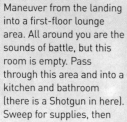 

Flee the area by heading down the open alley, and you'll face a citizen behind a barred gate, next to a Supply Crate. Open the crate as citizens in the background run across a drawbridge. Head up into the first tenement block, taking care to deal with the Headcrab menace on the landing.

Maneuver from the landing into a first-floor lounge area. All around you are the sounds of battle, but this room is empty. Pass through this area and into a kitchen and bathroom (there is a Shotgun in here). Sweep for supplies, then move across to a second apartment, where a battle rages on outside.

Leave quickly; you're looking for the stairs down to the doorway shown here. Outside you're on the other side of the gate where you talked to the citizen.

ADDITIONAL
INVESTIGATIONS

As you pass through the lounge and into the kitchen, peer out the window to see a Combine Soldier squad firing at citizens holed up in the tenement block to your left. There's nothing you can do to help them.

Peer through a window at the second apartment overlooking the courtyard you're trying to reach below, and you'll see more citizens running across a drawbridge. Further along is another window, and a Strider is laying waste to rebel forces along another street you cannot reach.

Cross the small courtyard, checking the bars ahead. Behind them is an area you'll reach soon and a drawbridge visible at the top of another building. For now, head into the last open doorway, meet up with some teammates, and dispatch a Combine Soldier at the base of the building's stairs.

Move into a small and partially destroyed room, gunning down a Soldier standing in the doorway, and claim the Supply Crate goods inside. Then return to the stairs and head up. Arm a close-assault weapon to use on Combine Soldiers who are throwing down citizens and executing them. Retaliate swiftly, then continue up as high as you can go.

TIP

You can save the two citizens on the stairwell from being executed if you're quick!

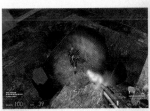 

At the top of the stairs, look across the landing for the open doorway and head through it to a burned-out floor. Do not drop through until you kill the Soldier below. Once on this level, head into the room with the open ledge overlooking the courtyard and drop the Soldier stuck in this area. Smash the Supply Crate.

Check a nearby side room for extra ammunition, then wait for the citizens to holler a password to their friends at the other side of the open ledge. A drawbridge quickly lowers, allowing you to access the opposite building. Run across quickly.

Once on the floor of the other building, exit via the doorway, and move along a series of 90-degree turns down some steps to a central stairwell, and then back up to a burning parasite rocket blocking your path. At the top of the stairwell, break out your favorite Fast Headcrab hunting tools. A couple are loose in the doorway; use your Flashlight to ferret them out.

As soon as you enter the blackened cement of the wrecked room beyond the doorway, turn right and look out. A Fast Zombie is ready to pounce on you and your team. Defeat it, then move to another hole in the ground, drop through, and immediately brace for another Fast Zombie. This one is on fire.

Drop through to another blackened chamber, then blast a couple of Fast Headcrabs as you step out to the base of the stairwell you couldn't maneuver through earlier. There's a Health Pack inside the elevator to grab, and a final few Headcrabs to squish.

Finally, move past the elevator and stairwell toward an open door. Pause to inspect a huge cluster of crates; this should increase your ammo levels.

Step out into the final courtyard in this cluster of buildings; you're on the other side of the second barred fence. Attack a couple of Combine Soldiers, being extremely careful to deactivate a Hopper mine. Check the rooftops for signs of Soldiers firing down, and use a Hopper to clear any foes. Finally, look to the green tenement building. The open door is your way out of here.

NOTE

Another exit takes you back to the building with the two huddled citizens, which is necessary backtrack if you failed to grab all the items.

A single Combine Soldier waits for death inside the burned shell of the green tenement. Cut him down, stride inside, then make a sharp right turn to an area of complete collapse. Strafe the Fast Headcrab bouncing around this area, then step into the room and up the rubble to an upper level. A welcoming committee awaits.

LAMBDA
LOCATION

At the top of the half-demolished building, a group of citizens stands near an opening in a wrecked wall, guarding items for your ongoing combat needs.

Be wary of stepping out onto the open rooftop of the building; scan the left side for a balcony where a Soldier moves, then across the drawbridge gap for two or three Soldiers, and a couple more Soldiers on the far rooftops ahead to the right. Take each down in a clockwise circle, using the wall parts to your right as cover. Then press the switch, bring down the drawbridge, and wait for enemy Soldiers to storm across. Fire an SMG grenade into the doorway or as they maneuver over.

Once the coast is clear, dash across the drawbridge to the balcony on the building opposite, and then peer through the door. Use the Magnum or Shotgun to blast the Soldiers in the burned room beyond. Grab the items on the right wall before dropping to the next level to take care of another Soldier.

Now continue down to the bottom floor, clearing the way for your team to drop down too (although you can send them in first). Shatter the Supply Crates in this area after dealing with another Soldier threat, then take the doorway into a maze of blackened corridors. At the next doorway, engage in a shoot-out with two more Soldiers.

If you can reach the end of this right wall corridor, look into the room below for a large combat between the undead and Combine. Throw a couple of Grenades to finish the action early, then back up; a couple of Fast Zombies come after you. When the undead are downed, you can drop into the hole, watching for Zombie Torsos or remaining Headcrabs, and quickly exit to a narrow corridor leading to a T-junction with a large spray-painted resistance logo.

To negotiate this wreckage, hug the right outer wall and have your team steam through the middle of this chamber so you can ambush a Soldier. Drop through a hole to another level, where there's a more open area with Soldiers running about beyond the debris you're hiding in front of. You could use Grenades, but it's easier to engage the enemies head-on.

LAMBDA
LOCATION

This one is in complete darkness. Before you exit this area, move up to the grating, and switch on your Flashlight to peer into the darkness. Bring out the Gravity Gun and suck the crates to the grating, then destroy them and suck back the goods.

To get past the debris, carry on, then turn and head up some steps to an open roof area. Be extremely careful; a couple of Barnacles hang from the ceilings around a blind corner. Blast them before you or your team are strangled, then search for an upper room with a Fast Zombie in it. Deal with it, then check the floor for a large hole.

You're almost out of this burned building. Move to a more intact area, and search the corridors for a stack of Supply Crates before moving into a room with another gigantic hole in the floor.

Peer down the hole; there's usually a two-Soldier squad firing back up at you. Fire an SMG Grenade to level them both, or just savage them with gunfire and drop down. This area is dangerous; when you reach the right-side corridor, lob a Grenade to the far end. You can also watch the flaming Zombies and Combine forces battle each other, then deal with the survivors (almost always the Zombies).

From this room, you can hear two sentry guns fire on a variety of rotting animated corpses. Wait until the Zombies are dead, then stand on the edge of the hole, suck up each sentry gun, and drop it on the floor you're standing on or down to the ground so it deactivates on its side. Don't fall through the floor, or you'll be cut up as the sentry guns activate again!

"IT IS FUTILE TO CRY FOR MOTHER'S MILK!"

MAP 55 | **CITY 17: STREET WAR V: (GENERATOR PLAZA)**

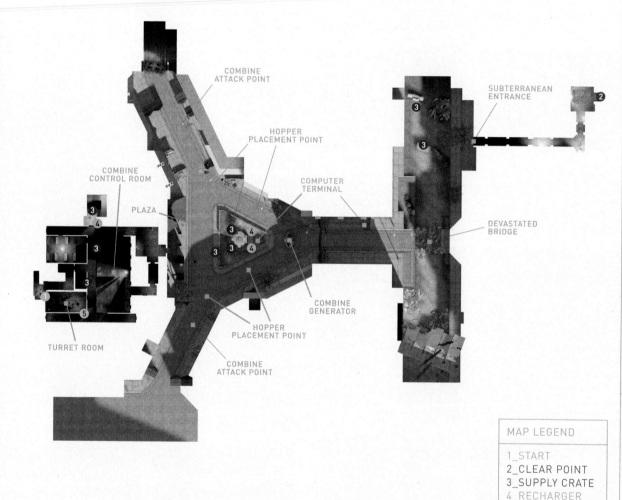

COMBINE
ATTACK POINT

HOPPER
PLACEMENT POINT

COMBINE
CONTROL ROOM

COMPUTER
TERMINAL

PLAZA

SUBTERRANEAN
ENTRANCE

DEVASTATED
BRIDGE

COMBINE
GENERATOR

TURRET ROOM

HOPPER
PLACEMENT POINT

COMBINE
ATTACK POINT

MAP LEGEND

1_START
2_CLEAR POINT
3_SUPPLY CRATE
4_RECHARGER
5_ALYX APPEARS

When the guns are out of commission, a side door opens and Alyx appears. "I've got Dr. Kleiner in a safe spot. Now we can join up with Barney!" she breathlessly announces. "There's a command center downstairs. I'm hoping to find information about generator locations."

If you have any teammates left, order them down the corridor you're not heading through. Then burst into a large sitting room with a couch and a trio of Combine Soldiers. Bring them down as your crew enters via a side door to cut them down, although you and Alyx can usually handle these troops yourself.

The rest of this area must be secured, so be prepared for a Soldier at each doorway as you pass through. You're heading for an open doorway to a small room with Rechargers on the far walls. Before you reach this point, make sure you've collected all the items you want from this floor; you won't be heading back here.

Enter the Recharger room, dose up, and go down the stairs. Prepare a Grenade for the Soldier standing between you and the Combine control room. As he backs up, blast him, then wait for Alyx to reach you.

Alyx and your teammates are positioned at two separate doorways. If they charge through the same narrow space, the Combine Soldiers in the control room beyond will concentrate their fire. As you step inside, cut down Soldiers in your firing line before stepping in to help Alyx (her pistol is deadly, but your machine guns are faster).

NOTE

You can wait by the doorway and let Alyx finish all the guards inside, but only try this if you're low on ammunition and pride.

With the Soldiers bleeding on the ground, Alyx steps up to the main monitor and checks it. "Well, we're in luck," she says, "there's a generator in the square outside. We're trying to disable as many as we can to loosen the Combine's grip on this sector. It'll take me a few minutes to expose the core, then I'll need you to hit it with a burst from the Gravity Gun." It seems like a reasonably solid plan. Take the new citizens who have arrived to the doorway leading to the plaza. Alyx has a simple request: "In the meantime, watch my back."

Dash out into the square. At the back of the triangle of grass is the generator, which houses a number of crates and Hoppers. Alyx swiftly moves to the generator and hacks in. Behind the square is the exit barricade you're trying to open. To the left and right are alleys with energy walls. Expect Combine resistance from these two areas, but only after you tag the Metro Cops up on a lookout post and in the square.

You have about a minute before Combine Dropships arrive with squads of Soldiers to disembark and rush your position. Do not let this happen! Increase your odds by locating all the available Hoppers in the area. Carry one across the right side of the plaza and place it on the ground by some wreckage at the narrowest point near the cybercafe (on your side of the wreckage so the Soldiers can't see it).

Then place the next one by more debris near the widening of the alleyway into the plaza. During this time, a Dropship flies high overhead.

The Dropship is depositing its squad of Soldiers at the end of the alleyway you should have primed with two Hoppers. Now move to the opposite side of the square and lay a mine on the cobblestone path to the generator, then lay another Hopper near the refuse bin at the base of the sloping alleyway. With your RPG ready, rush back to the low-walled cover of the middle ground and wait for a second Dropship to descend.

TIP

Don't waste your ammunition firing on the Dropships as they descend; they are impervious to small-arms fire.

Either while you place the Hoppers or while you're waiting for the Soldiers to arrive, a Cop on an upper balcony releases a couple of Manhacks. Destroy all the entities immediately; a Crossbow bolt to the Cop's chest works well.

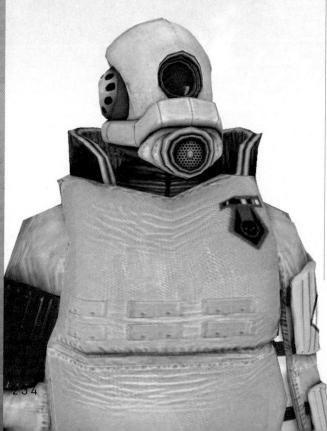

CAUTION

Although you wouldn't know it, the more enemies you kill, the more reinforcements arrive; this continues until the core of the generator is exposed. If you wish to save ammo, let your team do the fighting, and only act aggressively if a Soldier makes it to Alyx's location or is endangering a teammate's life.

TIP

During the battle, listen for Alyx shouting information to gauge how much more fighting is necessary:

"There goes the external shield": One-third of combat time is over.

"Inner shields are coming down": Two-thirds of combat time is over.

"That's it. The core is exposed": Back up and take out the generator!

Let the combat begin! Your job is to look down both alleyways and watch as Combine Soldiers attempt to maneuver down this path, using the debris and scenery as cover. Wait until they are at the near end of the alleyway (or you are under heavy fire) before returning fire. Make sure the Soldiers actually make it to the square's entrance so the Hopper explodes, and when the next wave arrives, hit them with rockets until they fall. Remember to switch directions. Toward the end of combat, Combine Elite, which you've only seen from a distance before, join the attack. A Hopper placed in the corridor to the generator sorts out the first wave of them.

TIP

Rechargers are available at the generator Alyx is working on, so move there quickly to replenish your health and suit.

ENTITY ENCOUNTER:

COMBINE ELITE

Clad in white armor and sporting a Pulse Rifle and a single red ocular sensor, the Combine Elite act in groups of their own kind, or sometimes lead squads of Combine Soldiers. Firing faster and more accurately than regular humanoid forces, they react to combat in a similar way to Combine Soldiers, and must be treated in the same careful and methodical manner. If you have a choice, deal with Elites before regular forces.

As Alyx finishes her infiltration of the generator's computer systems, the Combine attacks become more ferocious. The Hoppers are gone, so greet your foes with close-assault weaponry. Stay in the square and keep moving, dodging gunfire and dropping Soldiers and Elite. Note that each time an Elite falls, he drops Pulse Rifle ammo for the secondary orb fire. Use these to clear a number of enemies!

The combat should continue until most of your teammates are dead and any Combine forces heading for the generator area are defeated. Don't bother continuing to fight once Alyx calls to you for help; the stream of enemies is unending.

Once Alyx has shouted that the core is exposed, immediately arm the Gravity Gun and either suck the core orb out of there or blast it forward. As soon as you deactivate the core, the giant Combine wall barricade at the top of the courtyard swings open. You're still under fire, so immediately run through. It closes behind, allowing you a short breather; the Combine forces have been temporarily halted.

Alyx runs out to the rendezvous point to meet Barney. "Okay...Barney should be on the far side of that canal...." Alyx stops herself, realizing that the entire bridge area has been completely obliterated. "Well, there used to be a bridge here," she says before returning to a computer terminal to attempt to scout a new path. You have no choice but to drop into the dried-out canal bed. Alyx then disappears from view.

Alyx has disappeared, and there's no way to locate her. This is exceptionally bad news, but there's nothing you can do except continue looking for Barney. At the base of the dry canal, check the back of an old truck and near an overturned yellow car for Supply Crates. Then look for the brick sewer entrance in the opposite wall. The only way forward is down here, toward the barred gate.

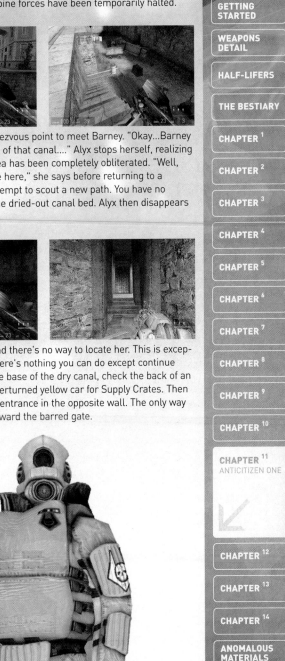

HλLF-LIFE²
PRIMA OFFICIAL GAME GUIDE

"FOLLOW FREEMAN!"

OVERVIEW ▮ The Street War continues and the tide appears to be turning. Your progress is made more frantic by the slippery floors of a sewer works and the climb through an industrial plant while attempting to locate incoming enemy fire. Assuming you survive, you appear back on the streets to meet up with Barney, but only after defeating a group of sharpshooters in snipers' alley.

The action continues as you and Barney progress to the city's museum, where a powerful suppressor cannon halts the rebels' progress. After dodging that fire, you enter the museum, shut off the three shield generators to reach the roof, down a Gunship, and turn off the suppressor.

Then you must secure the sky bridge. While Barney stays behind, you dash across the museum courtyard while fighting Striders. Next comes a claustrophobic rampage through an abandoned underpass and up through a parking lot; this leads to a final showdown in the plaza at the base of the Citadel. The Street War must be won!

INVENTORY PICK-UP

- Hoppers
- Sentry Turrets (hostile)

ENTITY ENCOUNTER
FRIENDLIES

- Resistance Citizens
- Barney Calhoun
- Dog

ENTITY ENCOUNTER
HOSTILES

- Manhacks
- Combine Soldiers
- Zombies
- Poison Headcrabs
- Headcrabs
- Barnacles
- Combine Elite
- Poison Zombie
- Fast Headcrabs
- Fast Zombies

ENTITY ENCOUNTER
HOSTILES (CONT.)

- Combine Gunships
- Sentry Turrets (hostile)
- Ground Turrets*
- Striders
- Combine APCs

* Indicates first exposure to entity

"GO AHEAD, DR. FREEMAN. BARNEY'S RELYING ON YOU."

MAP 56	STREET WAR VI: SEWERS AND INDUSTRIAL PLANT

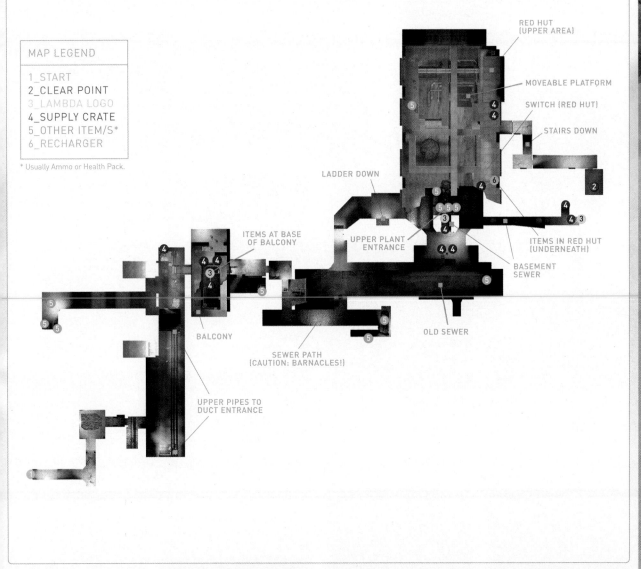

MAP LEGEND

1_START
2_CLEAR POINT
3_LAMBDA LOGO
4_SUPPLY CRATE
5_OTHER ITEM/S*
6_RECHARGER

* Usually Ammo or Health Pack.

RED HUT
(UPPER AREA)

MOVEABLE PLATFORM

SWITCH (RED HUT)

STAIRS DOWN

LADDER DOWN

ITEMS AT BASE
OF BALCONY

UPPER PLANT
ENTRANCE

ITEMS IN RED HUT
(UNDERNEATH)

BASEMENT
SEWER

BALCONY

OLD SEWER

SEWER PATH
(CAUTION: BARNACLES!)

UPPER PIPES TO
DUCT ENTRANCE

INTRODUCTION

GETTING
STARTED

WEAPONS
DETAIL

HALF-LIFERS

THE BESTIARY

CHAPTER 1

CHAPTER 2

CHAPTER 3

CHAPTER 4

CHAPTER 5

CHAPTER 6

CHAPTER 7

CHAPTER 8

CHAPTER 9

CHAPTER 10

CHAPTER 11

CHAPTER 12
"FOLLOW
FREEMAN!"

CHAPTER 13

CHAPTER 14

ANOMALOUS
MATERIALS

Open the barred gate to access a short drop down a brick gulley with a couple of Supply Crates at the bottom. Use the Gravity Gun to zap the crossbeam from a gate lock ahead, walk to the vertical planks, and blast them apart.

In this corridor, a trio of Manhacks attempts to cut you off. Introduce them to your Gravity Gun. Bars block the area ahead, so return to the original end of the corridor, and hop onto the pipes.

Keep your Gravity Gun handy and maneuver along the pipes. At the end of the corridor, a Manhack attacks from the left window. Destroy it, then head for the grating in the far wall and blast it apart. Scoot inside a duct, and take the left or right route around to the opposite side exit. Smash that grating open and drop down.

CHAPTER ¹²
ENCOUNTERS

Check the area to the left. You can hear the hum of Manhacks from a tunnel. Go in and destroy them as they tear through a barricade, then move to the end of the passage, where the remains of a citizen lie next to some items (usually an SMG). Move into the main corridor and check the stack of boxes on the high ledge. Suck the boxes off and claim the Supply Crate hidden here.

Step through the opening to the right, then be careful—you may be spotted by Combine Soldiers on an upper balcony. You're on a large stairwell balcony with a nasty drop in the middle. Blast the Combine Soldiers above, moving around the balcony as you do so. Then suck the Supply Crate and drop it at your feet before obtaining the items inside.

Continue down this balcony and stairs, dropping to the next floor and locating a Zombie near a broken balcony. Blast it down the stairwell. Walk around to the gap and drop to a lower area where you can see light from a side passage. A couple of Soldiers spot you. An SMG Grenade works well here. When in the balcony area, move to the light, and into the passage shown here.

LAMBDA
LOCATION

Below the balcony is a secret stash of Supply Crates left in a most precarious place. Look left and below, toward the rusting vertical pipe with the ladder on it, to spot the alcove with the goods on it, then jump onto the ladder (leap, then press E to grab the ladder). Go down and smash the crates, then return up the ladder.

In the illuminated passage, you find a locked door. A second door to the right is unlocked; open it and immediately train your gun around the right side of the door to plug a Poison Headcrab. A dead citizen is in the opposite corner; the Health Packs couldn't help him. Take them, and then peer through the window. A bar keeps the outside doors in the main passage shut. Suck the bar off the door and drop it.

It seems the sewer system is not under Combine control. Head around the corner and tear open a Soldier looking over a sewer channel. Watch from this balcony as Zombies attack a couple of Soldiers. One of them is grabbed by the neck, throttled, and sucked up into a Barnacle's waiting maw. Chaos reigns down here.

CAUTION

The dirt floor has a layer of scum and oily residue that causes you to lose traction as you move. Anticipate when to stop, because reactions are delayed on this surface.

Step to the right and around the corner to a dirt corridor with flickering side lights. A Headcrab leaps at you; dispatch it. At a junction farther ahead, two Barnacles hang from the ceiling. You can position yourself so a Headcrab leaps at you and is caught by the Barnacle's tongue, or just use a box as bait.

Investigate the far end of this corridor. There's a slumped body and a Combine Soldier attempting to ambush from the right side. Simply step back and watch the Soldier become entangled and yanked up into a waiting Barnacle; this saves on precious ammunition. Run around the right corner, up some steps to a dead end, and strike the support strut in the left-hand alcove to gain access to the supplies behind it.

Return to the middle of the side passage, feed a crate to the waiting Barnacle, and drop into the sewer water channel below. Or, you can destroy the Barnacle, wait at the top of the broken bridge, and strafe the Zombies without being harmed. When you've taken care of the undead, trek to the far end of the channel for a Health Pack before returning and heading into the square-shaped tunnel.

Step into this compact tunnel and strike down the Headcrab inside. To the left side is a ladder. Remember this, but continue through the tunnel until you reach another oily patch with a narrow double passage.

LAMBDA LOCATION

Enter the right side of the double passage and immediately check the right wall for a lambda logo. Hidden at the back of a tiny alcove is some ammunition. Use the Gravity Gun to suck it to you.

Be extremely wary! When you step onto the double passageway to inspect the Health Packs at the base of the lambda secret, a Poison Zombie appears. Close quarters and bad traction make this a frantic combat. Attack immediately.

Here's an odd occurrence: a series of pipes to bounce across, recounting the video game experiences you had as a youth controlling an Italian plumber. There's even a Headcrab between the second and third pipes that you can land on, and the attack kills it!

LAMBDA LOCATION

Cross the pipes to the end and break open your prize. There's another crate to your left, too. After restocking, return to the other end of the tunnel.

CHAPTER ¹²
ENCOUNTERS

Climb the ladder in the low-ceiling tunnel up a level, and then shoot a Poison Headcrab. Step out onto the upper walkway on the opposite side of the sewer channel and run under the archway back down to the sewer. There are two more Poison Headcrabs to smear. Drop to the Supply Crates in the well-lit entrance that leads to Pump Station 67. Slaughter the Headcrabs on the ground and inspect the middle passage ahead; a body holds a Shotgun and Health Packs.

Jump the masonry near the dead body and move into the base of a huge pumping chamber. Look up; that's where you're going. Walk up the slope to the tiny alcove left of the three small pipes ahead, and grab the Magnum shells stored here. Next, travel up to the sloping area near a red hut and look for a walkway across the other side.

Climb onto the walkway entrance on the opposite side to the red hut and walk down it. A second later, an explosion causes the walkway to crash down. Leap away and retrace your steps, then run and jump over the gap caused by the explosion. Hop the twisted mesh door at the end, and dive into the red hut for Supply Crates and two Rechargers.

You're being stalked by Combine Soldiers, and they have the height advantage. They appear from across and up on the other side of the chamber, or directly above you. Bring out your favorite weapon and flick the switch inside the hut. This brings a large cargo platform from the opposite side—the only way out of this predicament. Blast Combine Soldiers through the grating above you and across from you. Blow the explosive barrel off the platform before you run and leap on it, but keep a couple of barrels on the platform so you have some cover.

If you can, jump out of the moving platform into a nearby alcove to the right as it reaches the same level as some soldiers. From here, you can tackle the Combine from actual cover. After killing this group and before another wave arrives, run around the balcony to the far end of the pipe refinery area and locate the ladder shown here.

Climb to the top of the ladder and step out onto a mesh gantry just as the skylights disintegrate in a shower of glass and two Combine Elite rappel down to an upper walkway. You can't reach the walkway, so you must take out the Elite from your current position. Bursts of SMG fire or Magnum rounds do the trick. Then move along the white double pipes, turn right, and carefully run across the narrow girder, then up and left onto a side balcony.

Run across this balcony as more glass shatters above, and destroy more Elite. Aiming may be difficult under these circumstances, so continue climbing. Run across the balcony to the other side and locate the ladder on the opposite side of the pipe refinery. Climb it quickly to the top. From here, you're closer to the Elite (meaning you're also more susceptible to damage).

You have a lot of good options here: SMG Grenades, regular Grenades, peppering rounds of pulse or SMG fire, and shooting explosive barrels from the small stack to your left near the supplies. Defeat all enemies before you escape this area. Head down the ladder you just climbed, step onto a walkway halfway up, run to the other side, and smash open the two crates to the left. Then stop, look over the edge, and suck the Hopper out of the way so you aren't severely wounded by an explosion as you land on it.

With the Hopper detonated or hovering in your Gravity Gun's grip, head quickly down the stairs (you can exit with enemies still attempting to shoot you) and race to the bottom, where a rendezvous with Barney is finally near.

"DID YOU HEAR A CAT JUST NOW?"

MAP 57	**STREET WAR VII: SNIPER ALLEYS**

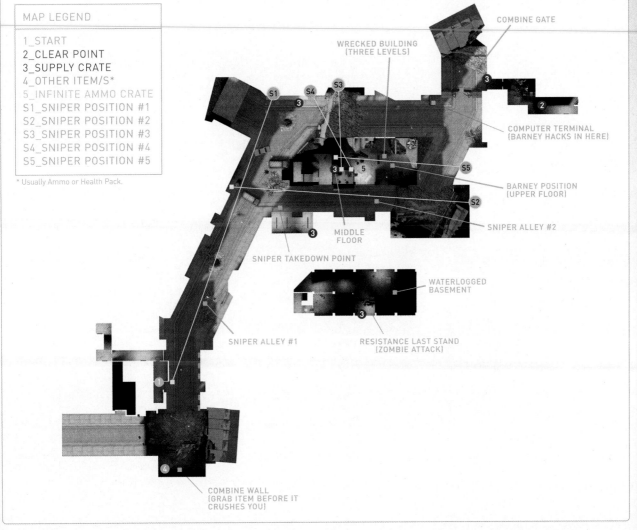

MAP LEGEND

1_START
2_CLEAR POINT
3_SUPPLY CRATE
4_OTHER ITEM/S*
5_INFINITE AMMO CRATE
S1_SNIPER POSITION #1
S2_SNIPER POSITION #2
S3_SNIPER POSITION #3
S4_SNIPER POSITION #4
S5_SNIPER POSITION #5

* Usually Ammo or Health Pack.

COMBINE GATE

WRECKED BUILDING
(THREE LEVELS)

COMPUTER TERMINAL
(BARNEY HACKS IN HERE)

BARNEY POSITION
(UPPER FLOOR)

SNIPER ALLEY #2

MIDDLE
FLOOR

SNIPER TAKEDOWN POINT

WATERLOGGED
BASEMENT

SNIPER ALLEY #1

RESISTANCE LAST STAND
(ZOMBIE ATTACK)

COMBINE WALL
(GRAB ITEM BEFORE IT
CRUSHES YOU)

The citizen at the base of the steps says, "You're Barney's old friend Gordon, aren't you? Maybe you can help him. Snipers trapped him on that warehouse - roof. He was going for a cache of explosives, but I guess he can't even get to them now. If you can find the Grenades, I'll bet you could get him loose." Words to live by.

Strafing at the last moment ensures the snipers never tag you, and this allows you to sprint to the truck at the end of the street. Move around it to the left, bring out your Grenade, and throw it into the open window shown in the screenshot. A second later, the Grenade detonates and the first Soldier sniper falls out. You can pick up the supplies from the crates at the end of the street, by his corpse.

ADDITIONAL INVESTIGATIONS

Throughout the Street War, Breen is still broadcasting, attempting to "reason" with you one last time. His rantings are saved for posterity: "I'd like to take a moment to address you directly, Dr. Freeman. Yes. I'm talking to you. The so-called One Free Man. I have a question for you. How could you have thrown it all away? It staggers the mind. A man of science, with the ability to sway reactionary and fearful minds toward the truth, choosing instead to embark on a path of ignorance and decay. Make no mistake, Dr. Freeman. This is not a scientific revolution you have sparked...this is death and finality. You have plunged humanity into freefall."

"Even if you offered your surrender now, I cannot guarantee that the Combine would accept it. At the moment, I fear they have begun to look upon even me with suspicion. So much for serving as humanity's representative. Help me win back their trust, Dr. Freeman. Help ensure that humanity's trust in you is not misguided and misplaced. Do what is right, Dr. Freeman. Serve mankind. Surrender."

Backtrack to the other alleyway on the right side of the street you came in from. Ahead in the distance is a building with four windows; the sniper is inside the open window second from the bottom. You can run the gauntlet, attempting to dodge him, or stand *exactly* by the storefront and aim at the top-most notch in the Citadel (see the second screenshot) and fire an SMG Grenade. The trajectory deposits the Grenade into the window.

As you pat yourself on the back for a takedown well executed, you're joined by a couple of citizens in this storefront. Ransack the place for Supply Crates before continuing down the sniper-free alley and into the open blue doorway to an office building.

As you head outside, turn right. A gigantic Combine wall holds some secrets. Sprint in and out of the Combine wall before it slams into the ground to grab the Batteries and other items, then return to the main street.

You're now at one end of a long, narrow street with a sharp-shooting Soldier at the other end. Just as with the snipers in Ravenholm, you must keep an eye open for their blue laser line, then sidestep out of the way when the line locks onto you.

A couple of Headcrabs and Fast Zombies lurch around in this gloomy area. Destroy them with your team's help, and then go to the wet basement.

Move to the lit barricade, where a badly wounded citizen gasps a message to you: "Help, help me! We thought we'd be safer down here. Little did we know the place was infested. The rest of 'em headed upstairs. They took their chances with the snipers. I guess they're still up there."

He isn't kidding about this infestation; stand and aim at the entrance with your team, away from the knee-deep water; as a half-dozen dead guys rise from this pool of filth. With your team covering each side, deal with any Headcrabs still alive after the Zombies fall. Continue to attack as Fast Zombies bound into the barricade. Cut them all down!

TIP

If the combat is too much, escape by smashing the wooden barricade to the left and diving into the water. However, you risk losing your team with this cowardly act.

As the Zombies lose their footing, step out toward the basement exit on your left and finish a couple more Fast Zombies that bound in. Climb the steps and open both the doors you couldn't access earlier; a citizen may be here to join you.

Continue up to the very top of the stairwell, which leads to a partially collapsed roof. You can't reach the upper floor yet, and there's a sizable Zombie presence here. You can see Barney crouching on the floor above; he's stuck. Don't make a move at the Zombies. A sniper to the left shoots down one of them, releasing its Headcrab. Deal with it, then mow down all the Zombies from cover.

With the undead defeated, step out to the right and throw a Grenade through the open window in the tenement block across from you. A second later, the sniper is blown out. You can now move into the collapsed roof area, pausing to gather more Grenades from the Infinite Ammo Crate, and zoom in on Barney. "Gordon!" he shouts. "I can't move—these snipers have me pinned down!"

Climb the remains of the steps to the upper floor. Some birds flap away, and a Combine Dropship hums low overhead, carrying a payload you haven't witnessed before: a Strider! This spells trouble ahead, but for now stay low and watch for another sniper in the same tenement block as the previous pest.

Once again, sidestep to the right and throw a Grenade at the easily visible open window shown here. There's no need to hold the button in. Just aim, throw, and wait for the detonation.

Now concentrate on the final sniper who's viciously blasting the area. To get into Grenade-throwing range, you must reach Barney's side. You'll be wounded by the sniper if you rush across small girder. Instead, grab the green cabinet and hold it in front of you (ideally without using the Gravity Gun), then cross the girder. The sniper's shots ping off the cabinet. Discard the cabinet and quickly lob a Grenade into the second window down from the roof, in the middle column.

That's all the snipers. Furthermore, you meet up with Barney. "It's good to see you, Gordon. It'll be good to have your help going into the Nexus up ahead." Barney calls other squad members to follow, and the team backtracks across the girder, optionally firing at any remaining Headcrabs hiding in the area.

CAUTION

Barney follows you for many battles to come and is an exceptional fighter. However, he isn't invulnerable, and the mission will fail if he goes down; only he can deactivate Combine terminals and open doors. If he complains of being wounded, stay close and protect him. Otherwise, use him to soak up enemy fire.

TIP

Restock with Grenades from the Infinite Ammo Crate before you drop from the building.

"Let's get going." Barney orders the team, and runs off the side of the building, down to the debris pile below. Follow him, turning right,

and dashing to the far side of the street level, near where the final sniper's outpost was located. "Let me get this gate. My Civil Protection status still gives me limited clearance." Barney taps into the computer terminal. Meanwhile, clear the area of any Hoppers.

"Did you hear a cat just now?" Barney asks you. "That damn thing haunts me," he admits, and you remember the conversation he had with Kleiner about the early teleportation testing that didn't achieve 100 percent success. The nearby gate grinds open. Move in, securing the Supply Crate, and blast the Poison Headcrab in the enclosed corridor.

CHAPTER¹² ENCOUNTERS

"ALL IN A DAY'S WORK, RIGHT?"

| MAP 58 | **STREET WAR VIII: SUPPRESSOR ASSAULT (EXTERIOR)** |

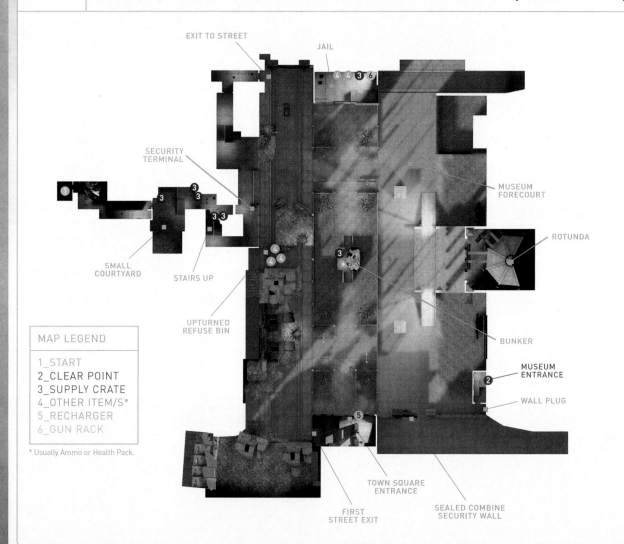

EXIT TO STREET

JAIL

SECURITY TERMINAL

MUSEUM FORECOURT

ROTUNDA

SMALL COURTYARD

STAIRS UP

UPTURNED REFUSE BIN

BUNKER

MUSEUM ENTRANCE

WALL PLUG

MAP LEGEND

1_START
2_CLEAR POINT
3_SUPPLY CRATE
4_OTHER ITEM/S*
5_RECHARGER
6_GUN RACK

* Usually Ammo or Health Pack.

TOWN SQUARE ENTRANCE

FIRST STREET EXIT

SEALED COMBINE SECURITY WALL

Step out of the connecting passage into a courtyard with tenement blocks all around you. A Combine Gunship hovers overhead as you and your team assemble. There's only one route out: toward the steps directly ahead.

Throw a Grenade over the low cement-walled staircase so it lands at the top of the stairs to knock out a sentry gun at the top. Switch to another weapon, and back up your team as they tackle the Combine Soldiers on the stairs.

Enter the building via the steps and clear the connecting corridor of Supply Crates and other scattered ammo. Check your team's location; it should be four strong, with Barney among them.

ADDITIONAL INVESTIGATIONS

After climbing a number of steps, you appear at a corridor with windows to the right overlooking a large courtyard. A squadron of Combine Soldiers scatter and a Gunship flies low across the square. Barney chimes in, "The bank or museum or something like that...whatever the hell it used to be, now it's a Nexus for Overwatch in City 17. It's the main source of pain for this part of town, thanks to a huge suppression device that's raining down hell from the roof of the place."

Barney continues with the game plan: "We'll have to get in that building to open it. Even then, the suppression device will, uh, suppress anyone coming through." A rooftop assault is called for, but first; "It draws power from inside the building, so that's where we've gotta go. All in a day's work, right?" Barney turns and begins to type the unlock codes for the nearby doors.

Wind your way down the steps, making sure that you remove any Hoppers from the ground to avoid taking damage. Once at street level, wait for your team, then step outside.

"So much for stealth. We've been spotted!" Barney hollers as the ground nearby begins to boil, and then a large line of superheated light blasts the ground, bathing it in white light and killing anything in the way. Move to the side as the strike occurs, and run down the street, ignoring the energy walls to the left that prevent you from heading straight to the building.

TIP

Your teammates are on their own here; your health is more important. Wait until you see the ground pulsate with heat, and *then* run past the area, out of its blast radius, before it fires. The shots actually show the path you must take through this town square.

Run across the right edge of the square, making sure you time your dashes so you aren't harmed by the incoming energy blasts. Move along the right side near the large hole in the ground, waiting for another blast to detonate before heading into an upturned container and snagging some Health Packs and items. Run toward the cover of the building ahead; it collapses a moment later, forcing you to the left.

With Barney close by, and perhaps a few citizens (usually they don't survive the Combine bombardment), time your runs out to the sidewalk near the center of the square, and then onward to the far corner of the area. Run past the pile of rubble, and you eventually reach a doorway to a building on your left. Open the door with Barney nearby.

When you enter the building, there are two Combine Soldiers to bring down; Barney can do it if you wish to conserve health and ammo. Or, you can roll a Grenade in and help your friend out. Blast both of them on their upper floor area, then visit the Health Recharger.

The side door gives you access to the other side of the energy wall you couldn't previously breach. Dodge a powerful blast near the park bench as you run toward the concrete bunker. As you near this building, bring out the guns and take care of the Combine Soldiers in this pit. Dash inside.

Run across the bunker, up the steps, and out to a dirt area between you and a building opposite. Run straight at the door to this building and prepare an SMG Grenade. Three Combine Soldiers open the door and try to take defensive positions to pin you at the bunker. Fire the SMG Grenade at the Soldiers as they open the door before they can disperse. Without a Grenade, rely on your rapid-fire weapons.

Open the door the Soldiers came out of and immediately gun down another Soldier; he's guarding four prisoners to the left and won't hesitate to kill them. Use the Crowbar or Gravity Gun on the lock, then corral the prisoners to your cause.

Grab the Health Pack and items from the table, and break open the Supply Crate for further goods. Then wait as your new team tools up with Combine Pulse Rifles from the weapon rack. Check your motley crew of survivors and lead them on.

You can order them out the door and into a firefight with Soldiers and Elite on the steps of the domed building while you bring up the rear. The team runs to the right of the steps, so you head left and catch any remaining Combine forces in the crossfire. It is best to keep your team alive, unless you're still badly wounded and can't afford to help them out.

Defeat all the Combine forces at the edge of this building before continuing to the far end. The horrific energy blasts have halted, but there seems to be no way into the building until you reach the far left corner. Behind an energy wall is a plug, and to the left, steps. Pull the plug by using your Gravity Gun to power off the wall, then rush up the steps and into the building.

"GREAT WORK, DOC! YOU STILL GOT THE TOUCH!"

MAP 59 | STREET WAR IX: SUPPRESSOR ASSAULT (INTERIOR)

MUSEUM LOWER LEVEL

SEALING DOOR #1

MUSEUM UPPER LEVEL

STAIRS TO ROOF

LARGE STORAGE ROOM (TRAP)

SHIELD GENERATOR #3

COMPUTER TERMINAL

ROTUNDA CHAMBER (LOWER LEVEL, SEEN FROM UPPER LEVEL)

SEALING DOOR #2

EXIT CORRIDOR

SHIELD GENERATOR #1

ROTUNDA CHAMBER (LOWER LEVEL)

MIDDLE STAIRWELL (LOWER)

MIDDLE STAIRWELL (UPPER)

JAIL AND COMPUTER TERMINAL

ENTRANCE CORRIDOR

LOWER CORRIDORS

SHIELD GENERATOR #2

SHUT-OFF SWITCH

LASER TRAP CHAMBER

MAP LEGEND

1_START
2_CLEAR POINT
3_SUPPLY CRATE
4_OTHER ITEM/S*
5_RECHARGER
6_GUN RACK
7_INFINITE AMMO RACK
8_RPG

☐ – – – ☐
Link between upper and lower levels

* Usually Ammo or Health Pack.

INTRODUCTION

GETTING STARTED

WEAPONS DETAIL

HALF-LIFERS

THE BESTIARY

CHAPTER 1

CHAPTER 2

CHAPTER 3

CHAPTER 4

CHAPTER 5

CHAPTER 6

CHAPTER 7

CHAPTER 8

CHAPTER 9

CHAPTER 10

CHAPTER 11

CHAPTER 12 "FOLLOW FREEMAN!"

CHAPTER 13

CHAPTER 14

ANOMALOUS MATERIALS

Head up the stairs into the building and move along the main corridor until you reach the store room. There, you can all tool up with extra items, including an infinite number of Grenades.

NOTE

Fill up with Grenades; the coming combat involves some specific Grenade placement.

GROUND TURRET

Now move into the small chamber with the sealed Combine door. In the corner of the room, Barney notices a square-shaped tile that activates when a team member trips the laser wire. "Uh-oh. Turrets." Barney makes a suggestion: "You've got the HEV suit, you deal with them. Then I'll work the security console." Defeat the ground turret with a Grenade roll while Barney attempts to deactivate the door, then step through to the main foyer of this huge building, which you discover is the old museum.

ENTITY ENCOUNTER:

GROUND TURRET

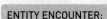

Ground turrets are interior gun emplacements set up to search for signs of movement on the floor they are guarding. Their sensors emit a constant range arc visible as blue laser light coming from what appears to be a floor tile. The turret then rises from the ground and a machine gun unleashes a fixed stream of bullets. Defeat it by activating the turret, stepping to the side out of its range, and rolling a Grenade (using 🖱) into the turret's exposed guts. Keep an eye out for the laser tripwires that warn you a ground turret is nearby.

Head into the main foyer and train your weapon upward. A squad of Soldiers is rappelling from the domed skylight, smashing the glass

as they drop–ideally into your SMG or Pulse Rifle shots. Any Soldiers that survive run to the large doorway with the Exit sign and an energy wall you cannot cross. Send your team in to finish them while you hide behind the rubble. Once done, move to the doorway just right of the Exit area, step through, then to the side, and roll a Grenade into another ground turret.

TIP

Barney is an exceptional fighter and tough. Put Barney in harm's way until he protests that he's heavily wounded. This is key to surviving these sections.

Step into a concrete corridor with a left turn at the end, and another annoying ground turret to deactivate. However, this time your posse is peppered with gunfire from a couple of Soldiers in the next corridor to come. Send your team to deal with them while you destroy the ground turret and mop up any remaining Soldiers in the corridor. Follow the corridor around.

CAUTION

In this close-quarter fighting, Soldiers with shotguns are the number-one cause of friendly fatalities, so concentrate any covering fire into the torsos of these enemy troops.

The corridor ends at a terminal and another prison with citizens waiting for freedom. Barney heads to the computer terminal to release them and power down the energy wall. This allows the team to tool up with weapons.

Leave the holding area and climb the stairs. Make a mental note of this location because you must hold it later in your Nexus destruction operation. For now, stop at the top of the steps and check the room beyond. There's a generator in here, but a blue laser crosses your path. This activates two ground turrets on either side of the room entrance. Hide your team back at the stairwell, then activate both turrets, run between them, and roll two Grenades immediately.

ADDITIONAL INVESTIGATIONS

The resistance is alive and well, and attempted to secure this building before; as vandalism on the outer wall shows the insignia of the Lambda.

Step into the room with the generator at the far end. Barney informs you, "I've got nothing to deal with those. What we need here is some kind of action at a distance." Produce your Gravity Gun and, just as you did back with Alyx, blast the energy orb out of the shield generator.

The building shakes. Before you remove the orb from the shield generator, use the HEV Suit and Health Rechargers in this room. After the deactivation, retreat out of the room; reinforcements arrive and head up the stairwell where you just entered. Jog back and throw a Grenade down to confuse and destroy this ambush attempt. Finish the remaining Soldiers from the top of the stairs.

Now head back into the generator room you secured, and go through the far left doorway and around the building passageway to a short exterior bridge. If you didn't take out the Soldiers on the stairs, this is where you'd be ambushed on both sides. Now all you need to worry about are a couple of Soldiers on the far side in the second section of the building. Cut them down and leave your team out on the bridge while you run through a tripwire and disable another ground turret.

Maneuver around the corridors until you reach an open doorway that Barney stands beside, checking the ground for a Hopper to remove. "Wow," he exclaims, "with that much security, there must be something good in there. Go for it, Doc. I'll wait here till you shut it down. Be careful!"

Enter the room, which is filled with Combine generator technology. If you've found a Hopper, suck it up and place it on the ground near the entrance. Then move left and leap on the side of a piece of machinery, heading past two laser tripwires on the ground. At the end of the machinery, about-face to the right, jump to the small metal platform, then right over more lasers, and follow the area in-between the shelving units. Suck up a Hopper on the left side of the unit, then crawl under the red laser tripwire.

CAUTION

Stepping through or into any of the red laser tripwires results in wall-mounted machine guns activating and cutting you down, wounding you severely. Replay this area again if you activate these deadly weapons.

CHAPTER 12
ENCOUNTERS

Return to the machinery chamber. More Combine Soldiers are coming to help the team you just destroyed. You and Barney (plus any surviving teammates) must hide in this chamber and guard both entrances. You'll hear when they arrive, because the Hoppers you rearranged explode, ideally taking one or two Soldiers with them. Finish the rest while using the machinery as cover.

Don't destroy this Hopper either; drop it on the other side after you crawl under the laser tripwire. Now turn right and inspect the group of machinery and pipes in this area. Nimble footwork is vital here; you need to locate the group of boxlike machine parts to the left of a door. Stand on the far left edge of them, and watch out for the laser tripwire millimeters to your right. Don't hit it!

Use the map to check your location, then leave the machinery room and go onto the balcony above the central foyer, down the steps, and up the other side. From these pillars, you can see another shield generator behind thick defenses (your next destination). Before heading that way, defeat the Combine troops pouring into the foyer below (the pillar and top of stairs can be used as cover). Grab the Elite's ammo.

From here you can move to the end of the boxlike machine parts, jump the gap to a generator-like device with a pipe on it, leap onto the pipe, and follow it to the far edge of the room, toward the wall. Now you can drop down with ease, run to the closed doorway, and open it by flicking the switch. However, before you do this, activate a Hopper in the exit to this chamber (the second Hopper you removed). Quickly place the other primed Hopper at the entrance once the switch is pressed, or just as you reach it during the laser avoidance maneuvers. Fill up at the Health Recharger, then press the switch.

TIP

During this foyer fight, an energy wall prevents you from heading onto the ground floor. To grab ammo, let all the enemies move through the wall, then shoot them, or suck items from fallen Soldiers by using the Gravity Gun.

Move down the now open corridor to the bust of Breen, and opposite that is a doorway to the second shield generator room. A quick blast with your Gravity Gun removes the orb (although you can suck it and use it as a projectile for the fight to come),

Follow the corridor round to this entrance. Inside, ransack the crates and items to the right side. Your way out is blocked by the sealed door at the opposite end of the room, and the original entrance also closes. You have been trapped inside this chamber. With Barney nearby, stand near the hole in the wall to the left of the door with the monitor near it, and throw Grenades at the incoming Combine forces massing near the door.

after which a stream of six Soldiers attempts to cut you down from the corridor. Keep them at bay at the doorway, killing any that enter, then retrace your steps. Make sure you drop the Combine Elite without dissolving him, as he drops Pulse Rifle secondary fire rounds.

While Barney attacks this hole, step back and place any available Hoppers in the room just in front of the two entrances. Prime them, and wait for the Combine's cutting tools to finish opening the door by the monitor. As it opens and the Hopper activates, throw in a Grenade to further wound the incoming Soldiers, then rush them with automatic weaponry. Quickly spin around, wait for the original door to open, and repeat this plan.

TIP

Try launching a rocket as the door opens for an even more impressive (but dangerous) takedown!

The Combine menace is defeated. Stock up on Grenades, then exit the far doorway into the passageway you just threw Grenades. Look for the two laser tripwires in front of the next doorway. Peer ahead into the next corridor to locate two ground turrets. Sprint through the tripwires, directly between the turrets, and immediately roll a Grenade into each turret's pit.

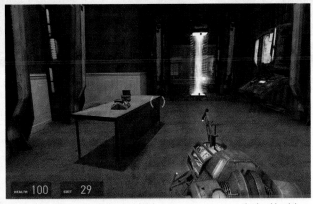

Now sidestep into the final shield generator room, nab the Health Pack and items on the table, and boost the final orb away from the energy conduit. The building shudders, and the generators power down. "That's it—they're all down!" Barney shouts. "That'll shut down the suppressor on the roof as well!"

Return to the main foyer. Head for the roof to commandeer a skybridge from Combine control. Barney follows you down the steps (now lacking the energy wall). Begin a firefight with Combine troops stationed at the exit doorway; cut them down with Grenades and quick shooting. Now is the time to utilize your Pulse Rifle's secondary fire.

Head through the exit doorway, shining your Flashlight along the floor ahead. You'll notice the Supply Crates and two Hoppers that can badly damage you or Barney if you don't deactivate them. Round the corner, and Barney works the computer terminal here, giving access to the roof stairwell. At this point, you're joined by more resistance fighters now that the building's energy walls are shut off.

Barney completes opening the gate. Dash into the base of a stairwell. An RPG lies on the ground, but don't switch to this weapon yet; climb the stairwell with your Pulse Rifle trained on the upper floors. Your team spots a few Soldiers. Rush them. Continue up and onto the museum roof. Barney stays behind.

"GOOD JOB, GORDON! I'LL SEE YOU ON THE GROUND!"

| MAP 60 | **STREET WAR X: MUSEUM ROOF AND SKYBRIDGE** |

CHAPTER ¹²
ENCOUNTERS

MAP LEGEND

1_START
2_CLEAR POINT
3_SUPPLY CRATE
4_RECHARGER
5_INFINITE AMMO
   CRATE

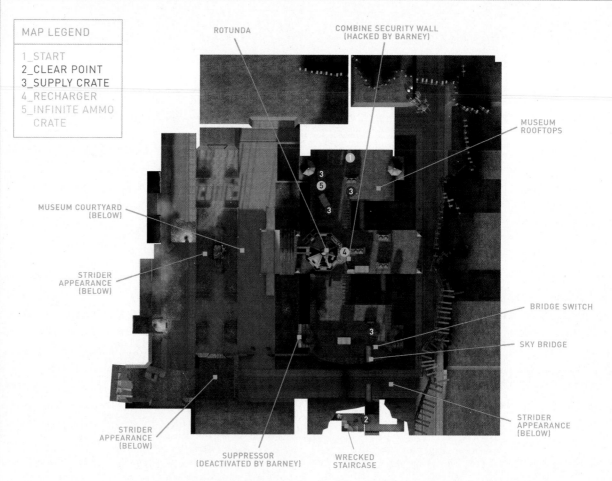

ROTUNDA

COMBINE SECURITY WALL
(HACKED BY BARNEY)

MUSEUM
ROOFTOPS

MUSEUM COURTYARD
(BELOW)

STRIDER
APPEARANCE
(BELOW)

BRIDGE SWITCH

SKY BRIDGE

STRIDER
APPEARANCE
(BELOW)

STRIDER
APPEARANCE
(BELOW)

SUPPRESSOR
(DEACTIVATED BY BARNEY)

WRECKED
STAIRCASE

Once on the roof, you see a Dropship hum overhead, transporting another Strider into combat below. You can't defeat either, so ignore them and check the immediate roof area for Infinite Ammo Crates. Locate them all.

A Combine Gunship has spotted you and your crew. Ignore your team (or instruct them to move into cover by pointing at the machinery near the dome and pressing Ⓒ), and begin your usual combat routine with this flying menace. Your position is important; use the machinery as cover and stay in the area right next to the RPG Infinite Ammo Crate near the right-side fence. The Gunship is closer now, and is laying suppression fire for a Strider in the combat below.

Switch to the RPG, and scout the area for a couple of Supply Crates. Stay away from some Combine stragglers and aim your RPG at them. When you reach the area to the left of the museum dome, you encounter a couple of Combine Elite. Use the RPG, then retreat to the first part of the roof; your progress is temporarily halted.

The extra cover and combat mayhem allows you to launch a rocket over the railing (point the weapon up at the sky). Once the rocket fires, steer it into the side of the Gunship as it passes around and over the courtyard. It circles you in a clockwise pattern, and although it is possible to blast it once it reaches the left side of the dome, it can easily strike you, so seek cover. You can also peek out just after the Gunship stops firing, and maneuver in a shot before it disappears behind the dome.

Continue this combat, firing over the railing and nailing the Gunship as it is preoc-cupied with the street war below. After a number of strikes, it explodes. You can also fire at the Striders in the street below, but this doesn't help your current situation; it only helps the resistance fighters tackling those beasts.

When the Gunship is down, you are free to move forward to the Combine gate Barney is franti-cally trying to override. At that moment, a Dropship deposits troops on the other side of the gate, which swings open. Send your teammates into the fray,

tackling all enemy Soldiers they can. You can lead the charge, because you need as many of your team as possible for the skybridge battle to come. Head past the Recharger onto the connecting walkway and bring down the last of the Combine Elite. Backtrack and use the Rechargers.

Your objective now is to take the skybridge. Force your team forward, over the walkway, and to the bridge entrance, which slides open. While waiting, slam a Crossbow bolt or RPG round into the Soldier atop the watchtower, then bring out the RPG. As enemy Soldiers try to reach the near side of the bridge, launch a rocket straight into them. Now let your team move onto the skybridge.

Just so you don't bear the brunt of the Combine Soldiers on the far side of this highly dangerous bridge, order all your team to charge the other side. As they move over, stay behind and launch a rocket (or two if possible) into the entrance they're running to; this should tear apart the waiting Combine Soldiers. Launch accurately and quickly, or you'll end up demolishing your own team! Then run to the end of the bridge, fire in an SMG Grenade to clear the remaining foes, and breath a sigh of relief; the skybridge is taken!

ADDITIONAL INVESTIGATIONS

The battle is far from over; if you peer across from the bridge before and after you run across it, you can see Striders engaged in fierce street battles with resistant fighters. The citizens need some extra help.

"DR. FREEMAN? IT'S A MESS OUT THERE."

| MAP 61 | **STREET WAR XI: MUSEUM COURTYARD STRIDER BATTLE** |

STRIDER

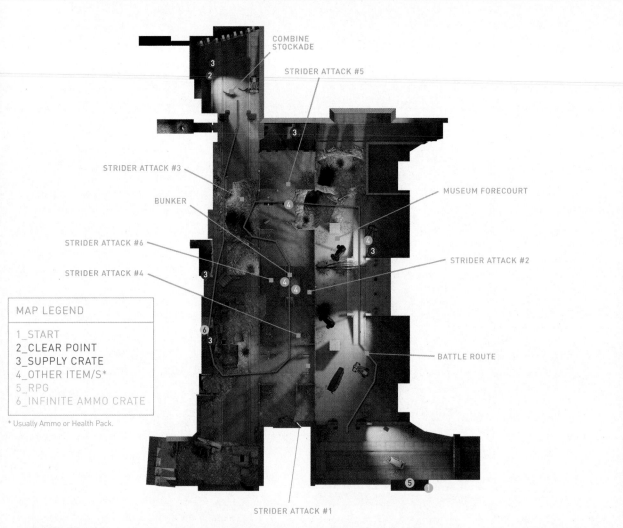

COMBINE STOCKADE

STRIDER ATTACK #5

STRIDER ATTACK #3

BUNKER

STRIDER ATTACK #6

STRIDER ATTACK #4

MUSEUM FORECOURT

STRIDER ATTACK #2

BATTLE ROUTE

STRIDER ATTACK #1

MAP LEGEND

1_START
2_CLEAR POINT
3_SUPPLY CRATE
4_OTHER ITEM/S*
5_RPG
6_INFINITE AMMO CRATE

* Usually Ammo or Health Pack.

Go through the entrance at the other side of the bridge, move to the half-destroyed stairwell, and peer down. Drop off to the landing below and go down the steps. You can leap over the stair railing and drop to ground level, which is quicker but results in damage. A citizen greets you at the building's exit, letting you know the resistance is fully engaged in Strider combat. Load up with rockets.

Head out the doorway and step into the museum square you infiltrated earlier. The energy walls are back up, but the main concern is two Striders cruising through the area and systematically destroying your forces. Immediately launch a couple of RPG rounds into its main body, and use the wreckage as cover when it spots you. Continue to pummel the beast until it falls near the museum steps.

CAUTION

Watch out for the beast's particle cannon which it launches on a parked Combine APC, or the Strider may just crash into the APC during combat. The wreckage can hit and kill you.

ENTITY ENCOUNTER:
STRIDER

This giant tripod attacks with two weapons mounted to its snout: a machine-gun-like rapid-fire weapon and a warp cannon. This cannon causes instant death (and scenic destruction) when it fires, so stay out of the shimmering light. Seek cover from the machine-gun fire, and stay away from the beast, because it also skewers human-sized foes with its sharp feet. Fire only powerful projectiles at Striders; RPGs, Grenades, SMG Grenades, or Pulse Rifle secondary fire orbs are all recommended. At least two, four, or six direct strikes are needed to topple one of these colossal fiends. The Strider only attacks you after you hit it, even if there are other targets in the area.

Amid the chaos and battle, dash along the museum steps, using the pillars and scenery as cover while a second strider moves into the area. You're exposed in the open, so head immediately toward the collapsed ground with the fires burning in it. A small sewer tunnel is visible as you arrive; sprint here to avoid further gunfire, and stock up on Health Packs and ammo.

NOTE

Striders constantly move into this battlefield because the Citadel can produce an infinite number of them. Don't try to strike down each one; escape is your only final option.

Be *extremely* careful when exiting the tunnel at the other side. Usually a Strider is extremely close by. Unless you've damaged the beast previously, save ammo and stay out of sight until it moves away, then scamper out and up to ground level, turning left. You should notice another Strider lolloping about on the courtyard's far side.

Sprint diagonally across the middle of this courtyard, heading directly for the bunker ahead and left of you. Time your run so you aren't strafed to death by Striders. Once inside the bunker, you have only a few seconds to grab items from fallen comrades; a Strider is likely to destroy the bunker's roof with a warp cannon shot.

Exit the bunker ready to execute some of the most daring moves yet. Wait for the barrage of machine-gun fire to stop, then sprint outside, searching for an area to use as cover. Unless you hear the Strider's warp cannon powering up, the bunker exit can be used as partial cover as you drop a second Strider; diving behind the trees also can give you a second or two of cover.

Your preferred fighting spot, however, is across the courtyard. Dash from the bunker, turn right, and run directly to the corner of the courtyard shown here. Once there, swing right and slow down to an area behind a load of debris. Resistance citizens drop in Supply Crates to your location. As this happens, switch to your Gravity Gun immediately; a blast rocks the cover you're in, and masonry falls all around. Don't stand near the walls, and stab 🖱 repeatedly to grab any falling concrete about to hit you.

After this near-death experience, you can stay at this point, running left and right in and out of cover, and using the Infinite RPG Crate to its fullest; blast Striders and return to cover to reload. When you're done demolishing, head left, watching out for a direct hit on an upturned container. Between Strider blasts (or after defeating one), grab the items from the container, then run left.

You're almost out of this mayhem. Run directly at the assembled Combine Soldiers and APC, and cut them down with a rocket or Pulse Rifle ordnance. Sprint into the gate area, especially if you're being targeted by a Strider, and use the APCs as cover. Step behind the barricade and search for the steps leading underground in the far left corner. Supply Crates are at the bottom.

"THIS CLOSE TO THE CITADEL, THEY'VE TURNED THE STREETS OVER TO STRIDERS!"

MAP 62 | **STREET WAR XII: STRIDER PATROL**

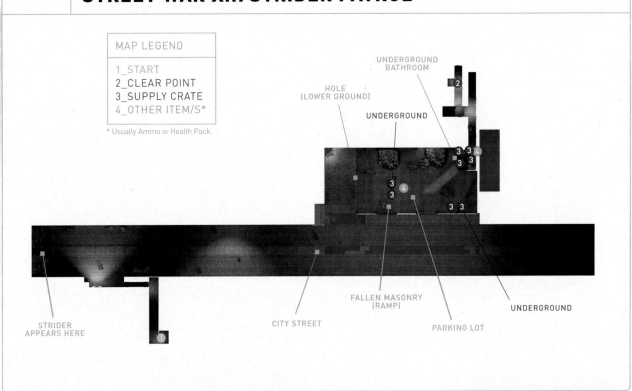

MAP LEGEND

1_START
2_CLEAR POINT
3_SUPPLY CRATE
4_OTHER ITEM/S*

* Usually Ammo or Health Pack.

UNDERGROUND BATHROOM

HOLE (LOWER GROUND)

UNDERGROUND

STRIDER APPEARS HERE

CITY STREET

FALLEN MASONRY (RAMP)

PARKING LOT

UNDERGROUND

At the base of the steps, you emerge in a giant underpass with bits of debris strewn everywhere. You are in extreme danger, so pay close attention. Turn right and sprint immediately toward the Soldier standing at the far end of the underpass. Do not slow down! A second later, the debris at the left end of the underpass is blown apart, and a Strider crashes through, firing directly at you! If you slow, even for a second, you can be mown down by Strider fire. Don't even try to fight the Strider.

Instead, concentrate on charging the Soldier and gunning him down before you reach him, then continue to run down the ramp to the left and into the hole in a nearby parking structure. The Strider will still be searching for you.

You're temporarily safe—from the Strider—so move into the hole and circle around this underground chamber to the exit on the opposite side of the room. As you move, try dropping an SMG Grenade directly into the doorway to destroy three incoming Soldiers before they disperse. Alternatively, use the exploding barrel and boost it into them with the Gravity Gun. This room also has Supply Crates and an item inside a bathroom sink. Climb the steps, turn to the next doorway, and throw a Grenade to unnerve another Soldier before cutting him down.

The particle beam of the Strider's warp cannon is powering up when you reach the open-air level of the ruined parking structure. The destruction is immense, but also helpful; the attack dropped a support beam to the ground on one side, allowing you to run up it to the next floor. Stay behind support posts when the Strider begins to fire at you.

As you reach the exit of this upper chamber, a Soldier heads in with a couple of Type II Scanners. Defeat the Soldier first if you can, then destroy both Scanners. You can conserve ammo by using the Gravity Gun to suck in a Scanner and bounce it off a nearby wall (or into the second Scanner).

Once at the top of the support strut, bring out the Gravity Gun to suck and destroy a couple of Scanners, then turn right and maneuver carefully across this topmost part of the parking lot. Being careful not to fall, move between Strider cannon fire, using support posts as cover. When you reach the end of the area, peer downward at a hole leading to a stairwell below. Move down these steps, attacking a Soldier if one appears.

Head up another flight of stairs; timing your move so the Strider stalking on the street outside doesn't spot you. At the top of the stairs, head right, down a joining corridor, until you reach an opening on the left. Be very careful here, because the Strider may see you. Try to launch a Grenade onto the upper structure roof, where a Soldier is attempting to snipe you. This detonates some barrels near him.

LAMBDA
LOCATION

The connecting passage between the parking structure and the final assault area holds a Lambda location that's easy to spot and on your way. Stop for a moment to reload from the Supply Crates here.

"AND IF YOU SEE DR. BREEN, TELL HIM I SAID, 'FU----.'"

MAP 63 | **STREET WAR XII: FINAL STAND**

CHAPTER ¹²
ENCOUNTERS

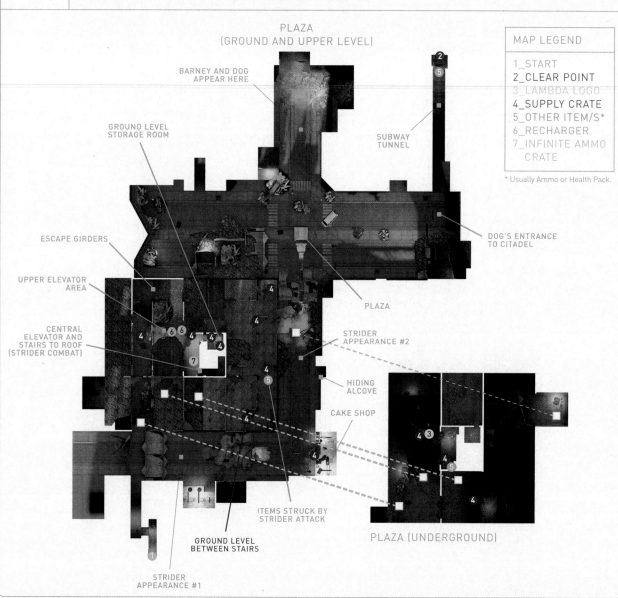

PLAZA
(GROUND AND UPPER LEVEL)

BARNEY AND DOG
APPEAR HERE

GROUND LEVEL
STORAGE ROOM

SUBWAY
TUNNEL

MAP LEGEND
1_START
2_CLEAR POINT
3_LAMBDA LOGO
4_SUPPLY CRATE
5_OTHER ITEM/S*
6_RECHARGER
7_INFINITE AMMO CRATE

* Usually Ammo or Health Pack.

DOG'S ENTRANCE
TO CITADEL

ESCAPE GIRDERS

UPPER ELEVATOR
AREA

PLAZA

CENTRAL
ELEVATOR AND
STAIRS TO ROOF
(STRIDER COMBAT)

STRIDER
APPEARANCE #2

HIDING
ALCOVE

CAKE SHOP

ITEMS STRUCK BY
STRIDER ATTACK

PLAZA (UNDERGROUND)

GROUND LEVEL
BETWEEN STAIRS

STRIDER
APPEARANCE #1

At the end of the corridor, you meet up with a citizen. "It's a mess out there," he informs you. "This close to the Citadel, they've turned the streets over to Striders. I think we can push 'em back if we get to high ground." You're almost at the Citadel wall. An explosion rocks the ground; batter through the wooden barricade immediately and head out to the wrecked street scene. Citizens join up with you again. Watch above as another Dropship carrying a Strider glides to a rendezvous point. You'll be fighting that Strider soon!

Your final push begins with an attack on an underground parking lot. You should by now understand the strengths of sending your team in first, so watch the combat from a safe distance, then follow your team inside, making sure you're not caught in a blast from a grenade rolled in by the enemy. In fact, if you catch enemies with your own grenades, you can even the score, and roll them under cars so they explode at the feet of the Combine Soldiers hiding behind the cars. Quickly secure one side of the parking area.

LAMBDA
LOCATION

The white van has some Batteries you can pick up between combat bouts, and even has a hidden lambda logo beneath the right brake light. Then move to the side and find a small dead-end area with more items to gather.

Work your way to the parking lot exit and bring down a couple of Combine Elite that assault your position. Up ahead is an area of rubble and a Strider moving down the street from right to left. Pluck up the courage and blaze a trail to safety as soon as the Strider passes so it doesn't spot you running and gun you down.

Sprint out and up the rubble, turn left onto the street, and immediately drop into an area of collapsed roadway. Dash under and out again, and blast a waiting Combine Soldier on the way. Seek cover from Strider attack at once by running straight for the cake shop building ahead. Blast the window and Supply Crates out to the right of the door and head through the opening you just made, claiming the items that spill out. Then rush behind the display rack at the back of the shop and hide from any Strider fire your team may be encountering.

TIP

During these Strider confrontations, don't shoot the Strider, or it will fire on you.

Peek out of the cake shop looking right and run forward, aiming to reach an alcove on the right side of the street as rubble and debris ahead is blown out of the away by a second Strider. Stay tightly packed against this alcove until it passes heading the way you just came. Only then is it safe to step out and seek cover.

The escape route is via another collapsed section of roadway leading into the other side of the underground parking lot. Once inside, wait until you see a Combine Soldier setting a bomb; it is possible to witness this and prevent a large explosion and a

portion of the lot sinking in with cars piling on top of the rubble. Attempt to maneuver toward the assembled Soldiers on the far side of this area, tackling them or forcing your team in. At the exit of the parking lot, wait for reinforcements by the Supply Crate.

Your plan is to seek higher ground and deliver some punishment to the Striders around the perimeter of this ruined building you're moving through. At the top of the parking lot ramp, watch out for the Soldiers on the roof wreckage above. Throw a Grenade or pepper the area with SMG fire. Turn right and head diagonally through the wreckage, plugging another foe on the roof as you go.

Move around, watching the rooftops for Soldiers, until you reach this wreckage-strewn entrance. Lob in a Grenade to scatter the Soldiers waiting inside. The survivors move up the stairs inside this entrance. Plug the Soldier on the roof above with a Crossbow bolt, then follow them in.

Step into the entrance and move to the left, circle-strafing so you can constantly watch the stairs on the other side of the entrance. Quickly stop to open the Supply Crate in the alcove here, then rush the stairs and tag the Soldiers at the top. A stack of crates is ahead; smashed them and grab supplies (or suck them with the Gravity Gun) without delay. Moments later, a Strider's particle cannon obliterates the ledge the crates are on.

Your assembled team can now be ushered to the area beneath a wrecked wall. On the way, a Soldier appears at a blown-out doorway, then another attacks from a second doorway. Keep to the right side of the debris and deal with the Soldiers on these balconies. Your team should be tagging any Soldiers in other areas and avoiding grenades. Your reason for staying to the right side becomes obvious when, moments later, the entire wall the Soldiers were standing on is destroyed by a second Strider cannon blast!

This strike is the timing you and your team need. As the smoke clears, rush the open doorway and step into a scene of complete destruction. While your team deals with nearby foes, stay in partial cover (don't move into the open area ahead just yet) and use the Crossbow to plug the Combine Soldiers hiding behind the debris ahead on the upper floor.

Now it's relatively safe to step into the open area, making sure the Soldiers on the roof above the entrance you can see to your left are removed. Quickly run to the entrance and hit the Supply Crates inside. As you emerge, check the skies. A final Dropship deposits another Strider nearby. That's three you need to kill!

Head up the right side of the ruins, up the slope of wreckage to the area where you fired the Crossbow, and move from debris to debris, blasting with SMG or Pulse Rifle rounds and dealing with a Combine Elite behind more wreckage. Turn left and blast an SMG Grenade into the remnants of an elevator foyer, then rush in and bring down any remaining Combine forces here. There's ample supplies and Rechargers in here, so fill up.

Check the elevator banks for a set of steps to the side leading up to the open-air rooftop that was once another floor of the building. Crouch at the top until a Gunship flies past; you don't need to attract its attention.

Move onto the rooftop and check your directions. Striders move on three of the four sides of this building's remains. Combine Soldiers appear on various rooftops too, but your team is dealing with them; leave them to attack while you select your first Strider. Fire an RPG at it from the upper roof, and concentrate your fire on this first Strider. Do *not* fire at more than one Strider at a time, or you'll be targeted by them, and there's no way to dodge both sets of attacks!

CAUTION

Don't try to escape prior to defeating the Striders. Their weapons will cut you down as you attempt to flee.

The remainder of the battle against the three Striders is fought from this vantage point, with you constantly moving back down to the elevator bank to the HEV Suit and Health Rechargers. Use the top of the stairwell as cover, and continue assaulting a single Strider until it falls. Reload at the Infinite RPG Crate on the rooftop, and use the lid (keep opening it) as a shield. Fire on the Striders in any order, but try executing them in the order shown in the screenshots here, because you'll have more cover to use when you move to the second and third Striders.

The resistance forces let out a cheer as the final Strider falls. All that remains now is to escape the rooftop. Do this by carefully moving across the zigzagging girders to the right of your rooftop vantage point. When the girder reaches the outer wall, drop to the street. You meet up with more citizens, who are pushing Combine remnants back to the very base of the Citadel.

You hear a voice over your suit's intercom: "Here, boy! Dog! Come back here, Dog!" It's Barney! "Damn it all...." Barney says in exasperation as Dog bounds out of the side street to your left, mashes the remaining Combine Soldiers, picks up a van, and hurls it at a final enemy cowering at the base of the Citadel ahead. Move up to the collapsed monument of the horseback rider.

"Gordon!" Barney explains his current predicament: "Dog came crashing through the plaza, knocking over walls and...I think he's looking for Alyx. He seems to have it set in his, uh, head that she's in the Citadel. I figured Alyx wouldn't want him getting any deeper in trouble, but...Hell, you try stopping him!" Barney turns as Dog begins to wrench the base of the Combine wall apart! "Hey, Dog! Not there! You can't get through that way!" The wall gradually lifts.

"Well I'll be damned." Barney is shocked at Dog's tremendous strength. "I think he wants you to go through, Gordon. You'd better hurry." Run to the opening Dog has created; it is a hole leading to what appears to be a tunnel.

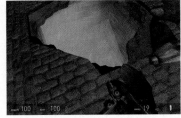

Jump down, just as Barney shouts a final message; "And if you see Dr. Breen, tell him I said, 'Fu----'." The wall crashes down, loudly cutting off Barney's words. The tunnel goes silent.

BENEFACTORY

OVERVIEW ▌ There's no turning back. You've reached the blackened heart of the Combine's enslavement plan for humanity: the Citadel of City 17. You cannot avoid gazing in wonder at the enormity of this spire of destruction. A spot of nifty footwork is required to enter the building via the digging chasm it has created. Then you must locate a conveyor belt and latch yourself onto an iron maiden, touring the depths of this hated place. After being stripped of weapons, you make a new physics discovery, and the results become your main armament as you head deeper into the Citadel, fending off Combine attacks and ignoring the Breen's continuous monologue. After rising through a giant elevator shaft, you locate a final conveyor system, and rise to the highest reaches of the Citadel.

INVENTORY PICK-UP

- Zero Point Energy Field Gravity Gun (Organic)
- Energy Ball

ENTITY ENCOUNTER
FRIENDLIES

- None

ENTITY ENCOUNTER
HOSTILES

- Headcrabs
- Scanners
- Stalkers*
- Combine Soldiers
- Combine Dropships
- Striders
- Dr. Wallace Breen (video feed)
- Combine Elite
- Manhacks
- Crab Synths*
- Mortar Synths*

* Indicates first exposure to entity

"THERE IS REALLY NO PLACE IN THIS ENTERPRISE FOR A ROGUE PHYSICIST."

With Dog closing the entrance and a rock fall blocking your way back to the city, the way forward is clear. Move along the tunnel until you reach the edge. Ahead is a gaping chasm, so awe-inspiring you may forget to pick up the Health Pack at the end.

Don't forget to look down and up at the true majesty of the Combine's Citadel, now revealed as a gargantuan digging machine miles in height and depth. You can't reach the other side of the tunnel, so carefully look around. Don't make any rash moves around this precipice. The drop is deadly.

NOTE

To give you an idea of the enormity of this monument, zoom in on the rocks below; amid the dust is wreckage of an oil tanker just visible at the base of the dig.

The only way is down, and not by dropping, but by a controlled descent. Step off the slope to the left, and slide down as rocks and dirt kick up and bounce down an infinite drop. Backpedal (S) as you reach the end of the slope and a more stable flat ledge, or you will accelerate over the edge and plummet to your death. Turn left, and nimbly walk along the narrow ledge to the left of the Citadel. Bring out your Crowbar.

A Headcrab hides in a fissure to your left. Immediately duck as the creature leaps, and it launches over your head into the giant pit below. If the Headcrab hits you, quickly defeat it with your Crowbar, then move to the end of the ledge. Turn right, and walk onto the jutting pipe. It creaks and collapses slightly; stay on it and don't slide off!

Your plan is to execute two well-timed leaps. The first is from the pipe to a moving blue platform on the edge of the superstructure. Jump as the platform moves upward so the fall doesn't cripple you. Then at the highest point of the blue platform's movement, leap again to the triangular ledge with the doorway and enter the outer shell of the Citadel. Follow the path between two giant walls of sleek, moving machinery, taking care not to stand under the triangular cylinders pumping up and down.

CAUTION

Gaps all around you lead to a chasm plummet. Be careful around the outer area of this monument!

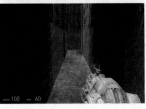

Look for a drop onto a very narrow passageway at the end of the walkway to the left. Drop a couple feet and follow the passage as it zigzags through a cathedral-like interior; look up at the mind-boggling structure above as you progress. Continue forward and left until you reach a large vertical light. You're almost out of this passage.

   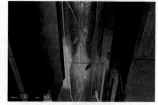

Continue into a large corridor with pieces of ground, wall, and ceiling missing. Cell pods clank along conveyor rods in the distance. Carefully follow the ground around to the left and search for a metallic plank; jump across to it, and then to the other side of this chasm.

A journey through a nightmarish cathedral of onyx begins. Amid the swirling pipes and dizzying heights, your iron maiden slowly floats on its conveyor belt, past a lone Scanner, and swings left into another gigantic fissure.

Peer out from the edge down a precipice even deeper than the outside digging mechanism. Little wonder the Combine call this area "the abyss."

The tour of the Citadel continues. A Combine Soldier guards a corridor below, and an emaciated *thing* slowly trudges across the ground on two stilts fused to its partially amputated legs. Two more of these pitiful fiends are hunched over a nearby computer. Your conveyor pulls you high up into the heavens of the fissure.

Maneuver around until you see a pod-cleansing mechanism spray liquid-hot metal into an iron-maiden-style device on a conveyor belt. Drop to the ledge and work your way along, then around a left corner to a small bridge. Combine iron maidens continuously move across this bridge on two conveyor belts, one heading left, the other right. The area ahead is a dead end. There is no way forward. You are trapped.

ENTITY ENCOUNTER:
STALKER

This withered slave is known as a Stalker. It appears that if you'd taken the train at the beginning of the adventure, Nova Prospekt scientists would have severed your higher brain functions, experimented on you in any number of foul and depraved ways, embedded a number of blackened nano-devices into your skin, and slowly watched you lose all your humanity. You'd then be known by the codename "Stalker," and sent on any number of menial duties inside this vast structure. Be glad you made friends with Barney; he's the one who saved you from this fate worse than death!

Or are you? It seems the only way forward is to jump into, and be clamped to, an iron maiden. Run to the opposite side of the bridge and turn around. When the next iron maiden arrives on the conveyor belt heading left, run to it and press E. You're then clamped into the pod.

 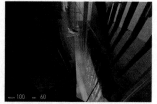

CAUTION

Clamp yourself to an iron maiden on the conveyor belt heading *left*. If you ride on the right one, you are cauterized and burned to death in a second.

The journey through the Citadel continues as you hum your way through a gigantic series of pod stations where prisoners are selected for various nefarious torturing. In the distance is another wretched skeleton busily keeping the Citadel working to the Combine's specifications. Be sure you look around; you have limited head movement.

Pass the skeletal Stalker, twitching under the watchful eye of the Combine, and glide onward, rounding a gigantic corner. Above you, Combine Dropships carrying squad containers sweep through, picking up their humanoid cargo to deposit them in the city below to attack your comrades.

Your pod swings low over the cranial surface of three lumbering Striders. Once these beasts trudge below you, the conveyor jerks to the right into another grand fissure, this one peppered with cell pods along the walls.

As you near the end of this gigantic corridor, a reactor coil roars to life and begins to hum with a bright white light shining between two power conduits. You can make out small balls of energy like the one you removed from the generator back in the battle for City 17's square.

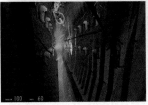

Your pod swings to a corridor filled with pods on each side. As you progress, you see Stalkers shuffling about decks near a Dropship hangar, working on the vehicle's superstructure. Floating past the dozens of Dropships ready for deployment, you're struck by the supreme and threatening power that the Combine possesses.

When you round a final corner, a black train trundles forward from the outside sectors, bringing in dozens more caged humans sedated and gibbering inside the prison pods. Look closely at the train, and you can view the railcars and their cargo. The train passes and the corridor closes in; you've reached the end of the journey.

"SUCH WILLFUL DISREGARD FOR HUMANITY'S FUTURE."

You are removed from your bonds with a thumping yank, and appear to be in some kind of observation chamber. A voice informs the Combine that your weapons have been neutralized, and all your available ordnance is ripped from your position and dematerializes before your eyes! When the energy beams rip into the Gravity Gun, however, the machine doesn't disintegrate. In fact, the energy conduits inside phase with the beams, and the weapon's orange glow changes to blue. The device falls to the ground. Pick it up.

INVENTORY ADAPTATION
ZERO POINT ENERGY FIELD MANIPULATOR

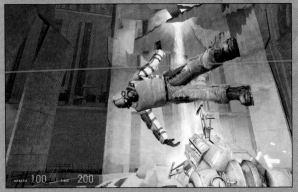

The Gravity Gun has been inadvertently changed. The flux capacitors were manipulated by Combine technology to allow both inorganic and organic materials to be manipulated. The upshot of this is that any enemy—whether human or machine—can be sucked, blasted forward, or abused as if it were a barrel or piece of debris. The offensive capabilities of this attack method are unsurpassed: you can "bowl" enemies into each other, carry a suspended enemy as a shield, or hurl scenic objects at your foes. Finally, the Gravity Gun's power to move heavier inorganic objects has also increased, and these make powerful projectiles.

Time to test the Gravity Gun on the Combine Soldiers running in to apprehend you. Suck one in, then blast him back into the other enemies to incapacitate them all. Or, at closer range, shoot a bolt of energy at a foe, sending him reeling (ideally into his squad).

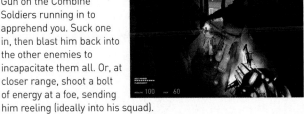

TIP

These are the two main strategies to employ whenever you encounter enemies: sucking them in (using them as cover) and boosting them back at other foes, or zapping all incoming enemies with a blast.

NOTE

Enemy troops drop grenades and weapons when you defeat them. However, none are as potent and easy to use as the Gravity Gun, so ignore the additional ordnance you obtain.

ADDITIONAL INVESTIGATIONS

Throughout your infiltration of the Citadel, you'll meet up with Wallace Breen a total of six times on the central computer monitors. His speech is a mixture of mockery and pleading, and has been transcribed at each point of interaction. Breen begins:

"Well, so this is Dr. Freeman at last. I wish I could say this was a pleasant surprise, but it's neither a surprise nor, as you will surely agree, very pleasant. Well...I am nothing if not pragmatic."

NOTE

If you can't stand listening to Breen any longer, rip the monitor and computer bank from the wall. This relieves some tension, and the objects can be used to hide behind or thrust into enemies.

After Breen's rant is silenced, move to the Combine Recharger device. These are dotted throughout the Citadel and offer up to 200 points of enhanced suit protection and up to 100 health. Make sure you visit each one.

Head out of the computer terminal area and onto a massive balcony with low fencing stopping you from plummeting over the edge. Another squad of Combine Soldiers (including a Combine Elite) must be quickly brought to their knees. Focus on the Elite first. You can even "play" with a remaining Soldier after the battle; catch him and then drop him over the balcony!

TIP

To stay in partial cover, suck up a dying enemy once this combat is over and carry him to your next confrontation. You have a ready-made projectile.

Head right, along the balcony, until you reach the end and another squad of Combine Soldiers to decimate. Continue around and wait for a Scanner to arrive, suck it up, and use it as a spontaneous bowling ball to knock over the incoming Soldiers.

ADDITIONAL INVESTIGATIONS

At the end of this balcony is another computer terminal with more of Breen's admonishments to listen to: "Under other circumstances I like to think we might have been able to work together in an atmosphere of mutual trust and respect. Certainly, judging from your brief tenure at Black Mesa while I was its Administrator, you showed every promise of becoming a valuable and productive contributor to the scientific process. And yet...I'm not sure what spurred you to it...but there is really no place in this enterprise for a rogue physicist."

Move past Breen's screens and into a chamber with a triangular platform and a giant stasis field in its middle. Soldiers begin pouring from the passage to your right. Deal with them as usual. However, if you toss them into the stasis field, their bodies float, twisting in the matter the field generates. But if you slam the Soldiers into the core of the field, they disintegrate. You can even step into the stasis field and float around, but don't enter the middle, or you'll be shredded instantly. When finished, push the Soldiers back along the passage to the right.

Round the corner, face a giant energy wall, and search for a way to switch it off. The answer lies in the small conduit with the ball of energy inside, to the left of two waiting guards. Suck the ball out of the conduit to deactivate the wall, step into the room, and release the ball so it hurtles into one of the troops in the same manner as your Pulse Rifle's secondary orb fire.

INVENTORY ADAPTATION
ENERGY BALL

The additional energy balls rising up the conduit behind the Soldiers can also be used as weapons; you now have an excellent projectile weapon that acts like the secondary fire capability of the Pulse Rifle. What's more, there are some amazing blurring effects if you're carrying a hovering ball and quickly move it around the screen! Pick up these balls from any energy conduit.

Pass the Recharger down the corridor to the right and stop when you reach a larger junction with another energy wall to deactivate. Destroy the enemies in this area, backing up to the initial room if you wish to seek cover. Once again, the small energy conduit is on your left. Suck out the ball, then step into the junction and look forward and to your right for signs of reinforcements. They will arrive in force. Toss them all about in a frenzy of well-timed Gravity Gun action.

CAUTION

Removing an energy ball from its small conduit deactivates an energy wall. But beware; shooting a ball back into the small conduit activates it again. Don't attempt this without realizing the ramifications of becoming stuck on either side of the energy wall!

TIP

Don't forget two interesting strategies: you can blast a foe over the railings into the main energy conduits that crackle up the walls in both of these areas (a sure-fire way to get rid of a Combine body), or ricochet an energy ball off the left wall of the initial conduit chamber before the Recharger so it bounces straight down the corridor (an expert way of demolishing enemies charging up there).

Pitched battles with Combine Soldiers continue as more reinforcements arrive from both directions and stop at the junction. Use cover if necessary and remain in this deadly combat until the Soldiers begin to back up. When you are able, move left down a large corridor to a small set of steps near a computer bank, finishing off the Soldiers here.

Pass the computer terminals and enter a narrower corridor with another Recharger on the right wall. It is imperative that you use this if you need it. Then continue deeper into the Citadel's constructs.

"I HAVE LAID THE FOUNDATION FOR HUMANITY'S SURVIVAL!"

ADDITIONAL INVESTIGATIONS

At the end of this narrow corridor, another dark room with two computer terminals opens up, and Breen cuts in to meet and berate you: "Your mentors are partly to blame, of course. My disappointment in Eli Vance and Isaac Kleiner is far greater than my sorrow over your unfortunate choice of career path. They threw away so much more than you. In a way, I suppose you could not have done otherwise. Who knows what seeds of icono-clasm they planted when you were young and gullible? But while they certainly share a great part of the respon-  sibility for the recent troubles, it is you alone who have chosen to act with such willful disregard for humanity's future."

Just like their teleport technology, Combine elevators take a while to deliver their cargo, and you must wait for the platform to arrive. During this time, expect extra Combine troop types to try defeating you. Scanners try to blind you; blast them into the conduits or Soldiers. More Soldiers arrive from corridors you cannot enter thanks to the energy walls blocking your path.

Next come a number of Manhacks; simply shoot them away into the conduits, suck and blast them as you've done before, or buzz-saw a few Soldiers with the Manhack sucked into your weapon.

You can shut Breen up by ripping the monitor or the large terminal console from its moorings and launching it into a collection of troops pouring into a central elevator shaft ahead. Or, you can blast the terminal into the large conduit that arcs upwards on both sides; the terminal disintegrates impressively.

TIP

Before you get on the elevator, make sure you've recharged at the base of the shaft.

Combat doesn't stop in this area. Soldiers come from three locations, all passages connecting to a central elevator. On the opposite side where you met the first Soldiers is a Recharger; use it between Combine incursions. Now prepare for quick combat, picking up more Soldiers and boosting them into their teammates, or dropping them off the edge of the central shaft.

Head to the center of this shaft, locate the switch, and press it. A large elevator descends.

Don't stay any longer than you need to; when the elevator arrives (look for the gap in the center of the room to be filled with the platform), hop on and ascend. This part of the infiltration can be tricky. Combine Soldiers attack from openings around the shaft perimeter, and it's difficult to see where they come from. Constantly circle and deal with enemies by either sucking them in or using the energy balls in the conduits as projectiles.

Force your way through to another narrow passage, and make sure you defeat the Combine Soldiers coming in from the energy wall junction, which you cannot access. Blast them back and continue.

Your ascension continues for a number of minutes, and the speed is agonizingly slow. It's a good thing you recharged before you got on the elevator. Yet more Soldiers appear from distant balconies, and you must defeat them all if you wish to avoid injury; a stream of energy balls is the best plan, but you can suck Soldiers and then throw them back at their brethren, or into the conduits as before.

You'll reach a second stasis field chamber. This is your last opportunity to defeat Combine Soldiers by throwing them into the field to disintegrate out of existence. Enemies attack you from the left, then the right. Deal with them in this area, running around the stasis field and sucking enemies through it for quick kills.

When you reach the top of the elevator (you'll see the platform if you look up, so position yourself looking forward as you arrive), immediately suck the energy ball out of the small conduit ahead and right to allow you access into the next chamber. Then deal with the Combine forces.

Head around the corner and catch up on all the latest Breen gossip, courtesy of two computer terminals. Rip them apart if you wish, but quickly look to the left, where there's an extremely long and immense corridor to move down. This is the interior of the Citadel, and perhaps the location of the Vances could be within your grasp.

ADDITIONAL INVESTIGATIONS

When the Soldiers have fallen, you can listen to Breen's increasingly annoyed pleadings: "Tell me, Dr. Freeman, if you can. You have destroyed so much. What is it, exactly, that you have created? Can you name even one thing? I thought not."

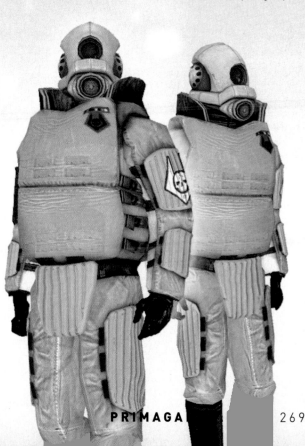

Embark on a long and frantic dash straight down this corridor, with little room for error. Meet the first set of Soldiers and blast them back quickly, and optionally use one of the bodies to soak up bullets fired from additional Combine forces as you reach the middle of the corridor. Pick up one of the large prison pods and use it as a shield, peeking around the sides to view incoming enemies, and then firing the pod straight at them.

Make an instant sidestep left or right at the end of the corridor before a bridge. A Strider will cut you down in seconds if you don't immediately take cover behind the stationary prison pods. With no more Combine Soldiers to bother you, engage this Strider in combat. Peek out from the cover of the pods, suck in a ball from the conduit in the crevasse in front of you, and shoot it directly at the Strider's head and gun.

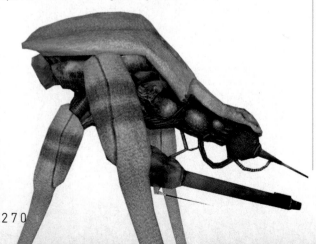

Continue this combat, darting back into cover, then out again to suck an orb and fire it at the Strider. Wait until the Strider finishes firing a salvo, and remember you can grab an energy ball and return to cover, biding your time before you fire it. Eventually, the Strider splits apart and comes crashing to the ground.

CRAB SYNTH

MORTAR SYNTH

ADDITIONAL INVESTIGATIONS

Amusingly, you can pick up one of the collapsed appendages of the Strider and boost it up into the giant monitor containing Breen's final thoughts: "I have laid the foundation for humanity's survival–and not as we have narrowly defined ourselves, but as something greater than we ever could imagine. Something we can only now begin to glimpse."

With Breen finished, turn left and check the large energy wall. The small conduit, with multiple balls writhing inside, can be breached. Suck out the first ball, and the wall remains; all orbs must be sucked and deposited away from the conduit for the wall to dissolve. Then step into a large groove behind the wall, move to the Recharger and use it, and then move to another bridge where Combine iron maidens maneuver along conveyor belts.

It appears you have no option but to restrict yourself into the Combine iron maiden and ride it to whatever fate the Combine command has deemed for you. Press E and hitch a ride along to a junction. Your pod waits as a Stalker passes you by, spasmodically twitching at your presence. You trundle left.

You continue along a bottomless fissure of black metal to a junction where a red laser activates a camera. The camera scans you and your pod changes direction. It seems you are climbing. Your pod moves right, toward crisscrossing series of platforms. Strange and fearsome new forms stride across these balconies, while Stalkers remain at terminal controls watching their march.

ENTITY ENCOUNTER:

CRAB SYNTHS

ENTITY ENCOUNTER:

MORTAR SYNTHS

Although these things are like the Stalkers, you have only the briefest glimpse of these strange and inhuman contraptions. It is worth studying these previously unseen Combine forces: self-replicating and parts-replacing synths, the backbone of the Combine's subsequent armies. Crab Synths, with their sharp mandibles, are close-quarter ripping fiends, while Mortar Synths use biomechanical armaments and shells to wreak havoc.

As the sun begins to glint off the onyx structure of doom you're weaving through, a squadron of Dropships powers up and flies through a central window and out into the skies. They are on their way to crush the human resistance.

Your final moments are spent gazing with incredulity at the Combine's circle of black death and the lights of City 17 below. You're ascending rapidly now, heading up to the heavens, and approaching cloud cover. The air begins to thin. Up you hurtle, before finally blacking out...

H λ L F - L I F E ²
PRIMA OFFICIAL GAME GUIDE

DARK ENERGY

OVERVIEW ▮ After being captured and hand-delivered to Wallace Breen by Judith Mossman, an argument about the future of mankind begins in earnest. At the crescendo of this battle of words, a traitor turns on her former master, and Breen escapes to the main reactor of the Citadel. Doggedly refusing to let him escape, you and Alyx give chase, uncovering the true face of the Combine. Your tasks end with a tumultuous ascension of the reactor spire, where Breen is stopped and the shocking conclusions of your mercenary activities are revealed.

INVENTORY PICK-UP

- None

ENTITY ENCOUNTER
FRIENDLIES

- Alyx Vance
- Doctor Eli Vance
- Doctor Judith Mossman

ENTITY ENCOUNTER
HOSTILES

- Combine Soldiers
- Combine Elite
- Dr. Wallace Breen
- Combine Advisor*
- Combine Gunships

* Indicates first exposure to entity

It is useless to struggle. You are immobilized except for the ability to move your head. A Combine Elite takes your Gravity Gun from you. The traitorous Mossman appears, telling you not to struggle. You glide out into a spacious corridor, automatically following Mossman.

The procession moves toward Breen's sanctum. Combine Elite guards are posted on either side of the chamber's entrance. An Elite has already entered the chamber with your Gravity Gun. As the sun sets behind the giant vertical window, you're led inside.

ADDITIONAL INVESTIGATIONS

Breen is inside the chamber talking at the imprisoned Eli Vance. You, Gordon Freeman, enter. A soldier hands Breen the specialized Gravity Gun they have seized from you. "What's this? Put it over there." Breen quickly gestures.

Mossman tries to make the point that Eli needs to live to finish his research, but Breen dismisses the idea and says, "Eli...if you won't do the right thing for the good of all mankind, maybe you'll do it for one of them." Breen is talking about Alyx. He threatens to send both Alyx and Eli into the dark side of a combine portal. Mossman pipes up: "It isn't necessary–" "I agree," Breen interrupts, "it's a total waste. Fortunately, the resistance has shown it is willing to accept a new leader. And this one has proven to be a fine pawn for those who control him."

Turning to you Breen begins to bargain; "How about it, Dr. Freeman? Did you realize your contract was open to the highest bidder?" "Gordon would never make any kind of deal with you!" Alyx shouts. Breen presses a button that starts the pods moving. But as he does, Mossman steps forward and electrifies the control panel with Alyx's EMP device. The intercom explodes.

"They know you betrayed them." Breen pleads, "they'll turn on you! Judith, Dr. Mossman, please!" "I'm sorry, Wallace. You're all out of time." Mossman replies. Mossman starts to push the buttons to release Alyx and your pods, but as she does, Breen grabs the Gravity Gun. He fires it, to devastating effect.

When the smoke clears, Breen has fled to the elevator shaft behind you. However quick you are to react, you cannot catch him. Mossman shouts, "There's no time, Alyx. He's on his way to the portal...you have to stop him." She hands Alyx the EMP device. Trying to take it all in, Alyx says to her father, "Dad, I'm not saying goodbye."

"No! Never!" Eli responds. Run to the elevator with Alyx, who jimmies the lock.

Alyx thanks you for saving her, then the elevator reaches Breen's location. Step out into his personal command module, down an ornate carpet, where Breen is talking to a green sluglike entity on a screen.

ENTITY ENCOUNTER:
COMBINE ADVISOR

Behold a face of the Combine; a giant, green, sluglike entity with the gift of telekinesis appears for the briefest of moments on Breen's largest computer monitor. It blinks out of view a moment later.

Breen has mistakenly discarded the Gravity Gun as he fled the area. Pick this up immediately and follow Alyx's advice; power up your suit to maximum capacity at the Recharger, then enter the elevator. Moments later, you are transported to the base of the reactor.

INTRODUCTION / GETTING STARTED / WEAPONS DETAIL / HALF-LIFERS / THE BESTIARY / CHAPTER 1–14 / ANOMALOUS MATERIALS

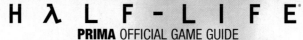

Head right, passing a computer terminal, and wait for a descending piston arm. Run across it to the balcony on your right. Combine Soldiers quickly appear. Demolish them quickly.

TIP

Your race to the top of the spire is against Breen in his sphere. To ensure victory, stay above Breen; speed and careful maneuvering are key here.

Move up and around in a continuing counterclockwise path to a set of three conduits. Suck the orbs out of the first, then step into the area, swing around to the left, and prepare to repel the Soldiers streaming in from a corridor behind you. Use the Plexiglas sides of the conduits as cover and the orbs as projectiles.

TIP

Ricochet the orbs off walls to hit enemies out of your direct line of sight.

Continue across the conduits, deactivating them by sucking the orbs out. Swing right as you reach the final conduit, aiming up into the balcony above at additional Combine attacks; suck up and drop Soldiers, or use an orb to clear them away.

Step out from the conduits and locate the black arm rising and falling in the corner. Step onto the top of it and ride it up to the next balcony.

TIP

Quickly check on Breen's progress; if he's at the same height or higher, get moving!

A squad of Combine Elites and Soldiers temporarily halt you. They step in from a side corridor, which, like all the others, has an energy wall at its entrance and cannot be entered. Topple the Soldiers off the sides or into each other, then step across the narrow plinth to the next part of the balcony ahead and left.

Move around until you reach a jutting walkway leading directly to the central fusion tower. Step onto it and carefully move to the edge. Wait for a spinning platform to lock into place for a second. Step onto that, and you're whisked up to a high platform on the spire. Get off and recharge your suit; this is critical.

Work your way around the narrow and confusing platforms in the middle of this structure until you reach another arm. Stand atop it to move up to another high platform. Prepare for more Combine combat and the arrival of Breen's bubble.

Move farther around until you reach a platform leading to the outside of the fusion reactor, marked "1." Engage in another round of Combine combat. The walkway shelters you somewhat, or you can use an Elite's body as a shield. Step onto the outer balcony, head right, and then up to another gigantic arm; ride this to the reactor's top.

Attack a quartet of Gunships flying out from the Citadel's containment areas below. Use the orbs in the conduits nearby and shoot them directly at the ships; it only takes three orbs to destroy each Gunship.

Your attack is simple. Shoot the orbs at the fusion reactor's core. This causes instability and blocks Breen's escape. After a couple of shots, some metal shields appear, but blasting them with an orb shatters them. Time your attacks after this so the orb passes between the spinning shields and directly into the core. There's no need to destroy each individual shield. Keep this up until the core explodes after approximately three to six shots.

G-MAN
ABOUT TIME AND SPACE

The top of the fusion spire begins to pulse, crackle, and detonate. The spire then bursts outward in a gigantic explosion, and Alyx can just be heard over the top of it: "Come on, Gordon! We've got to get out of here! Maybe we still have...."

Alyx stops talking. The fireball freezes a second before engulfing you. A gaunt man in a gray suit appears, and finishes Alyx's sentence for her: "...Time, Dr. Freeman? Is it really that time again? It seems as if you only just arrived."

 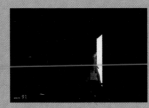

"You've done a great deal in a small timespan," the man continues. "You've done so well, in fact, that I've received some interesting offers for your services. Ordinarily, I wouldn't contemplate them, but these are extraordinary times."

Time and space congeal into an inky blackness. The G-Man continues, "Rather than offer you the illusion of free choice, I will take the liberty of choosing for you...if and when your time comes round again. I do apologize for what must seem to you an arbitrary imposition, Dr. Freeman. I trust it will all make sense to you in the course of...well..."

The G-Man pauses to gaze at you.

"I'm really not at liberty to say."

"In the meantime..." his voice trails, as a door of white opens, "This is where I get off."

The G-Man strides through the doorway.

Everything fades to black.

ANOMALOUS MATERIALS

Research has uncovered further instability with your HEV Suit that may result in enhanced or odd gameplay experiences.

G-MAN ABOUT TOWN: CHECKLIST

The entity keeping an omnipresent watch over your movements follows you throughout your adventure in and around City 17. His locations have been pinpointed in a checklist.

ANOMALOUS MATERIALS

LOCATION #1: WAKE UP AND SMELL THE ASHES

In a wild hallucination prior to you waking up on the train.

LOCATION #2: CHAPTER 2, A RED LETTER DAY

On a monitor screen in Kleiner's lab after Barney finishes at the terminal.

LOCATION #3: CHAPTER 3, ROUTE KANAL

On a television the Vortigaunt is watching, inside the red train carriage.

LOCATION #4: CHAPTER 4, WATER HAZARD

Standing on the pier in front of Station 7.

LOCATION #5: CHAPTER 4, WATER HAZARD

Flickering on a giant monitor attached to the high-rise building.

LOCATION #6: CHAPTER 4, WATER HAZARD

On a small gantry near the second covered bridge.

LOCATION #7: CHAPTER 6, "WE DON'T GO TO RAVENHOLM"

Walking into a train tunnel beyond the railcar blocking the railroad.

LOCATION #8: CHAPTER 9, NOVA PROSPEKT

Looking through a window near a pair of double doors, on a monitor screen.

LOCATION #9: CHAPTER 11, ANTICITIZEN ONE

On a television at the ruined foyer of a tenement block.

LOCATION #10: CHAPTER 14, DARK ENERGY

At the top of the Citadel Spire, stopping time and exiting into space.

CONSOLE COMMAND TRICKERY

Enable cheats by bringing down the console command prompt and typing "sv_cheats 1."

BINDING AND FINDING

bind <key> <command>: This binds a console command to a key. Note that if the command has arguments, quotes must be used. For example: bind x "impulse 101"

find <keyword>: This searches for all console commands that contain the keyword. For example: "find wireframe" returns all console commands related to wireframe.

Commands with numeric value: Experiment with that number for different (and sometimes desirable or undesirable) effects.

GAMEPLAY ENHANCEMENTS

COMMAND	EFFECT
god	You don't receive damage.
buddha	You receive damage, but won't die.
infinite_aux_power	Grants infinite power for your suit's functions: Sprinting, Flashlight, and Swimming.
impulse 101	Immediately stocks all weapons and ammunition.
notarget	Enemies do not attack you.
npc_kill	Instantly kills any nonplayer character in your target reticle.

SCREENSHOT ENHANCEMENT

COMMAND	EFFECT
impulse 200	This removes the weapon model.
cl_drawhud 0	The HUD is completely removed.

GOOD, OLD-FASHIONED MALARKEY

COMMAND	EFFECT
noclip	Allows you to fly through the world, including all walls and floors.
ch_createairboat	Instantly creates the airboat.
ch_createjeep	Instantly creates the scout car.
impulse 102	Skulls

DEVELOPER TOOLS

COMMAND	EFFECT
mat_wireframe 1	Constructs the world in wireframe.
vcollide_wireframe 1	Draws physics object wireframes.
showtriggers_toggle	Draws game triggers.
mat_normalmaps 1	Draws normal maps.
mat_normals 1	Draws surface normals.
mat_fastnobump 0	Turns off bump mapping.

COUNTER STRIKE SOURCE

In addition to *Half-Life 2*, your copy of the game comes with an enhanced version of the popular team first-person shooter game, *Counter-Strike Source*. The following pages show you how to connect and start your own server by using Steam.

STEAM

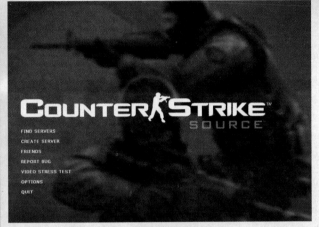

Steam's main menu screen and game list.

Steam is Valve's convenient method of meeting and chatting to friends online, hosting multiplayer game sessions, and finding or joining a variety of standard and customized multiplayer games for *Half-Life 2*, *Counter-Strike*, and other Valve games. It also provides exclusive games and game updates automatically.

- Play the latest Valve games
- Find your friends
- Find the best servers
- Get automatic updates
- Chat with friends, even when in-game
- Receive Steam-only special offers

To take advantage of Steam's features, Steam will convert your Valve games (and any other mods you have installed) to the Steam format and store them in the Steam directory. After this conversion process, your computer needs to be connected to the Internet to play and download Steam games.

INSTALL STEAM
Connect to the Internet and go to www.steampowered.com to download or update to the latest version. When prompted, create an account name and password.

ACCESSING STEAM
Steam runs in the Notification Tray, located in the right corner of the Windows taskbar. To access Steam or to quit, right-click on the Icon. You can also access Steam from the Windows XP All Programs menu (from the Desktop, click Start → All Programs → Steam).

MAIN MENU

PLAY GAMES
Choose a game from the Games menu. My Games lists Valve games installed on your computer. Available Games lists Valve games that you can play using Steam. To add a game to the My Games list, you need the original CD product key as it appears on the CD case.

BROWSE GAMES
Choose this option to check out all the available Valved games that you can download and play. Some are free, others are not. If you already own a game package, a message appears to let you know.

FRIENDS
Quickly find friends online. To build your friends list, you'll need to know your friendsí e-mail, user name, or first/last name. When you've added friends to your list, you can choose to be notified when they are online.

SERVERS
Connect to multiplayer games online and find your favorite servers. Select a column heading to sort the list for easier browsing. To find a game by specific criteria, select Change Filters. You can also add/remove column headings by right-clicking on the category bar.

Favorites: For quick access to a specific game server, right-click on the server name and select Add Server to Favorites. The server will be available in the Favorite folder.
History: Quickly locate a recently accessed server.
Spectate: Watch games, study strategies, and get into the action from a variety of camera angles.
LAN (Local Area Network): Browse servers running on your local network.
Friends: Find friends currently playing a game.

SETTINGS
This allows you to change your Account settings (if you wish to use another name), your Internet connection, the interface and Steam box that appears when you run the program, any skins you want to cover the Steam information boxes that appear, and the language.

NEWS
Keep up with the latest Steam news, including client updates, new game releases, events, contests, and much more.

SETTING UP A CS SOURCE SERVER

When you launch *Counter-Strike Source* and reach the main menu screen, you are presented with a number of options. These are:

- Find Servers
- Create Server
- Friends
- Options
- Quit

The Find Servers choice is the same as the general Servers option in Steam, as is the Friends choice. Options and Quit are the same as in *Half-Life 2*. Create Server is of most interest.

There are two tabs: Server and Game. Server allows you to pick a map of your choice (and remember, more maps are available all the time to download via Steam). The Game option allows the largest number of choices to be made, which are detailed here:

Hostname: The name of your server. Call it anything you like.
Max. Players: The default is 32, which is large enough for the maps provided. Increase or decrease depending on how many other players you wish to have join your server.
Server Password: Optionally add this to keep your server private. Remember to tell your friends what the password is.
Time per map (minutes): Default is 20. This is how long you'll spend on a particular map before continuing to another location.
Win limit (rounds): Default is 0. The number of rounds it takes for a team to emerge as an overall winner.
Round limit (rounds): Default is 0. The number of total rounds in the match you're hosting.

Time per round (minutes): Default is 5. This is how long a round takes (if no team wins earlier).
Freeze Time (seconds): Default is 6. This is how long each team remains frozen to allow for purchases at the start of each round.
Buy Time (minutes): Default is 1.5. This is how long you can spend buying ordnance as the round begins.
Starting money: Default is 800. The amount of money each team member begins with.
Footsteps on/off: Allows you to hear or mute approaching enemy footsteps, which affects strategies and ambush plans.
Death camera type: Choose from "Spectate anyone," "Spectate team only," or "First-person only." This determines what players dying in a fight can see for the remainder of the round. Switching to "Spectate team only" allows you to stop dead players from telling living ones where enemies are.
Disable chase/death cam: On/off. Allows you to turn the chase/death cam on or off.
Friendly fire on/off: Switch to on and everyone gets hurt by everything!
Kill TKers on next round on/off: Kicks off Team-Killers from your server when switched to on.
Kick idlers and TKers on/off: Instantly kicks those who have an entity on the battlefield but don't move, or those killing members of their own team when switched to on.
Kick after (x) hostage kills: Default is 5. If you are playing a map with hostages, and a player kills a number of them, the player can be banished.
Allow Flashlight on/off: Enables the Flashlight; good for lighting up dark rooms.

RETURN TO THE SOURCE

Now that your server is up and running, you can begin to learn the ins and outs of the various stages that shipped with the game. The following pages detail the best choke areas, sniping holes, and ambush points in the game.

AZTEC   MAP TYPE: DEMOLITION

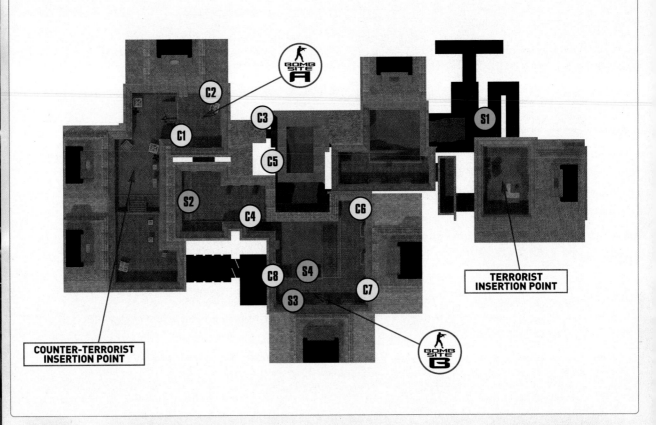

COUNTER-TERRORISTS

Mission: Terrorists want to bomb the Aztec ruins. Eliminate the terrorists and defuse the bomb if planted.

Overview: Unlike some maps that feature clear defensive positions around the bomb sites, this one offers no such amenities. In fact, both bomb sites are relatively open, making them difficult to lock down. Instead of standing out in the open and waiting for the terrorists to arrive, move your defenses away from the bomb sites and along the major passages and identifiable choke points. When playing with skilled teammates, consider implementing a roving defense. This works best when splitting into two squads and patrolling the areas around each bomb site.

TERRORISTS

Mission: Enter the ruins and plant the bomb at site A or B. Stop the counter-terrorists from defusing the bomb.

Overview: Simply reaching the bomb sites can prove far more dangerous than assaulting them. The lengthy passages and pitch-black interiors are ideal camping spots for CT snipers and campers. Stick to the shallow streambed where at least you have a fighting chance of overcoming the CT defenders. Regardless of which path you take, stay close to your teammates. If you run off by yourself, you're likely to fall prey to a CT ambush.

KEY LOCATIONS

Bomb Site A
Close to the CT insertion point, bomb site A offers little for defenders. With the exception of a large crate and a few stone blocks, there aren't many places to hide or take cover. As a result, the bomb site is difficult to camp. Defenders are better off holding

the surrounding paths. There are three main entry points to the site, but CT defenders should worry mostly about the two arched passages.

Bomb Site B
Like bomb site A, this site offers little protection. In fact, the site is open to long-range attacks from the opposite side of the large courtyard, making it exceptionally difficult to defend. The stack of stone blocks offer a bit of protection, but defenders can't

stage any surprise attacks from them. Fortunately for the CTs, the attack usually comes from one general direction. Still it's important to scan the nearby staircase leading down to the shallow stream below to prevent enemies from assaulting the site at close range.

Camping Spots

C1

This is the best camping spot for covering bomb site A. Crouch behind the slanted stone slab and aim toward the bomb site. You can't see enemies as they enter one of the two nearby passages, but you can engage them as soon as they approach the target area. Whether they're planting a bomb or defusing one, hold your fire until they begin their task, then let loose with an automatic burst. This position also allows you to hit attackers moving up the stone steps to the left. Enemies moving from this direction are more likely to spot you, so listen for incoming footsteps and be ready to move if you come under fire.

C2

If C1 is already occupied, hide behind the large crate in the corner to cover bomb site A. In addition to covering the bomb site, this position allows you to see a wider angle of the surrounding area, including the steps to the right as well as the arched passage ahead. However, this also makes you easier to spot. So use the crate more for cover than for concealment. Strafe out to attack your opponents, and strafe back behind it for cover and reloading.

C3

For the CTs, covering this bridge is essential in preventing terrorist rush attacks on bomb site A. Fortunately, this is a pretty easy choke point to defend. Simply take a position in the dark passage and aim out the arched doorway ahead to pick off enemies as they attempt to cross the rope bridge. Intense firefights often develop over this bridge, so be ready to strafe to the left or right to avoid incoming fire. If possible, bring a teammate along so you can lay down an endless stream of automatic fire—while one reloads, the other one fires. Stay back in the dark passage and avoid moving out toward the bridge. Otherwise you can be hit by enemies firing from the shallow streambed below.

C4

Another important choke point for the CTs to cover is the stone stairway leading up from the streambed. Crouch at the top of these stairs and aim down the steps. From this position you also can cover the base of the ramp leading up to bomb site B. Terrorists moving along the streambed to either bomb site move from the left, so be ready to pick them off as they come into view. When holding this position, make sure that the nearby covered walkway and the rope bridge near C4 are adequately covered. If these areas aren't controlled, you stand a good chance of being flanked from the left. Keep an eye on your radar to get a rough estimate of where your team is positioned.

C5

If the CTs can get here early in the round, this position behind a stone block is excellent for covering the streambed as well as the rope bridge above. The streambed is wide open offering little cover. This stone block is one of the few spots that provides any sort of protection, and it has a good angle as well. Move in behind this block and aim down the streambed to pick off incoming terrorists from a distance. If you come under fire, crouch to avoid taking damage.

C6

By positioning yourself on this large stack of crates in the corner of the courtyard, you're treated to a great distant view of bomb site B and the nearby covered walkway. However, the best application for this spot is to ambush enemies advancing through the nearby doorway. Aim down into the gap between the two wooden doors and wait for an opponent to move into view. A quick burst from your weapon is bound to catch him by surprise.

C7

Like the other site, there aren't too many defensive options for directly covering bomb site B. This corner position is one of the only spots that provides some protection and concealment. Squeeze in between these two stone blocks and the wall, then aim out into the courtyard. When playing as a CT, the terrorists are most likely to attack the site along the pathway leading from C6, so keep your sights trained in this direction. However, assaults also could come from the nearby ramp leading up from the streambed, so don't neglect this area either.

C8

Another option for covering bomb site B is to crouch in the nearby doorway, between the wooden doors. This angle gives you a clear view of the bomb site without exposing yourself to incoming fire from the opposite side of the courtyard. This spot works best for CTs in the opening moments of a round. If you hold this position much later, you run the risk of being attacked from behind.

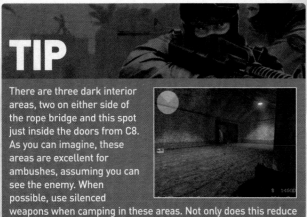

TIP

There are three dark interior areas, two on either side of the rope bridge and this spot just inside the doors from C8. As you can imagine, these areas are excellent for ambushes, assuming you can see the enemy. When possible, use silenced weapons when camping in these areas. Not only does this reduce the sound of your weapon, but it also eliminates muzzle flash, something that would give away your position in these pitch-black interiors.

Sniping Positions

S1

The terrorists can benefit from this position early in a round, using it cover the streambed while teammates advance. From this spot you can easily hit CTs at the far end of the L-shaped bend in the streambed. This area is often accessed by CTs hopping off the rope bridge in an attempt to attack terrorists on the move. Take your time to center your sights and squeeze off a round as soon as your target stops. Unless you're really good, hitting a moving target at this range is extremely difficult—even with the scope.

S2

The covered walkway ahead is high traffic area for both CTs and terrorists, making this an excellent sniping position for both factions. Its close proximity to bomb site A makes it a good defensive position for shutting down this long path. By zooming in, you can cover the passage all the way to the crates at C6. But before you get too cozy, make sure the nearby choke points are covered by your teammates to prevent getting flanked.

S3

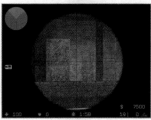

By moving out of the doorway at C8, you get a good view of the whole courtyard. Although little cover is available, the long-range capability can greatly benefit the defense of bomb site B. For instance, enemies in the covered walkway on the opposite site of the courtyard are difficult to see and hit with conventional firearms. But with the aid of a scope, you can easily zoom in and pick them off. However, if the bomb site is rushed, retreat to another position–you won't last long once the battle moves to short range.

S4

Similar to the spot at S1, this position works well for covering the shallow streambed. This spot is particularly good for CTs defending the lower path leading toward bomb site B. Set up in the middle of the streambed against the far wall and aim past the camping spot at C5 toward the L-shaped intersection ahead. This where most terrorists first appear, whether they're moving along the streambed or dropping down from the rope bridge. You also can look up to spot enemies moving along the covered walkway. Unfortunately, this is where you'll most likely be attacked from too. This area is boxed in, offering no quick way to escape, so use this position only when the walkway above is covered by teammates.

COUNTER-TERRORIST TACTICS

Two Squad Roving Defense

Loitering around the bomb sites doesn't serve your team well. Take the fight to the terrorists and sweep the predictable avenues of attack. At the start of a round, split into two squads. While one squad moves toward bomb site A...

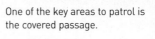

...the other squad moves toward bomb site B.

One of the key areas to patrol is the covered passage.

COUNTER STRIKE SOURCE

The rope bridge is another potential site of enemy movement.

At the top of the stairs, turn right and move toward the wide archway leading to bomb site A.

When your squad encounters the enemy, report your position to the other squad and request assistance.

Upon entering the bomb site, take time to secure the area. Peek behind the stones and crate before planting the bomb.

In most instances, this allows you to hit the enemy from two directions at once, bringing a quick end to the enemy's assault.

When it's clear, place the bomb in the center of the site.

TERRORIST TACTICS

Bomb Site A Assault
Bomb site A can be tough to reach. Not only is it close to the CT insertion point, but most of the paths leading into it are likely to be filled with CT defenders. Your best option is to move along the streambed.

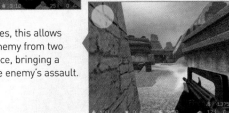

Now take cover behind the stone at C1 and aim toward the bomb. Pick off the incoming CTs from this position as they move into view.

Bomb Site B Assault
While it's possible to rush bomb site B, you're likely to face heavy resistance just as you're about to plant the bomb. So use the path along the streambed—it's a longer route, but ultimately it's the safest option.

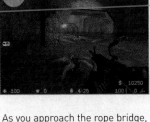

As you approach the rope bridge, watch the area above near C3. Defenders can fire through the gaps in the wooden planks. Move through this area to avoid getting bogged down in a firefight where the CTs have the definite height advantage.

Watch the usual camping spots for CT defenders while moving along the stream.

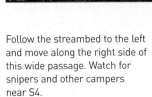

Follow the streambed to the left and move along the right side of this wide passage. Watch for snipers and other campers near S4.

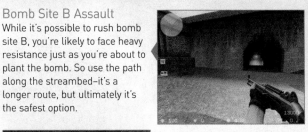

As you move toward the bomb site, watch the stairway along the right. The CTs are likely to enter the streambed at this point in an attempt to halt your advance.

Turn right to take the stone staircase up to C4. Before advancing to the top, make sure there's not a CT camper aiming down at you.

Continue to the stone ramp leading up to the bomb site. By now you'll probably encounter some defenders. Deal with them before advancing to the top.

When you reach the top, scan the surrounding courtyard for imminent threats.

Once all enemies have been cleared from the area, plant the bomb.

While your team takes positions around the bomb site, move over to the corner at C7 and wait for the CTs to counterattack.

CHATEAU MAP TYPE: **DEMOLITION**

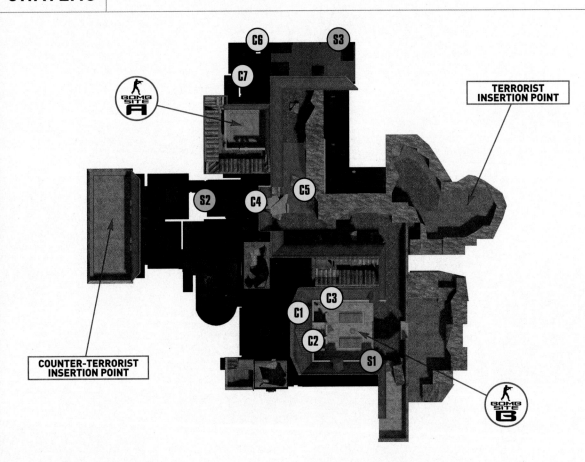

COUNTER-TERRORISTS

Mission: Terrorists are attempting to bomb the chateau. Secure both bomb sites and defuse the bomb if planted.

Overview: The chateau is full of potential ambush spots, but try to focus on the major choke points, primarily around bomb site B. If you have enough manpower, you can cover bomb site A from the windows overlooking the courtyard, but get there fast–terrorists love to rush this site. While most of the team will be busy securing the two bomb sites, if possible, send a teammate or two outside to roam the outdoor tunnels and canals. The chateau is easy to defend if you can keep the terrorists out, but if they manage to infiltrate the

hallways, the round can quickly become a free-for-all death match–like firefight.

TERRORISTS

Mission: Enter the chateau and detonate a bomb in the atrium or outside courtyard.

Overview: The odds are against the terrorists from the start. The quickest option is to rush bomb site A and hunker down for an immediate CT counterattack. But an even better tactic is to infiltrate the chateau through the nearby windows (at bomb site A) and take the fight inside. Once inside the chateau, you can tilt the odds in your favor by attacking from unpredictable directions and ultimately causing panic and confusion among the CT ranks.

KEY LOCATIONS

Bomb Site A

This U-shaped courtyard is close to the terrorist insertion point, making it a popular site to rush. However, if the CTs get here first, they can lock it down by covering from the 10 windows overlooking the site. Each window is a potential entry point, making defending this site from the courtyard a risky challenge. Defenders are better off taking positions inside the building and covering from the windows–preferably the upper floor windows.

Bomb Site B

If defended properly, this second courtyard can also be a tough nut to crack. The CTs are most likely to reach this site first, giving them ample time to lock down the surrounding choke points. The site is ringed by a couple of walkways, one at ground floor and another one level up. These dark walkways are the best option for covering the open courtyard. The two main entry points to this site are on opposing sides of the courtyard on the ground floor. One of these passages leads to the basement (with the wine vats), while the other leads into the chateau's interior. Upstairs, another entry point leads into the chateau. To effectively defend the site, you must cover all three entrances.

TIP

For beginners, navigating the dark rooms of the chateau can be overwhelming. Fortunately several signs point you to the bomb sites, helping alleviate some of the confusion.

Camping Spots

C1

This upstairs window overlooking the bomb site A courtyard is a good spot for CTs to take early in a round. If the terrorists choose to rush the site, they'll arrive along the lengthy canal at the far end. This spot gives you a good view of the ramp leading up to the site as well as the courtyard below. The window provides partial concealment, so don't shoot it out until you have a target in your sights.

C2

From the window at C1, you can also move outside onto the nearby balcony.

Step out onto the windowsill and inch along a narrow ledge toward the balcony and jump into the position.

The low stone wall running along the perimeter of the balcony obscures your view of the courtyard below, so hop up on this ledge to cover the bomb site. This leaves you open to return fire, but also gives you the chance to drop back down into the balcony for cover. Pop in and out of cover during a firefight. Keep an eye on your right flank–the stone ledge is broken here and if you're not careful you could fall off the balcony. This break in the low wall also makes it possible for enemies in the corner below to hit you. Watch for enemy activity along this side.

TIP

Continue along the narrow ledge ringing the courtyard to take position in this corner. This spot gives you a clear view of the courtyard, but offers no cover. Don't stay here too long.

C3

Locate this piece of broken stone in the corner of bomb site A.

Crouch behind this stone to cover the courtyard. This is a good spot for terrorists to take after the bomb has been planted. For best results, plant the bomb so it's within a line of sight of this position. From this partially concealed spot, you stand a chance of remaining hidden while CTs scour the courtyard for the bomb. Wait until they stop by the bomb and open fire.

By aiming up, you can see the window at C1. When counterattacking, CTs may jump out of this window to reach the courtyard. Try to pick them off as they drop to the ground—they won't know what hit 'em.

TIP

By crouching behind this piece of stone, you can withstand the bomb's blast, but only if you've sustained no more than minimal injuries during the round.

C4

This upstairs position is a major choke point that CTs can use early in a round. The crack in the wall is a favorite entry point for terrorists looking to assault bomb site B, or those trying to enter the chateau. Crouch in the darkness and aim toward the large crack. Don't shoot the wooden planks blocking this gap—these slow down the terrorists, giving you a few more seconds to catch them in this narrow crack while they break inside.

By creeping forward, you can scan the alley outside and fire down on the terrorists as they move up the pile of rubble. But you're better protected (and concealed) by hanging back in the dark room and waiting for the terrorists to fill your sights. If possible, use a silenced weapon to avoid giving away your position.

C5

Here's another option for covering the alley near C4. Exit the crack in the wall and take a position along the large chunk of stone in the adjoining alleyway. Keep an eye on the crack in the wall at the end of this alley—this leads into the basement. But the most important passage is the one to the right. Terrorists looking to rush bomb site B usually file through this passage on their way to the crack in the wall. Halt their advance with a burst of automatic fire.

C6

Due to the tight confines and three possible entry points, bomb site B has no definitive camping spots. However, you can try to hold this spot in the short stairwell next to the basement passage. This works well for the CTs in the opening moments of a

round. As the terrorists file in through the basement, mow them down with a machine gun or blast them with a shotgun as they pass through the adjacent walkway. Don't hold this spot too long; you can be hit from behind by any enemies that access the upper walkway circling the bomb site.

C7

Along with the crack in the wall at C4, the basement is another popular entry point for terrorists. Take a position at the top of the stairs and aim down into the room. Both entry points are along the right side of the room, so be ready to gun down the enemies as they move around the large wine vats. If the enemy pushes forward, fall back toward bomb site B and consider taking up a position at C6.

Sniper Positions

S1

This upstairs window is great for covering the lengthy canal leading to bomb site A. Move along the right side of the window and crouch for increased accuracy and better concealment. By peering through the scope, you can see to the end of this narrow passage. Engage targets before they get too close. Otherwise your enemies can return accurate fire into the window. If your position is discovered, move to one of the other windows on the top floor and engage the enemies down in the courtyard from a new spot.

S2

Here's another option for CTs covering the crack in the wall near C4. Set up in the room below and crouch in the far corner. Aim your rifle at the crack in the wall and wait for a terrorist to appear on the other side. The wooden planks blocking the passage buy you some time to adjust your aim. These planks also help keep you out of sight, so try to drop your targets before they break through. Use a semiautomatic sniper rifle such as the SG-550 for a good balance of accuracy and rate of fire.

S3

 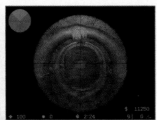

From this spot in the basement you can cover the long tunnel system leading toward bomb site B. This spot works best for CTs, as the tunnel ahead must be accessed by all terrorists moving along this side of the chateau. Whether they're heading toward the crack in the wall or the basement, they must pass through this tunnel. Crouch next to the large wine vat in the corner and set your sights straight ahead. This position works best if a buddy armed with an automatic weapon accompanies you. He can fire a wild burst of suppressing fire while you pick off the enemies. A friend can also prevent you from getting flanked or rushed.

COUNTER-TERRORIST TACTICS

Upstairs Defense

When playing as a CT, stick to the upper floor. Not only does this give you a height advantage over the terrorists below, but it's also the quickest way to move between the two bomb sites. This is essential when responding to the planting of a bomb. From bomb site B, locate the upper floor passage leading into the chateau.

Follow the passage beyond and cross these planks spanning a gap in the floor. If you get turned around, watch for the occasional signs posted next to the doorways.

Continue into this room with the large hole in the floor. Watch for terrorists hiding among the rubble while passing through.

Move to the window at C1 and peek outside. Line up your shot before shooting out the window.

Pick off any defenders you can see from this window before dropping to the ground.

When you reach the ground, scan all corners and neutralize any more terrorist campers. Find the bomb and rush over to it.

Have your team cover you while you defuse the bomb. The same path illustrated here can be used to reach bomb site B, so get familiar with it. If you're low on manpower, patrol this upstairs area to watch both bomb sites.

TERRORIST TACTICS

Bomb Site A Rush

Of the two sites, bomb site A is the best one to rush because it's close to the terrorist insertion point, and if you're quick, you can get there before the CTs can defend it. Before the round begins, select your pistol or knife to increase your speed and dash for the passage ahead.

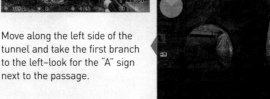

Move along the left side of the tunnel and take the first branch to the left—look for the "A" sign next to the passage.

Exit the tunnel and approach the lengthy canal to the left.

Although it's unlikely that any CT snipers are in place yet, always move along the right side of this canal to avoid being targeted by any opponents in the window at S1.

Rush up the ramp and aim into the window at C1. If the CTs are on their way, they're most likely to attack through this window.

Once your team has gathered near the site, plant the bomb while they cover you.

Now move to one of the nearby lower floor windows and shoot it out.

Climb through the window and find a good position on the interior to cover the bomb. Move away from the window and exterior wall before the bomb explodes to avoid sustaining heavy damage.

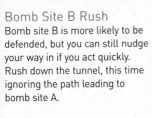

Bomb Site B Rush
Bomb site B is more likely to be defended, but you can still nudge your way in if you act quickly. Rush down the tunnel, this time ignoring the path leading to bomb site A.

Follow the tunnel around to the right and look for the passage on the left. Run to this passage before you can be hit by any CT snipers in the basement at S3.

Turn right into the parallel passage and enter this hole in the wall leading into the basement.

If you're carrying the bomb, let your team move ahead into bomb site B and clear the surrounding walkways.

Quickly enter the courtyard and plant the bomb in one of the corners.

Scan the basement for any CT campers hiding among the vats, then continue up these steps while watching for attacks near C7.

Follow closely behind and order your team to fall in, so they can cover you while you plant the bomb.

Move up to the second level and take cover behind one of the pillars while keeping your sights on the bomb. Hold your fire until a CT approaches the bomb, then open fire while his back is turned.

COBBLE

MAP TYPE: DEMOLITION

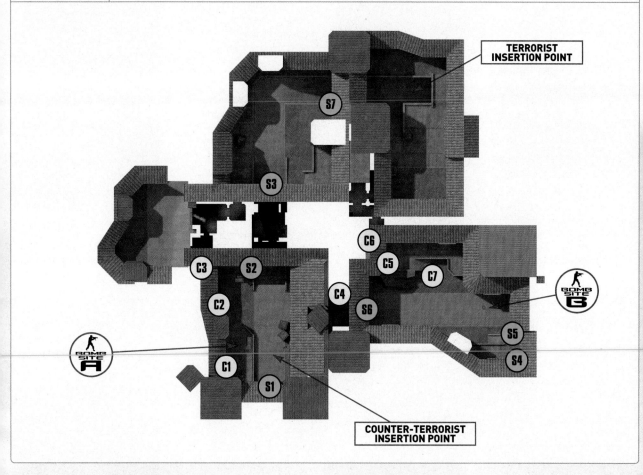

TERRORIST INSERTION POINT

COUNTER-TERRORIST INSERTION POINT

COUNTER-TERRORISTS

Mission: Terrorists intend to destroy vital supplies. Prevent them from detonating a bomb at either bomb site.

Overview: The strong defensive positions of both bomb sites usually prompt the terrorists to rush, in an attempt to catch your team before proper defenses are established. Instead of splitting your team between two sites, pick a single bomb site to defend. You can always counterattack later.

TERRORISTS

Mission: A fortified castle holds supply crates you want to destroy. Enter the castle and detonate the bomb at one of two sites.

Overview: When playing as the terrorists, teamwork is extremely important. Try to get your team to rush one of the bomb sites, preferably from multiple directions. This is the best way to get the upper hand over the sniper-heavy CT positions. If the team splits up, you'll be picked off one-by-one. Strength in numbers is the key here.

KEY LOCATIONS

BOMB SITE A

Bomb site A is on a raised platform in the same courtyard as the CT insertion point. The site is crowded by several crates, providing adequate cover and concealment for defenders. However, the area surrounding the raised platform is an open kill zone, making it a perilous area for attackers to cross. Defenders can cover all three major approaches to the site at long range.

BOMB SITE B

A short hallway separates bomb site B from bomb site A. The actual site is located at the far end of this large courtyard, offering multiple long distance angles for both attackers and defenders. The two separate entry points to this courtyard can be covered from the bomb site and the nearby elevated platform. Attackers should expect at least one sniper covering this area.

CAMPING SPOTS

C1

Climbing up on the large crates overlooking bomb site A is one option for covering the site and the courtyard.

Crouch-jump onto the crates to work your way to the top.

Once on top, you have a clear view of the courtyard and the bomb site below. The downside is that everyone in the courtyard can see you too. When taking this position, make sure you have a good, accurate rifle. Submachine guns and shotguns won't deliver the accuracy you need to cover the three entry points.

C2

For a more concealed position, hide behind this bush along the same wall as the bomb site. From this position you have a clear view of the doorway leading from bomb site B. This is a good position for terrorists guarding bomb site A, as most CTs approach through the opening ahead. The bushes won't block any bullets, but they make you harder to see. The CTs (in their green camouflage) blend in even better.

C3

By camping inside this narrow passageway leading to bomb site A, you'll rack up some kills when playing as a CT. Out of the three entry points, this one is the most popular for incoming terrorists. By shutting down this passage, you force the terrorists to take one of the two other paths leading out into the open courtyard, where they encounter your team's snipers and other defenders.

C4

Once the bomb is placed, this dark hallway between the two bomb sites is a great ambush spot for terrorists looking to prevent a CT counterattack. If you're defending bomb site A, move along this crate and get a good view of the partially open double doors. If your budget is limited, a submachine gun or shotgun is effective from this spot.

When defending bomb site B, turn around and aim toward the open doorway leading from bomb site A. This allows you to catch incoming CTs as they rush through the doorway.

C5

The most likely path for terrorists assaulting bomb site B is through the nearby passage. Hide along the side of this crate near the passage and hit the terrorists in the back as they rush the bomb site. Use a silenced weapon to avoid giving away your position.

C6

Taking a position in this passageway is a great way to stem the flow of terrorists into bomb site B. However, expect heavy resistance, especially if the rest of your team successfully locks down bomb site A. That leaves this passage the only path into bomb site B. Due to the tight confines and short range, this is a great spot for a shotgun or a heavy machine gun.

However, terrorists can catch you off guard by peering through this metal grate at the end of the passage. Look beyond this grate for movement and prepare to open fire as terrorists round the corner.

C7

If used in conjunction with C5, this spot at the bottom of the ramp can be used to catch attackers in a cross fire. However, if defending alone, avoid this spot as it puts you in the path of attackers moving toward bomb site B.

SNIPING POSITIONS

S1

By hiding in the shadows next to this closed wooden door, you can cover most of the bomb site A courtyard. From this position you can cover the underpass area straight ahead and the hallway passage to the right. Your major blind spot is to the left. Attackers can access the bomb site without you even knowing about it. Take this position only when teammates are present to cover the raised platform and the passageway to the left.

COUNTER STRIKE SOURCE

S2

This spot is opposite S1 at far end of the courtyard. Crouch between the crates on your right and the railing on your left to get a decent view of the raised platform. The tree ahead obscures your view to some degree, but it also makes you harder to see. Always remain crouched while in this spot, or else you risk exposing yourself to attacking troops moving up the ramp to your left.

The doorway to the left also poses a threat, but as long as you stay crouched you should remain concealed.

This leads into a small room with a couple of windows overlooking the adjacent courtyard.

S3

Climb this ladder in the underpass near bomb site A.

This is a good position for both CT and terrorist snipers defending bomb site A. However, this is an obvious sniping position, so expect to face resistance. If you suspect your position has been flanked, keep an eye on the ladder leading up into the room, or abandon the position altogether.

S4

This is the most comprehensive and flexible sniping position covering bomb site B. Climb the steps leading up to the raised platform right next to the site.

By aiming across the courtyard you can spot this passageway–a major thoroughfare for attacking terrorists. The large platform offers no real protection other than the thin guard rail. However, you can strafe back and forth to evade incoming fire–this is an effective tactic while loading a fresh round into your bolt-action sniper rifle. You also can cover the wooden double doors at the end of the courtyard.

S5

Here's a more specialized spot for covering bomb site B. Squeeze into this small nook between the closed doors and the raised platform. From this spot you have a clear shot of the double doors at the far end of courtyard. This position can be used by both sides, but works well for terrorists defending the site after the bomb has been placed. Surplus CT defenders from bomb site A usually counterattack through these doors. The major downside of this position is that your peripheral vision is completely cut off. Use this position only when you have teammates covering the site from different angles.

S6

This is another sniper spot for bomb site B that can be used by attackers and defenders. Crouch between the double doors and aim directly at the site. This can be used by CTs to pick of terrorists planting a bomb. But attackers can also use it to pick off various defenders camping the bomb site.

S7

Beneath the underpass near the terrorist insertion point, a ladder leads up into a room overlooking the nearby courtyard. Although this courtyard does not contain any critical areas, it's a good place to engage enemies moving about the map.

The same room contains another ladder leading up to a third-story room. From this window you have a better view of the courtyard below. You can also spot the windows of sniping position S3. Terrorists can use this spot to pick off any CT snipers defending the underpass leading into bomb site A.

COUNTER-TERRORIST TACTICS

BOMB SITE B RUSH

Make securing bomb site B your primary goal at the beginning of each round. But move fast to get there before the terrorists do. As soon as possible, move through the doorway on the right.

Rush through the dark hallway connecting the two bomb sites.

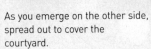

As you emerge on the other side, spread out to cover the courtyard.

Keep your eyes on the raised walkway to your left. If terrorists arrive in the next few seconds, they'll come from here.

Cautiously move up the walkway and take a position inside the passageway at C6. Hold this position until you encounter the enemy or receive new orders from your teammates.

BOMB SITE B COUNTERATTACK

If you're guarding bomb site A and the terrorists plant the bomb at bomb site B, stage a quick counterattack. Instead of moving through the nearest and most predictable path, take the long way around. Begin by moving through the nearby underpass.

Move up the ramp on the other side and veer to the right.

Find this passageway to the right and enter.

Turn right inside and follow the corridor—the path is clearly marked.

You eventually exit into the courtyard. Scan the area below and take out any defenders from a distance—watch for snipers at the far end and deal with them as quickly as possible.

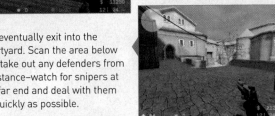

When it's clear, rush toward the bomb site and find the bomb. Whoever has a Bomb-Defusal Kit should defuse it. Provide cover while the bomb is defused to win the round.

TERRORIST TACTICS

BOMB SITE A ASSAULT

Bomb site A is on the opposite side of the compound. To hit this site, rush in before the CTs can establish a solid foothold on the surrounding area. Begin by moving through the nearby underpass. Equip your pistol to move faster.

As you spot the windows of sniping position S3, strafe left and right to throw off the aim of any CT snipers lurking inside.

Immediately move for this passage to the right of the underpass.

As you enter this passage, equip your primary weapon and prepare to encounter CT campers.

Upon exiting into the courtyard, scan the area opposite of the doorway.

Then turn to the right to spot bomb site A.

Cautiously approach the raised platform and order your squad to gather around for the site's defense.

Crouch-jump onto the large stack of crates next to the bomb site, proceeding to the top. Plant the bomb up here. This buys your team some extra time as the CTs search for the bomb.

Move back into this corner so you're partially covered from incoming fire. Aim down and cover the crates below—this is the only way up to the bomb.

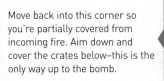

BOMB SITE B ASSAULT

Bomb site B is closer than site A, but expect plenty of resistance along the way. As soon as you can, move up the narrow passage to the left of the insertion point. Order the rest of your team members to follow—you'll need them.

The cramped passageway is a popular spot for CT campers. Help your teammates clear a path and continue outside into the courtyard.

Before rushing for the bomb site, scan the area below and engage any more defenders. Retain the high ground until the area is clear.

Cautiously approach the crates stacked around the bomb site. Strafe from side to side to locate any CTs hiding behind them.

Plant the bomb behind one of the crates. This keeps you covered from any immediate CT counter-attacks. Now pick a good camping spot and help your squad secure the courtyard.

This open doorway leads into the passage connecting to bomb site B. Take a left at the intersection just inside.

When you exit the passage, focus on the raised platform next to the bomb site. Keep moving while scanning for CT snipers. Whatever you do, don't stop!

Descend the ramp and scan the area near the double doors for any more defenders.

DUST | MAP TYPE: **DEMOLITION**

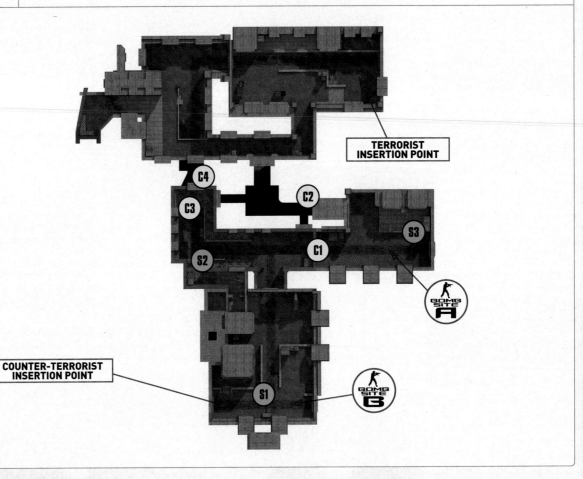

TERRORIST
INSERTION POINT

COUNTER-TERRORIST
INSERTION POINT

COUNTER-TERRORISTS

Mission: Eliminate hostile forces. Stop them from deploying or detonating the bomb at bomb sites A and B.

Overview: If the CTs act quickly, they have a good chance of shutting down all passageways leading to the two bomb sites. Two main choke points are in the underpass and in the tunnel. In addition to two areas, it's important to defend the bomb sites as well. The map's lengthy passages make for several effective sniping positions, allowing CTs to hold back and engage the terrorists at long range.

TERRORISTS

Mission: Plant the bomb at weapons stockpile A or B. Prevent counter-terrorists from disarming it.

Overview: There are only a few paths to the bomb sites, making it difficult to avoid CT ambushes. The best option is to avoid open areas and take the fight to the CTs at close range. The dark tunnel system in the map's center is a key location to control. Securing this area provides passage to both bomb sites and allows the terrorists to avoid getting caught in the open by CT snipers covering the underpass.

KEY LOCATIONS

BOMB SITE A

Bomb site A is usually a major point of contention as the terrorists rush to bomb it and the CTs attempt to secure it. There are only two main entry points: one through the tunnel and another through the large wooden doors. The area surrounding the bomb site is loaded with crates, providing defenders with plenty of cover and concealment.

BOMB SITE B

Right next to the CT insertion point, bomb site B is tucked away from the map's major choke points. Because CTs have plenty of time to adjust their defenses, terrorists usually skip this site–especially when playing against bots. Like the other site,

there are two major entry locations, requiring defenders to scan two different directions. Pay attention to the narrow passage on the side–this is a popular route for sneak attacks.

CAMPING SPOTS

C1

By crouching in between the large wooden doors at bomb site A, you can cover several incoming paths. When defending from this position, it's best to have a good rifle. Submachine guns and shotguns don't provide the long-range accuracy needed to engage distant targets. If a teammate is placed at C2, you can effectively lock down bomb site A.

C2

This spot is close to C1, but just inside the tunnel. From here, CTs can cover one of two major choke points as terrorists flow into the tunnel. Crouch next to the crate and aim straight ahead. Terrorists usually move through the passageway to the right. If you see nothing, back up behind the crate and aim out through the opening near the double wooden doors. Either way you can cover both paths leading into bomb site A. This is a good spot to take early in a match, when you can't afford larger and more accurate weapons. Terrorists also can use this spot to secure bomb site A once the bomb has been placed. Automatic weapons and shotguns work well here, especially when faced with large coordinated rushes by the opposing team.

C3

This position overlooks the underpass, the map's other major choke point. However, from this spot you can't see down into the underpass. Still it's a good spot to ambush terrorists as they rush toward the bomb sites. Automatic rifles work the best. Bring some grenades along to toss down on your enemies.

Use this spot to cover the tunnel from a different angle. If a teammate is placed at C2, you can pinch the enemy at both sides. Use a sniper rifle to scan down the tunnel and pick off terrorists as they turn their backs and move toward bomb site A.

C4

Another option for covering the underpass is to move down in it. This works for both sides. Try using a sniper rifle to pick off enemies from a distance. You have a long line of sight from this position, giving you slight advantage against those with less accurate weapons.

You also can try to ambush enemies at close range. Several crates and nooks in the underpass provide plenty of cover for surprise attacks.

SNIPER POSITIONS

S1

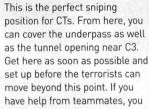 

You can adequately cover bomb site B from this position at the top of the short steps. Aim out into the archway and wait for enemies to move into view. If needed, drop back near one of the crates near the bomb site for better cover and concealment. While you're aiming into the archway, you could be flanked from the left, so keep an eye on this area as well. Better yet, have another teammate cover or patrol the narrow passageway to the left.

S2

This is the perfect sniping position for CTs. From here, you can cover the underpass as well as the tunnel opening near C3. Get here as soon as possible and set up before the terrorists can move beyond this point. If you have help from teammates, you can pin the terrorists in the underpass and pick them off one at a time. Bring some grenades and flashbangs to add to the confusion.

If terrorists exit through the tunnel, back up behind the nearby crate. This provides adequate protection, but limits your line of sight to one direction. Aim along the walkway heading toward the bomb sites and pick off terrorists as they turn their backs. If you have teammates covering bomb site A from C1, you can catch enemies in a wicked crossfire. You also can pick off terrorists trying to infiltrate bomb site A through the wooden doors. If your position is assaulted, retreat through the nearby passageway and take a position near bomb site B.

S3

The best way to defend bomb site A with a sniper rifle is to get as far back from the entry points as possible. Get on the platform near the bomb site and move to the back along the right side. Hop on the small ledge and move to the back wall.

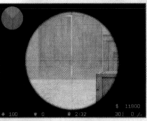

Turn around so the large crate is on your right and the double door entrance is ahead in the distance. From this spot you can focus your sights on the small opening between the doors. The crate on your right keeps you safe (and concealed) from enemies moving in from the tunnel entrance.

If you're defending by yourself, you need to cover both entrances. Inch forward, past the crate, until you can get a good view of the tunnel entrance. Engage enemies in the tunnel before they infiltrate the bomb site. Otherwise you have to engage them with your pistol, or any other weapons you can scrounge.

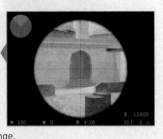

COUNTER-TERRORIST TACTICS

CHOKE POINT CRUNCH

THE TUNNEL

Act quickly to close off the map's two main choke points. Pick a good submachine gun or automatic rifle and make a break for the main archway leading out of bomb site B.

Rush past the wooden doors leading into bomb site A, and approach the nearby tunnel opening, aiming toward the C2 camping spot.

Cautiously enter the tunnel and move toward the crate. You're likely to bump into terrorists at this point, so stay sharp.

If it's clear, take a position near the crate and aim down the tunnel.

THE UNDERPASS

While part of the team covers the tunnel, the rest of the team should focus on the underpass. From the insertion point, move along the left side and approach the narrow passageway.

Race down this narrow passage. It's the most direct path to the sniping position at S2.

Depending on the weapon you're using, you may want to hang back at S2 and pick off incoming terrorist from a distance.

Entering the underpass allows you to get a more distant view of the incoming terrorists, but you'll lose sight of the tunnel entrance near C3.

With the help of your teammates, hold this position and repel the enemy advance.

Weave around a series of corners, turning right, left, and left again until you spot the opening overlooking the underpass.

You also can jump down onto the nearby crates to get a better line of sight down the underpass.

TERRORIST TACTICS

BOMB SITE A ASSAULT

The quickest way to bomb site A is through the tunnel system. Rush up the steps on the left and turn left down the nearby passageway.

Cautiously enter the tunnel and turn left at the intersection.

When it's clear, continue down the tunnel leading into bomb site A. Watch for snipers and other defenders on the raised platform ahead.

When it's clear, cover the teammate with the bomb while he plants it.

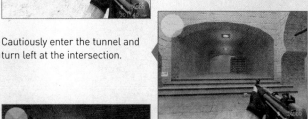

Follow the passage around to the right and focus on the tunnel entrance to the left.

Before rushing to the bomb site, peek down the passageway to the right and engage any CTs camping near the wooden door.

Peek out the tunnel exit and scan the large open area around the bomb site. Pick off any defenders you can see from a distance before moving out into the open.

Now take a position among the nearby crates and aim out toward the wooden doors. Keep an eye on the tunnel entrance as well to secure the bomb site.

BOMB SITE B ASSAULT

Take the underpass route to bomb site B.

Follow the path through the underpass and turn left to move up the ramp.

Move through the sniping position at S2, and enter the passageway behind it. Take a left, a right, and another right to reach the narrow passage running along the bomb site.

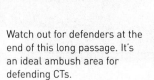

Watch out for defenders at the end of this long passage. It's an ideal ambush area for defending CTs.

As you enter the underpass, watch out for incoming CTs on the path ahead and on the sniping position at S2.

At the top of the ramp, turn around and aim toward S2. Move along this pathway and clear it of any CT defenders.

Sidestep out into the open, scanning the bomb site for any more defenders. Step softly to avoid alarming any defenders aiming at the main archway entrance.

Rush over to the bomb site and plant the bomb. Crouch behind one of the crates to avoid getting caught by enemy fire in the event of an immediate counterattack.

Now secure the bomb site and keep an eye on both main entrances.

DUST2   MAP TYPE: DEMOLITION

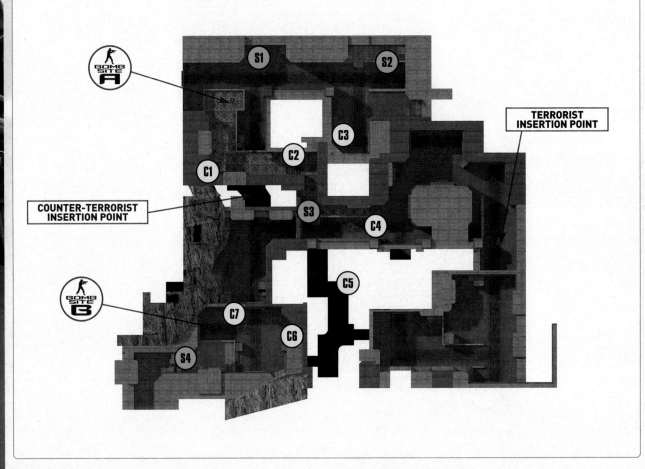

COUNTER-TERRORISTS

Mission: Terrorists are attempting to detonate a bomb at site A or B. Eliminate terrorists and prevent bomb detonation.

Overview: Both bomb sites are relatively close together, allowing the possibility of a roving defense strategy. Still, it's a good idea to keep at least one scout near each site to report the positions of the terrorists. Use the lengthy passageways to your advantage by positioning snipers in key locations.

TERRORISTS

Mission: Detonate the bomb at site A or B. Prevent counter-terrorists from eliminating your team or defusing the bomb.

Overview: Staying out of the crosshairs of CT snipers is one of the most challenging aspects of this map. Avoid open areas as much as possible and vary your attack patterns. Concentrate on taking bomb site B; it's relatively easy to reach and easier to defend.

KEY LOCATIONS

BOMB SITE A
This bomb site is located on a raised platform next to the counter-terrorist insertion point. Although the site can be directly accessed only from two directions, it can be covered from several nearby locations. The crates and barrels provide plenty of cover for defenders, making it easy to stage ambushes.

BOMB SITE B

Bomb site B isn't too far from the CT insertion point either, giving CTs only a few seconds to set up defenses before they can expect an attack. Due to the constricted entry points, this site is easier to lock down. As in Dust, the wooden doors leading into the

site are partially open, creating a narrow gap. Along the same wall is a hole that can be accessed from the other side by climbing on a series of crates. Finally there's the tunnel entrance, just opposite of the raised platform.

CAMPING SPOTS

C1

From this corner position near bomb site A, you can guard both access points. Move into the corner and hop behind the small bench. You're pretty much wedged into this spot, but if you lay down enough firepower, it won't matter. The clutter of the crates and the bench can make you hard to spot, especially if enemies approach from the left.

C2

Here's another camping spot near bomb site A. This position allows you to overlook the ramp leading up from the CT insertion point, often hitting the incoming attackers in the back. The only problem is that your right flank is open to attack, unless a teammate is covering from C1.

C3

Not far from the terrorist insertion point, this is one of the map's major choke points. CTs can use this spot to intercept terrorists moving toward bomb site A. If possible, try to move in front of the dark passageway and aim at the partially open doorways at the end.

C4

Here's a choke point that the terrorists can use to their advantage. Move up against the wall and aim at the doors at the bottom of the ramp. If you're quick enough to get into position you may hit some CTs moving from their insertion point. By

concentrating automatic fire in the small crack between the doors you can effectively shut down this passage. The same is true for CTs camping on the other side.

C5

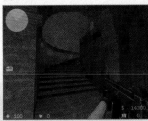

This darkened tunnel-like structure is another spot for CTs to catch terrorists on the move. Begin by moving up the short stairs, but stop before your reach the top. Aim to the left and gun down terrorists as they rush in through the nearby passage. Staying low on the stairs buys you some time, as the ambushed terrorists attempt to adjust their aim.

C6

Hide inside this nook near bomb site B to surprise incoming attackers. By sidestepping left you can glance through the open doors to the right, and blast enemies that attempt to enter. This spot also gives you a good view of the hole in the wall just

above the bomb site. Novice attackers moving from the tunnel to your left probably won't spot you as they rush for the bomb site.

C7

This is one of the most obvious camping spots on the map, so it's not a good idea to use it when playing with your peers. However, it can still surprise the bots in single-player games.

Access it by crouch-jumping up on the crates on the opposite side of the wall.

Climb through the hole in the wall and drop down on the high crate on the other side. From here you can cover the entire bomb site area, but you're also highly visible, making you an inviting target for enemies.

SNIPING POSITIONS
S1

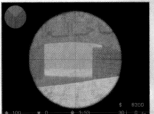

Use this spot to help cover bomb site A. Aim down into the low area that serves as the CT insertion point and pick off incoming enemies. You also can cover the walkway above, leading to the bomb site. Scan to your left to avoid getting flanked. There probably won't be too much traffic from this direction, especially if it's late in the round.

S2

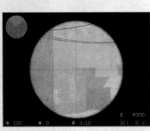

Both sides can use this position to cover bomb site A. Peer through your scope to spot a red barrel (in the foreground) on the raised platform. This barrel is right next to the bomb site's target. Use this barrel to adjust your aim and wait for a target of opportunity to wander into your sights. Whether it's a CT disarming a bomb or a terrorist placing one, they usually stop next to this barrel, allowing you to drop them with one well-placed shot.

S3

Here's a nice counter-terrorist response for the camping spot at C4. Just inside the double doors, take a position along the ledge above. Aim at the narrow passage ahead. This narrow passage connects to an area next to the terrorist insertion point. If you can get into position quickly, you can pick off a few terrorists as they filter through. Due to the limited width of the passage, they usually move through in single file—the perfect opportunity to skewer a couple of terrorists with one bullet.

S4

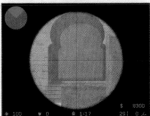

Although bomb site B is compact and cluttered, taking this position at the back of the raised platform gives you the perfect view of the tunnel entry point. In fact, you can see a good distance into the tunnel. Use this opportunity to pick off incoming enemies before they move into the bomb site. Chances are they won't be able to see you tucked away in the corner among the crates. Even if they do respond, the range is in your favor—unless they have a sniper rifle too.

COUNTER-TERRORIST TACTICS

RAPID RESPONSE TEAM
Before moving out, decide who is guarding which bomb site. If you have the manpower, consider using any remaining members as a rapid response team. The idea is to move around the center of the map and engage the terrorists. If a bomb is placed, you can then move to the site to secure and defuse.

Always make sure at least one team member has a Bomb-Defusal Kit. This buys you some extra time, which can be important especially if you have to fight your way to the bomb.

Hold near these double doors just outside the CT insertion point. This places you between the two bomb sites, giving you adequate response time to both locations. Listen for hints on the radio as to where the attacks are coming from and respond—preferably before the bomb is placed.

In the event that the bomb is planted, secure the particular site and cover the team member with the Bomb-Defusal Kit.

CAMPING A DROPPED BOMB

On some occasions you take out a lone terrorist with the bomb, causing him to drop a brown backpack–this contains the explosives.

Immediately order the rest of your team to the bomb's position. Wherever the bomb is, all terrorists will soon follow. The bomb sites are safe as long as the bomb stays under your control, so there's no risk in pulling other team members off guard duty. Covering the bomb is the top priority.

Watch where your team members set up and work out the best angle for maximum coverage. Eventually some poor terrorist will walk into your ambush. Take out all terrorists to win the round.

TERRORIST TACTICS

BOMB SITE A ASSAULT

The quickest way to bomb site A is through the narrow passage next to the insertion point. Turn left on the nearby ramp and jump over the ledge to reach it quickly.

Rush through this dark tunnel before the CTs can set up defense at the far end of the next long corridor.

Keep an eye on the double doors ahead while rushing forward. Sidestep to the corridor's right side to access the walkway running along the downward slope.

While moving along this walkway, stay up against the right wall to limit your exposure to any CTs lurking near the doors below.

Strafe around this corner to the right. The bomb site is around the next corner.

When it's clear, rush over to the bomb site and plant the explosives. If possible, have a teammate cover you.

Slowly sidestep around the next corner to the left and scan the area around the bomb site. Pick off any defenders from a distance, using the corner and nearby crates for cover.

Now dig in for a CT counter-attack. Get a good view of the underpass, as most forces probably will come from this direction, fresh from guarding bomb site B.

BOMB SITE B ASSAULT

Head for this tunnel entrance not far from the terrorist insertion point–it's clearly marked as a passage to bomb site B. If you have a flashbang, toss it in before entering. This helps spoil the plans of any ambushing CTs.

Inside the tunnel, keep an eye for CTs down the stairs to the right. Then take the passage to the left.

Sidestep out into this opening leading into bomb site B. Look for defenders on the raised platform ahead. If you encounter resistance, stay in the tunnel and pick off all visible CTs from a distance.

Cautiously exit the tunnel (C6) and scan the area to the right, near the double doors. Also look at the nook near the tunnel entrance.

When it's clear, jump down among the crates and plant the bomb.

Move up onto the raised platform and scan the area near the bomb site. Some CTs may be hiding among the crates.

Rush over to the nook at C6 and watch the bomb site. Stay concealed as much as possible and engage CTs as they turn their backs on you.

HAVANA

MAP TYPE: **HOSTAGE RESCUE**

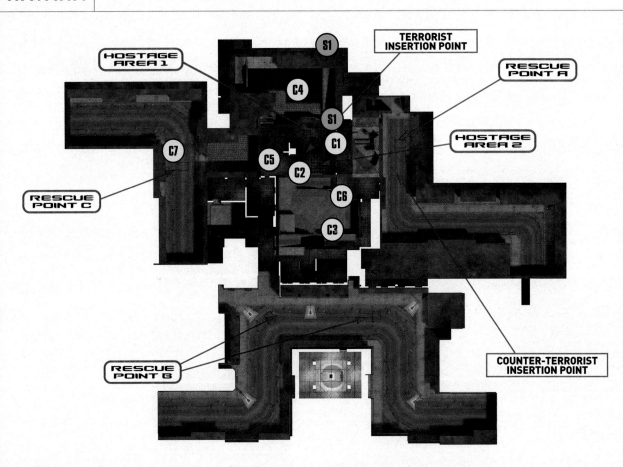

COUNTER-TERRORISTS

Mission: Terrorists are holding hostages in an abandoned villa. Raid the house and rescue the hostages.

Overview: Because the hostages are in one general area, the CTs' best option is to stick together and rush the hostage areas. In large matches, consider splitting the team into two squads, one responsible for securing the hostages and another team to secure a designated path to one of the rescue points.

TERRORISTS

Mission: Counter-terrorists have discovered the villa safehouse. Protect the hostages there. Eliminate the counter-terrorists.

Overview: The dilapidated mansion provides multiple opportunities to catch the CTs in ambushes, but don't wander too far from the hostage areas. One or two terrorists can cover both hostage rooms adequately. Concentrate the rest of your defenses around the perimeter of the two courtyards.

KEY LOCATIONS

HOSTAGE AREA 1

Think of this as the green hostage room. It's in the upper level of the mansion, on the opposite wall from hostage area 2. The hostages are in front of an open balcony overlooking a courtyard—the one with the gazebo. This room has two entry points on either side. The large balcony is open to gunfire from the courtyard and surrounding upper level walkways outside.

HOSTAGE AREA 2

The yellow hallways lead to this hostage room. Like the previous room, this one has two entry points on either side. The two large glass windows can't be broken, so the room is secure from gunfire originating from the courtyard.

RESCUE POINT A

This point also serves as the CT insertion point. The rescue point is in the middle of the street, making it easy to cover from all directions.

RESCUE POINT B

This point is easily distinguished by the "Viva Fidel" graffiti on the nearby wall. When rescue point C is out of question, this spot is a good alternative for CTs moving through the courtyard near hostage area 1.

RESCUE POINT C

This is the closest rescue point to the hostage rooms. CTs can reach this point by jumping out of an upper story window near hostage area 1 and rushing through the alley and out into the street.

CAMPING SPOTS

C1

When defending hostage area 1 from within the room, always take a position along the inside wall. This provides the most cover from the adjacent hallways. Stick to the corners to avoid falling prey to incoming fire from the courtyard. If possible, cover this room with a buddy. While crouching in one corner, aim at the opposite entrance near your teammate. If he aims at the entrance next to you, you can cover each other's backs. In the event

that CTs storm the room, don't remain still. Instead, retreat to one of the hallways and prepare to counterattack while the CTs secure the hostages.

C2

Here's another position for terrorists defending the hostages. In hostage area 2, pick a corner next to one of the entrances and crouch along the outside wall. If you're on your own scan left and right to cover both entrances. Watch your radar while listening for footsteps. If the rest of your team is dead or out of the area, patrol between the two hostage rooms. The CTs will attack at some point, and it's best to avoid getting stuck in a corner.

C3

Both teams can use this spot on the opposite side of the courtyard from hostage area 2. While you can't shoot through the windows in the hostage room, you can cover the courtyard below, including the staircase to the left.

C4

Here's another option for covering hostage area 1. From the upper walkway of the adjacent courtyard, jump over to the top of the gazebo. From here you have a good view of the courtyard as well as the open balcony of the hostage room. However, use this spot sparingly. The opposition can hit you from multiple positions. For better concealment, drop to the ground and enter the gazebo. The darkness keeps you well hidden, but your view of the hostage room is greatly reduced. Still this can be a great spot to cover the courtyard from, especially if you're using a silenced weapon.

C5

This window looks down into an alley that leads to rescue point C. For terrorists this can be a good spot to catch CTs moving on the street below in the opening moments of a match. Later use this position to block CTs from escaping through the window. Crouch-jump into the window and turn around. If you come under fire, back up to fall out of the window. On the ground, take cover behind the trash bin and aim up at the window to catch any CTs that follow you.

C6

This stairway near hostage area 2 is a good choke point for the terrorists. When CTs take a direct path to the hostage rooms, they move through this courtyard and rush up these steps. Take a position at the top of the steps and mow them down with automatic fire.

C7

Rescue point C is a hot spot for both sides due to its close proximity to the hostage rooms. Both sides can use this spot to cover the upper floor window near hostage area 2. Use an accurate rifle when taking this position. You don't want to hit any hostages.

SNIPING POSITIONS
S1

 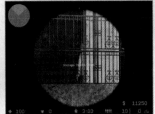

If you're a good sniper, try this position for covering hostage area 1. Move to the opposite side of the adjacent courtyard and take a position in the far dead-end corner. Back into the little nook in the corner to provide partial cover for your right flank. Aim at the balcony across the courtyard to get a clear view of both hostages. When playing as a terrorist, wait for a CT to stop next to one of the hostages. Zoom in, line up your sights, and squeeze the trigger. Counter-terrorists can use this position too, both to attack defenders and to cover the assault by other teammates. You could also use the area below S1 as a sniping position, but visibility of hostage area 1 isn't as clear as it is upstairs.

S2

This is a counter-sniping position for S1. When you're playing as a CT, S1 is likely already occupied, or soon will be. Move to rescue point B and enter the damaged building leading into the courtyard. Stop short of stepping out into the open and stay in the shadows. Crouch and peek between the pillars and get a good fix on S1 at the top of the stairs. Zoom in to get a clear view and fire. If you miss, back up into the shadows to prevent being seen.

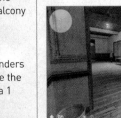

COUNTER-TERRORIST TACTICS

QUICK ASSAULT

With the support of your team, speed through and rescue the hostages before the terrorists can get their act together. Begin by moving through the alley near the CT insertion point.

Hang a right through the small yellow room that leads out into the courtyard.

Hold near the opening into the courtyard and help your team drop any resistance. Scan the perimeter before rushing outside. If a large firefight ensues, continue while the rest of your team occupies the terrorists.

Rush up the stairs and avoid stopping during your ascent. Jump if needed to avoid incoming fire.

Turn right at the top of the stairs and enter this hallway.

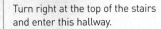

Cautiously approach hostage area 1 and toss in another flashbang. Enter and clear the room, securing the hostages as quickly as possible.

Before jumping through the window, scan the area below (near the trash bin) for any campers. Glance farther down the alley and into the street as well.

Move to hostage area 2 first. While rushing forward, equip a flashbang and toss it into the room. Switch back to your primary weapon and clear the room. Secure the hostages and proceed to the next hostage room.

Return through hostage area 2 and spot the window in the adjoining hallway–labeled C5 on the map.

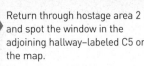

Crouch-jump through the window and turn around to make sure all hostages are behind you. Scan the window above to make sure no terrorists are on your tail.

Before you reach the end of the alley, strafe around the corner and glance down the street. Sidestep through rescue point C to successfully win the round. Try to accomplish this plan in less than 90 seconds.

TERRORIST TACTICS

HOSTAGE ROOM PATROL
Instead of staying in one position, keep moving between the two hostage rooms.

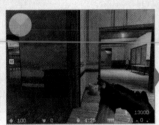

Watch both rooms by sidestepping left and right in one of the adjacent hallways.

You eventually run into one of the CT members trying to run off with your hostages.

ROVING DEFENSE
If the hostage areas are covered by teammates, take to the courtyards and scan for enemies.

Keep patrolling the courtyards while keeping an eye on the two hostage areas.

Unless you have plenty of teammates, forget camping the rescue points. The CTs have three points to choose from, giving them pretty good odds of missing you. If you do camp a rescue point, make sure the other points are covered too. Your best bet is to stick close to the hostages and prevent the CTs from securing them.

ITALY   MAP TYPE: HOSTAGE RESCUE

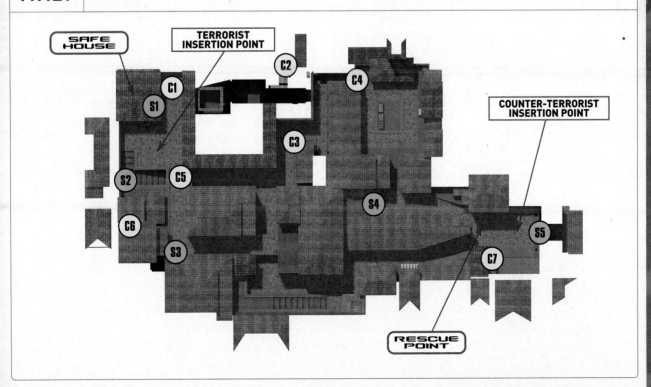

SAFE HOUSE

TERRORIST INSERTION POINT

COUNTER-TERRORIST INSERTION POINT

C1
C2
C4
C3
S1
S2
C5
S4
C6
S5
S3
C7

RESCUE POINT

COUNTER-TERRORISTS

Mission: Enter and sweep terrorist safehouse where hostages are held. Rescue hostages by returning them to the extraction point.

Overview: Plenty of paths lead to and from the safe house, but all paths converge on only one rescue point. It's important to have at least one team member stay behind and prevent this area from falling into terrorist hands. Vary your routes to the safe house each round and try to stick together as a team. Move through areas such as the apartment and the wine cellar to avoid getting caught in the ambushes along the narrow streets. Escort the hostages back to the rescue point through these same areas.

TERRORISTS

Mission: Guard the hostages. Eliminate counter-terrorists before they can enter the safehouse and perform rescue.

Overview: The terrorists can either hunker down near the safe house, or move out and try to ambush the CTs in the streets. If manpower allows it, a combination of both tactics works well. The problem with a roving defense are the multiple paths that the CTs can take. You could wander around the whole map and never spot a single CT. For that reason, try to stick near the safe house or the rescue point. You're guaranteed to run into the enemy at these areas.

KEY LOCATIONS

THE SAFE HOUSE

The hostages are kept in a safe house next to the terrorists insertion point. These two hostages are on the first floor, tucked in the corner next to a large crate. The crate's position makes the hostages hard to see when you enter the room from the adjacent hall.

The other two hostages are on the second floor—turn right at the top of the stairs to see them. A large radio in the corner pumps out Italian opera music, adding a bizarre element to the atmosphere. But the music actually works in favor of the CTs, as it helps drown out the sound of incoming footsteps.

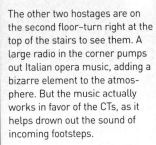

TIP

In addition to the downstairs entrance, you can access the safe house through an upstairs window by climbing onto this stack of crates.

Crouch-jump to the top of the stack. If you're assaulting the building as a CT, make sure a teammate covers your back while you climb the crates.

At the top, crouch-jump across to the windowsill—a regular jump won't cover the distance. Once you reach the windowsill, crouch to crawl through the window.

THE RESCUE POINT

The only hostage rescue point on this map also serves as the CT insertion point. Two long streets funnel into this open area, making it easy to cover by either side's snipers. CTs should secure this area for the duration of a round to prevent terrorists from setting up. Otherwise, returning to this spot with hostages in tow is dangerous.

CAMPING SPOTS
C1

This dark corner just outside the safe house is an excellent position for terrorists. From this corner you can hit anyone who tries to enter (or exit) the groundfloor entrance, while the shadows help conceal you. However, you don't have much in the way of cover, so make your shots count—a shotgun works well for solely covering the nearby door. But a longer-range weapon is more appropriate for a more generalized defense. If possible, use a silenced weapon to keep your target guessing. CTs also can use this spot to secure the outside of the house while the hostages are rescued.

C2

While hiding in this little nook my seem obvious, you can still surprise a few players. Instead of opening fire as your enemies run by, wait until they pass, then move into the dark passageway and open fire on them from behind. However, this relies on

you not being spotted in the first place. So stay crouched at bottom of the steps and hold your fire. Even if passing enemies glance in your direction, they may not see you. But don't take any chances. If an enemy stops in front of the doorway, blast him.

C3

This is a good choke point for terrorists to hold. Take a position near this corner and aim through the narrow passage ahead—just beyond is the open marketplace. CTs moving along this side of the map must pass by this entrance, giving you the

opportunity to fire on them. As a result, this is often the site of some intense gun battles. Bring along some flashbangs and grenades to get the upper hand.

C4

Take cover along the side of this barrel and aim into the market-place. If the terrorists have teammates at C3, this is the perfect spot to catch CTs in a cross fire. The marketplace is a major thoroughfare, and this is one of the best camping spots.

By holding in this corner you can cover two passages leading to the safe house. Although this is an ideal spot for terrorists, CTs can use it to pick off any unsuspecting roving defenders.

C5

This position, just a few steps from the terrorist insertion point, overlooks another narrow passage, serving as a good ambush spot. In addition to covering the passage, you also can cover the exit from the wine cellar by aiming down and to the

right. It's not a great angle, but at least you can see some movement, allowing you to turn around and hit them as they move up the stairs behind you.

C6

The wine cellar is a popular route for CTs, whether they're infiltrating the safe house or escorting the hostages back to the rescue point. Early in a round, hold in this dark corner and aim for the doorway—this is where CTs enter. For best

results, use an automatic rifle, but a submachine gun works well too. Use this same spot later in the round too, assuming the CTs move the hostages through here. Instead of covering the doorway, aim to the left and hit the CTs as they enter—just watch your aim around the hostages.

However, the raised platform nearby offers a bit more protection and distance. Crouching behind the guardrail makes you harder to see. This is a good spot for CTs to pick off terrorists attempting to gain control of the rescue point.

C7

If you choose to camp the rescue point, this corner near the two entries is a good spot—especially if your weapon has limited range. This can work equally well for both sides.

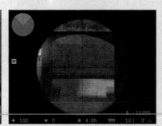

SNIPING POSITIONS
S1

By peering out this window in the safe house, you can see all the way down the darkened path ahead. This is an ideal kill zone for a terrorist sniper. Once CTs enter the passage, there's little opportunity for cover, allowing you to pick them off one-by-one. For best results, hold your fire until they're about a quarter of the way into the passage. They may retreat and choose another path if you open up too early.

TIP

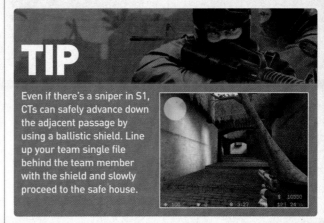

Even if there's a sniper in S1, CTs can safely advance down the adjacent passage by using a ballistic shield. Line up your team single file behind the team member with the shield and slowly proceed to the safe house.

S2

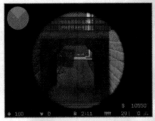

This position covers the same passage as C5, but provides a long-range approach ideal for a sniper. Peer through the scope and pick off CTs advancing at the far end. The only obstacle is a large crate on the right side. Even if CTs take cover behind this crate, you can pin them, forcing them to stay put or attempt another route. However, this position is relatively open to attacks coming from the wine cellar. If this happens, switch to your pistol and retreat to the safe house. Don't get caught in a firefight with CTs at close range, because you probably won't survive.

S3

CTs that enter the apartment at S4 emerge from this open doorway just ahead. Keep your scope centered on this passage and pick off any CTs as they come into view. If the CTs get bottle-necked near the doorway, you could take out a couple with one shot. However, due to the relatively short range, an accurate automatic rifle can work well here too.

S4

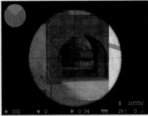

Whether playing as CTs or terrorists, this is a good spot for covering the rescue point. CTs can reach this spot by climbing up the nearby stack of crates and hopping through the window. Terrorists can reach it by entering the doorway near S3 and moving through the apartment. This apartment entrance makes the spot open to attacks from behind, so listen for incoming footsteps while holding this position, and peek to the right every now and then.

TIP

If you don't have a sniper rifle, try camping below the window at S4. Push back into the darkness among the crates, and aim down the path leading to the rescue point. However, this isn't a good spot for terrorists because you stand the chance of blasting the hostages trailing behind any CTs. But CTs can use this spot to help secure the rescue point.

S5

By holding this spot at the back of rescue point, you can cover both streets that branch off into the distance. You won't have the protection or concealment of any objects, but if you're good with the rifle, you can pick off any threats from a distance before taking too much damage.

Aim left to cover the street leading from the wine cellar area.

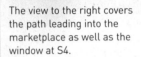

The view to the right covers the path leading into the marketplace as well as the window at S4.

TIP

Terrorists sniping from S5 need to watch their shots. If a hostage is behind a CT, your bullet may pass through the CT and continue into the hostage, potentially injuring or killing him. For this reason, avoid using high velocity sniper rifles such as the AWP.

COUNTER-TERRORIST TACTICS

THE WINE CELLAR ROUTE

Try taking the wine cellar route to avoid some of the more obvious choke points and sniper positions. Begin by taking the left street from the CT insertion point. Stay along the left side and climb these steps.

Turn right to spot this short bridge. If you see resistance in the alleyway below, keep moving–you don't want to get caught in a firefight here.

Enter the nearby doorway and descend these short steps.

Sidestep into the wine cellar and scan the corners–particularly the one at C6. If your team has any extra flashbangs, this is a good room to use one on. Otherwise, save them for the safe house assault.

Cautiously work your way through the cellar and watch for terrorists moving through the passage ahead.

Strafe around the next corner to spot the doorway leading outside.

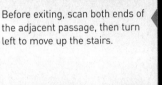

Before exiting, scan both ends of the adjacent passage, then turn left to move up the stairs.

Turn right while ascending the stairs to spot the safe house. Keep your sights on the upper floor window and hammer any resistance with automatic fire.

SAFE HOUSE TAKEDOWN

Although it's possible to enter the safe house through the upper floor window, it's not the quickest way to overwhelm the defenders with maximum firepower. Instead, go through the front door. Begin by sidestepping into the front hall and gun down any campers at the far end.

Stay clear of the next corner and equip a flashbang. Throw it at the wall inside the next room, causing it bank off the wall. Rush along the right side of the hallway before it goes off and switch back to your primary weapon.

The occupants of the next room will be blind for a few seconds, so rush in and sweep all corners. Stay away from the base of the stairs and move to clear the corner near the two hostages–there may be a terrorist hiding behind the crate.

With the first floor clear, approach the base of the stairs and equip another flashbang. Toss it up into the room as shown, bouncing it off the far wall, then sidestep right before it goes off. If this is your last flashbang, you automatically switch back to your primary weapon.

Rush up the stairs while the occupants are blind, and aim to the right. Scan all corners including the spot near the window. While your teammates secure the hostages, watch for terrorists moving from the adjacent hallway near S1. Once the area is clear and the hostages are secure, choose a way back the rescue point. The path through the apartment is always good. Try to avoid the marketplace.

TIP

If hostages were injured during a gun battle, avoid leading them through paths where they have to drop out of windows. If their health is low, even a short fall could kill them.

TERRORIST TACTICS

CAMPING THE SAFE HOUSE

When you don't have the manpower to guard the map's various choke points, fall back into the safe house. The first lines of defense should be the spot at C1 and the balcony above. The front entrance can be covered adequately from these two spots.

The window overlooking the step leading up from the wine cellar is another good position.

Upstairs, use this hostage for cover and pick off the CTs as they move up the steps.

Place another team member at the end of the hallway on the first floor, covering the main entrance. In later rounds, use a heavy machine gun to cover this entrance. Even if a flashbang is thrown into the room, the blind gunner still can lay down an impenetrable wall of lead.

In the next room, use the large crate for cover and take up positions near the two hostages.

This position at the top of the stairs is also good. From here you can cover the room below as well as the upstairs window should any CTs attempt to enter this way.

OFFICE   MAP TYPE: **HOSTAGE RESCUE**

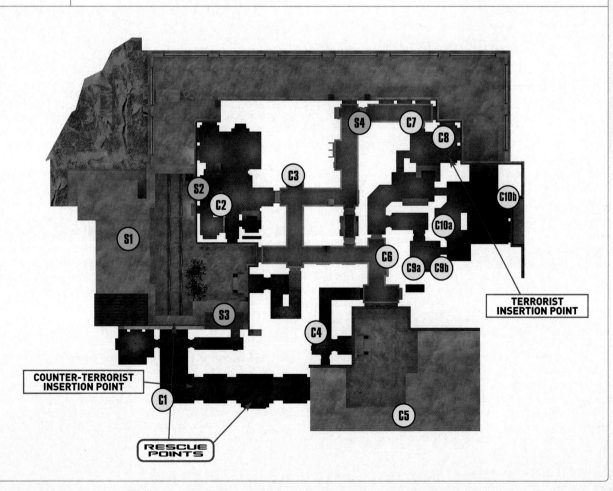

S4 C7 C8

C3

S2 C10b

C2 C10a

S1 C6 C9a C9b

TERRORIST INSERTION POINT

S3

C4

COUNTER-TERRORIST INSERTION POINT

C1 C5

RESCUE POINTS

COUNTER-TERRORISTS

Mission: Four hostages are being held inside a small office complex in two separate locations. Neutralize any terrorist threat, and bring the hostages back to one of two rescue points.

Overview: With the advantage of numerous entry methods, your team can choose a total of seven different openings (mostly windows) to gain entry to the office interior. Once inside, ideally in groups of two, it is imperative to move swiftly through the initially confusing corridors, working out sniping angles and learning where the terrorists are likely to ambush you. There are only two ways to reach the hostage areas, though, which are where you should expect the most vicious firefights.

TERRORISTS

Mission: Two pairs of hostages are being held in an office complex in two separate but adjacent areas. Prevent them from being rescued by repelling all attacks from the outside.

Overview: As there are a number of different ways to enter the building you're holed up in, most of your team should stay in relative proximity to the hostages. Use the numerous items of cover and long corridors to watch and ambush from. You can effectively choke your foes in the main and side halls of the office if your team is likeminded. Only venture out into the open if you're chasing hostages, or are completely overrunning the opposition.

KEY LOCATIONS

THE PROJECTOR ROOM

Two of the hostages are standing in the shadows along the projector room's south wall. The projector room is accessible through two entrances: via the storage room (which is likely to be a prime ambush spot for the terrorists), or the terrorost insertion point to the north. The hostages are in shadow, and the room itself is also likely to have at least one terrorist in position to cut down rescuers.

TERRORIST SPAWN

The other two hostages are hanging around the office's northeast area, where many of the terrorists spawn. However, unlike the projector room, the hostages are easy to spot and can be rescued via the side hall to the north, or the main hall to the south, and up a side corridor. Once again, expect the heaviest terrorist resistance at this point. Watch the sofas and blind corners for ambushes.

THE RESCUE POINTS

Keep one or two teammates in a sniping or camping position near the two rescue points, located at either side of the counter-terrorist insertion point in the garage. The two separate locations make it easier to return the hostages, as you have a choice of corridors to move through, but it is also difficult to defend. The front yard is especially open, allowing retaliation from either side.

CAMPING SPOTS

C1

Always have one of your CT teammates hang back in the corner of the garage to provide suppressing fire on teammates returning with hostages, or terrorists sneaking around your insertion point looking for a hiding place. This corner provides ample views of the entire garage which looks left out to the front yard and right to the end of the garage.

C2

Usually a counter-terrorist hidey-hole, this desk in the front room isn't likely to be guarded by terrorists, although they are likely to pour in from the side hall ahead of you. This makes a perfect place to camp out and tag incoming terrorists. You can head here later if you're a terrorist, and learn that the enemy is bringing hostages back this way. You aren't likely to be ambushed from behind, either—perfect!

C3

For the terrorist team, this is an excellent place to crouch down and prepare for the firefight to come, as it provides numerous opportunities to tag counter-terrorists trotting up the stairs on the opposite (south) end of the corridor. Keep the CTs at bay here with crossfire; the choke point at the crossroads is the place all terrorists must learn. You can also bring down CTs with hostages from here, too.

C4

You can leap on top of this crate and ambush counter-terrorists trying to sneak their hostages through the backyard area, through the window and into the yard, or down the stairs.

C5

If you receive a leg-up from your compadre, you can smash the window and enter a small windowed alcove south of the backyard (where you can snipe across to position C6). The backyard is an under-used area ripe for an ambush. Terrorists can rush this area, smashing the window to the north, and throw a flashbang into the CTs entrance corridor to dissuade them from heading in this direction.

C6

Although a good sniper from S1 can wing you all the way to this location, the terrorists need to keep this area ready with a camper that can check the main corridor and the backyard area. Two terrorists training their weapons down a corridor can tag as many CTs as possible early in the round.

C7

Waiting at this junction allows you to listen for incoming CTs (after you've retreated from position S4, for example), and dispatch them quickly and effectively, using the entrance to the terrorist insertion point as cover. However, you can expect incoming fire from CTs heading up from the main hall, so watch your positioning. This is not only a good camping spot, but an excellent escape route; you can only be attacked from two locations.

C8

If all of your terrorist teammates decide to sit and wait at the insertion point ("spawn camping"), then anywhere in this zone is a possibility. It allows partial cover behind the sofas, and you can dart between the hostages for extra cover. You can tag counter-terrorists running in from a number of directions from here, but the lack of real cover and escape routes means you must be on your toes.

C9A AND B

The storage room ambush is perfect if you and your terrorist posse have enough teammates to back you up; decide whether to spawn camp at the beginning of the round. There are excellent opportunities to tag CTs as they round the corner, and crouching behind the boxes provides some cover. However, there's little room to escape from this point, so only attempt to camp here with extra help.

C10A AND B

Counter the CTs by positioning a couple of terrorists in this area, along with the adjacent camping positions. Crouching near the sofas watching the hostages allows you to quickly blast incoming enemies

from the right door, while the terrorist hiding behind the projector can cover the left door as there's an excellent view of the corridors outside this room.

SNIPING POSITIONS

S1

Two exceptional spots. You have a full view of the front yard (which you can drop down on), the exits, the windows, and the entire main hall. Cause havoc for terrorists everywhere by heading here quickly. Terrorists can use this later in the round to annoy CTs bringing hostages home.

The third area in this sniping position is outside, above the stack of crates in the open front yard. Move here and you'll have the ability to quickly dash to and fro, peering into windows. There's also a good potential for escape, by either going around the ledge or dropping down.

S2

Near the CT insertion point, head across the front yard and up the ladder to secure this spot looking across the side hall. Move to the right as you reach the top and your teammates can still enter the building.

S3

Head up to this window from the CT insertion point and you have a great view of the front yard, across to the window leading to the front room. Although it's a reasonable sniping spot, terrorists can really use it toward the end of the round to gun down CTs with incoming hostages.

S4

As most CTs will receive damage by the time they reach the main hall, this is a great place from which to finish them off at the start of a round. You can blast CTs coming in from the bathroom or side hall. The left wall acts as partial cover, and you can even retreat back to the CT insertion point if you're overrun.

COUNTER-STRIKE SOURCE

COUNTER-TERRORIST TACTICS

WINDOW DRESSING

CTs have numerous methods of entering the offices. Choose how many teammates are making the journey, and where they are going, then move! Climb the ladder at the left side of the front yard.

To the right of the front yard ladder is an entrance to a lower-level passage heading left, around to the northwest part of the map. Here, climb a second ladder into the corner of the front room. This takes time.

The main entrance is north of the CT insertion point. Head east, into the entrance, and around the stairwell, watching for ambushes. This is the "amateur" method of gaining entry, and is easily repelled.

TIP

You can use the snow-covered crates to the left of the main entrance to climb onto the ledge, and then enter by smashing either of the two windows. You're likely to be shot at if you take the right window. Or, you can break a window to attract terrorist attention, and enter from a different area or ambush them!

The front room is the preferred way of entering the office complex, due to the cover and the quick entry. Crouch on a desk and give your team suppressing fire as they advance, if you're first.

BACK WAY FORWARD

The other method of entering the office is via the small steps at the east end of the garage (this is the other way to bring hostages back). Varying your entry points annoys and confuses the terrorists, so never use the same entry method twice. If you can reach the top of the steps, you can stay near the main hall and lay down suppressing fire.

AN EXCURSION IN DIVERSION

CTs or Ts can prowl the garage corridor itself, waiting for hostages to arrive, or helping fellow teammates out. The crates in this area and the stairwell entrance should be guarded if this is an agreed escape route.

TIP

Your CT team can easily infiltrate the office with minimal casualties if you all storm the building in a similar area, or create a diversion in another area. Mix up your intrusion methods for best results.

TERRORIST TACTICS

OFFICE HAVOC

Those unsure of the map should remain near their hostages and ready themselves to repel the enemy by hiding behind partial cover.

The area between the main hall and the storage room is a high-traffic choke point. With two teammates here and a supply of grenades, you can annoy the CTs.

USING THE BACK DOOR

Early in the round, remember you can smash the backyard glass and jump down and attack CTs coming up the steps from the side. Better yet, remain atop the stairs and gun down CTs as they disperse into the backyard or exit at the top of the stairs. Retreat to the storage room if you're overrun. If no targets present themselves, you can even head to the CT spawn and round to attack from behind!

The Projection Room is your last stand, as it's the room that's most difficult to reach. Make sure at least one teammate waits here, camping near a door or at the C10 locations.

ON THE PROWL

Later into the round, try to head back to the CT insertion point and pinpoint the hostage rescue points, using cover and stopping the CTs from victory.

HOSTILE CAMPING

These are all high-traffic areas; the storage room and main hall areas can expect the most traffic and damage. Learn the choke point at the storage room's west exit and the bathroom area, and position your terrorists here accordingly.

PIRANESI   MAP TYPE: **DEMOLITION**

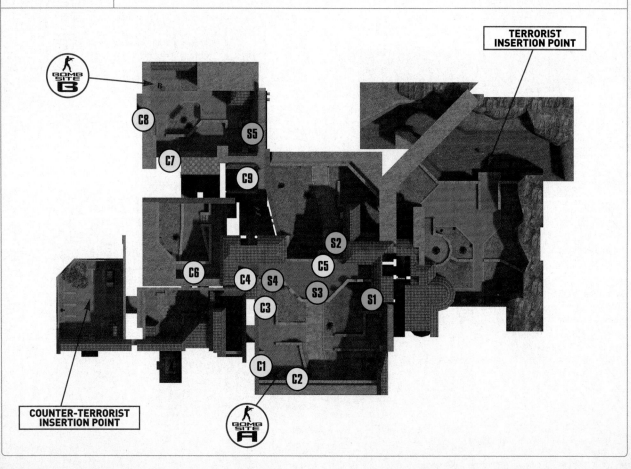

COUNTER-TERRORISTS

Mission: Terrorists are planning to bomb the Villa Piranesi. Stop them from detonating the bomb at either site.

Overview: This castle-like map is full of narrow passages and several typical sniping positions, making it easy to defend. However, multiple passages lead to the two bomb sites. So unless you have a large enough force, it's difficult to shut down all choke points. In such cases, stick to the bomb sites and wait for the terrorists to come to you. When defending from the exterior, choose a rifle with good accuracy and plenty of power. Most engagements around the bomb sites take place at long range, so plan accordingly. Meanwhile, stick to submachine guns and shotguns when patrolling the cramped corridors.

TERRORISTS

Mission: Enter the villa and set a bomb at one of two sculptures. Stop the counter-terrorists from defusing it.

Overview: Staging direct assaults on either of the bomb sites is a quick way to get your team killed. Even if you rush, the CTs can get to both sites slightly ahead of you, giving them enough time to take defensive positions. So instead of taking the most predictable paths, try to stay within the castle's walls as much as possible. This keeps you out of the snipers' sights while giving you a fighting chance to reach the target areas. Try storming the sniping positions ahead of your assault in an attempt to clear out any defenders, and bring along plenty of grenades.

KEY LOCATIONS

BOMB SITE A

Bomb site A is about equidistant from the CT and terrorist insertion points, making this large courtyard a frequent spot of intense firefights—especially in the opening moments of a round. This courtyard can be accessed from three major entry points, not to mention the various windows overlooking the area. The elevated walkway on top of the tall wall (near S4) is a popular spot for snipers, so defenders should take the high ground early and hold it. Those defending near the bomb site can take cover among the large crates, and engage attackers at short range. This isn't an easy site to defend on your own, but with a couple teammates helping out, you should be able to lock down this courtyard.

BOMB SITE B

Even if the terrorists rush to this site, it's likely that the CTs already defend it. The site is tucked away in the corner of this courtyard, set on a slight hill overlooking all three potential entry points. Hedges and darkened doorways provide defenders with plenty of cover and concealment. The elevated ledge at S4 also offers excellent coverage of the entire courtyard for snipers. So if this site is well defended, attackers definitely have their work cut out for them.

TIP

Throughout this map, various signs point toward the two bomb sites. They're labeled with illustrations of a globe and a sundial, associated with the sculptures found at each site. Signs with the sundial point to bomb site A, while signs with the globe point to bomb site B.

CAMPING SPOTS

C1

Look for this stack of crates in the corner of the bomb site A. Crouch-jump on the crates to get to the top.

This camping spot gives you a clear view of the bomb site as well as the courtyard below. As a result, this is a good position when defending the site on your own. However, use it more as an observation post than an actual combat position—snipers on the wall to your left have no problem taking you out. If you come under fire, drop to the ground and take cover by one of the nearby crates or behind the sundial sculpture.

C2

Here's another option for covering bomb site A. Crouch in the far corner (across from C1) along the wall and aim toward the center of the site. From this angle you can cover the nearby entry point while remaining mostly concealed to the rest of the courtyard. This is a good option if your weapon lacks the power and accuracy needed to engage enemies effectively at long range. So if you're stuck with a weak submachine gun or a shotgun, try holding in this corner.

C3

This corner spot is out of the way, giving you a chance to surprise attackers as they rush toward bomb site A. While this corner lacks cover, it does offer a good elevated view of the lower part of the courtyard. Pick off enemies as they move across the ramp on the opposite side. CTs can use this spot early in a round as the terrorists attempt to rush the site.

C4

Look for the scaffold along the wall in this room and climb the ladder to the top. Now aim into the adjacent hallway, using the bucket and wall lamp for partial cover. Sidestep out to the left to see around the lamp. From this angle, you can fire down on your enemies before they enter the room. If you come under fire, take cover behind the bucket–do the same when changing clips. This is a great ambush spot for CTs, especially if the terrorists move through the interior passages toward either of the bomb sites.

C5

Farther down the hall from C4 is this large stack of crates. Either stay on the floor and peek around these crates, or climb to the top. If you peek around the crates you stand a better chance of survival, especially if you're not too good of a shot. But if you're feeling confident, climb the stack of crates and aim down on your opponents. This can take them by surprise as they enter the room, requiring them to aim upward. Use this brief window of opportunity to your advantage and blast them before they can get their crosshairs centered on you. Try using a shotgun or submachine gun to cover this passage.

C6

Holding on this balcony is a good spot for defenders trying to lock down bomb site B. The walkway running beneath it is a major path leading into the site. It's also the quickest path linking the two bomb sites, making this a valuable position for both sides. The spot is best used when enemies are moving from bomb site B to bomb site A. This allows you to pick them off while they're moving away from you. However, it can be difficult to see enemies moving from bomb site B due to the darkened passage ahead. In fact, they'll probably see you before you see them. If you come under attack, crouch against the stone ledge and move to a new position before popping up to return fire.

C7

Chances are your enemies won't see you in this darkened doorway near bomb site B unless they carefully scan this corner. While this spot doesn't provide a wide view of the surrounding courtyard, it offers a decent view of the bomb site, allowing you to

pick off enemies that move in to plant or disarm the bomb. Whenever possible, use a silenced weapon to avoid giving away your position.

C8

Here's another dark doorway position, right next to bomb site B. Press up against the right side of this wide doorway while aiming toward the globe sculpture. This spot is a good for ambushing the enemy at close range, but you can't see most of the courtyard. For best results, use a shotgun or a powerful automatic weapon when holding this position. Once your position is given away, you won't have long before your opponent shoots back. So make your first shot count.

C9

This darkened passage is a major choke point leading into bomb site B. This path is often taken by terrorists early in the round, so CTs should get here quickly. Use the darkness for concealment and open fire as soon as your enemies come into view. With some luck you can pin the enemy advance in the courtyard beyond, allowing a sniper teammate at S2 to catch them in a crossfire. If the enemy force is overwhelming, retreat to bomb site B and take up a defensive position there.

SNIPING POSITIONS
S1

This narrow window overlooking the courtyard near bomb site A is a decent sniping position, but the site is mostly obscured by a large tree. However, terrorists may still find this spot useful for picking off CT defenders on the opposite side of the courtyard. This is most useful in the early moments of a round as CTs move through the dark archway next to the bomb site. Even if your enemies uncover your position, they'll have a hard time threading their bullets through the narrow rectangular window.

S2

Although the courtyard below contains no crucial objectives, it's one of the major thoroughfares for players moving between the two bomb sites. This elevated position is custom made for covering this high traffic area. Because most potential targets

will be running, stay away from the slow-firing sniper rifles unless you're an expert. Instead, pick a good assault rifle and use short automatic bursts to knock down your enemies. Keep an eye on the passage to your right to avoid getting flanked.

S3

This spot isn't far from the crates at C5. A series of rectangular windows lines the side of the hall, overlooking bomb site A. As in S1, the narrow windows make you difficult to see and hit. So stay back in the hall, where it's darker, and avoid stepping into the window. This position range's isn't too extreme, so you can get by using an assault rifle here. However, the persistent sound of automatic fire and muzzle flash may give you away. Move between the different windows to keep your enemies guessing. This spot's main weakness is its hallway location, making it possible to get flanked from both sides while you gaze out the window. So use this spot only if you have a teammate watching your back or if you have a good idea where your opponents are located.

S4

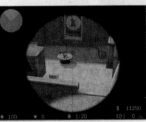

The top of this wall provides a great view of bomb site A as well as the opposite courtyard covered by S2. When covering bomb site A, crouch between the wall's stone crenellations and aim down into the courtyard below. When defending the site as a terrorist, make sure you have a good view of the bomb. This way you can pick off CTs as they rush to disarm it. Wait till they stop and crouch next to it, then let loose with a lethal head shot. Like S3, this spot is along a walkway and has the potential of being flanked. So keep an eye on the two suspicious passages and be prepared to fall back in the opposite direction.

TIP

This map features many steep drops, so look at your health before leaping. Even seemingly short drops inflict some damage, and you don't want to die as the result of a fall.

S5

This ledge overlooking bomb site B is accessed through the adjacent interior hallway. No guardrail prevents you from falling, so be careful when moving onto this narrow perch. This spot gives you a nearly complete view of the courtyard below as well as the bomb site. However, the general lack of cover and concealment make you easy

to spot and hit. Use this spot sparingly and don't stay here once your position is revealed. Fire one clean shot, then get away, either by dropping to the ground or racing back into the hallway.

COUNTER-TERRORIST TACTICS

INTERIOR COUNTERATTACK

If the terrorists plant a bomb at one of the sites, you need to counter-attack before it detonates. The map is full of potential ambush spots, but if you stick to the interior hallways you can avoid getting picked off by terrorist snipers. From bomb site B, move down the path to the left leading to the interior.

Enter this arched passage on the left side and follow the hallway beyond.

Move down this narrow hallway, keeping an eye open for enemy movement ahead.

Before descending these steps, carefully scan the area below for any terrorist campers.

At the bottom of the stairs, take a right and follow the sign to bomb site A.

Sidestep into this passage and watch for terrorist campers at the end and along the walkway to the right.

When it's clear, move toward the arched passage on the left. If you have any, equip a flashbang or grenade and toss it toward the bomb site.

Quickly enter the bomb site and clear it of any terrorist defenders. Don't forget to scan the crate at C1.

Upon entering the next room, scan to the right and look for campers hiding by the table or along the stairs. When it's clear, move forward to the passage marked with an A.

Scan the next passage ahead for CT defenders, but most of them probably are clustered around the bomb site.

Find the bomb and defuse it while your team members cover. Always carry a Bomb-Defuse Kit to speed up the process. So whether counterattacking bomb site A or B, stick to the interior hallways. It's not the quickest route between the two areas, but it's one of the safest.

TERRORIST TACTICS

BOMB SITE A ASSAULT

To avoid getting picked off by CT defenders from a distance, take the long way around to bomb site A. Begin by moving toward the passage marked with a B.

Continue toward the arched passage leading into bomb site A. Scan the opposite end of the courtyard and pick off any CT defenders you can see from a distance.

Cautiously enter the bomb site while scanning in all directions. Pay close attention to the areas near the crates.

Go downhill around this passage. Move quickly before the CTs can take up defensive positions in the courtyard beyond.

Plant the bomb in the dark corner near the large stack of crates at C1.

Stop short of entering the courtyard and turn left to enter this passage.

Now climb up onto the crates and wait for the CTs to counter-attack. Use the crates for partial concealment and pick off the opposing forces as they rush over to the bomb.

Take the steps up and follow the corridor.

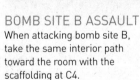

BOMB SITE B ASSAULT

When attacking bomb site B, take the same interior path toward the room with the scaffolding at C4.

Move past the crates at C5 and scan the next room for CT campers—remember to check the scaffold at C4.

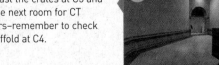

This time, turn right and head up the stairs.

Move down this narrow hallway and watch for movement along the passages to the left.

When you reach the small ledge at S5, step out and scan the area below. Pick off any CT defenders from a distance, then return to the hall.

Follow the corridor until it exits into the courtyard.

Once again, scan the courtyard, in particular the areas you couldn't see before from S5.

Move up this pathway toward the bomb site. Watch for campers in the two darkened doorways.

Plant the bomb in the narrow doorway so you have a good view of it from C8.

Once the bomb is planted, order the squad to hold near the site. Take a position at C8 and wait for the CT counterattack.

YOU'VE GOT THE GAME ▶